Economic Foundations of Law

The secon ... nalysis of
the major ... rocedure,
corporatio ... ent trends
in legal sc ... aversion,
efficiency, ... s of scale,
thus ensur

Accessi ... examples
and explar ... it explains
all the pri ... st in a sea
of jargon. ... including
an explan ... settlement
negotiatio ... s examples
drawn fro ... akers, and
how law f ... of subjects
as diverse ... adoptions,
the marke ... es of racial
profiling. ... .

A deta ... be of great
value to b

Stephen ... a Ph.D. in
economic ... Wayne State
Universit ... w and labor
economic

Birmingham · Chester · Guildford · London · Manchester · York

The revised edition of *Economic Foundations of Law* provides an economic analysis of the major areas of the law: property law, contracts, torts, criminal law, civil procedure, constitution law and financial markets, taxation and labor law. In line with current trends in legal scholarship, discussion is focused on economic principles such as risk, transaction, opportunity cost, moral hazard, rent-seeking behaviour, and economics. This ensures the reader stays fully up to date.

Accessible, comprehensive and well written, this book uses extensive practical examples and illustrations to illustrate key points. Unlike other texts on law and economics, it explains all the principles of economics used in the book. This ensures the reader is not lost in the theory. There are numerous applications to lawyers and the legal profession, such an explanation of why partners in a law firm do not tell their associates about litigation while a lawsuit is pending. The chapter on informal property rights has sections from the California gold rush, sharecropping agreements, whaling, the Shakers and how firms divide profits among the partners. There are detailed discussions of topics such as the proposed market for transplantable human organs, the market for babies, the market for bail bonds, the unanticipated effects of Megan's law, and issues of crime. Fully updated and revised, the text includes a new chapter on labor law. A well-structured yet wide ranging economic analysis of the law, this textbook will be useful for both undergraduates and postgraduates.

Stephen J. Spurr has a J.D. from the University of Michigan Law School and a Ph.D. in economics from the University of Chicago. He is a professor of economics at Wayne State University. He has published many articles in the areas of economic analysis of law, and statistics in economics journals.

Economic Foundations of Law

Second edition

Stephen J. Spurr

Routledge
Taylor & Francis Group

LONDON AND NEW YORK

First edition published by South Western College Publishers, Mason, OH, 2005
Second edition published 2010
by Routledge
2 Park Square, Milton Park, Abingdon, Oxon. OX14 4RN

Simultaneously published in the USA and Canada
by Routledge
270 Madison Avenue, New York, NY 10016

*Routledge is an imprint of the Taylor & Francis Group,
an informa business*

© 2005, 2010 Stephen J. Spurr

Typeset in Times New Roman by Glyph International Ltd.
Printed and bound in Great Britain by TJ International Ltd, Padstow, Cornwall.

British Library Cataloguing in Publication Data
A catalogue record for this book is available from the British Library

Library of Congress Cataloging in Publication Data
A catalog record has been requested for this book

ISBN: 978-0-415-77852-7 (hbk)
ISBN: 978-0-415-77853-4 (pbk)
ISBN: 978-0-203-84691-9 (ebk)

To Laura

Contents

Illustrations

Tables

Acknowledgments

A few years ago I asked a friend who had just finished a textbook on intermediate microeconomics what the opportunity cost of the book had been, in terms of forgone journal articles. He ignored my question, and I was wise enough not to press him on it. Now I understand his response; this is a question that no textbook author wants to think about carefully. A textbook is a massive undertaking, an all-consuming endeavor. If you try to relax, or do something else before it is finished, you are squarely confronted by the fact that it is incomplete and may, in fact, never be completed if you lack the stamina to see it through.

I would like to acknowledge the outstanding teachers I have had in both economics and law, in addition to those at the University of Chicago. My interest in economics began in classes at Oberlin with the late Ben Lewis, Hirschel Kasper, Thomas Dernberg and Art Wright. Ben Lewis was a pioneer in economic analysis of law, and Hirsch Kasper introduced me to labor economics. I also benefited greatly from professors at the University of Michigan Law School, especially the late Alfred Conard, Luke Cooperider, Sam Estep, Frank Kennedy, Theodore J. St. Antoine, and James J. White. The late Gerald L. Wallace was a fascinating teacher in the Graduate Tax Program of New York University Law School. I especially want to thank Walter Oi, of the University of Rochester, who made very helpful comments on several chapters while declining any compensation from the publisher for his review. Finally, I would like to express my gratitude to two great economists, now deceased, who were also human beings of the highest caliber: Peter Pashigian and Sherwin Rosen.

S.J.S.

Introduction

For the rational study of the law the black letter man may be the man of the present, but the man of the future is the man of statistics and the master of economics.

(Oliver Wendell Holmes, *The Path of the Law*, 1897)

Economic analysis of law: its growth and consequences

In February 1982, I was sitting in a classroom at the University of Chicago, in a graduate course in public finance taught by Arnold Harberger. He was explaining the economic consequences of certain provisions in U.S. tax law that allow producers of oil and gas to use percentage depletion rather than cost depletion. I found myself riveted by this material, since I had worked on a legal case involving percentage depletion for over a year, as a lawyer in New York. I knew (or so I thought) as much as a lawyer can know about the tax provisions, their legislative history, and the policy arguments for and against percentage depletion. Yet that class gave me insights about the consequences of the subsidy that is percentage depletion, the merits of the policy arguments, and the different analyses of the tax issues by accountants, lawyers, and economists that I would never have gained if I had spent my entire career in this area of practice as a lawyer. It was for me a powerful and strangely affecting experience.

Somewhat later I took a course in the economics of regulation from Sam Peltzman. One day he explained that the problem of pollution can be viewed as one of incomplete property rights, to which economists had proposed an elegant solution: creating marketable licenses to pollute. Hearing this, I could not suppress a smile, since I knew from my experience in law and business that, for political reasons, such a proposal would have no chance of being adopted.

Today, of course, there are well-established markets in sulfur emissions and many other types of pollution rights. Economic analysis of law has prompted many other innovations that I would then have thought equally improbable: government auctions of broadcast frequencies, oil drilling rights, and massive deregulation of trucking, airlines, telecommunications, banking, and other industries. My mistake had been to underestimate the power of an idea.

Economic analysis of law has been a revolution – not one marked by sudden, violent change, but a bona fide revolution nonetheless. Since it has been such a gradual, incremental process, the magnitude of the changes it has wrought is often overlooked. Economic analysis was first introduced into the classroom at the elite law schools, most notably Chicago and Yale, and subsequently percolated down to the others. Now in virtually any classroom in the top eighty law schools, the discussion may be laced with terms like risk aversion, efficiency, opportunity cost, moral hazard, rent-seeking behavior, economies of scale, and the like.

Almost any recent issue of a major law journal will include articles employing economic analysis, often including diagrams and a formal mathematical model. The use of rigorous econometric and statistical methods is now routine in the top twenty law journals. *Black's Law Dictionary*, the staple of law students for generations, now has enough definitions of economic terms to provide a glossary for a principles of economics text. A study that measured the influence of the economic approach by the frequency of use of economic terms in law review articles found that the influence of economics has continued to grow steadily.[1]

Resistance to economic analysis of law

As noted above, it is clear from measures such as journal citations and the frequency of references to economic terms in law review articles that the influence of economic analysis on legal research has been increasing continuously over time. However, it is also true that there has been vigorous resistance to it in some quarters. A prominent professor of contract law[2] once called for a "nonproliferation treaty" for economic analysis, thus consigning it to the fold of nuclear, chemical, and biological weapons. It is worth while to reflect on various possible reasons for this opposition.

First, it is not surprising that there would be resistance from many law professors who were neither trained in economics nor encountered economic analysis when they were law students. Few are pleased to learn that proficiency in their line of work requires a major new investment in human capital, or that there has been some depreciation of their previous work (in this case, their contributions to legal scholarship). Presumably, though, opposition of this type has declined over time, as the share of law school faculty who have seen economic analysis as law students has increased.

Another important reason for opposition is a concern that allowing economics to infiltrate the law school curriculum would "open the floodgates" to every other discipline, thus preventing law schools from carrying out their essential mission. According to this view, that mission is both to train students to become lawyers and to certify them, i.e., to sort them according to quality. (To help with the second objective, most law schools require all first-year students to take the same courses.) If we allow economics to enter the classroom, the argument runs, we can count on the subsequent entry of sociology, political science, psychology, history, and every other subject. The classroom would soon become a Tower of Babel, or psychobabble. The model that law professors have in mind is that different disciplines will petition for, and ultimately receive, equal access, just as legal protection against discrimination has been granted first on the basis of race or national origin, then gender, then physical disability, and (most recently) sexual orientation.

This fear of a loss of control of the curriculum is attributable to the fact that, historically, the study of law has not followed the rules and conventions of the natural and social sciences. Legal research has not been subject to peer review or Occam's razor;[3] hypotheses have not been required to be testable (capable of being disproved) or, when they are, have usually not been tested by experiments or empirical work that would meet the standards of the social sciences. Consequently law professors, while representing a large share of the best and brightest in academia, tend to be less familiar than other academics with the rigor of the market discipline imposed by an open marketplace of ideas. Physics, for example, has been greatly influenced by mathematics, and in some areas by chemistry, but not very much by other fields, simply because to date physicists have not found other fields helpful in advancing their research. Archeology is now being informed by chemistry, to analyze the remains of ancient human groups to determine their diet. In other words, science is opportunistic.

The success that has been enjoyed by economics in legal research is not likely to be replicated by many other fields. In science there is equal opportunity, but that does not guarantee equal achievement.

One sometimes hears the suggestion that economic analysis of law, or economics itself, is "conservative," i.e. it tends to uphold the status quo, to support the privileged and powerful, and provides a rationale for the oppression of low-income persons, minority groups, and the dispossessed. This argument is more likely to occur to lawyers than to those in other fields, since lawyers are trained to be advocates; indeed, the original idea of an attorney was that he was an agent. However, this claim reveals such a profound ignorance and misunderstanding of economics that it is difficult to know where to begin with a rebuttal. It is axiomatic that research constrained by political considerations is bad science; in fact it is not science at all. The advice of one renowned economist is to "let your interests and passions guide you in choosing the questions you ask, but keep those passions out of the answers you form."[4]

It should also be noted that there is much important work in economic analysis of law that would not be well received by many who consider themselves politically conservative. We will see in the chapter on torts that Easterbrook et al. (1980) have argued on behalf of the common-law rule against a right of contribution among joint tortfeasors, a position favorable to plaintiffs. Becker and Stigler (1974) proposed that a lawyer who brings a class action be allowed to retain the full amount of the recovery. Donohue and Levitt (2001) found that the Supreme Court decision in Roe v. Wade, by legalizing abortion, accounted for about half of the overall decline in the crime rate between 1991 and 1997. Ayres and Waldfogel (1994) found discrimination by judges against Black males, in the setting of bail bonds. The argument that economic analysis is tailored to a particular ideology is refuted by a cursory review of the literature.

Finally, a basis for opposition that is far more compelling than those considered above is a concern that the economist's objective of efficiency is too restrictive to be a satisfactory guide to policy. One might argue, for example, that the law should assign substantial value to a person's individual privacy – to her personal dignity, and right to be free from governmental intrusion by searches and seizures, or monitoring – but that economics does not recognize the importance of this principle. However, this objection is based on a misunderstanding of the role of efficiency in economic analysis. Efficiency is not a criterion that can be used to determine priorities among competing interests such as the right of privacy, freedom of expression, or measures of national output such as gross domestic product. All these values are accommodated under the heading of utility. In other words, economic analysis takes the relative importance of these values as given, i.e. determined elsewhere, and seeks to maximize the utility or well-being of society, subject to that determination. Economics can also enable us to identify, and often measure, all the costs and benefits of a specific proposal, such as a roadblock and search of all vehicles on a highway, and this analysis is generally quite useful in helping us decide whether the proposal should be adopted.

In any case, as previously noted, the opposition to economic analysis has not been able to thwart its long-run progress. As a measure of the change that has occurred, consider how a provision in a standard consumer contract would be analyzed, in either the classroom or a law review article, in, say, 1970 and today. Suppose, for example, an individual who purchased a product on credit from a department store challenged the right of a finance company to collect from her, under the "holder in due course" doctrine, when the product she bought was defective. In 1970 the contract would have been classified as a "contract of adhesion," i.e., a contract made between parties of unequal bargaining power. Since the buyer had much less bargaining power than the department store seller, a progressive judge would be inclined to construe the contract against the seller, and perhaps to even declare the objectionable clause (the provision giving a purchaser of the buyer's note the right to be a holder in due course) invalid, on the ground that it was "unconscionable." On the other hand, a more conservative judge would be inclined to enforce the provision, to uphold the sanctity of contract. Generally the analysis of either type of judge would not delve into the economics of the transaction at all.

Today we recognize that a provision like the holder in due course rule may be efficient, indeed that it could actually benefit buyers as a group, by making their promise to pay more liquid – more like cash. We now consider the possibility that a rule like this reduces the cost of financing installment sales, by making suits for collection less costly and more likely to succeed. Finally, we understand that restrictions on contracts that may be imposed by courts or legislatures may, and usually do, affect market equilibria on various margins. For example, abolition of the holder in due course rule may make it more costly to sell goods for credit. Sellers might therefore respond by either charging a higher rate of interest, or imposing higher standards on those who want to buy on credit. Consideration of broader economic effects, or indeed any effects beyond those on the transaction being reviewed, was almost unheard of in 1970, but is the norm today.

Another major development has been the advent of a number of peer-reviewed journals specializing in economic analysis of law.[5] There is a trend for legal scholars to publish an increasing share of their work in these refereed journals rather than in the student-edited law reviews, the traditional outlet for legal research. Once the number of researchers and the body of work in this field passed a given threshold, it was inevitable that a formal scholarly association would follow. In 1991 The American Law and Economics Association was founded to coordinate research efforts in the economic analysis of law. This association currently has approximately 1,000 members, including law professors, practicing lawyers, judges, and economists. There is also a European Association of Law and Economics, which was founded in 1984 and is now well established, a Canadian Law and Economics Association, and an Australian Law and Economics Association.

A development concurrent with, and related to, the growth of economic analysis was the gradual evolution of law schools from inward-looking teaching institutions to research institutions with active ties to other parts of the university. In the years immediately following World War II, tenure at a law school was essentially automatic for any new instructor who was a reasonably good teacher, even at the top law schools. (The hiring decision was based almost entirely on the applicant's academic record in law school.) Today a law professor at a school in the top fifty must usually have several publications to earn tenure. Increasingly, there is an expectation that the candidate's research will meet the standards of the social sciences, and that at least some of her work will be in peer-reviewed journals.

During earlier years law students may have considered economic analysis to be something like a parlor game – a fascinating exercise, but something they would leave behind once they had graduated and entered into practice. Today, however, that approach would be quite ill advised, because there is an excellent chance they will encounter applications of economics in law practice. There has been a trend of increasing reliance by the U.S. Supreme Court on publications that apply the rigorous analytical methods of the social sciences. Another important development has been the appointment to the executive branch and the federal bench of individuals whose decisions are frequently based on applications of economics. With respect to the federal judiciary, this group includes Guido Calabresi and Ralph Winter of the Second Circuit, Alex Kozinski of the Ninth Circuit, Douglas Ginsburg and Stephen Williams of the DC Circuit, Richard Posner and Frank Easterbrook of the Seventh Circuit, the Supreme Court Justice Stephen Breyer, and many others.

There is still some entrenched opposition to economic analysis of law in isolated pockets, but the remaining opponents now appear more and more like Don Quixote, or the few Japanese soldiers found in the caves of Iwo Jima and elsewhere many years after the formal surrender of Japan, unaware that World War II was over. For all practical purposes, this battle is also over. Indeed, some would argue that the extent to which economic principles are included in the teaching and research of a law school's faculty is a good measure of the school's quality. All indications are that the role of economic analysis in the study of law and the formation of public policy will continue to grow in the future.

An example: the value of a professional degree

To illustrate the use of economic analysis in law, let us consider a specific example of an area, divorce law, which is being influenced by economics. Currently, however, there is considerable variation in the courts' propensity to apply economic principles. A 1985 New York case, O'Brien v. O'Brien,[6] involved the issue of the value of a professional degree. Eighteen months after their wedding, the O'Briens moved to Mexico so that Mr. O'Brien could attend medical school. Mrs. O'Brien worked as a teacher to finance her husband's medical education during most of their nine-year marriage. The year he graduated from medical school Mr. O'Brien filed for divorce. Since the couple had not acquired many tangible assets, the amount of Mrs. O'Brien's recovery depended largely on whether she would be compensated with a share of the value of her husband's medical degree.

From an economic standpoint, it is clear that Mr. O'Brien's medical education increased his productivity, or "human capital"; the value of his medical degree was the present value of the expected increase in his lifetime earnings. In 1998, for example, the median earnings of a physician were $160,000, while those of a college graduate were $42,692. Thus, assuming relative earnings have not changed much between 1985 and 1998, and that Mr. O'Brien would have the career of an average physician, his medical degree increased his annual earnings by approximately $117,308.[7] If we further assume a career length of twenty-five years and a real interest rate of 2 percent, the present value of this asset turns out to be $2,290,258 in 1998 dollars. We obtained this figure by applying a formula that converts an annuity received for n years into a current lump-sum payment of equal value:

$$V = X \left[\frac{1 - \frac{1}{(1+r)^n}}{r} \right]$$

where V is the value of the asset (the degree), X is the annuity (the amount received each year), r is the real rate of interest, and n is the number of years the annuity will be paid. In this case $X = \$117,308$, and we assume the real rate of interest is 2 percent, so $r = 0.02$, and $n = 25$.

The New York Court of Appeals fully recognized the value of the wife's contribution, but also acknowledged that the courts had not generally considered a professional degree or license to be "property" that could be divided between the parties to a divorce case. However, the Court managed to circumvent this limitation of the law by holding that the

New York statute applicable to marital property settlements was not bound by the traditional legal definition of property. Thus Mrs. O'Brien was entitled to compensation for her support of her husband's medical education.

The law in this area is not yet settled, but it appears to be moving in the direction of incorporating the economic insight of the Court in O'Brien v. O'Brien, that a professional degree can be an asset of substantial value.

Why this book was written

I decided to write this textbook because, when I began teaching my course in economic analysis of law, none of the existing textbooks was exactly what I wanted. Polinsky's book[8] was excellent, but at that time too short and limited in scope, and Posner's *Economic Analysis of Law*, as remarkable as it is – a bold, pioneering work and a source of much inspiration to me over the years – took for granted that the reader had considerable knowledge of both law and economics.[9] So after two or three iterations, I decided to assign, instead of a text, a packet of about twenty readings from articles and book chapters. It soon became clear that this was not the way to go. For one thing, I got the distinct impression that the students were not reading the articles, perhaps because they were rational, and understood that the law of eventually diminishing marginal product would set in long before they reached the end of a twenty-page paper in an economics journal, never mind a forty-page article in a law journal. Moreover, I heard myself advising students that, given everything else they had to do during the semester, it was probably not cost-effective for them to read all the way through, say, Coase's *Problem of Social Cost* – they could read it later, in the summer or in graduate school. Another factor was the cost and bother involved in getting copyright approvals: one very prestigious university demanded $30 per student for permission to distribute copies of a famous law review article about how the law should protect entitlements. So there was nothing left to do but write a book.

The purpose of this text is to provide examples of applications of economic principles in a number of major areas of law – property law, trusts and estates, torts, contracts, civil procedure, criminal law, taxation, and corporate law. Clearly a comprehensive discussion of any of these areas would be a book by itself. A reviewer of this text asked how one could "do justice" to the subject of taxation in a chapter of thirty pages. The answer, of course, is that one can't – and shouldn't try to. This chapter should not be viewed as a substitute for a course in taxation and public finance, but rather as an illustration of economic principles underlying some controversies in tax law.[10]

The student will learn that economics is not external to the law. Today one cannot indulge the notion that law is a separate, independent body of knowledge, and consider economics as being like physics, the province of the expert witness who is invited on to the stage only to provide us with information that is essentially factual, and should then quickly depart. The student will find that the same principles and themes recur again and again, in very different settings. The free-rider problem explains not only the doctrine of attorney work product set forth in Hickman v. Taylor, but also the rules of contract law on when the buyer must provide information to the seller, and the opposition of economists to anti-takeover statutes that require advance disclosure to the public by those who plan to acquire control of a corporation. A knowledge of law that does not recognize these common themes falls far short of understanding; it is like an overstuffed steamer trunk, crammed full of arbitrary rules, ill-fitting corollaries and random exceptions. Such knowledge, like the steamer trunk, is hard to transport, in the sense that it is both hard to remember, and leaves the lawyer at a loss when she encounters a set of facts slightly different from those examined in her study of law. My hope is that this textbook will make at least a small contribution toward enabling present and future lawyers, who as judges and legislators are the principal architects of law, to become social engineers, fully prepared to apply economic principles to their work.

Supplements to this textbook: the glossary and the *Instructor's Manual*

The glossary and *Instructor's Manual* are designed to meet the special requirements of a textbook on economic analysis of law. One would expect that very few instructors, if any, have equal confidence in their teaching of the economics and law components of all the topics covered in this book. Accordingly, the glossary and *Instructor's Manual* are designed not only for students, but also to provide key legal terms for the economist and key economic terms for the law professor. The glossary includes definitions, not only of the terms used in the textbook, but also of other economic terms, such as "economies of scope," and legal terms, such as "hearsay," that the reader may find useful. The *Instructor's Manual* has answers to all the questions at the end of the chapters. These answers are substantially more detailed than usual, so an instructor who is unfamiliar with the underlying material can rely on them for a complete explanation, and need not hesitate to include them in an examination.

References

Ayres, Ian, and Joel Waldfogel, "A Market Test for Race Discrimination in Bail Setting," 46 *Stanford Law Review* 987–1047 (May 1994).

Becker, Gary S., and George J. Stigler, "Law Enforcement, Malfeasance and Compensation of Enforcers," 3 *Journal of Legal Studies* 1–18 (January 1974).

Cooter, Robert, and Thomas Ulen, *Law and Economics* (Glenview, IL: Scott Foresman, 1988; 4th ed., Boston, MA: Pearson Addison Wesley, 2004).

Donohue, John, and Steven Levitt, "Legalized Abortion and Crime," 116 (2) *Quarterly Journal of Economics* 379–420 (2001).

Easterbrook, Frank, William M. Landes, and Richard A. Posner, "Contribution among Antitrust Defendants: A Legal and Economic Analysis," 23 *Journal of Law and Economics* 331 (1980).

Ellickson, Robert C., "Trends in Legal Scholarship: A Statistical Study," 29 *Journal of Legal Studies* 517–543 (January 2000).

Garner, Bryan A., ed., *Black's Law Dictionary* (7th ed., St. Paul, MN: West Group, 1999).

Kelso, Charles D., "The 1981 AALS Conference on Teaching Contracts: A Summary and Appraisal," 32 (1) *Journal of Legal Education* 616 (April 1982).

Parkin, Michael, *Economics* (Reading, MA: Addison-Wesley, 1990).

Polinsky, A. Mitchell, *An Introduction to Law and Economics* (2nd ed., Gaithersburg, MD: Aspen Publishing, 1989).

Shapiro, Fred R., "The Most-cited Legal Scholars," 29 *Journal of Legal Studies* 409–426 (January 2000).

Starnes, Cynthia, "Divorce and the Displaced Homemaker: A Discourse on Playing with Dolls, Partnership Buyouts and Dissociation under No-fault," 60 *University of Chicago Law Review* 67–139 (winter 1993).

Table of cases

1 Principles of microeconomics (I)

Welcome to the study of economic analysis of law! If you can master the material in this chapter and the next one, you will find all the applications of economic principles in the remainder of this text straightforward. The approach to the study of law taken in this text, and in the research referred to below, represents the future of legal scholarship.

These first two chapters introduce some fundamental economic principles. The basic tools of price theory – supply and demand curves, and the like – are humble and deceptively simple, and it is easy to underestimate the power of these ideas. A lack of understanding of these principles often leads to the adoption of inefficient and sometimes disastrous policies – government subsidies of crops and inefficient firms, protectionist policies in foreign trade, and the like. Outside the United States, of course, the ignorance of economics has resulted in mass starvation and blighted lives for millions living in poverty. Thus we can begin to appreciate the value of price theory by considering the consequences of making decisions without it.

In this chapter we will examine demand and supply curves, how price and the amount of the good sold are determined in a competitive market (with an application to the market for lawyers), elasticities, and the effects of government intervention in the market via taxes, subsidies or price controls. We develop these foundations of price theory only to the extent they are helpful for the analysis of law set forth in the chapters that follow. Readers who are familiar with price theory at the level of a college course in intermediate microeconomics may wish to skip the first two chapters, and proceed immediately to the chapter on an introduction to the legal system.

A basic principle: the fungibility of money

A good is "fungible" if units of the good are regarded as indistinguishable from one another, and thus freely exchangeable. Money is fungible. A's $1 bill is for all practical purposes identical to B's $1 bill. The idea of fungibility has important economic implications. Many state lotteries have been adopted in part because of political support resulting from promises made to the public that all net revenues of the lottery will be used only for public education. Suppose a state spends $500 million a year on its public schools, raising the funds from a property tax. The voters of the state approve a state lottery, relying on the promise that all net revenues of the lottery will be spent on public education. The lottery has $200 million in net revenues in its first year, and all of it is spent on the public schools. Suppose, however, the state now takes $200 million of its property tax revenues that were previously spent on education, and spends them instead on road repairs. In this case the total spending on education has not increased; the problem is that money is fungible.

Now suppose that, without a lottery, the state would have continued to spend $500 million on public education. However, there is a lottery, and its net revenues for the year are $800 million, all of which must be spent on education. In this case the lottery actually increases spending on education by $300 million. Even though money is fungible, a restriction or earmark that causes expenditures to be greater than they would otherwise be does have an effect.

Let us return to the previous example, where the lottery raised $200 million specifically for public education, but total spending on schools ($500 million) did not increase at all. Do things like this really happen? As it turns out, it is unusual to find such extreme examples of fungibility. There have been a number of studies of the effect that earmarking funds for public education has on total educational spending. One study[1] found that between 50¢ and 70¢ out of every dollar earmarked for education ends up in local school districts, notwithstanding the fungibility of money. Governments are usually not brazen enough to offset the additional funds completely. This has been attributed to the "flypaper effect," i.e. the idea that money often sticks to the wall in the place where it is thrown. The idea is that government spending for a particular purpose, like public education, that has been promoted by an interest group, like the education lobby, tends to increase total expenditures for that purpose, because (1) the interest group will follow through to make sure the new funds that have been committed are not offset by an equal reduction of funds somewhere else, and (2) the government does not want to disappoint the interest group, because the interest group will then lose interest in supporting government programs. There is something like an implied contract that the government will not "double-cross" the interest group by reducing its spending to fully offset the new spending program that has been approved.

Cost

Let us now consider a basic economic term that is often misunderstood – the idea of cost. When an economist uses the word "cost," a layman, or beginning student, often assumes he means the financial cost – the cost in terms of money. However, when the word "cost" is used in a discussion among economists, it does not even occur to them that it means only the financial cost. For cost is a very broad idea in economics: depending on the situation, the cost of a given action may include money, time, emotional stress, discomfort, the risk of physical injury or criminal prosecution, or other undesirable consequences.

In general, the cost of an action is the value of the best opportunity that is lost by taking that action. In other words, it is the value of the best alternative to the action being considered. Suppose Bill, a college student, is trying to decide what to do with his life. He is considering several alternative occupations: law, dentistry, accounting, and becoming a high-school cross-country coach. Among these alternatives, the two he finds most appealing are law and becoming a cross-country coach. In this case the cost of choosing law is that he will not be able to coach cross-country. His decision whether to enter law school should turn only on whether law is more attractive to him than coaching cross-country. The other alternatives to law are irrelevant to his decision because they are dominated by the option of coaching cross-country.

The cost of going to college, rather than going to work immediately after high school, includes not only the out-of-pocket expenses for tuition, books, and the like, but also the loss of earnings one could have had by working full-time instead of attending classes.

There is also a psychic cost, namely the effort involved in studying and learning new and often difficult material. High school graduates go to college because the benefits they expect from college, in terms of increased earnings and greater knowledge, exceed these expected costs.

As the preceding example suggests, an important component of the cost of an action is the time it takes. Businesses whose workers must frequently wash their hands, like those involved in food preparation and health care, must decide whether their employees will use paper towels or electric hand driers to dry their hands. Manufacturers of hand driers contend that they cost less than paper towels, but their calculation does not consider the value of the time an employee requires to dry his hands. If the services of the average employee are worth $30 an hour to the employer, and the use of an electric hand drier takes a minute longer than paper towels, this represents an additional cost of $1/60 \times \$30 = \$.50$ each time an employee dries his hands. When this additional cost is considered, paper towels may be less expensive to an employer than electric hand driers.[2]

Sometimes one hears the expression "sunk cost." A sunk cost is a cost that has already been incurred and cannot be recovered. The key thing to know about a "sunk cost" is that it is not a cost at all. The cost of an action, or decision, is the opportunities that are sacrificed, or the resources that are consumed, by taking that action or making that decision. One should act if the benefits of the action being considered exceed its costs. If, on the other hand, the costs of the proposed action exceed its benefits, one should not do it. If an expenditure has already been made, and would not be increased or reduced by an action being considered, it is not a cost of that action, and is not at all relevant to whether that action should be taken. Suppose your father was a physician, and for as long as you can remember, everyone in your family expected that you would also become a physician. After college you entered medical school (mostly because everyone expected you to do so), and your family eventually paid $200,000 for your medical school education. However, after graduating, you realized that what you really wanted to do, or at least consider seriously, is to become a writer. How should you decide what to do – whether to become a writer or pursue a career in medicine? In particular, should the $200,000 your family paid for your medical education be a consideration? In fact it should not be. The $200,000 is gone and cannot be recovered; in economic terms, it is a sunk cost.

We may also note that economists use the terms "cost" and "revenue" in ways that are sometimes different from the way those words are used by others, such as accountants and tax lawyers. This is illustrated in the example below.

The economist's definitions of cost and revenue

The following example illustrates the difference between the definitions of cost and revenue used by the economist and the accountant, and the meaning of opportunity cost. Suppose Mr. X buys a parcel of land for $20,000 because he suspects there is oil under the property. To finance his oil exploration venture, he borrows $300,000 from a bank at an interest rate of 5 percent per year. He then buys oil drilling machinery for $200,000, and spends $50,000 more on materials and supplies, all of which are consumed during the year. He also hires two workers at a salary of $25,000 each.

During the year he discovers reserves of oil on the property, which increases its market value to $1 million. However, he does not sell the property. At the end of the year, the oil drilling machinery is worth $140,000 because of depreciation and ordinary wear and tear.

Although Mr. X works full-time in the oil drilling venture and owns the business, he does not receive any salary. Mr. X is trained as an engineer. If he were not working full-time in this oil drilling business, he could earn $50,000 a year working for a corporation. The question is, what is his profit (or loss) for the year?

An accountant would say that Mr. X has a loss, determined as follows:

Total revenue = $0

$$- 50,000 \text{ (cost of labor)}$$
$$- 60,000 \text{ (depreciation of oil drilling machinery)}$$
$$- 50,000 \text{ (cost of materials and supplies)}$$
$$- 15,000 \text{ (interest)}$$
$$= (\$175,000)$$

i.e., a loss. An economist, on the other hand, would say that Mr. X has a profit, determined as follows:

Total revenue = $980,000 (the gain from appreciation of the land, $1,000,000 − $20,000)

$$- 50,000 \text{ (cost of labor)}$$
$$- 60,000 \text{ (depreciation of oil drilling machinery)}$$
$$- 50,000 \text{ (cost of materials and supplies)}$$
$$- 15,000 \text{ (interest)}$$
$$- 50,000 \text{ (the value of the time of Mr. X)}$$
$$= \$755,000$$

i.e. a substantial profit.

Note that there are two differences between the calculation of profit made by the accountant and the economist. Unlike the economist, the accountant does not treat the appreciation in value of the land as a gain, because there has been no sale of the land. Also, unlike the accountant, the economist treats the value of the time of Mr. X – the income he sacrifices by working in the oil business – as a cost.

Now suppose instead that Mr. X was able to start his business without borrowing any money, because his grandmother had left him a trust fund, from which he withdrew the $300,000 required to finance the oil drilling project. Should we then eliminate the deduction of $15,000 for the cost of interest? We should not. Even though Mr. X does not have to borrow the money, by investing it in his business he has foregone the opportunity of investing it in a bond that would earn interest at 5 percent per year.[3] Since this opportunity that is sacrificed is a real economic cost, it is still appropriate to subtract the $15,000 to reflect the cost of using these funds.

In discussions of firm costs one often encounters references to "economies of scale." Below we consider economies of scale, and two related ideas: economies of scope, and learning-by-doing.

Table 1.1 Economies and diseconomies of scale

Quantity produced	Total cost	Average cost
0	30	
10	90	9
20	140	7
30	180	6
40	220	5.5
50	250	5
60	330	5.5
70	420	6
80	560	7
90	630	7
100	750	7.5

Economies of scale

There are economies of scale when the long-run average cost of production declines with the amount produced. In Table 1.1 average cost declines in the range from 0 to 50 units, but increases over the range from 50 to 100 units. We would say there are diseconomies of scale over the range from 50 to 100 units.

There are a number of different reasons for economies of scale:

1. One important factor is specialization and division of labor. In a famous passage in the Wealth of Nations, Adam Smith explained how "the important business of making a pin is … divided into about eighteen distinct operations which, in some manufactures, are all performed by distinct hands." If one worker tried to do all these operations himself, he would produce much less efficiently, since he would continually have to put down the tools required for one task, to pick up another set of tools required for another task. Also he would probably do each operation less skillfully than he could if he did the same operation repeatedly. Consequently eighteen workers dividing the labor of making pins would produce far more than eighteen times the number of pins that could be made by a single worker.
2. There are indivisibilities of certain factors of production or, putting it differently, certain inputs may have unavoidable "excess capacity." A photocopying machine suitable for a firm of twenty lawyers does not cost ten times as much as a photocopier purchased for a firm of two lawyers; it may cost less than twice as much. Moreover the photocopier purchased for the larger firm probably will not require ten times as much space, nor require ten times as much labor to maintain it, nor use ten times as much electricity. Perhaps the two-lawyer firm could have their photocopying done by an outside firm like Kinko's, but this would involve a transaction cost not borne by the firm with its own photocopier.
3. Inputs are generally less expensive when purchased in large quantities. The purchaser of 10,000 envelopes will pay less per envelope than one who buys 100 envelopes, since the cost of the transaction – making the purchase – can be spread, or as the economist would say, amortized, over a larger number of envelopes.
4. Some economies of scale are a result of the statistical law of large numbers. Loosely speaking, the weak law of large numbers states that the average value of a sample of objects chosen randomly from some population is likely to be closer to the true mean

of the population, the larger the size of the sample. For example, there is much less variation in the death rate of a large population like the United States – i.e., the number of deaths per year divided by the population – than in the death rate of a small town. The current death rate of the U.S. population is about eight per thousand per year, and does not change much from year to year. In a small town with a population of 500, however, there may be only one death in one year, but seven in the following year, and four the year after that, etc. (a small town is a very small sample of the U.S. population). Because of the law of large numbers, there is less variation in the demand for milk by the customers of a large supermarket than by the customers of a local convenience store. Therefore if, for example, the supermarket sells on average ten times as much milk as the convenience store, it does not have to stock its shelves with ten times as much milk. The convenience store must carry more inventory relative to its sales since there is far more variation in the demand of its customers.[4]

Diseconomies of scale

Table 1.1 shows that there are diseconomies of scale over the range from 50 to 100 units. In general, there are diseconomies of scale if it takes more than twice the inputs to double the firm's output. What would explain diseconomies of scale? Students often think they would result from efforts to produce more than a plant's capacity, but this is incorrect, since in the long run we assume the firm is using a plant of optimal size for the level of output being considered. Some economists argue that once a firm reaches a certain size, it becomes difficult (costly) for managers to obtain good information about the firm's operations, or monitor the work of employees, or to organize and coordinate activities.

Diseconomies of scale may also arise because of unions. Unions are more likely to attempt to organize the workers of a large firm than a small firm; the reason is that for the union there are economies of scale in organizing workers. The costs of a firm whose workers join a union will generally increase as the union seeks higher wages and fringe benefits for its members; moreover, a union can call a strike, and cause the legal expenses of a firm to increase for various reasons.

George Stigler noted that very large firms do not do well in industries where rapid changes are required by changes in style or fashion, like women's apparel, women's shoes, or novelty toys. Walter Oi pointed out that entrepreneurial ability is subject to the law of eventually diminishing marginal product. If there is one fixed factor (entrepreneurial ability), the marginal product of other factors such as land, labor and capital, must eventually decline as more of these factors are hired. If only one executive can be in charge of the firm, he will become less informed and less effective when the firm continues to grow beyond a certain size.

Economies of scope, economies of scale and learning-by-doing

There are economies of scope when two different products can be produced at lower cost by one firm than by two firms, each producing one product. Since firms in the beef industry obtain the hides of steers as a by-product, they may be able to produce beef and leather at lower cost than two firms, each producing one of these goods, assuming the same inputs are used in each production arrangement. A single oil refinery can produce heating oil, gasoline and jet fuel at a lower cost than three firms making these products separately. Conversely in some situations there are diseconomies of scope. Kim (1987) found that it cost 41 percent more for a railroad to transport both passengers and freight than if these tasks were done separately by two railroads.

Economies of scale and economies of scope refer to conditions in effect at a particular time, with a given technology. For example, there are economies of scale in the automobile industry, because today the average cost of an automobile is lower for a firm that produces one million vehicles than for a firm that produces only ten of them. This comparison involves only a change in output, not a change that occurs over time; we are considering a movement along a long-run average cost curve, rather than a shift of the curve.

We can also consider changes that occur over time. "Learning by doing" refers to a downward shift of the long-run average cost curve that occurs when workers learn from experience how to produce goods more efficiently. A lawyer who has done three or four house closings (the investigation, negotiations and paperwork required to complete the sale of a house) can do another one much more efficiently than a lawyer doing his first closing. Long-run average cost curves also move downward because of technological change. It costs less to manufacture an automobile today than it did thirty years ago at any level of production, because of technical advances such as computer programs, lasers and robots.

Demand curves and supply curves

Demand curves

Let us now consider the definition of a demand curve. A demand curve for some good or service X shows the amount of X that is demanded at different prices.[5] There are individual demand curves and market demand curves; a demand curve may represent the demand for X of an individual consumer, or it may represent the demand for X of a large population of consumers in a given market area, such as the Denver metropolitan area. Some period of time is implicit in the demand curve; for example, a demand curve may show the monthly demand for avocados in the Denver metropolitan area. A market demand curve is constructed by summing horizontally the individual demand curves of each consumer in the market. For example, suppose Ann and Bob are the only two buyers of product X in the market. At a price of $10, Ann will buy six units of X, and Bob will buy ten units. Therefore at a price of $10, the market demand curve will have a total amount demanded of sixteen units. At a price of $6, Ann will buy nine units of X, and Bob will buy twelve units. Thus another point on the market demand curve will be where the price is $6 and the quantity demanded is twenty-one.

Let us consider a demand curve for avocados per month of an individual in Denver. What exactly is it? His demand curve represents not only the number of avocados he will buy per month at different possible prices, but also, and equivalently, the value of avocados to him. Parenthetically, the word "value" always has a precise meaning in economics: it is the maximum amount the individual is willing to pay for the object. Assume the first avocado is worth $8 to this person, the second one is worth $6, a third one would be worth $5, a fourth $2, and a fifth or further avocados would be worth zero. Now suppose the market price of avocados is $4. Under these circumstances he would buy three avocados. The total value to him of these avocados is $8 + $6 + $5 = $19. He must pay $12 to purchase them, so he has realized a gain from this exchange (which is known as consumer surplus) of $7. The total value of the avocados to him of $19 equals the area under his demand curve from the origin out to the third avocado. Thus the demand curve is a curve of marginal value, or marginal social benefit; by "marginal value" we mean value "at the margin," i.e., the value,

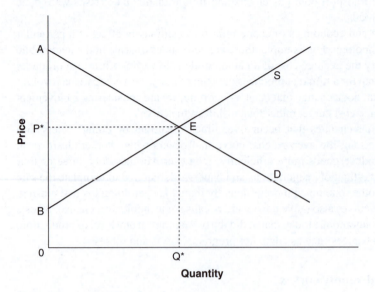

Figure 1.1 Supply and demand curves; market equilibrium.

given the current amount, of one more unit of the good. When this person has no avocados, the marginal value of an avocado to him is $8; when he has one avocado, the marginal value is $6, and so forth. The area underneath a curve of marginal value equals the total value. This observation applies to market demand curves as well. In Figure 1.1, the total value of Q* goods to consumers equals area AEQ*O, the total area under the demand curve from the origin to Q*.

It is customary[6] to draw demand and supply curves with the quantity of the good on the horizontal axis, and value or price on the vertical axis.[7] A critical feature of demand curves is that they are downward-sloping. The demand curve of an individual for, say, refrigerators, slopes down because the first refrigerator has more value to the individual than a second one. A market demand curve is also downward-sloping, which implies that if the price of a good declines, the quantity demanded will increase.

Of course the demand for a good is affected by factors other than its price. For example, an individual's demand for a good may be affected by his income, the prices of other goods that are substitutes or complements, his information about the good, or by an expectation on his part that the price of the good will change. What happens to the demand curve if there is a change in some factor *other than price* that affects the quantity demanded? A change in some variable that affects the amount demanded, but is not shown on either axis of the demand curve, causes a *shift* of the demand curve. For example, if we consider a market demand curve for avocados, an increase in the income of the population will cause the demand curve to shift to the right, since at any price more avocados will be demanded. Note that a decline in the price of avocados will also increase the amount demanded, but this corresponds to a *movement along the demand curve*, rather than a *shift* of the curve. Similarly, since rental cars are complementary to air travel, an increase in airline fares will probably cause the demand for rental cars to shift to the left. Some new information about eggs, i.e. scientific studies linking egg consumption to higher levels of cholesterol, will cause the demand curve for eggs to shift to the left. The size of each of these changes – whether movements along the demand curve or shifts of the curve – is measured by a number called an elasticity, which we will examine below.

Here we may introduce a distinction between the intensive and extensive margins, that applies to market demand and supply curves. The word "intensive" means "increasing in degree or amount," while "extensive" means "characterized by extension." A change on the intensive margin is a change in the level of activity by those currently participating in the market, while a change on the extensive margin is a change in participation: either entry into the market, or exit from it. When the price of avocados falls, someone who previously bought two avocados per week might increase his purchases to three avocados; this is a change on the intensive margin. Another person, who was not buying avocados, might respond to the decline in price by deciding to buy some; this is a change on the extensive margin.

Supply curves

The supply curve for a good X represents the cost of producing each additional unit of output; stating it differently, a supply curve is a curve of marginal cost. Marginal cost is the cost of producing one more unit of the good, given the current level of output.[8] Some period of time is implicit in a supply curve, just as it is with a demand curve. Suppose a firm's total cost of production is $100 for ten units per month, $112 for eleven units per month, and $126 for twelve units per month. Then the marginal cost of the eleventh unit is $12, and the marginal cost of the twelfth unit is $14.

While a demand curve represents the maximum amount the buyer is willing to pay for the good, a supply curve represents the minimum amount the supplier will accept for the good. At each level of output, the supply curve shows the price the producer must receive, i.e., the absolute minimum amount, to produce that additional unit of output. If A's supply price for doing tax returns is $50 per hour, he will insist on that amount, and of course would gladly accept a higher rate.

As with demand curves, there are supply curves for individual persons or firms and there are market supply curves. A market supply curve is constructed by summing horizontally the individual supply curves of all persons or firms providing the good to the market. Since a supply curve shows the marginal, or additional, cost of each unit, the area under the supply curve equals the total cost of all units of the good. Referring again to Figure 1.1, the total cost to firms of producing Q* goods equals area OBEQ*, the total area under the supply curve, from the origin to Q*.

A change in a factor other than price that affects the amount supplied will cause a shift of the supply curve. For example, a general increase in the wages of the workers in an industry will cause the market supply curve to shift upward. On the other hand, technical progress – a reduction in the costs of production – will cause the supply curve to shift down.

Supply, like demand, is affected by an expectation that the price of the good will change. On January 1, 1992, Russia announced that prices of goods and services would no longer be subject to price controls. This announcement had been expected by suppliers, and the anticipation of it had caused many firms to withhold their goods from the market, resulting in severe shortages prior to the announcement. The firms decided to wait until the price controls were removed before selling their goods, so that they could sell at the much higher market price.

The distinction between intensive and extensive margins applies to market supply curves as well as market demand curves. For example, suppose the supply curve in Figure 1.1 represents the supply of nursing services in the United States. If the average hourly wage for registered nurses increases, say from $20 to $25, there will be an increase in the amount of nursing services supplied. On the intensive margin, nurses may choose to work more hours (or, in some cases, fewer hours). On the extensive margin, there will be changes in the decision to enter or leave the market. Some persons who were originally trained as nurses, and who subsequently left nursing, will be drawn back into it. Some nurses who had previously planned to retire will decide to postpone their retirement. There may well be an increase in immigration, as nurses from other countries like Canada, the Philippines or India, decide to emigrate to the United States. Finally, there will be an increase in enrollment in nursing schools.

Compensating differentials

Let us consider more closely the factors that determine the supply of labor to an occupation, or to a specific job. A particular job will have amenities or disamenities, i.e., favorable or unfavorable working conditions, that have some value (positive or negative) to workers. The term "compensating differential" or "equalizing difference" refers to an upward or downward adjustment of the wage, reflecting any amenities or disamenities of the job. Recall that the labor supply curve shows the wage required to induce a worker to do a job. If working conditions are especially unpleasant or risky, the labor supply curve for that job will be higher than it is for the average job. Adam Smith pointed out that the executioner is paid more than other workers with the same skills because his work is distasteful.[9] Coal miners earn a higher wage than workers with comparable skills because coal mining is dirty and dangerous work. Nurses on the night shift receive a wage premium since working at night is disruptive to sleep and to interaction with others. The labor market provides compensation for risks of various kinds. One example is physical risk: police officers on the bomb squad are paid more than those with routine duties. Before the development of modern navigation systems for airplanes, pilots were paid more for flying at night and over mountains. There are also compensating differentials for income risk: construction workers in the private sector generally have a higher wage than state employees because they face a higher probability of layoffs.

In Chapter 8, on torts, we will see that the wage premiums that compensate workers for physical risks have been used to estimate tort damages for loss of life.

Conversely, there is a negative compensating differential for jobs with especially attractive working conditions; other things equal, the supply curve is lower (people are willing to work for a lower wage) for jobs on cruise ships or in Caribbean resorts. Wages are also lower in jobs that enable the worker to improve his productivity and earning capacity (which economists call general human capital) by, for example, learning computer or word-processing skills that increase his value to many potential employers.

Thus if Ms. Jones has a choice between one position with money income of $35,000 and disamenities valued at minus $3,000, and another position with money income of $30,000, and amenities worth $3,000, we assume she will choose the second one. In other words, we assume that an individual chooses the job that will maximize her total real income, instead of considering only the job's money income.

The equilibrium of a competitive market

Now that we have examined both market demand and supply curves, we can consider how they jointly determine the price of the good and the amount sold. In a competitive market, the

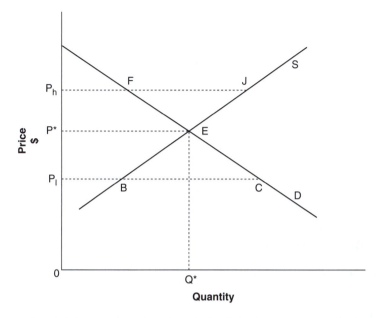

Figure 1.2 The equilibrium of a competitive market.

equilibrium price, and the equilibrium quantity sold, are determined by the intersection of the market supply and demand curves. In Figure 1.2, the demand and supply curves intersect at point E, and this determines both the market price P* and the quantity sold Q*. Notice that at a price lower than P*, such as P_l, the amount demanded, P_lC, exceeds the amount offered for sale by suppliers, P_lB. Accordingly if P_l were the market price some of the buyers, in the amount BC, would not be able to obtain any goods. Yet we know that the value of the good to these buyers is represented by the height of the demand curve above the line segment BC, and in this region the demand curve is everywhere higher than P_l. We would expect that some buyers would then offer to pay sellers a premium – a price greater than P* – to avoid having to go home with no merchandise. This will cause upward pressure on the price. On the other hand, if the price happened to be above P*, such as P_h, the amount offered for sale by suppliers, P_hJ, exceeds the amount demanded at that price, P_hF. Thus if P_h were the market price some of the sellers, in the amount FJ, would be unable to find buyers for their goods. Yet we know that the amount the sellers are willing to sell the good for is represented by the height of the supply curve below the line segment FJ, and in this region the supply curve is everywhere lower than P_h. Under these conditions one would expect that some sellers would offer discounts to avoid being left with their inventory. This would cause downward pressure on the price. Accordingly if the current market price happens to be something other than P*, market forces will tend to push the price back toward equilibrium.

Price ceilings

Sometimes the law prevents the price from moving toward equilibrium. For example, some cities have statutes on rent control that make it unlawful for landlords to charge more than

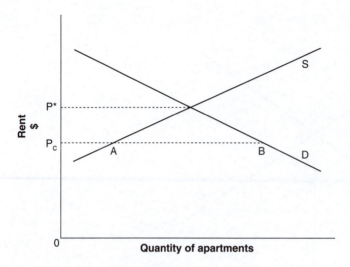

Figure 1.3 The effects of rent control, a price ceiling.

a specified amount, which is often much less than the equilibrium rental. Rent control is an example of a "price ceiling." In Figure 1.3, P_c is the maximum rent allowed by law. At P_c there is excess demand for apartments in the amount AB, yet buyers cannot legally compete for apartments by raising their bids above P_c. In this kind of situation competition among buyers who do not want to be excluded will be diverted into other channels. One form of competition is waiting in line; in many cities with rent control, apartments have long waiting lists. Another way of competing is through the quality of the buyer; a landlord who chooses a tenant from hundreds of applicants will be inclined to choose one whom he finds personally attractive: perhaps someone who is quiet, or highly educated, or from an ethnic or religious background favored by the landlord, or an applicant without small children, who may be expected to cause more wear and tear to the apartment. Thus, as has often been noted, low-income persons and members of minority groups, whose types by definition are underrepresented in the landlord population, do not necessarily benefit from rent control.

A price ceiling can also be avoided by "black market" transactions: applicants may surreptitiously give landlords "key money" to move ahead of others on the waiting list, or may agree to purchase worn-out furniture from the landlord at inflated prices. The point is that competition among buyers for the scarce commodity cannot be suppressed by law, and will, without fail, find a way to express itself.

Rent control laws have some effects that develop over time (there is a general distinction between static and dynamic analysis: a static analysis examines market forces at a given point in time, while a dynamic analysis considers changes that occur over time). In the case of rent control, owners of apartment buildings have little incentive to maintain their buildings, since they will receive a rent of only P_c rather than P^*. Consequently many property owners simply allow their buildings to deteriorate to the point where their rental value reaches P_c. On the extensive margin, some owners will convert their apartment buildings to office space, or to other uses that are not subject to rent control ordinances. In addition, developers may well choose not to construct new buildings in areas where there is rent control.

Table 1.2 Market demand and supply curves

Units ($000)	First	Second	Third	Fourth	Fifth	Sixth
Marginal value (height of demand curve)	40	30	20	15	14	12
Marginal cost (height of supply curve)	6	10	12	14	16	20

In Chapter 5 on property law we will encounter other price ceilings in a number of different contexts: in the procurement of transplantable human organs, in the adoption of babies, and the protection of endangered species such as African elephants.

An important feature of competitive equilibrium is its effect on social welfare. Competitive equilibrium maximizes the net social benefits of exchange, i.e., the total social benefits of exchange, minus the total social costs. Net social benefits are maximized when, in deciding how much output to produce, suppliers produce more output as long as the social value of an additional unit of the good (the height of the demand curve) exceeds its social cost (the height of the supply curve); when total output reaches a point where this is no longer true, production should cease. The optimal level of output will emerge as the natural outcome (the equilibrium) of a competitive market.

Suppose the height of the demand and supply curve for different amounts of the good are as shown in Table 1.2. Note that the fourth unit is the last one for which the height of the demand curve exceeds the height of the supply curve; thus four units of output will be produced in equilibrium. The social value of four units of output is

$$(40 + 30 + 20 + 15) = \$105$$

and the social cost is:

$$(6 + 10 + 12 + 14) = \$42$$

Therefore the net social benefit from producing and selling four units of output is $63. If only three units were produced, the net social benefit would be $(90–28) = \$62$, and if five units were produced, the net social benefit would be $(119–58) = \$61$. Net social benefits are maximized when suppliers produce and sell exactly four units, and this will occur in equilibrium.

One normally thinks of demand and supply curves as being continuous, rather than the discrete step functions shown in Table 1.2. Figure 1.4 shows the competitive equilibrium for continuous demand and supply curves. The net social benefit of a market in avocados is represented by the area AEB, which equals (1) the area under the market demand curve AEQ*O (representing the total social value of the avocados) minus (2) the area under the market supply curve BEQ*O, (representing the total social cost of the avocados). Subtracting the total social cost from the total social value yields the net social value, or net social benefit, of having a market for exchange of the avocados.

The market for lawyers

Let us now apply the ideas introduced above to a real-world example: the market for lawyers in the United States. Figure 1.5 shows the supply curve for legal services in the United States. The wage of lawyers is on the vertical axis, and the amount of legal services provided is on

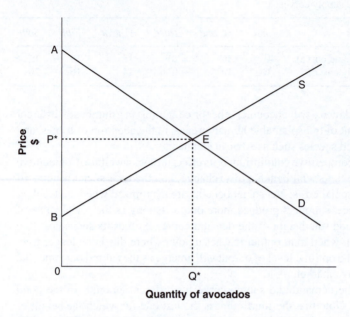

Figure 1.4 The net social gain from a market for avocados.

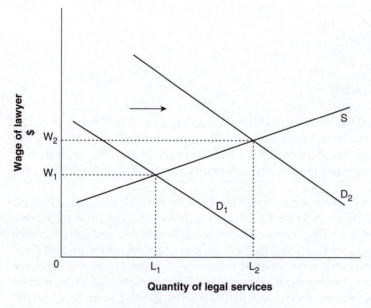

Figure 1.5 An increase in demand for legal services.

the horizontal axis. The amount of legal services could be measured, for example, in millions of man-hours of legal work per year. If there is an increase in demand for legal services, as there was between 1975 and 1987, the relative wage of lawyers will increase, and more legal services will be provided. In Figure 1.5, the demand curve shifts from D_1 to D_2, the wage increases from W_1 to W_2, and the quantity of legal services increases from L_1 to L_2.

On the intensive margin, lawyers may choose to work longer hours. On the extensive margin, more college graduates will choose to enter law school. Some individuals who were trained as lawyers but left law practice may be attracted back into legal work, and some older lawyers who were previously planning to retire may now decide to postpone their retirement. Overall, in the United States the number of lawyers per capita doubled between 1967 and 1979, and increased by almost an additional 50 percent between 1979 and 1987.[10]

To provide the additional lawyers for the U.S. economy, there were changes in law schools at both intensive and extensive margins. The number of law schools grew at an annual rate of 2.35 percent from 1967 to 1975, and then slowed to 0.64 percent, reaching a peak of 175 schools in the mid-1980s. Over the same period, the average size of each law school increased by 75 percent.[11] Most of the adjustment occurred at the intensive margin, since change at the extensive margin is more costly: it takes time to plan and build a new school, recruit faculty and students of high quality, assemble a library, and the like.

The factor market

The law of (eventually) diminishing marginal product

Economists assume that the process by which a firm uses "inputs" or "factors of production" such as land, labor, and capital to produce final output can be represented by a production function. If q is the level of output, and $a, b, c,$ and d are the amounts of inputs used by the firm, we can write the production function as:

$$q = f(a, b, c, d)$$

which simply means that the amount of output produced by the firm over a given period of time is a function f of the quantities of $a, b, c,$ and d used in the production process.

If we hold constant the amounts of all inputs but one, input a, we can express the output of the firm as a function of that one input:

$$q = f(a)$$

The *marginal product* of a is defined as the increase in total output the firm would obtain by hiring one more unit of a, holding fixed the amounts of all other inputs:

$$MP_a = \frac{\Delta q}{\Delta a}.$$

Table 1.3 shows in a hypothetical example how the marginal product of a changes as more units of a are employed by the firm, and Figure 1.6 shows how the level of output of a firm, q, might change as the firm used more units of a. The marginal product of a, $\Delta q / \Delta a$, is in fact the slope of $q = f(a)$.[12] Note that in Table 1.3 the marginal product $\Delta q / \Delta a$ increases at first, then subsequently declines from seven to six when the fourth unit of the factor is hired. Also in Figure 1.6, the slope of the total product curve q increases at first, but then declines at a_1. This change occurs because of the famous law of eventually diminishing marginal product. According to this law, as more and more units of a factor a are hired by a firm, holding fixed the amounts of all other factors, the additional output obtained by hiring an additional unit of factor a must eventually decline.

Table 1.3 Hypothetical schedule of marginal product of
factor *a*

Units of factor hired	q = Total output	Change in output (marginal product, Δq/Δa)
0	0	
1	4	4
2	9	5
3	16	7
4	22	6
5	27	5
6	30	3
7	32	2
8	33	1

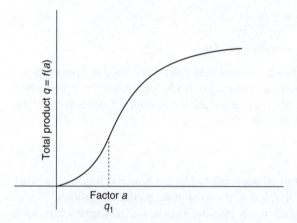

Figure 1.6 Changes in total product as more of a factor is hired.

In Figure 1.6 the amounts of all factors other than *a* are held fixed. Now what would happen if the amounts of the other factors changed? An increase in the amount of another factor, *b*, might increase the marginal product of *a*; if this is true, we would say that factors *a* and *b* are *complements*. We would expect that factors are complements in many cases. If a law firm increases the amount of on-line legal materials available to its lawyers (court cases, statutes, regulations, law journal articles, etc.), the productivity of its lawyers will increase. Conversely, the value of those materials to the law firm will increase if the firm hires additional lawyers. Assuming *a* and *b* are complements, we can draw different total product curves for *a*: $f_1(a), f_2(a), f_3(a)$, corresponding to increasing amounts of *b*: b_1, b_2, and b_3. This is shown in Figure 1.7.

How much of an input will the firm hire?

When we examined the decision a firm makes on how much output it will produce, we concluded that to maximize profits, the firm would produce at the level of output where marginal revenue equals marginal cost. Another question we might ask is how much of

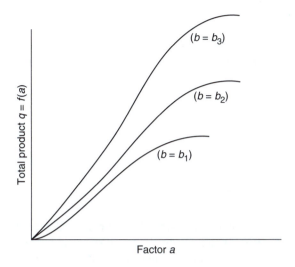

Figure 1.7 Total product curves for different amounts of a complementary factor.

each input (of land, labor, capital, etc.) should a firm hire in order to maximize profits? Of course, the amount of inputs a firm hires will determine the amount of output it produces (through the firm's production function), so we would hope to get the same answer – the same level of output – if we pose the question in terms of inputs rather than outputs. And, of course, we do.

When we considered what the optimal level of output would be, we concluded that an additional unit of output should be produced and sold if, and only if, the additional revenue thereby gained (marginal revenue) was greater than the additional cost of producing that unit (marginal cost). It turns out that when we consider how much of each input the firm should hire, we should follow the same rule. An additional unit of an input should be hired if, and only if, the additional revenue thereby gained (which is called marginal revenue product) is greater than the additional cost of hiring that unit (called marginal factor cost).

The marginal revenue product of an increase of an input equals the change in the firm's total revenue divided by the change in the amount of the input: $\Delta TR / \Delta a$. Note that this fraction can be written as:

$$\frac{\Delta TR}{\Delta a} = \frac{\Delta TR}{\Delta q} \cdot \frac{\Delta q}{\Delta a},$$

where the first term on the right-hand side represents the change in total revenue divided by the change in the amount of the product produced and sold, or marginal revenue, and the second term is the change in total product divided by the change in the amount of the factor used, or marginal product. Thus:

marginal revenue product = marginal revenue × marginal product.

Now let us consider an example of how much of a factor – in this case labor – a firm will hire.

Suppose a rental car agency must decide how many customer agents to hire to staff one of its local offices. The salary of a rental agent is $100 per day. If the office has many potential

Table 1.4 Hypothetical schedule of marginal revenue
product of labor for car rental agents

No. of rental agents	Total rental revenue per day ($)	Marginal revenue product per day ($)
0	0	
1	90	90
2	200	110
3	340	140
4	430	90
5	500	70
6	550	50
7	580	30

customers, the additional revenue to be gained by hiring a second agent may well exceed the revenue obtained from hiring the first agent. If there is only one agent, she would not be able to answer the phone and serve customers who walk in, simultaneously. If the office has only one agent, customers may have to wait a long time to be served, and they may decide to go elsewhere (never to return). In Table 1.4, the marginal revenue product of a second agent exceeds that of the first agent, and the marginal revenue product of a third agent is greater still.

There will be some number of agents that is optimal for the rental office, holding fixed the amount of its other factors, e.g., the size of the rental office, its location, inventory of vehicles, advertising expenditures, telephone lines, computers, fax machines, and the like. Table 1.4 indicates that for this particular office the optimal number of agents is three. The marginal revenue product of a third agent, $140, exceeds her marginal cost of $100, while the marginal revenue product of a fourth agent, $90, would be less than her marginal cost. If there are already three agents in the office, who can handle most of the customer traffic, a fourth agent may not have much to do for most of the day. With the fourth agent, this rental office would be subject to the law of eventually diminishing marginal product. Note also that the marginal revenue product of the fourth agent would surely increase if the firm were to increase the amount of complementary factors at the rental office, e.g., by adding more vehicles and telephone lines, or by doing more advertising.

Next we consider how a change in the price of a factor affects the firm's decision of how much of that factor, or other factors, it will hire.

Substitution and scale effects of a change in factor price

The substitution effect

A change in the price of a factor has both a substitution effect and a scale effect. The substitution effect arises because at a given level of output, a firm will be inclined to hire more of a factor whose price has fallen, and less of a factor whose price has increased. This obviously has implications for the amount of other factors that the firm hires. If, for example, the price of capital falls, or the productivity of capital increases, which effectively reduces the price of the services of capital, one would expect the firm to substitute toward capital and away from labor. With the advent of bar code technology, stores do not need as many workers to mark prices on goods, or to add up the prices of goods at the cash register. The introduction of automatic teller machines greatly reduced the need for bank tellers.

Since the objective of a firm is to maximize profits, the firm will seek to minimize costs at every level of output. Therefore if the price of an input increases, the firm will tend to substitute toward the use of other inputs. If, for example, the cost of labor increases, a firm may substitute toward capital and hire fewer workers. Laws that were intended to improve working conditions for migrant agricultural workers in the United States required the owners of farms to provide them with housing and other amenities. As a consequence, many farms decided to buy machinery to harvest their crop rather than hire migrant workers.

Another example is the salad bar. In many restaurants in the United States, a customer who wants a salad goes to the salad bar to prepare it himself. In restaurants that do not have a salad bar, a restaurant employee prepares the salad in a bowl, and serves it to the customer at his table. Salad bars are generally found in countries where wages are high, like the United States. The use of a salad bar enables the restaurant to reduce its use of labor, but allows the customer to obtain a larger salad than he would get otherwise. In high-wage countries it costs less to give the customer more lettuce, tomatoes, croutons, etc., than it would to hire the labor to prepare a salad. In countries in which the cost of labor is low, like China, restaurants will not use a salad bar.

The same analysis applies to the automated telephone service (called automated interactive voice-response systems), which can be used either to receive calls ("If you wish to refill a prescription, press 1; if you wish to talk to a pharmacist, press 2 …") or to make calls. In high-wage countries, firms will substitute away from using their employees to make calls toward these services, or will hire individuals in low-wage countries to talk on the telephone. In low-wage countries firms can minimize costs by having their own employees talk to the firm's customers.

A similar observation applies to the web sites of many companies. Often the web site encourages a customer to contact the company with an email, rather than by a phone call, by making the phone number difficult for the customer to find. Customer requests made by email can be handled with fewer employees than such requests made by phone.

Web sites of companies with employees in low-wage countries are more likely to invite customers to contact them by phone.

The scale effect

That is the substitution effect. What about the scale effect of a change in factor price? This arises because a change in the price of a factor affects the firm's desired level of output. A supermarket that adopts bar code technology (an effective decline in the price of capital) will be able to lower its prices and thus attract more customers and expand its operations. It will then employ more managers, truck drivers, workers to stock its shelves, etc. Similarly, a bank that installed automatic teller machines was able to, in effect, reduce the price of its banking services by improving their quality: a customer could now make withdrawals at any time of the day or week, rather than just during regular banking hours. A bank that effectively reduces its price will be able to increase its output. Thus a bank would attract more customers, and would need to hire more loan officers, secretaries, security guards, etc.

An increase in wages increases the costs of a firm, which means the firm must raise its price, in which case its sales and output will decline. Because its output has declined, the firm will hire fewer amounts of factors such as labor and capital. Conversely, a decline in wages leads to an increase in sales and output. A hotel chain that hires immigrant workers at a low wage will be able to offer lower room prices to guests, and thus will obtain more business than its competitors. The hotel chain will then need to increase its use of other types of labor – security guards, plumbers, electricians, and others.

Another way to understand the scale effect is through the effect of a change in factor price on the amounts of other factors employed by the firm. To understand this, suppose a firm received an addition to its capital from out of the blue, as a gift. If capital and labor are complementary factors – the usual case – this increase in capital would increase the marginal product of the labor employed by the firm, which would induce the firm to hire more labor. When the firm hires more labor, the marginal product of its capital will increase, leading the firm to acquire more capital, which in turn increases the marginal product of labor. Of course this sequence of events does not continue indefinitely; the firm will converge to a new equilibrium with larger amounts of capital, labor, and other factors.

Now imagine that the initial change is a decline in the price of capital. In this case there is both a substitution effect, which induces the firm to substitute toward capital and away from other factors such as labor, and a scale effect, which will affect the amounts of other factors desired by the firm. Since the price of capital falls, the firm will respond by buying more capital. Assuming capital and labor are complementary factors, the marginal product of labor will increase, and the firm will wish to hire more labor. This effect will work in the opposite direction from the substitution effect.

In general, the scale effect can be greater or less than the substitution effect. If the overall result of a decline in the price of capital is that the firm employs less labor, we say that capital and labor are gross substitutes. If the overall result is that the firm hires more labor, we say that capital and labor are gross complements.

We could also ask a more theoretical question, namely what happens if there is no scale effect, so that the firm's output remains the same. Suppose again there is a decline in the price of capital. If the firm would then wish to hire less labor, we would say that capital and labor are net substitutes. If the firm would wish to hire more labor, we say that capital and labor are net complements.

Isoquants

We can analyze the question of how much of each factor of production the firm should hire with the use of curves called isoquants. The word "isoquant" is derived from Latin words meaning "equal or same quantity." Isoquants are curves that show all the different combinations of inputs that can be used to produce a given level of output. In Figure 1.8, there are two inputs: labor per year is the input on the horizontal axis and capital per year is on the vertical axis. The diagram shows three isoquants representing three different levels of output. The isoquant for $Q = 100$ units of output shows that this quantity of output can be produced with five units of capital and two units of labor, or alternatively with two units of capital and four units of labor.

The problem facing the firm is how to maximize the output it produces for a given total expenditure on factors of production, or (stating the same problem differently) how to minimize the total cost of factors of production that will yield a given level of output. Suppose we have only two factors of production, capital, K and labor, L. The cost of a unit of capital per unit time is r, and the cost of a unit of labor per unit time is w. The total amount spent by the firm on factors of production, which we will call C, is $rK + wL$. We can represent all the possible combinations of factors that can be purchased for a given total expenditure C by something called an isocost line, meaning a line showing the same or equal total cost at

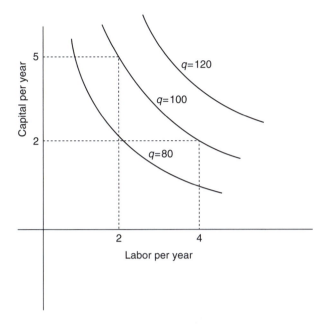

Figure 1.8 Isoquants for three levels of output.

all points on the line in Figure 1.9, at point A the firm would be spending all of C on capital, and at point B it would be spending it all on labor. Since we know that $C = rK + wL$, and at point A we know that $L = 0$, the amount of capital purchased at point A is C/r. Similarly, since we know that $C = rK + wL$, and at point B we know that $K = 0$, the amount of labor purchased at point B is C/w. Also, since $rK = C - wL$, we know that:

$$K = \frac{C}{r} - \frac{w}{r}L$$

Thus the slope of the isocost line is:

$$-\frac{w}{r}$$

Now what would happen if the wage increased from w to a higher wage, w_2? In this case the point where the isocost line crosses the horizontal axis would shift inward from C/w to C/w_2, 95 shown in Figure 1.9. The isocost line now points more steeply toward labor, since labor has now become more expensive. Similarly, suppose the cost of capital increased from r to a higher rent, r_2. In this case the point where the isocost line crosses the vertical axis would decline from C/r to C/r_2, which is shown in the diagram. The isocost line now points more steeply toward capital, since capital is now more expensive.

For a given total expenditure C spent on factors of production, the firm would want to produce as much output as possible. Note in Figure 1.10 that the firm could produce eighty units of output by operating at either of points F or G; however it could produce 100 units of output by operating at point E*. Since in order to maximize profit it wants to maximize the output it produces for a given level of expenditure on factors, it will produce at point E*, hiring

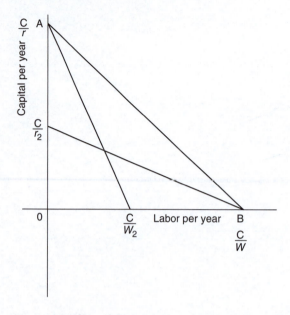

Figure 1.9 Effect of changes in the price of a factor on the isocost line.

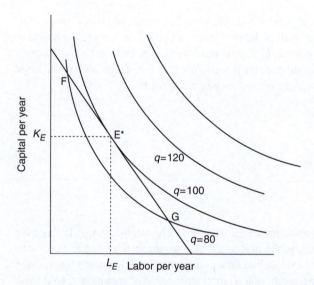

Figure 1.10 Maximizing output for a given level of expenditure on factors.

K_E units of capital and L_E units of labor. Note that it would like to produce 120 units of output for the level of expenditure C, but this higher isoquant cannot be attained from this isocost line.

Finally, Figure 1.11 shows how the firm that wants to produce 100 units of output would respond to different relative prices of capital and labor, in choosing how much of each factor to buy. If the relative wage of labor is high, as on isocost line IC_1 the firm will choose point E_1,

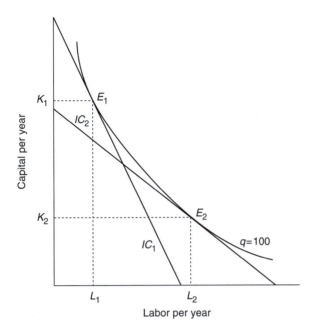

Figure 1.11 How the firm's choice of inputs responds to different factor prices.

and hire K_1 units of capital and L_1 units of labor. If, however, the relative wage of labor is lower, as on isocost line IC_2, the firm will choose point E_2, and hire K_2 units of capital and L_2 units of labor. Recall from the discussion earlier in this chapter that the substitution effect of a change in factor price shows how the firm would change its purchases of factors if it stayed at the same level of output where it was operating before the change in factor price. Here the firm's response to a reduction in the relative price of labor, going from isocost line IC_1 to IC_2, would be to increase its purchases of labor from L_1 to L_2, and reduce its purchases of capital from K_1 to K_2.

These represent the pure substitution effects of the change in relative factor price. There will also be scale effects. If, for example, the wage of labor falls, the costs of the firm fall, and it will choose a higher level of output. This means a shift to a higher isoquant.

The effects of a tax

In a preceding section we considered the consequences of a price ceiling imposed by law. The government can also intervene in a market by imposing a tax on a good, or by providing a subsidy to encourage its consumption. In this section we will consider the impact of a tax in general terms. In the following section we will analyze the effects of a subsidy.

Let us consider an excise tax, which is a tax of a fixed dollar amount on each unit of a good. The economic effects of an excise tax are shown in Figure 1.12. A tax puts a wedge between the market demand and supply curves, to the left of their intersection. The way to understand a tax is to consider the following equation:

The amount paid by the buyer = the tax + the amount received by the seller

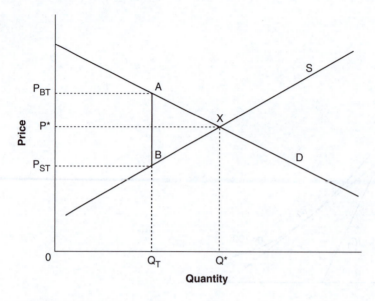

Figure 1.12 A tax.

In Figure 1.12, the amount paid by the buyer is AQ_T, the amount received by the seller is BQ_T, and the tax is AB. If there were no tax the amount paid by the buyer would be P^*, which would also be the amount received by the seller. Note that the tax has several consequences: (1) it reduces the amount of the good sold, from Q^* to Q_T, (2) it increases the amount paid by the buyer, from P^* to P_{BT}, and it reduces the amount received by the seller, from P^* to P_{ST}. The amount of tax revenue collected by the government equals the tax AB multiplied by the quantity of the good sold OQ_T, which equals the area of the rectangle P_{BT} AB P_{ST}.

It is important to note that this is only a "partial equilibrium" analysis of the effects of the tax. That is, we know that two groups have left this market: the buyers who occupied the portion of the demand curve AX, and the sellers who occupied the portion of the supply curve BX. To determine the full impact of this tax, we would have to examine the effect of the increase in demand by these buyers in the other markets that they switched to, and the effect of the increase in supply in other markets by the sellers.

Changes in these other markets could affect the equilibrium in this market. For example, suppose there is an increase in demand in another market for a factor of production (e.g. labor) that is used to make this good. The increase in price of this factor would then cause an upward shift in the supply curve of this good. To trace the effects of all these changes would require a general equilibrium analysis, which calls for mathematical techniques beyond the scope of this book.[13]

The effects of a subsidy

In Chapter 12 on taxation we will examine the preferential tax treatment of some activities, such as oil and gas exploration. Firms in this industry can take advantage of favorable provisions in tax law such as percentage depletion and the intangible drilling allowance. This preferential tax treatment amounts to a subsidy (a grant of money from the government)

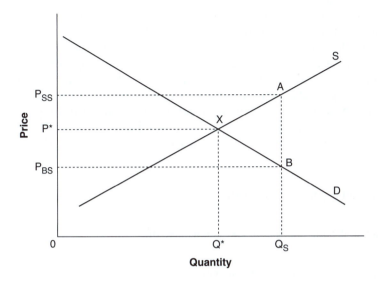

Figure 1.13 A subsidy.

for this type of business activity. Figure 1.13 shows the impact of a subsidy. A subsidy acts as a wedge between the market demand and supply curves, to the right of their intersection. A subsidy can be understood by considering the following equation:

The amount received by the seller = the amount paid by the buyer + the subsidy

In Figure 1.13, the amount received by the seller is AQ_S, the amount paid by the buyer is BQ_S, and the amount of the subsidy is AB. Again, if there were no subsidy, the amount received by the seller would be P^*, which would also be the amount paid by the buyer. Note that the subsidy has several consequences: (1) it increases the amount of the good sold, from Q^* to Q_S; (2) it increases the amount received by the seller, from P^* to P_{SS}; and (3) it reduces the amount paid by the buyer, from P^* to P_{BS}. The total amount paid by the government in subsidies equals the subsidy AB multiplied by the quantity of the good sold OQ_S, which equals the area of the rectangle $P_{SS}AB\,P_{BS}$.

Again, however, this is only a partial equilibrium analysis of the subsidy. To determine the full impact of the subsidy, we would have to consider that two groups have left other markets to enter this market: the sellers along the portion AX of the supply curve, and the buyers along the portion BX of the demand curve. A general equilibrium analysis would take into account the effects of the decrease in demand and supply in the markets that these groups came from.

Elasticities

Next we consider the subject of elasticities. Why are elasticities important? Suppose you were an executive vice-president of a large soft drink company. It would be important to you (and to your career) to know the answers to certain questions, such as: How much would the sales of your product decline if a competitor reduced the price of its soft drink by five percent? Or, what would happen to the sales of your product if you increased its price by five percent?

Or, what would happen to your sales in a particular community if the median income of that community increased by 10 percent, because of economic growth? A knowledge of elasticities would enable you to answer all these questions precisely.

Many different types of elasticities are used in economics, but all of them have one thing in common: each is a percentage change in something, divided by a percentage change in something else. For example, the elasticity of demand for a good X with respect to its price is a fraction, equal to (1) the percentage change in the amount of X demanded, divided by (2) the percentage change in the price of X. Suppose the price of artichokes increases from $2.00 per pound to $2.20, and the number of artichokes purchased per month in San Diego then declines from 10,000 to 9,500. There has been a percentage change in the price of artichokes of:

$$\frac{\Delta P}{P} = (2.20 - 2.00)/2.00 = 0.20/2.00 = 10\%$$

and a percentage change in the amount of artichokes demanded of:

$$\frac{\Delta Q}{Q} = (9,500 - 10,000)/10,000 = -500/10,000 = -5\%$$

Therefore the elasticity of demand for artichokes with respect to their price is:

$$\frac{-5\%}{10\%} = -\frac{1}{2}.$$

This particular elasticity – the price-elasticity of demand – is the most widely used elasticity in economics. It is especially important because it indicates how sensitive, or how responsive, the amount demanded of a good is to its price. The price-elasticity of demand for a good can be anywhere between 0 (perfectly inelastic) and – infinity (perfectly elastic). If the elasticity is 0, an increase in the price of a good has no effect whatever on the amount demanded; this is shown in Figure 1.14 as the demand curve D_0. If the elasticity is $-\infty$ (negative infinity), a very small increase in the price of the good causes the demand to decline to zero; this is shown in Figure 1.14 as the demand curve D_1.

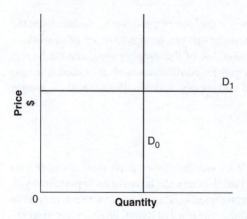

Figure 1.14 Perfectly inelastic and infinitely elastic demand curves.

If the elasticity is between 0 and -1, we say that demand is "inelastic;" if the elasticity is between -1 and $-\infty$, we say that demand is "elastic."

Note that the price-elasticity of demand is always negative (unless it is zero). This follows because it represents a movement along a demand curve. Since demand curves are downward-sloping, when one moves up the curve, the price increases, so ΔP is positive, but the quantity demanded falls, so ΔQ is negative. Conversely, when one moves down the curve, the amount demanded increases (ΔQ is positive), but the price falls (ΔP is negative). Thus the sign of the percentage change in quantity demanded, $\Delta Q/Q$, is always the opposite of the percentage change in the price, $\Delta P/P$; when one is positive, the other must be negative. Thus the price-elasticity of demand, which is $\Delta Q/Q$ divided by $\Delta P/P$, is always negative.

It is important to be aware that the way a change in price of a good affects the total revenue from its sales depends on the price-elasticity of demand. Namely, if the price-elasticity of demand is less than -1, like for example -1.5, total revenue declines when price increases, and increases when the price falls. This happens because if the price elasticity of demand is less than -1, an increase in price by one percent reduces the amount demanded by more than one percent, so total revenue, the product of price and the amount demanded, falls. Conversely, if the price-elasticity of demand is greater than -1, like for example, -0.5, total revenue increases when the price increases, and decreases when price falls. Let us consider some examples.

Suppose first that demand is elastic. The price of a good is \$10, the amount sold is 200, and the price-elasticity of demand of the good is -1.5. Note that total revenue is now $10 \times 200 = \$2,000$. Now suppose the price of the good increases to \$12, a price increase of $2/10 = 20$ percent. Since the price-elasticity of demand is -1.5, the quantity demanded will fall by 30 percent of 200, or sixty. Total revenue is now $12 \times 140 = \$1,680$, less than the prior amount of \$2,000. Since demand is elastic, there are good substitutes for the product, and buyers will not tolerate an increase in price.

Now suppose demand is inelastic. The price of a good is \$10, the amount sold is 200, and the price-elasticity of demand of the good is -0.5. Total revenue is still $10 \times 200 = \$2,000$. Now suppose again the price of the good increases to \$12, a price increase of 20 percent. Since the price-elasticity of demand is -0.5, the quantity demanded will fall by 10 percent of 200, or twenty. Total revenue is now $12 \times 180 = \$2,160$, greater than the prior amount of \$2,000. Since demand is inelastic, there are no good substitutes for the product, and buyers will not reduce their purchases very much despite the increase in price.

There have been empirical studies of the price-elasticity of demand of every good and service imaginable. For example, the elasticity of demand has been estimated to be -3.04 for furniture, -0.03 for wheat, and -1.50 for marijuana. What determines the magnitude of the price-elasticity of demand for a product or service? While a number of factors could be cited, by far the most important consideration is: how good are the substitutes for the product? Things that do not have good substitutes, like wheat, salt, and insulin, tend to have low (in absolute value) elasticities. Thus, when the price of one of these commodities increases, there is not much decline in demand; a diabetic will not reduce his consumption of insulin very much when its price increases. On the other hand, things that have good substitutes, like wool, tend to have large elasticities. In general, the price elasticity of demand is lower the broader the category of the good. There may be good substitutes for a Hershey Bar, a specific type of chocolate bar, but if we consider a broader category, all chocolate, the substitutes are not as good, and if we consider an even broader category, all types of candy, the substitutes are even less satisfactory. So the demand is less elastic the broader the category.

If better substitutes for a product become available, the elasticity of demand of the product will increase. Consider, for example, the elasticity of demand for first-class postal service by the U.S. government. Frank Wolak (1996) found that this elasticity increased (in absolute value) from −857 in 1986 to −1.13 in 1994. During this period there was increasing use of a number of substitutes for first-class mail, especially electronic mail, fax communications, and less expensive long-distance telephone service.

In general, elasticities of supply and demand are more elastic with respect to price, the longer the period of time involved. Both supply and demand are more elastic in the long run than in the short run. If the price of gasoline increases abruptly, people might not reduce their purchases of gasoline very much in the short run, because it is difficult (costly) to make adjustments – an individual cannot easily change the distance he has to commute to his job, it would be costly for him to sell his automobile quickly, it is not easy for him to change his routines of shopping and recreational trips, and so on. However in the long run, (assuming the increase in the price of gasoline is permanent) when his automobile has expired, he could replace it with a smaller and more fuel-efficient vehicle, and when the lease of his apartment ends, he can choose another apartment that is closer to work, and so forth. With regard to the elasticity of supply, if there is an increase in the price of gasoline, it is difficult (costly) to increase supply substantially in the short run, because of limitations in the amount of accessible oil reserves and in the capacity of refiners, but in the long run, more resources can be invested in exploration, more refineries can be built, and so there will be a greater increase in supply than in the short run.

If the supply of or demand for a good is very inelastic, there will be greater variation in its price than otherwise. For example, the demand for various forms of energy – gasoline, electricity, natural gas, and heating oil – tends to be inelastic in the short run because consumers do not have much ability to substitute between fuels when the price of one increases. In the United States most gasoline is used by automobiles and light trucks, and if the price of gasoline suddenly increases, people must still commute to work, drive approximately the same distance on business trips, and are generally unable to switch quickly to a vehicle that is more fuel-efficient than the one they have. Consequently there is considerable variation in the price of gasoline when there are disruptions in supply resulting from shutdowns of refineries or pipelines. In Figure 1.15 below the demand curve is inelastic, while in Figure 1.16 it is elastic. The supply curve shifts upward to the same extent in each diagram. Note how the price of the inelastic good in Figure 1.15 increases more than the price of the elastic good in Figure 1.16.

Similarly, if the supply of a good or service is essentially fixed, like the supply of motel rooms in Santa Barbara on a given day, we might expect substantial variations in price when there are fluctuations in demand. The variation in prices may be less if the sellers have some monopoly power – in Alaska there might be a considerable distance from one motel to the next – or if buyers or sellers do not have good information about alternatives. The supply of labor to the construction industry tends to be more inelastic for occupations to which entry is restricted by licensing laws, e.g. plumbers and electricians. We would expect the wages of such occupations to vary more in response to changes in demand, than wages of occupations that anyone can enter. Perloff (1980) found that licensing laws were responsible for large increases in wages of construction workers in the late 1960s and early 1970s.

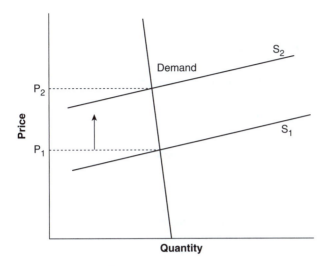

Figure 1.15 Effect of a decline in supply when demand is inelastic.

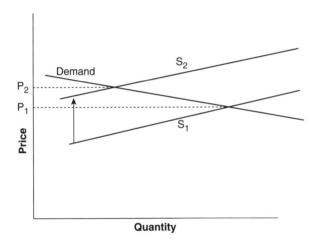

Figure 1.16 Effect of a decline in supply when demand is elastic.

Cross-price elasticities

As noted above, elasticity is a general concept, and there are many useful elasticities other than the price-elasticity of demand. Another important one is the cross-price elasticity of demand, which is the elasticity of demand for one good, X, with respect to the price of another good, Y. This elasticity equals the percentage change in the amount of X demanded, divided by the percentage change in the price of Y. Suppose the price of swordfish increases from $4.00 a pound to $4.80, and the amount of yellowfin tuna demanded per week in Blue Hill, Maine, consequently increases from eighty pounds to eighty-four pounds. There has been a percentage change in the price of swordfish of:

$$\frac{\Delta P}{P} = (4.80 - 4.00)/4.00 = 0.80/4.00 = 20 \text{ percent}$$

and a percentage change in the amount of yellowfin tuna demanded of

$$\frac{\Delta Q}{Q} = (84 - 80)/80 = 4/80 = 5 \text{ percent}$$

Therefore the cross-price elasticity of yellowfin tuna with respect to swordfish is:

$$\frac{5\%}{20\%} = .25.$$

Note that this elasticity is positive. In general, the cross-elasticity of demand can be positive, negative, or zero. It may be negative, for example, when two goods are often jointly consumed. An increase in the price of corned beef will tend to reduce the amount of cabbage consumed. If this elasticity is negative, we say that the goods are complements. If it is positive, the goods are said to be substitutes.

Income-elasticities

Another important elasticity is the elasticity of demand[14] with respect to income, which for a good, X, is the percentage change in the amount of X demanded, divided by the percentage change in income. Suppose an individual's annual income increases from $20,000 to $40,000, and he then increases his consumption of lobsters from four to twelve per year. The percentage change in his income is $(40,000 - 20,000)/20,000 = 100$ percent, and the percentage change in his lobster consumption is $(12 - 4)/4 = 200$ percent. His income-elasticity of demand for lobsters is then 200 percent/100 percent $= 2$. This elasticity may be positive, negative, or zero, depending on how the consumption of the good changes in response to the change in income. Goods which have a positive income-elasticity are called "normal" or "superior" goods, and those whose income-elasticity is negative are called "inferior" goods. These terms are purely descriptive, and carry no connotation of approval or disapproval of the goods. Indeed, it has been argued that economics is an inferior good. There is relatively little interest in economics during periods of prosperity; during recessions, however, the opportunity cost of taking classes is lower, and more people are inclined to take courses and buy books on economics.

Income-elasticity is a "local" property. By that we mean that for the same individual, a good can switch from being a normal good to an inferior good, or vice versa, as his income changes. If Mr. Blue's income is $20,000, hamburger may be a normal good; if his income increases slightly, he will buy more hamburger. If, however, he gets a major promotion so that his income increases to $60,000, he may decide to substitute filet mignon for hamburger; hamburger is now an inferior good.

When a consumer's income increases, and her total expenditures therefore increase, it is not possible for her to reduce spending on all goods at the same time. Therefore, the broader the category of a good, the more likely it is to be a normal good. For a particular consumer at a given level of income, "hamburger" may be an inferior good, but "meat" is less likely to be an inferior good, and "food" is quite likely to be a normal good.

Why elasticities are important to economic analysis of law

Many controversial issues in the economic analysis of law are, at bottom, disputes about elasticities. Let us consider a few examples.

In Chapter 10 on criminal law we consider the elasticity of the murder rate with respect to the probability of execution, given a conviction of murder. This is simply the percentage change in the number of murders per capita, divided by the percentage change in the number of executions per conviction. Of course, many commentators have argued that this elasticity is zero, i.e., that the murder rate is not at all affected by the probability of execution.[15]

In the chapter on property law, we will consider the elasticity of the supply of transplantable human organs with respect to the amount (if any) paid for them. This is the percentage change in the amount of organs provided to recipients by donors, divided by the percentage change in the compensation paid to donors or their families. Some commentators have argued that this elasticity is zero, or perhaps even negative, while a number of economists contend it is likely to be positive.

In the chapter on criminal law there is a section on Lojack, an innovation in law enforcement that increases the probability that automobile thieves are apprehended. In this section we consider the elasticity of supply of crimes. The issue we examine is: when the expected punishment for auto theft increases, how does this affect the supply of other crimes? That is, do criminals, recognizing that the costs of stealing automobiles have increased relative to the expected benefits of this activity, respond by diverting their efforts to other types of property crimes, e.g., burglary, shoplifting, stealing laptop computers, and the like? Here we are seeking to determine the elasticity of the supply of other property crimes with respect to the price (cost) of auto theft.

In another section of this chapter we consider the effect of the size of a state's prison population (prisoners per capita) on its crime rate. We might expect a relatively large prison population to reduce crime, either through the deterrent effect of longer prison sentences or through incapacitation (i.e., persons cannot commit crimes while in prison). Some have argued that a policy of law enforcement that relies heavily on imprisonment doesn't work, since the crime rate in the United States has not declined much, if at all, in recent years even though the rate of incarceration has more than tripled. However Levitt (1996) finds the expected negative effect; he calculates the elasticity of violent crime with respect to the size of a state's prison population to be −.40.

Income and substitution effects

The effects of a change in price of any good or service can be decomposed into two effects: an income effect and a substitution effect. The substitution effect is the effect of a pure change in price. Suppose a lawyer goes to Belize four times a year to do scuba diving, and the cost of each trip is $3,000. Suppose also that because of a decline in air fares, the price of a trip falls to $2,000. Since the price of a trip to Belize has declined, the lawyer might decide to take more trips; this is the substitution effect. Since demand curves are downward sloping, an individual may well increase his consumption of a commodity when its price declines.

What then is the income effect? The basic idea is that a change in prices can affect an individual's real income. To see this, suppose an individual's money income doubled, while the prices of all goods and services remained the same. Now suppose instead that the individual's money income stayed the same, but the prices of all goods and services were cut in half. Clearly this change would have exactly the same effect as a doubling of money income. Thus a change in prices affects an individual's real income.

Now let us return to the example of the lawyer who goes to Belize four times a year. Recall that because of a decline in air fares, the cost of each trip has declined from $3,000 to $2,000. Note that if the lawyer continues his practice of taking four trips to Belize a year, it would cost him $4,000 less to do so. Thus the decline in price has in effect increased his income by $4,000. This increase in income will cause changes in the amounts he spends on various goods and services. He will buy more of the commodities for which his income-elasticity is positive (normal goods), and less of the commodities for which his income-elasticity is negative (inferior goods). For example, if cognac is a normal good and subway travel is an inferior good, he will consume more cognac and take fewer subway rides. If vacation trips to Belize are a normal good for the lawyer, there is a positive income effect that will reinforce the substitution effect: both effects will tend to increase the number of his annual trips to Belize.

The effects on an individual's income of a change in price are greater when the good whose price has changed represents a relatively large share of his total expenditures, like housing, or a large share of his income, like his labor services. Thus a decline in the price of housing substantially increases the individual's real income, and an increase in the price of his labor, i.e., an increase in his hourly wage, will have the same effect. Clearly the income effect of a change in one's wage will be greater for a full-time worker than for a part-time worker. If Ms. X's wage increases from $20 to $25 per hour, her income would increase by $200 a week if she works 40 hours, but by only $50 a week if she works ten hours.

For most workers, all or almost all their income is derived from the sale of their labor, often to a single employer. For such individuals, the income effect of a change in their wage may be quite large – it may even be large enough to overcome the substitution effect. To understand the income and substitution effects of a change in the wage, let us divide the total time available to a worker into two parts: (1) the time he spends working, and (2) his "leisure time," i.e., the time he spends outside the labor market. Leisure time is usually assumed to be a "normal" good, i.e., a good with a positive elasticity of income. Thus if Ms. X's income increased because she won the California lottery, we would assume that she would "buy" more leisure time; that is, she would work less. Note that in this case, there is a (large) positive income effect, but no substitution effect, since there has been no change in Ms. X's wage.

Suppose, however, that Ms. X's wage increases from $20 to $25 per hour, and that she works forty hours per week. Now there is both an income and a substitution effect. Her income has increased by $200 a week, or by $10,400 a year. The substitution effect arises because the price, or cost, of her leisure time has increased. The cost of taking an additional hour of leisure time is the wage she could have earned by working that hour.[16] That cost has just increased from $20 to $25. When the price of a good increases, the usual response of a customer is to buy less of it. Thus the substitution effect of an increase in the wage will induce the worker to "buy" less leisure – or to work more. However, we must also consider the income effect. Since the worker has more income – $10,400 more a year – she will be inclined to buy more of all normal goods, including leisure; that is, she will tend to work less. Thus the net effect of an increase in the wage on the number of hours worked is indeterminate. If the income effect outweighs the substitution effect, the worker will work less. If the substitution effect outweighs the income effect, the worker will work more.

We will encounter the distinction between income and substitution effects in Chapter 8, on torts, in reference to a worker's expected date of retirement, and in Chapter 12, on taxation, in the discussion of charitable contributions.

Bibliography

Buck, Bob, "The Price of a Safe Landing," *New York Times*, March 18, 2006, p. A27.

Evans, William N., and Ping Zhang, "The Impact of Earmarked Lottery Revenue of K-12 Educational Expenditures," *Education Finance and Policy* 40–73 (2007).

Kim, H. Youn, "Economies of Scale and Scope in Multiproduct Firms: Evidence from U.S. Railroads," 19 (6) *Applied Economics* 733–741 (June 1987).

Levitt, Steven D., "The Effect of Prison Population Size on Crime Rates: Evidence from Prison Overcrowding Litigation," 111 (2) *Quarterly Journal of Economics* 319–351 (May 1996).

Marshall, Alfred, *Principles of Economics: An Introductory Text* (1890).

Oi, Walter, "Heterogeneous Firms and the Organization of Production," 21 *Economic Inquiry* 147–171 (1983).

Pashigian, B. Peter, "The Market for Lawyers: The Determination of the Demand for and the Supply of Lawyers," 20 *Journal of Law and Economics* 53–85 (1977).

Perloff, Jeffrey M., "The Impact of Licensing Laws on Wage Changes in the Construction Industry," 23 (2) *Journal of Law and Economics* 409–428 (October 1980).

Rosen, Sherwin, "The Market for Lawyers," 35 *Journal of Law and Economics* 215–246 (1992).

Singhal, Monica, "Special Interest Groups and the Allocation of Public Funds," 92 (3–4) *Journal of Public Economics* 548–564 (April 2008).

Smith, Adam, *An Inquiry into the Nature and Causes of the Wealth of Nations* (1776).

Wolak, Frank A., "Changes in the Household-level Demand for Postal Delivery Services from 1986 to 1994," unpublished paper, Department of Economics, Stanford University (December 1996).

Problems

1. Consider two individuals who want to get a tuneup for their cars in the morning before going to work: Bill Fletcher, a lawyer who earns $120 per hour, and Dave Miller, a bill collector who earns $60 per hour. They each have to choose between the following three garages offering tuneups, which have the following prices and waiting times. Which garage will each of them choose? Explain why in detail.

Table 1.5 Different prices and waiting times for a tuneup

Garage	Price of tuneup ($)	Waiting time (minutes)
Jiffy	20	5
Toughie	12	10
Mel's	8	15

2. Suppose the monthly demand for fax machines in a small city can be expressed by the equation $P = 600 - 30Q$, and the monthly supply can be expressed by the equation $P = 100 + 20Q$. What is the equilibrium price and quantity sold of fax machines?

3. The following statement is taken from the *Wall Street Journal*, March 30, 1966: "A retired Atlanta railroad conductor complains that he can no longer visit his neighborhood tavern six times a week. Since the price of his favorite beer went up to 30¢ a glass from 25¢,

he has been dropping in only five times a week." Assuming the man in question consumed the same amount of beer per visit before and after the price change, calculate the elasticity of his demand for tavern-dispensed beer.

4. Mr. Z buys twelve bottles of champagne a year when the price is $45 per bottle. The following year the price of champagne increases to $55 and he buys eight bottles. What is the price-elasticity of his demand for champagne?

5. Consider the cross-price elasticity of demand for air travel and rental cars. Would you expect it to be positive, negative, or zero? Your answer should explain exactly what the cross-price elasticity of demand is.

6. Suppose in Wayne County the income-elasticity of demand for Palm Pilots is 0.25. If Wayne County income increases by 20 percent, what is the percentage change in demand for Palm Pilots?

2   Principles of microeconomics (II)

This chapter will complete our introduction to some important basic principles of microeconomics. In this chapter we examine some extensions of, and departures from, the standard static competitive paradigm. We will examine monopoly, cartels, rent-seeking behavior, moral hazard, adverse selection, and public goods. We will also consider different types of capital, the determinants of interest rates, the rate of return on a security, preferences on risk, and how to determine the present value of future payments.

Monopolies and cartels

There is a monopoly in a market or industry in which only one firm produces a product for which there are no good substitutes (so demand is relatively inelastic), and in which there are significant barriers to entry that prevent other firms from entering the market to compete. A monopoly charges a higher price than the price that would emerge in a competitive market, and produces less output than the amount produced in a competitive industry.

It will be helpful to elaborate somewhat on the comparison of a monopoly to a firm operating under perfect competition. Consider first a firm in a perfectly competitive environment. A market approaches the ideal of perfect competition if: (1) the product is supplied by many firms, and no firm has a significant share of the market; (2) the product is purchased by many buyers, and no individual buyer has a significant share of the market; (3) the product is homogeneous, so that to each buyer, the product of one firm is a perfectly good substitute for that of another firm; (4) firms can easily enter, or exit from, the industry; and (5) both buyers and sellers have access to good information, so that if one firm were selling the product at a higher, or lower, price than others, all buyers would immediately find out about it.

Figure 2.1 shows the by now familiar equilibrium of a competitive market, in which the supply and demand curves intersect at the point E, and the amount Q^* is produced and sold at the price P^*. Figure 2.2 shows the equilibrium of a competitive firm supplying its output to the market shown in Figure 2.1. The firm will produce and sell the amount, q_f^*, the amount at which the firm's marginal revenue just equals its marginal cost. Note that to this firm, the demand curve appears to be a horizontal line at the price P^*; this is so because the firm can sell as much output as it wants at the price P^*. This market price will not be affected by the amount sold by the firm. Under perfect competition the price-elasticity of demand of the firm's demand curve approaches $-\infty$.[1] Since the products of other firms are a perfect substitute for the product of any given firm in the industry, any firm that raises its price above P^* will lose all its business.

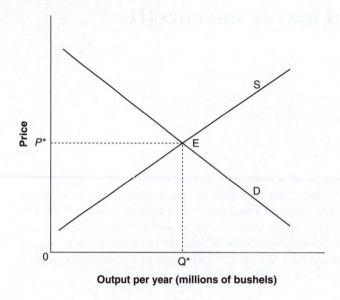

Figure 2.1 The equilibrium of a competitive market.

Figure 2.2 A firm in a competitive market.

A comparison of the two diagrams raises an obvious question, however: how is it possible that the demand curve facing the competitive firm in Figure 2.2 is a horizontal line, while the market demand curve shown in Figure 2.1 is clearly downward-sloping? The answer is that the two diagrams are drawn to a different scale, since the output of the competitive firm is infinitesimally small compared to total market supply and demand. For example, if the product in question is a given type of apple, Figure 2.1 might show millions of bushels of

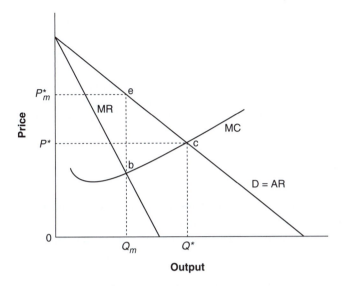

Figure 2.3 A monopoly.

apples, while Figure 2.2 would show hundreds of bushels. If an individual farmer were to increase his output of apples tenfold, he would be causing the market supply curve to move a small distance to the right from point E, and thus the intersection of supply and demand would move down the demand curve, but this move would be so small that the price would not fall perceptibly below P^*. Thus the firm operating under perfect competition perceives no change in P^* no matter how much it produces for the market.

Now we should consider the equilibrium of a monopoly, shown in Figure 2.3. A firm may have a monopoly, or substantial market power, if there is some barrier to entry that prevents other firms from entering the market to compete with it. The monopolist, like the competitive firm, maximizes profit by choosing the level of output where its marginal revenue equals its marginal cost. The equilibrium price P^*_M is determined by the price on the demand curve corresponding to this level of output.

Note that the demand curve facing the monopoly is downward-sloping. This is so because the market demand curve does not have to be drawn on a different scale for a monopoly. Unlike the competitive firm, the monopoly is not small relative to total market supply and demand; indeed a pure monopoly represents the sole source of supply to the market.

The point that is crucial to understand about monopoly (and the economic rationale for antitrust law) is that it is inefficient. The monopoly equilibrium is inefficient because at Q_m the social value of an additional unit of output, equal to the height of the demand curve $Q_m e$, exceeds the social cost of producing that unit, equal to the height of the firm's marginal cost curve $Q_m b$. Efficiency would require the firm to increase its output, in order to maximize the net social benefit, i.e. total social benefit minus total social cost. That would be accomplished at Q^*, the level of output corresponding to point c, where the marginal social benefit (the height of the demand curve) just equals the marginal social cost (the height of the firm's marginal cost curve). Thus the monopolist produces too little output (Q_m rather than Q^*), and charges too high a price (P^*_m rather than P^*).

Relation between marginal and average amounts

The juxtaposition of Figures 2.2 and 2.3 provides an opportunity to introduce a simple rule that will improve the reader's understanding of various diagrams presented in this textbook. First, however, it is important to understand that the demand curve for the product sold by a firm is a curve of average revenue.

By definition, the average revenue of a firm is its total revenue from sale of a good divided by the quantity sold, which equals the price of the good. We can show that this is true as follows: if P is the price of the good, Q is the quantity sold, TR is the firm's total revenue, and AR is its average revenue, then:

$$AR = \frac{TR}{Q} = \frac{P \bullet Q}{Q} = P$$

Since the demand curve facing a firm shows the price corresponding to different amounts of the good sold, the demand curve is a curve of average revenue.

The general relationship between marginal and average amounts can be summarized as follows:

1   If the marginal amount is less than the average amount, the average amount will decline.
2   If the marginal amount is greater than the average amount, the average amount will increase.
3   If the marginal amount equals the average amount, the average amount will not change.

This relationship can be illustrated by a baseball player's batting average. Suppose in the middle of the baseball season, a player's batting average is .250 just before he starts a game. Suppose during the game he is at bat five times, gets one hit, and strikes out the other four times. Then his marginal batting performance for the game is 1/5, or .200. This will cause his season (overall) batting average to fall below .250. Alternatively, suppose he gets two hits, and strikes out the other three times. Then his marginal batting performance for the game is 2/5, or .400. This would increase his batting average. Finally, suppose he came to bat only four times, got one hit, and struck out the other three times. Then his marginal batting performance would be .250. In this case his batting average of .250 would be unaffected.

We can now examine Figures 2.2 and 2.3 to see whether these rules are reflected in these diagrams. In Figure 2.2, showing a firm under perfect competition, the demand curve, or average revenue curve, facing the firm is horizontal, i.e., it stays the same for all quantities sold. Since average revenue doesn't change over the entire range of the firm's output, it must be true that marginal revenue always equals average revenue for the firm operating under perfect competition.

In Figure 2.3, showing a monopoly, note that the demand, or average revenue, curve declines as the quantity sold increases. Note also that marginal revenue is less than average revenue over the whole range of output, which means that average revenue must be falling – as indeed it is. The reader will find that this relationship between marginal and average amounts holds true generally, and is reflected in diagrams throughout this textbook.

Cartels

A cartel is a group of independent firms that attempt, by a collusive agreement, to behave as a collective monopoly. The members of a cartel may be buyers or sellers. In a cartel of sellers,

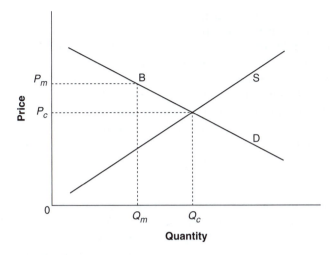

Figure 2.4 A cartel.

the firms may agree to charge a price above the competitive price, or to restrict output below the competitive level of output. A cartel may also divide a market among its members, so that each member has a monopoly of the share of the market assigned to it. The market might be divided geographically, or along product lines, or by groups of customers. In 1897 E. I. du Pont de Nemours & Co. and several other American firms engaged in the manufacture of explosives entered into an agreement with a group of European companies that explicitly assigned most of the countries in the western hemisphere to the American firms, and other parts of the world to the European firms. A division of the market can also be made along product lines: if there are only two firms providing telephone service in a country, they might agree that one firm will acquire a monopoly of long-distance telephone service while the other takes local telephone service. Finally, a cartel can agree to divide customers among its members; in one case several laundries agreed that each laundry would keep its current customers, and would not attempt to attract customers away from the other laundries.[2]

Let us consider a cartel of sellers that agrees either to charge a price above the competitive price or to restrict total output. In Figure 2.4, a competitive industry would produce output of Q_c at a price P_c. If all the firms in this industry banded together to form a cartel, they might agree to restrict their total output to Q_m, or might agree that each firm would charge a price of P_m. In either case the result is the same, assuming all firms in the cartel abide by the agreement: the cartel will operate at point B on the market demand curve.

Game theory and the prisoners' dilemma

In the cases of both pure competition and monopoly, the environment of a firm is fixed. Under pure competition, a firm faces an exogenously determined market price; under monopoly, it faces a market demand curve. There is, however, an intermediate region in which the firm's environment is not fixed, namely when it is one of a small number of firms in a market. In this case, what the other firms do, in terms of choosing a level of output, prices, advertising, whether to open a new store, and the like, often depends on what the firm under consideration does. This area is the province of game theory. Game theory is used to analyze the behavior of individual economic agents, whether persons or firms, in a setting where what others do both affects what you do and is affected by what you do.

Consider a well-known game known as the prisoner's dilemma. Suppose two men, A and B, decide to rob a gas station. After the robbery the police investigate, and find some evidence suggesting that A and B were involved in the robbery, but not enough to obtain a conviction. In such a case it is standard practice for the police to interrogate the two suspects separately. Often they will tell each suspect that the other suspect already has confessed, or is about to do so, and that he will provide enough information about the crime to ensure that both of them will be convicted. Moreover, they assure each suspect that if his confederate confesses and he does not, his sentence will be far more severe than his confederate's. If, on the other hand he confesses promptly and provides full information, the court will take his cooperation into account in determining his sentence.

This predicament can be modeled as a game, in which the two robbers are "players." In this particular game each player has two choices or "strategies" – confess or don't confess. This game can be solved by looking for a Nash equilibrium, a solution algorithm named after the mathematician who discovered it, John F. Nash, Jr. (1928–). In a Nash equilibrium, each player chooses the strategy that gives him the highest payoff, given the strategies chosen by the other players, and every player's beliefs in what the others will do must be borne out. In the prisoners' dilemma game shown in Figure 2.5, we follow the game theory convention that the payoff to the player on the left, suspect A, is given first, while the payoff to the player on top, suspect B, is given second. Thus in row 2, column 1, the payoff to A for not confessing is -10, while the payoff to B for confessing is -1. A chooses the row (top or bottom), and B chooses the column (left or right).

In this game, the Nash equilibrium is shown in the cell at the upper left: confess, confess. This is so because if B chooses left, A's best choice is confess, while if A chooses top, B's best choice is confess. None of the other cells qualifies as a Nash equilibrium. For example, consider the cell at the bottom right (don't confess, don't confess). If B chose the right column, A would choose the top, not the bottom. What is noteworthy about this outcome is that both players would be better off if they could agree to choose the outcome (don't confess, don't confess). Thus choices that are privately optimal for each player can lead to an outcome that is not in the best interests of either player.

The prisoner's dilemma has been applied to many examples of behavior of firms and individuals, e.g., the decision by the members of a cartel whether to honor the commitments they made to charge a high price or restrict output, or instead "chisel"; an arms race

| | Suspect B | |
	Confess	Don't confess
Confess	−8, −8	−1, −10
Don't confess	−10, −1	−2, −2

Suspect A (row labels at left)

Figure 2.5 The prisoners' dilemma.

Union has

	No lawyer	Lawyer
No lawyer	57	75
Lawyer	46	65

Employer has

Figure 2.6 Percentage of discharge grievances sustained for the union in 755 arbitrations.

between two nations; advertising by competing firms; whether countries will take measures to reduce their own contributions to climate change; and the use of performance-enhancing drugs by athletes. It has been argued that sometimes the decision to hire a lawyer is an example of the prisoner's dilemma! Block and Stieber (1987) analyzed the outcomes of arbitration proceedings involving discharge grievances. Union contracts often provide that if an employee is discharged by the employer, and he believes that his discharge is unjustified, he can file a formal grievance against the employer. If the grievance cannot be resolved through negotiations, it is presented to an arbitrator for a decision. Block and Stieber calculated the probability that the discharge grievance would be denied (the employee would lose) as a function of whether each party retained a lawyer to assist in presenting the case to the arbitrator. Their results are shown in Figure 2.6. The diagram indicates that when only one party hired a lawyer, the probability that the arbitrator would decide in its favor increased substantially, in comparison to the scenario where neither party hired a lawyer. For the union, this probability increased from 57 percent to 75 percent; for the employer, it increased from 43 percent to 54 percent. When both parties hire a lawyer, the probability that the union prevails (65 percent) is only a little higher than if neither side had hired a lawyer (57 percent). Thus, although it is clearly a good idea for each side to hire a lawyer, provided the lawyer's fee is not too large, it appears that both parties would be better off if neither hired a lawyer and the employer made a side payment to the union to compensate the union for the difference between 57 percent and 65 percent. (We are assuming that there are no systematic differences among the cases in each of the four cells.)

One should not conclude from this analysis that expenditures on lawyers are socially wasteful. We will return to this subject in Chapter 9 on the economics of litigation. There we will review a literature that finds that the extent to which a nation provides protection of personal and property rights is crucial to its productivity and economic growth. These fundamental legal safeguards are provided and enforced by lawyers.

Rent-seeking behavior

From time to time we will refer to "rent-seeking behavior." The purpose of such behavior is to acquire something of value that is not subject to price competition, rather than do something that is economically productive. For example, the executive of a U.S. steel company might spend his time (1) learning how to reduce the costs of producing steel, or to improve its quality; or (2) lobbying for tariffs, quotas, or other regulations that would protect his firm's steel from foreign competition. Alternative (2) is rent-seeking behavior; its sole purpose is to transfer wealth, rather than create it. Rent-seeking behavior by a firm is a waste of resources, whether the firm seeks an advantage for itself or is simply trying to prevent others from obtaining an advantage at its expense.

Capital; human capital

Capital has been defined[3] as anything, other than a free human being, that yields productive services beyond the current period.[4] Capital goods can be distinguished from consumer goods, like a hot dog, which once consumed is gone. A refrigerator, for example, is clearly a form of capital, since it provides valuable services for many years. However, the definition of capital clearly covers much more than machinery and equipment. It includes, for example, the customer goodwill created by certain types of advertising. Advertising was originally treated as a current expense of a business, until it occurred to economists that the benefits of advertising were often realized by the business in future years, as well as the year in which the advertising was done.

Another very important type of capital is human capital. An investment in human capital is an investment made in a person, that increases his or her expected real income. An individual acquires human capital when he increases his productivity and earning capacity through education or on-the-job training, or acquires knowledge that improves the quality of his life, or carries out activities that improve his physical or mental health. The value of a professional education is often measured (crudely) by determining the present value of the resulting increase in the individual's annual earnings over the remainder of his working life.

Physical capital declines in value through wear and tear and obsolescence. Human capital also declines, when knowledge is forgotten or becomes obsolete. Since there are frequent changes in tax law, the human capital of a tax lawyer depreciates more rapidly than that of a lawyer whose practice is centered around contract or criminal law. We would therefore expect tax lawyers to attend more seminars in continuing legal education than other lawyers, to maintain or increase their human capital.

Anyone who has the impression that human capital is a more ethereal and less important form of wealth than tangible assets would be greatly mistaken. In 1994, the total wealth per capita in North America was estimated to be around $379,000, 76 percent of which ($289,000) was in the form of human capital.[5] The extreme poverty of some underdeveloped nations like Rwanda and Bangladesh is attributable more to their population's low endowment of human capital – widespread illiteracy, and a lack of the knowledge or skills required to be productive in a modern industrial economy – than to their lack of material wealth.

Some groups have found human capital to be a more secure form of wealth than physical assets. Political refugees, who often lose the physical wealth they had in the countries they leave, tend to concentrate on accumulating human capital in the countries to which they emigrate.[6] The emphasis placed on education by certain ethnic minorities may be partly attributable to a history of persecution and the likelihood of confiscation of their physical assets.

The present value of future payments

In this section we will learn the general technique that is used to compute the present value of payments to be received, or made, in the future. This method is used, for example, to determine damages in personal injury cases attributable to future medical expenses, lost earnings, and lost household services. It can also be used to determine the value of a professional degree in a divorce case.

Suppose someone deposits some money in a savings account or certificate of deposit for one year, and receives no interest until the end of the year. Let P be the amount deposited today, r the rate of interest paid by the bank, and F_1 the amount of principal and interest the bank will pay back to the depositor one year from now. Then:

$$F_1 = P + Pr \tag{1}$$

For example, if we deposit \$1,000 in a savings account at a rate of interest of 6 percent, after one year we should receive from the bank $\$1,000 + (1,000 \times (0.06)) = \$1,060$.

Looking at this transaction from another angle, the present value of the right to receive \$1,060 one year from now is \$1,000. In terms of equation (1), since $F_1 = P(1+R)$,

$$p = \frac{F_1}{1+r}$$

Now if we invest our money for two years, and interest is compounded annually,[7] how much can we expect to receive two years from now? We know that after one year we would be entitled to receive F_1 from the bank, so we could deposit that amount in the savings account for another year. Then, at the end of the second year, we would be entitled to receive $F_2 = F_1 + F_1 r$. For example, if r still equals 6 percent, we would receive $\$1,060 + (1,060 \times (0.06)) = \$1,123.60$.

Again we can look at things from the opposite direction, to compute the present value of the right to receive an amount two years from now. Since $F_2 = F_1 + F_1 r$, $F_2 = F_1(1+r)$, but since $F_1 = P(1+r)$ we can substitute for F_1 in the expression for F_2, to obtain $F_2 = P(1+r)^2$. We can now solve for P in terms of F_2:

$$P = \frac{F_2}{(1+r)^2}$$

From this formula, if we know F_2, the amount that will be received two years from now, we can determine its present value P.

We can, of course, repeat this process for as many additional years as desired. For example, since $F_3 = F_2 + F_2 r$, we can substitute for F_2, and eventually solve for P in terms of F_3:

$$P = \frac{F_3}{(1+r)^3}$$

Proceeding in this manner, we find that, in general, the present value of the right to receive the amount F_t, t years from now, is:

$$P = \frac{F_t}{(1+r)^t}$$

For example, the present value of the right to receive \$1,000 twenty years from now, if the rate of interest is 6 percent and amounts saved are compounded annually, is:

$$\frac{\$1000}{(1.06)^{20}} = \$311.80$$

Now suppose we would like to determine the present value of the right to receive a payment *A* every year, forever. Let us assume this payment is made at the end of each year, that interest is compounded annually, and the rate of interest is *r*, now and in the future. Then the present value of the right to receive annual payments of *A* forever is:

$$P = \frac{A}{1+r} + \frac{A}{(1+r)^2} + \frac{A}{(1+r)^3} + \frac{A}{(1+r)^4} + \dots \tag{2}$$

where the infinite series continues forever. However, it happens that we can express the value of *P* in a much more convenient manner. Consider the expression we obtain if we multiply *P* by $1/(1+r)$:

$$\frac{P}{1+r} = \frac{A}{(1+r)^2} + \frac{A}{(1+r)^3} + \frac{A}{(1+r)^4} + \frac{A}{(1+r)^5} + \dots \tag{3}$$

Now let us subtract equation (3) from equation (2). If we do so, we obtain:

$$P - \frac{P}{1+r} = \frac{A}{1+r} \tag{4}$$

If we multiply equation (4) by 1+r, we get:

$$(1+r)P - P = A \Rightarrow P + \mathrm{P}r - P = A \Rightarrow P = \frac{A}{r} \tag{5}$$

From this formula we can determine the present value of the right to receive an annual payment *A* forever, if we know the interest rate *r*. For example, the present value of the right to receive $1,000 every year at the end of each year, assuming the rate of interest is 6 percent now and in the future, is $1,000/0.06 = $16,666.67$.

Now suppose we want to determine the present value of the right to receive an annual payment *A*, not forever but for a finite number of years. Calculations like this are often required in finance, or in personal injury cases, when an economist must determine the present value of lost earnings over an individual's remaining expected work life. Let us first consider the present value of an infinite stream of payments *A* that will begin, say, thirteen years from now:

$$P_{13} = \frac{A}{(1+r)^{13}} + \frac{A}{(1+r)^{14}} + \frac{A}{(1+r)^{15}} + \frac{A}{(1+r)^{16}} + \dots \tag{6}$$

This is easily seen to be the stream of payments (2) multiplied by: $1/(1+r)^{12}$. This makes sense, because we are simply moving the infinite stream of payments (2) twelve years into the future. But this gives us an idea on how we can find a compact expression for a finite stream of payments of *A* lasting for only twelve years:

$$P_F = \frac{A}{1+r} + \frac{A}{(1+r)^2} + \frac{A}{(1+r)^3} + \frac{A}{(1+r)^4} + \dots \frac{A}{(1+r)^{12}} \tag{7}$$

Since, according to (5), the infinite series (2) that begins one year from now equals A/r, the infinite series (6) that begins thirteen years from now must equal:

$$\frac{1}{(1+r)^{12}} \bullet \frac{A}{r}$$

But then the finite series of payments for twelve years (7) must equal:

$$\frac{A}{r}\left(1 - \frac{1}{(1+r)^{12}}\right)$$

And, in general, a finite series that begins one year from now, and ends n years from now:

$$\frac{A}{1+r} + \frac{A}{(1+r)^2} + \frac{A}{(1+r)^3} + \frac{A}{(1+r)^4} + \cdots \frac{A}{(1+r)^n}$$

will equal:

$$\frac{A}{r}\left(1 - \frac{1}{(1+r)^n}\right)$$

Interest rates

The preceding discussion of present value referred to "the" rate of interest, as if there were only one rate. However, it is obvious from everyday experience that there are many different rates of interest. In several chapters of this book[8] we will have occasion to consider interest rates, and how they are affected by changes in the law. What explains the differences among interest rates? We will see that the interest rate on a given loan is determined by (1) the rate of inflation, (2) the risk of default (nonpayment), (3) the term, or length of time, of the loan, and (4) the tax treatment of the interest on the loan, to the lender and borrower.

With respect to the first factor, the rate of inflation, we must make a distinction between real and nominal interest rates. The nominal rate of interest is the rate in nominal (money) terms, i.e., the rate stated in the loan agreement. The real rate of interest is the nominal rate of interest minus the rate of inflation.[9] Inflation is the rate of change of the general price level over time. For example, the inflation rate is three percent if the average rate of increase of money prices of all goods and services in the economy is 3 percent per year. Let i be the nominal rate of interest, r the real rate of interest, and π^e the expected rate of inflation. Then (confirming our definition of the real rate of interest), according to a well-known identity known as the Fisher equation:[10]

$$i = r + \pi^e$$

Thus if the real rate of interest is 3 percent, and the expected rate of inflation is 10 percent, the nominal rate of interest will be 13 percent. In certain countries like Brazil and Israel the rate of inflation has at times exceeded 100 percent per year, and consequently nominal interest rates have also been greater than 100 percent.

The rate of interest will be greater, the greater the risk of default by the borrower. There is virtually no risk of nonpayment of a short-term loan to the U.S. government, in the form of a ninety-day Treasury bill. On the other hand, the risk of default on a consumer loan for an automobile is substantial, so the interest rate is much higher. This consideration also explains why a second mortgage usually has a higher interest rate than a first mortgage. Suppose a house is subject to a first mortgage of $100,000 and a second mortgage of $30,000. The homeowner defaults, and the house is subsequently sold at a foreclosure auction for $120,000; the expenses of foreclosure are $20,000. In this case the first mortgage would be fully repaid, but the holder of the second mortgage would get nothing.

The interest rate also depends on the term of the loan. If the rate of inflation is currently low, but there is a concern that it may increase within a year or two (perhaps because the government is expected to increase the money supply to help pay for large deficits), the interest rate on a five-year bond will exceed that on a one-year bond.

Finally, the interest rate will be affected by tax treatment of the loan. The interest on municipal bonds (loans to state and local governments) is exempt from federal income tax, while the interest on corporate bonds is fully taxable income. Consequently the equilibrium rate of interest on municipal bonds is always lower than the rate on corporate bonds.

Efficient capital markets

In Chapter 11 on corporations we will consider some implications of the theory of efficient capital markets, or efficient markets theory, and it is appropriate to introduce the theory now. However, it will be helpful to define some terms before we do so. First, the capital gain (or loss) on a security is just the change in its market price over time. If I buy common stock of Ford Motor Company for its current market price of $30 per share, and one year later its price is $35 per share, I have a capital gain of $5 per share for the year. We may also define the rate of return from holding a security, such as stock or bonds. The rate of return on a security over some period of time equals the sum of (1) the capital gain on the security during the period, plus (2) any cash payments derived from it, such as dividends or interest, all divided by (3) the initial purchase price of the security. In symbols:

$$\text{the rate of return} = \frac{P_{t+1} - P_t + C}{P_t}$$

where P_t is the price of the security at the beginning of the period, P_{t+1} is its price at the end of the period, and C is the total cash payments received by the holder during the period from t to $t+1$. According to the theory of efficient markets, equilibrium prices in a financial market are determined so that the expected return on a security equals the optimal (best possible) prediction of the return. Putting it differently (and perhaps more clearly), the current market price of a security reflects all the information that is available to the public.

There is also a somewhat stronger version of the theory, which is that prices in an efficient market (and capital markets are assumed to be in this category) reflect the true (intrinsic) value of the securities. That is, in capital markets prices are always accurate, and fully reflect the underlying factors (called market fundamentals) that affect the future stream of income to be expected from the securities.[11] The theory of efficient markets will be important, for example, to the discussion of takeovers and insider trading in the chapter on corporations.

Externalities

Many issues in law and economics involve externalities. An externality arises when the actions of one economic agent affect the environment of another in some way other than through a change in prices. Important examples of externalities are pollution and congestion. A number of externalities arise from the purchase of gasoline for automobiles: air pollution caused by emissions, with contributions to global warming, increases in traffic congestion and motor vehicle accidents. Cul-de-sacs (residential streets with dead-ends) have little traffic and are perceived to be safe, but they impose a negative externality on nearby areas, by funneling traffic on to other routes, and limiting the access of emergency vehicles to neighborhoods.

One important type of externality is a network externality. In a network externality, the value of a good to the consumer either increases or decreases the more the good has been purchased by other consumers. An example is the telephone. In modern industrial countries, almost everyone has a telephone, but in some parts of the world, such as rural Afghanistan, telephones are relatively rare. A telephone is not much good if all the people you might want to call do not have a telephone. Suppose the number of telephones owned by all the people in your group of family and friends increases from fifty to 100. Now you can make twice as many calls as before, and the value of a telephone to you has approximately doubled. Computer software has the same positive network externality. A word-processing software package is worth more to an individual user the more that other people have the same software, so that one can transfer and receive documents with a larger group of users. When there is a positive network externality, the demand curve of each individual for the good shifts to the right the more consumers have purchased the good. Thus the market demand curve for the good, which is simply the horizontal sum of all individual demand curves, also shifts to the right. Goods with a positive network externality are sometimes called "bandwagon" goods, because they are worth more, the more consumers hop on the bandwagon.

For some goods there is a negative network externality. The value of a lift ticket at a ski resort is lower the more people have purchased it, because there is more congestion – longer lines waiting for the lift and more people on the slopes. The feeling of prestige and pride in being a member of an elite group declines the easier it is to gain admission to the group; consequently such goods are sometimes called "snob" goods. Membership in the National Baseball Hall of Fame of the United States would be much less impressive if anyone with a .250 lifetime batting average qualified for admission. After nearly 90 percent of Harvard's class of 2001 graduated with some form of honors, Harvard decided to limit the number who could graduate with honors to 60 percent. For goods with a negative externality, the demand curve of each individual for the good shifts to the left the more consumers own the good. Thus the market demand curve for the good, which is simply the horizontal sum of all individual demand curves, also shifts to the left.

Attitudes toward risk

In this book (for example, in the chapters on property law, torts, and criminal law), we will frequently use certain terms that describe an individual's attitudes toward risk, or risk preferences, in particular, "risk-neutral," "risk-averse," or "risk-lover." To explain these terms, we must first define the "expected value" of a gamble (a term from probability and statistics). The expected value of a gamble is the weighted sum of the values of the possible outcomes, where each outcome is weighted by its probability. Consider, for example, the flip of a fair coin, in which the individual gets $100 if tails comes up, and $200 if heads comes up. The expected value of this gamble =

$$\left(\frac{1}{2} \times \$100\right) + \left(\frac{1}{2} \times \$200\right) = \$150$$

An individual who is risk-neutral is indifferent if asked to choose between the gamble and its expected value; in this case, he would be indifferent between an offer of this gamble and an offer of a certain payment of $150. However, a person who is risk-averse would prefer the certain $150, and a person who is a risk-lover would prefer the gamble. For an individual who is risk-averse, the degree of risk aversion is determined by the "certainty-equivalent" amount, i.e., the certain amount that would just make the person indifferent between it and the gamble. For a person who is only moderately risk-averse, the certainty-equivalent might be $140. A person who is more risk-averse might strongly prefer the $140 to the gamble; for this individual, the certainty-equivalent might be $120. If offered a certain payment of only $110, even this person would choose the gamble instead.

For a person who is risk-averse, income has diminishing marginal utility, i.e., the more income he has, the less he gains from an additional dollar. Now it is easy to understand that tangible goods have diminishing marginal utility; for a household, a third car usually has less value than the second, and the second less than the first; indeed this is why demand curves for cars (and for all other goods) are downward-sloping. The application of this principle to money is less obvious, because money has so many different uses. In the above example, diminishing marginal utility of income means that the risk-averse person prefers the certain payment of $150 to the gamble, since the value of the additional $50 that could be won is less than the value of the $50 that could be lost.

Most people are risk-averse, at least when they respond to risks that are large relative to their total wealth. Thus, although people may wager small amounts in office pools or casinos, they will also buy insurance for risks involving disability, loss of life, their vehicles, business, or house. In the theory of finance everyone is assumed to be risk-averse.

Markets with incomplete information

As noted above in the discussion of monopoly, the analysis of competitive markets assumes, among other things, that buyers and sellers have complete information about the product being sold. In the next section we consider the topics of moral hazard and adverse selection. These are problems of opportunistic behavior, which arise when one participant in a market has better information than another. In these situations, the party with superior information is apt to take advantage of the uninformed party, and, as we shall see, this behavior interferes with the market's ability to arrive at an efficient outcome.

Moral hazard

Moral hazard is the inefficiency that arises when someone does not bear the full cost of his actions. When someone enjoys the full benefits of an action but bears none or only part of its costs, he may pursue that action beyond the point of efficiency, i.e., beyond the point where its net social benefits (total social benefits minus total social costs) are maximized. In the context of insurance, moral hazard arises because a person's behavior will change after he is insured, in such a way as to increase the probability or amount of a loss. A person who has insurance on his automobile will take fewer precautions to prevent its theft than if he had no insurance; he may be less apt to lock the car, close all its windows, park it in a well-lighted area, and so forth.

Insurance companies try to minimize moral hazard through the use of coinsurance and deductibles. Under coinsurance the insured party bears a specified percentage of the loss, like 10 percent, whereas with a deductible, the insured bears a fixed dollar amount; for example, the insurance policy may cover the amount of a loss minus $500. Since with a deductible or coinsurance the insured party bears part of the loss, he is more likely to take precautions that reduce the likelihood of loss.

Note that there would be no problem of moral hazard if all the parties involved had perfect information. If the insurance company could perfectly (and costlessly) observe all the actions of the insured person, it would charge a slightly higher premium each time the person neglected to lock his car, or fail to take other precautions. In this case the insured person would bear the entire cost of his actions, and would take the optimal level of precautions.

Of course, moral hazard is a very general concept, and is not restricted to problems involving insurance. It applies to any situation in which an action is separated from its costs. In 2003 the Michigan Education Association proposed taking funds from the school districts that had stayed within their budget and accumulated "rainy day funds" to allow for unforeseen emergencies, in order to give them to "hardship" schools that had exceeded their budget and were in debt. This is a classic example of moral hazard; it penalizes the school districts that were fiscally responsible and rewards the districts that did not maintain a balanced budget. Under this proposal the actions of the profligate school districts (spending beyond their budget) were separated from their costs (laying off teachers, freezing salaries of administrators, eliminating programs, and the like).

Another example involves the associate lawyers of a law firm working on a litigation. It often happens that the partners of the law firm who are in charge of the case are actively involved in settlement negotiations with the other side, while the associates are writing briefs, researching the law, organizing the testimony of witnesses and exhibits, and otherwise preparing for trial. It is customary for the partners to keep the associates completely in the dark about the progress of settlement negotiations. The reason is moral hazard: if an associate knew that there was a high probability that the case would be settled, she would be less likely to prepare diligently for trial, since in the event of a settlement none of her work would be used. However, it is always possible that the negotiators will fail to arrive at a settlement, in which case the firm's lawyers would have to go to trial inadequately prepared. The associate would not bear the full cost of her shirking; that cost would be borne first by the law firm's client and then by the partners of the firm (some of this cost is likely to be passed on to the associate, who could be rebuked or fired). Because of this prospect of moral hazard, the partners find it expedient to keep the associates completely uninformed about the progress of settlement negotiations.

In this text we will encounter numerous examples of moral hazard, many of which, like the "fisheries problem" considered in Chapter 4, are problems arising when property rights are incomplete.

Adverse selection

Adverse selection is opportunism at the extensive margin. More precisely, it is the tendency for less desirable, or low quality types to enter a market, and for more desirable, or high quality types to leave it, because of an inability to distinguish one type from another, i.e., because of a lack of information. An example of adverse selection is afforded by the recent experience of the New York State Bar Association with health insurance.

The New York State Bar Association provided group health insurance with Empire Blue Cross and Blue Shield to all of its members. The fee charged for this insurance was based on the average level of health care use by all the Association's members. If a lawyer had chronic health problems, it was to his advantage to join the Association and pay the fee. Over time the Association acquired a disproportionate share of lawyers with serious health problems, making it necessary to increase the health insurance fee. However, the increase in the fee made membership unattractive to lawyers who were in relatively good health, so they often declined to renew their memberships. Consequently the average level of health care use increased, requiring further increases in the health care fee, resulting in a greater exodus of healthy lawyers. Finally, in 1991 Empire Blue Cross and Blue Shield withdrew from the program. This is a classic example of the dynamics of adverse selection.

As with moral hazard, adverse selection would not arise if perfect information were available without cost to the insurance company. An insurer with complete knowledge of health risks would charge each customer a premium based on the expected health care costs for that individual; in this case no customer would gain an advantage, or be put at a disadvantage, by being in the health plan. In fact insurance companies do collect information on persons applying for health insurance, by requiring them to fill out an application, provide access to their medical records, and take a physical exam. Insurers generally exclude from coverage all pre-existing medical conditions, and may charge different premiums depending on an applicant's age, gender, and certain other characteristics. However their ability to charge rates based on the individual's characteristics may be limited by regulation that deems that practice to be "discrimination." For example, members of the Christian Science Church do not accept medical care in the event they are injured in an automobile accident. One might therefore expect Christian Scientists to drive more carefully than others, and to be less likely to have accidents. In many states, however, an automobile insurance company would not be allowed to offer a lower premium to a Christian Scientist, since that would be deemed impermissible discrimination based on one's religious beliefs.

Because the information about applicants obtained by insurance companies is imperfect, there remains a problem of adverse selection. This explains why premiums for group medical insurance are generally lower than those for individual medical insurance. Group medical insurance by definition covers all the members of a group, viz. all the employees of a firm, so the group covered by the insurance tends to be a representative sample of the population. Of course, this analysis did not apply to the New York State Bar Association, but that is the exception that proves the rule: for many members of the Association there was no independent significance to being a member apart from coverage under its health insurance plan. Another example of adverse selection is provided in one of the chapters on property law, describing the history and evolution of the American religious sect known as the Shakers.

Public goods

A public good is a good with a most unusual property: namely, when it is used or consumed by a person, that use or consumption does not reduce the amount of the good that will be available for others. The goods we usually consider in economics do not have this property. For example, if A eats a hot dog, there is nothing left for B. The traditional example of a public good is a lighthouse. The beam of a lighthouse on the coast of Maine can be seen by all vessels within its range; the fact that one freighter sees it does not prevent another from seeing it (unless, of course, one freighter happens to be blocking the other's view, and in that case, the lighthouse is no longer a public good). A theorem of mathematics is a public good. If I use the chain rule of calculus to work out a problem, that in no way prevents you from using it in your research. Another way to describe a public good is to state that the marginal cost of its consumption by another user is zero.

Public goods often have the characteristic of being nonexclusive.[12] A good is nonexclusive if, once the good has been provided to a group, it is impossible to exclude some members of the group from its benefits while providing it to others. Consider a government program to eradicate an agricultural pest. This is clearly a public good, since eliminating blight from the crop of one farmer does not in any way reduce the ability to provide the same benefit to another farmer. This good is nonexclusive since the government cannot limit the benefits of the program to certain farmers, e.g., those who would be willing to pay a fee.

The ability to exclude persons from enjoying the benefits of a public good may change with technological advances. At one time a television network could not prevent persons within the range of its signal from watching its programs, but technology was developed that now enables it to do so.

An example of a public good that we will consider later is a published court decision – a legal precedent. A written judicial opinion provides information about the law to anyone who reads it. The fact that it enlightens one lawyer does not prevent it from enlightening another. (Legal precedent is of course also a capital good, since it provides informational benefits for many years.) Scientific and technical knowledge, art, music and literature all provide examples of public goods.

It is noteworthy that the same object can be a public good at one moment and a private good a few hours later. At 3:00 A.M. the George Washington Bridge in New York City is for all practical purposes a public good. Since very few vehicles are on the bridge at that hour, the social cost of having an automobile cross it is approximately zero.[13] At 8:00 A.M. on a weekday, however, the bridge is no longer a public good. Since thousands of people wish to use the bridge at that hour, there is a substantial opportunity cost of having, for example, Mr. A's vehicle cross the bridge; that prevents another driver from crossing it in his place.

There are certain economic problems that are unique to public goods. One issue involves the social value of a public good. This is important because, until we know the value of different amounts of the good, e.g., national defense, scientific research, and the like, we cannot determine how much of it should be provided. Now the value of something that is not a public good, like a hot dog, is easily determined; it is the maximum amount that anyone is willing to pay for it. But how does one determine the value of a public good like, say, a national park? The social value of a public good equals the sum of its values to each person who would benefit from it. Recall that the height of a market demand curve represents the social value of each additional unit of the good. Therefore the market demand curve for a public good is constructed by adding *vertically* the individual demand curves of all persons for that good. For simplicity, assume there are only two persons in the economy, A and B. Figure 2.7 shows the individual demand curves for A and B, respectively, and

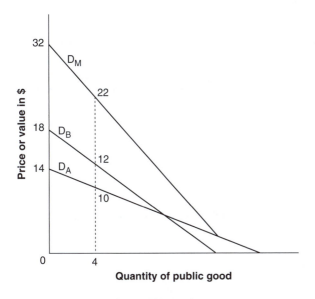

Figure 2.7 Demand for a public good.

Table 2.1 Constructing market demand curves for a public and a private good

Value (height of individual's demand curve)	Additional units of the good								
	First	Second	Third						
Mr. C	14	12	8						
Ms. D	10	9	6						
Ms. F	13	7	5						
Market demand curve (public good)	37	28	19						
Market demand curve (private good)	14	13	12	10	9	8	7	6	5

the market demand curve constructed by adding these two demand curves vertically. The diagram assumes that the value of a fourth unit of the public good is $10 to A and $12 to B. Since A and B are the only two persons in the economy, the social value of this unit is $22.

In most of this book, the goods we analyze are not public goods. Recall that for such goods, the height of the market demand curve represents the value of that additional unit to the person who values it most highly. For these nonpublic goods, the market demand curve is formed by summing the individual demand curves horizontally, rather than vertically. Let us now suppose there are only three individuals in an economy, Mr. C, Ms. D and Ms. F. The values they attach to additional units of a good consumed per month are shown in the first three rows of Table 2.1. Rows 4 and 5 of this table show the height of the market demand curve for each unit if (1) the good is a public good, or (2) the good is a private good. If we also know the marginal cost curve of the good, we can determine the amount that will (or should) be produced. For example, if the cost of producing the public good is $25 per unit, two units of the good should be produced. If the cost of producing the private good is $7.50 per unit, six units of that good will be produced.

Appendix 2.1 Continuous compounding

In the discussion of the present value of future payments in the text, we assumed that compounding of the amounts invested was done only once a year. Now let us suppose that compounding is done more frequently. Let us assume that compounding occurs n times a year, where P is the amount currently invested, r is the annual rate of interest, and we want to determine the accumulated value of principal and interest after x years. In this case the effective rate of interest for $1/n$ of a year is r/n, and over the period of x years, compounding will occur a total of nx times. Therefore Fx, the accumulated value of the amount invested after x years, will be:

$$F_x = P\left(1 + \frac{r}{n}\right)^{nx} \tag{1}$$

For example, if $1,000 is invested at a 6 percent annual rate of interest, compounded monthly, the value of principal and interest after two years will be:

$$F_2 = \$1,000\left(1 + \frac{0.06}{12}\right)^{(2\times12)} = \$1,127.16$$

Note that this amount is greater than the accumulated value if compounding were done annually, which we previously determined to be $1,123.60.

Now suppose that compounding is done daily. If $1,000 were invested at a 6 percent annual rate of interest compounded daily, the accumulated principal and interest after two years would be:

$$F_2 = \$1,000 \left(1 + \frac{0.06}{365}\right)^{(2 \times 365)} = \$1,127.49$$

Finally, suppose that compounding is continuous, i.e., that the number of intervals n approaches infinity. In this case we choose the limit of Fx as n approaches infinity. Note first that expression (1) can be rewritten as:

$$F_x = P\left(1 + \frac{r}{n}\right)^{\frac{n}{r}(rx)} \tag{2}$$

It is a fact of mathematics that as $y \to \infty$

$$\left(1 + \frac{1}{y}\right)^y \to e$$

where e is the transcendental number 2.71828182, that has the property that $\log(e) = 1$. Consequently if we consider n/r to be y, we notice that as $n/r \to \infty$ the limit of expression (2) can be rewritten as:

$$F_x = Pe^{rx} \tag{3}$$

Thus if $1,000 is invested at a 6 percent rate of interest compounded continuously, the accumulated value after two years will be:

$$F_2 = (\$1,000)e^{(0.06 \times 2)} = \$1,127.50$$

Note that this is very close to the amount obtained from daily compounding, $1,127.49. We can now also determine the present value of a payment x years from now when there is continuous compounding, since expression (3) indicates that $P = F_x e^{-rx}$. We will use such an expression in Appendix 5.1 (in Chapter 5, "Problems of incomplete property rights"), when we analyze the problem of when a tree grown for its value as lumber should be harvested.

Bibliography

Block, Richard, and Jack Stieber, "The Impact of Attorneys and Arbitrators on Arbitration Awards," 40 *Industrial and Labor Relations Review* 543–555 (July 1987).

Ehrenberg, Ronald G., and Robert S. Smith, *Modern Labor Economics: Theory and Public Policy* (8th ed., Reading, MA: Addison-Wesley, 2003).

Mishkin, Frederic S., *The Economics of Money, Banking and Financial Markets* (5th ed., Reading, MA: Addison-Wesley, 1998).

Pashigian, B. Peter, *Price Theory and Applications* (2nd ed., Boston, MA: McGraw-Hill, 1998).

Stigler, George J., *The Theory of Price* (3d ed., New York: Macmillan, 1966).

World Bank, *Expanding the Measure of Wealth: Indicators of Environmentally Sustainable Development* (Washington, DC: World Bank, 1997).

Problems

1. Explain why Empire Blue Cross and Blue Shield decided to drop health insurance cover for the 700 lawyers who were members of the New York State Bar Association. Make sure your explanation is in economic terms, not in the language of the "man on the street."

2. Table 2.2 appears in the textbook *Price Theory and Applications* by Peter Pashigian. It refers to the number of days per season spent on the disabled list by various pitchers who signed multi-year contracts after they became eligible for free agency in 1976. Explain everything that is going on here.

Table 2.2 Time spent on the disabled list before and after free agency

Status of pitchers	Average No. of days disabled before free agency	Average No. of days disabled after free agency	Change (%)
Remained with their original team	3.66	9.57	167
Joined another team	5.12	28.07	448

3. Suppose Monty Hall offers Bill Davis a choice between two alternatives: (*a*) a gamble, where the probability of winning $400 is three to four, and the probability of winning $100 is one in four; and (*b*) a guaranteed payment of $318. Mr. Davis chooses alternative (*b*). Is he risk-neutral, risk-averse, or a risk preferrer? Explain.

4. Suppose that, if Bill becomes an actor, there is an 90 percent probability that his income will be $20,000 and a 10 percent probability it will be $200,000. (*a*) What is Bill's expected income as an actor? (*b*) If Bill becomes an accountant, his income is certain to be $37,000. Suppose that, apart from the money, Bill is interested equally in acting and accounting. Bill chooses to become an accountant. Can we tell whether he is risk-averse, risk-neutral, or a risk lover? Explain.

5. Suppose there are only three persons in an economy: Mr. A, Ms. B, and Ms. C. Indicate the height of the demand curve for the first three units of the good described in Table 2.3 if (*a*) it is not a public good; and (*b*) it is a public good.

Table 2.3 Constructing market demand curves for a public and a private good

Value (height of individual's demand curve)	Additional units of the good			
	First	Second	Third	Fourth
Mr. A	16	13	8	
Ms. B	11	9	6	
Ms. C	14	12	5	

3 Introduction to the legal system

This chapter introduces some legal terminology that is used throughout the text, and some basic features of the legal system. At the same time we will show how economic analysis can be used to explain these features, which might otherwise seem completely arbitrary.

We first consider the different stages and different possible outcomes of a lawsuit (a civil action). We examine the doctrine of precedent, how a lawsuit may create a precedent, and the body of all precedents, which is known as the common law. We also consider an economic analysis of the doctrine of precedent developed by Landes and Posner.

There are substantial differences in the burden of proof applicable to different legal controversies. We consider an economic explanation for these differences, to illustrate how economics is used to analyze procedural issues.

Finally, we consider the design of the U.S. Constitution. The founders believed that, to provide a legal foundation for the nation's economic growth and development, the Constitution had to depart from the scheme of the Articles of Confederation, by transferring vast governmental powers from the states to the federal government. At the same time, the founders thought it imperative to ensure that this transfer of power would not lead to an undue concentration, or (in economic terms) a monopoly, of power in the central government. Accordingly, many provisions of the Constitution were designed to prevent that outcome. We will analyze the sections of the Constitution that are intended to thwart the acquisition of a monopoly of governmental power.

Although the specific institutional features we describe are those of the U.S. legal system, the issues that arise apply to any legal system.

Litigation and the court system

A lawsuit is called an "action" by lawyers. An action is viable only if it is based on a valid legal claim, or "cause of action." We can, and should, divide all actions between civil and criminal cases, since the substantive and procedural rules applicable to them are completely different. In a civil action a plaintiff files a lawsuit against one or more defendants; in a criminal case the accused party is the defendant, and the plaintiff is the government.

After a case is filed, it will be scheduled for a trial by either a judge or jury, and unless it is previously settled, it will be tried to verdict. Figure 3.1 shows various possible stages in the life of a lawsuit (a civil action), which are explained below. It should be noted that there are possible litigation events that are not shown in the figure. At any time during the litigation, the case may be settled by the parties, or abandoned by the plaintiff; moreover, a wide variety of procedural motions may be filed by either party, and there may be hearings on such motions.

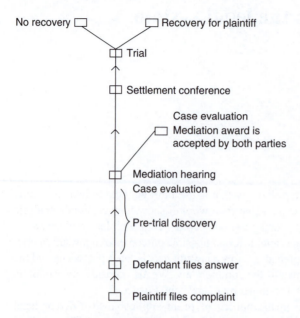

Figure 3.1 The life of a lawsuit.

After an action has been filed, the parties will engage in "pretrial discovery." In the process of discovery, each party obtains information from the other side by various means, such as interrogatories (written questions); oral depositions, in which witnesses are required to testify under oath; and the discovery of documents and things (physical evidence). These methods of discovery enable both sides to become fully informed about the merits of a case at a minimum cost. Again, the case may be settled at any stage until the judge or jury returns a verdict.

Because of the cost of litigation, there are many rules and practices designed either to avoid it altogether, or to resolve lawsuits that have been filed without incurring the expense of a trial. An example of attempts to avoid litigation is the language in many contracts requiring that any disputes that may arise must be submitted to binding arbitration. We will consider two examples of practices that are designed to avoid trials in pending cases: the offer in compromise and court-annexed mediation.

An offer in compromise may be made in the federal courts under Rule 68 of the Federal Rules of Civil Procedure. This rule provides that if a defendant makes a formal settlement offer to the plaintiff, the plaintiff must pay the costs incurred by the defendant after the offer is made unless (assuming the case is tried to verdict) the judgment at trial exceeds the amount of the offer. For example, suppose (1) the defendant makes a formal settlement offer of $500,000, (2) the plaintiff refuses it, and (3) after a trial the jury awards the plaintiff $400,000. In this case the plaintiff's award will be reduced by the costs incurred by the defendant after the offer was made. The idea behind the offer in compromise is that the plaintiff's action of rejecting the offer is not justified unless the offer is less than what he would obtain from a trial. Consequently, unless the offer is less than the trial judgment, the plaintiff should bear the full social costs of his decision to reject it.

Court-annexed mediation is really a form of nonbinding arbitration. In this procedure, which is required by some courts and voluntary or unused in others, both parties appear before a mediation panel at a hearing, which is briefer and more informal than a trial. After the hearing the panel proposes an award, and each party decides independently whether to accept or reject it. If both parties accept the mediation award, the case is resolved, and the defendant pays the plaintiff the amount of the award. If, however, either party rejects, the case proceeds on toward trial. If the case is subsequently tried to verdict, a penalty is imposed on the party who rejected the mediation award, unless the party does better at trial than he would have by accepting the award.[1]

Whether a procedure like court-annexed mediation reduces the costs of litigation depends on several factors, e.g., the cost of the procedure, whether the procedure is mandatory or voluntary, and how often it succeeds in resolving the case or at least prompting an early settlement.[2] If a procedure involves substantial costs, is mandatory, and rarely resolves the case, it will simply increase the costs of litigation (one consequence of this may be that fewer lawsuits are filed). If, on the other hand, a procedure frequently succeeds in resolving cases, it will reduce the costs of litigation (and one consequence may be that more lawsuits are filed).

Once a decision is made by a trial court, it can be *affirmed* or *reversed* on appeal. For purposes of illustration, we consider here the organization of the federal courts; there is a parallel system of state courts in every state. In the federal court system there are three levels. At the bottom is the trial court, which is called the federal district court. A plaintiff or defendant who is dissatisfied with the verdict of this court may appeal to the next level, the Circuit Court of Appeals. There are now thirteen courts at this level: one for each of eleven regions, or circuits, plus the District of Columbia and the Federal Circuit Court of Appeals.[3] The Sixth Circuit, for example, includes Michigan, Ohio, Kentucky, and Tennessee. At the highest level is the U.S. Supreme Court.

In all legal systems a party who is dissatisfied with the decision of the trial court has either an absolute right of appeal or a right to discretionary review, meaning that the appellate court decides whether it will review the case. In the federal court system in the United States, a party who is dissatisfied with the decision of the federal district court has a right to appeal to the Circuit Court of Appeals, but a subsequent appeal by either party from the Circuit Court to the Supreme Court is subject to discretionary review. One reason for this scheme is that it is important for the Supreme Court to limit the number of cases it considers. The Supreme Court would be inundated with cases if parties had an absolute right to have their cases reviewed by the Court. A plaintiff or defendant who is dissatisfied with the decision by the Circuit Court usually applies to the Supreme Court for appellate review by filing a writ of certiorari.[4] However, the Supreme Court agrees to decide only a small fraction of the cases submitted to it for review – currently less than 10 percent.[5]

Box 3.1 How the Supreme Court decides whether to grant certiorari

There are nine Justices on the U.S. Supreme Court. The Supreme Court grants certiorari (agrees to hear an appeal) if at least four Justices vote in favor of it. There have been a number of studies of the factors that lead the Court to grant certiorari. Factors that have been found to be important include the following:

1   The U.S. government has requested certiorari.

2   Briefs have been filed by amici curiae (friends of the court – someone who is not a party in the case) either in support of, or in opposition to, certiorari. The likelihood of certiorari being granted increases with the number of amicus briefs filed. The number of amicus briefs filed is a rough index of the importance of the case.

3   There is a conflict in decisions among lower courts. This conflict may be one between two or more federal Circuit Courts of Appeals, between two or more state supreme courts, between a federal court and a state court, or between the lower court and the appellate court in the case being decided, that is, the appellate court has overruled the trial court.

4   There is a conflict among the justices of the court immediately below, i.e., they decided the case by a split vote.

5   There is a conflict between the decision of the court below and a Supreme Court decision. The Supreme Court cannot allow lower courts to disregard or defy its decisions.

6   There is a conflict between governmental agencies.

7   The issue is important.

8   There is no need for more extensive consideration of the issue by the lower courts. Sometimes, even though there is a conflict among the lower courts, the Supreme Court may not want to resolve it yet, because the issue has not had enough "seasoning." The idea is that the Court can make a better decision if it has the benefit of the views of many different courts on the issue in question.

Of the factors listed above, the one that probably has the greatest likelihood of inducing the Court to grant certiorari is a request by the U.S. government.

Researchers have considered whether the votes of individual Justices are motivated by an "error-correction strategy." According to this hypothesis, a Justice will vote to grant certiorari if he believes the decision of the lower court should be reversed, and to deny certiorari if he believes the lower court decided the case correctly. However, some commentators have pointed out that this approach seems a bit shortsighted; in reality, a Justice's vote is likely to be influenced by what he expects the full Court to do if certiorari were granted. Even if a Justice disagreed strongly with the decision of the lower court, it seems unlikely that he would vote for certiorari if he knew that he was in the minority, so that the full Court would be likely to affirm the lower court decision, thus making it a far more influential precedent. Similarly, a Justice who agreed with the decision of the lower court, and knew that he would be in the majority, might vote for certiorari to establish the rule decided below in a Supreme Court decision. Palmer (1982) states that this idea of "strategic voting" generates two hypotheses: (1) other things being equal, Justices would be more likely to vote for certiorari when they disagree with the decision of the lower court; and (2) other things being equal, Justices would be more likely to vote for certiorari when they later end up in the voting majority of the Court. He found statistical evidence supporting both of these hypotheses.

Precedents and the common law

Once the case is finally decided, it may be published as the opinion of the court.[6] If so, it becomes a precedent which is useful as a guide to courts which have to decide similar cases in the future. Under the doctrine of precedent, or *stare decisis* (to stand by things decided), a court is obliged to follow an earlier decision made by another court if that decision basically involved the same issue as that arising in the case at bar. The rule of law which constitutes the "precedent" is known as the "holding" or *ratio decidendi* (the "reason for deciding").

According to the doctrine of precedent, cases must be decided the same way when their "material facts" are the same. The holding of a case, then, consists of its material facts plus the decision based on them. In addition to its holding, a decision may often have an *obiter dictum* ("a thing said by the way") – an incidental observation or remark made in passing, which is not binding upon future courts. Examples of *obiter dicta* would include a proposed rule of law offered as an analogy or illustration, or an alternative rationale suggested for the decision, which is not finally adopted, or an indication as to how the court would rule if the facts were different. The reason why *obiter dicta* are not regarded as binding authority is that they may have been made without thorough consideration of the relevant case law and of all the implications that would follow if they became a precedent.

Once a case has been suggested to a court as a precedent, it can be *followed, distinguished*, or *overruled*. A prior case will be distinguished if the court feels that the principle announced by that case is not directly applicable to the issue arising before it. If, on the other hand, the court feels that the rule of the prior case is applicable, but that that case was wrongly decided, it may decide to overrule the prior case, thereby destroying its value as precedent.[7]

Another issue is the effect the overruling of a court decision has on other cases. In principle, a decision could be overruled "prospectively"; that is, the new rule of law would apply only to future cases, not the case in which the question is litigated. The courts have, however, recognized that prospective overruling would greatly diminish the incentive of a litigant to challenge an existing rule of law. How many litigants would be willing to bear the risk and cost of litigating to overturn a rule of law if they could not reap the benefits of doing so?

The body of all precedents is known as the common law. It is a stock of knowledge about legal rules and obligations. Turning to economic analysis, let us consider the idea, developed by Landes and Posner, that the body of legal precedent is a form of capital. Capital has been defined as anything, other than a free human being, which yields productive services beyond the current period. Precedent qualifies under this definition since a case can provide useful information about rules of law for many years. It should, however, be noted that the stock of legal capital can depreciate; a case may be overruled by a subsequent court or by legislation, or may become obsolete because of changes in the environment. There is an impressive body of case law concerning the effect of blood tests on the probability of paternity, but now this territory is ruled by DNA evidence.

New precedents are added to the stock of legal capital through litigation. More law will be produced by litigation when the demand for information about legal rules is large relative to the supply. In areas where there is not much knowledge of the law, there is uncertainty, which often results in litigation. Much of our law of mortgages was generated during the Great Depression, when there was an exceptional demand for information about rights of foreclosure, etc. Much of our law of impeachment and the scope of executive privilege was developed during the last years of the Nixon administration and the second term of the

Clinton administration. Thus rules of common law tend to be generated in areas where they will have the greatest social value. It should also be noted that a precedent is a pure public good, since its use by many lawyers and judges does not diminish the ability of others to apply it to future controversies.

The doctrine of precedent would seem to enhance efficiency because it enables judges to limit their consideration to issues which have not previously been analyzed by other courts. If ten courts have decided that a train engineer is negligent when he fails to blow the whistle before a crossing, it is efficient for the eleventh court to abide by their decision on this point, and limit its consideration to the novel issues presented in the case.

Landes and Posner measured the value of a court decision as precedent by counting the number of times it was cited by subsequent courts. This method has also been used to determine the scholarly value of the work of economists and other scientists. The underlying assumption here is that on average, an individual's work is more significant the more often it has been cited by others working in the same field. Indeed, at some universities the number of citations of an individual's work is considered together with other factors in deciding whether to grant him tenure, or to promote him from associate to full professor.

Landes and Posner found that the rate of depreciation of precedent is relatively low – between four and 5 percent. This may explain why the income of a lawyer tends to decline relatively slowly with advancing age, relative to other occupations where the rate of depreciation of knowledge seems higher, e.g. biochemistry or computer science. According to the theory of human capital, people will invest in additional human capital to improve their productivity, thereby maintaining or increasing their income. If an individual's professional knowledge depreciates at a high rate, his income will decline rapidly when he ceases to invest in supplemental training.

As a person approaches the age of retirement, he has less incentive to invest in human capital because the period over which he can realize the benefits of his investment is so short. Thus in an occupation in which human capital seems to depreciate rapidly, one would expect earnings to fall sharply as the person approaches the age of retirement. Figure 3.2 shows how the annual income of two professions – law and computer science – might change with the age of the worker. The lawyer's income declines less rapidly with age because of the lower rate of depreciation of his human capital.

Different standards of proof

The standard of proof (sometimes called the plaintiff's "burden of proof") is different in different types of legal controversies. In civil cases, the plaintiff prevails only if his position is supported by a "preponderance of the evidence" or, alternatively, "the greater weight of the evidence," anything beyond 50 percent (if the plaintiff achieves exactly 50 percent the defendant wins). In certain types of civil controversies, the plaintiff's proof must meet a standard of "clear and convincing evidence," which is higher than the preponderance standard, but has not been quantified by the courts. This standard applies when the plaintiff must prove a case of fraud, or show that a document which appears to be a deed was actually intended to be a mortgage, or to prove a claim against a decedent which was not presented to her during her lifetime. Finally, in criminal proceedings it is necessary to prove the guilt of the accused "beyond a reasonable doubt." Here again the courts have refused to quantify this standard, although it is greater than clear and convincing evidence.

How can one explain these differences in the burden of proof? It has been argued that the explanation lies in differences in the cost of error. In a civil case two types of mistakes

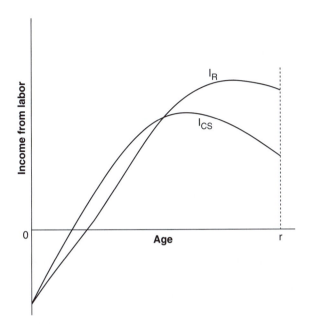

Figure 3.2 Hypothetical age–earnings profile of a lawyer and a computer scientist.

are possible: the court might grant an award for the plaintiff when it should not (a Type 1 mistake), and might hold in favor of the defendant when it should not (a Type 2 mistake). Suppose the social cost of a Type 1 mistake is $400, but the cost of a Type 2 mistake is $100. Now suppose the court is 75 percent convinced that the defendant should be held liable. If the court rules for the plaintiff, the expected loss is:

$$(0.75 \times 0) + (0.25 \times (-400)) = -\$100$$

On the other hand, if the court holds in favor of the defendant, the expected loss is $(0.75 \times (-100)) + (0.25 \times 0) = -\$75$. So it is efficient to rule in favor of the defendant, even though the court is 75 percent sure that the defendant is liable! For this particular example, it turns out that the court should rule for the defendant unless it is more than 80 percent certain that the defendant is liable. Thus a rule allowing a plaintiff to prevail only if he satisfies an 80 percent standard of proof would be efficient.

It has been argued that in most civil cases, the cost of a Type 1 mistake is probably about the same as that of a Type 2 mistake; thus it is appropriate to rule for the plaintiff if the court is more than 50 percent persuaded of the defendant's liability. In the special kinds of civil cases described above involving a claim of fraud and the like – it may be that the cost of a Type 1 mistake, i.e., holding an innocent defendant liable for fraud, is substantially greater than the cost of a Type 2 mistake, so that a higher burden of proof is appropriate.

It would certainly seem to be true in a criminal case, that the cost of an erroneous conviction is much greater than the cost of an erroneous acquittal. The cost of a wrongful acquittal is just the general reduction in the deterrent effect of the law, while the cost of a wrongful conviction includes the social cost of punishment. To the extent that punishment involves imprisonment, the social cost includes the actual cost of the incarceration and the loss of the defendant's productivity, both during his prison term and later, if his job opportunities are diminished by a stigma resulting from his conviction. Thus it would take several acquittals to be as costly as one erroneous conviction, and the reasonable doubt standard may be justified. A decision theorist would say that these situations involve an "asymmetric loss function."

A recent study of forecasts made by weathermen on television found that the probability of an incorrect forecast of rain was much greater than the probability of an incorrect forecast of fair weather, presumably because the loss function of the viewer is asymmetric. The cost of being caught unprepared in a thundershower exceeds the cost of carrying an unnecessary umbrella.[8]

The U.S. Constitution

At this juncture it is useful for us to consider briefly the purpose and design of the U.S. Constitution. It is appropriate to do so now, since we will need to refer to provisions of the Constitution in the chapters on property law, the economics of litigation and criminal law, and elsewhere in this book.

We first consider how the Constitution was shaped by the vested interests and economic views of the framers and their political opponents. In this section we evaluate the hypothesis of an influential American historian, Charles Beard, who was evidently the first person to provide an economic interpretation of the Constitution. In the second section we will analyze the Constitution as a plan to thwart the acquisition of a monopoly of governmental power.

The Beard hypothesis

The idea of analyzing the Constitution in economic terms is generally credited to the historian Charles Beard (1874–1948).[9] Beard viewed the Constitution as the outcome of a power struggle between one group that has been described as owners of personal property – those with businesses based on money, public securities, manufacturing, trade, and shipping – and another group described as owners of real property – small farmers and debtors. Beard argued that it served the economic interests of the owners of personal property for the Constitution to depart from the scheme of the Articles of Confederation, by transferring most governmental power from the states to the federal government. That is, of course, exactly what the Constitution did. Thus in Beard's view the Constitution chiefly represented the interests of owners of personal property, and its adoption was largely attributable to their skillful advocacy and lobbying efforts.

The interests of the owners of real property had been reflected in the Articles of Confederation, adopted in March 1781. Under the Confederation the states had the right to issue their own currency and regulate commerce. Some states, like Rhode Island, had enacted laws that intervened in private contracts, either by suspending the debtor's obligation to repay, by allowing debtors to pay with goods rather than money (tender laws), or by allowing loans to be paid with paper money rather than specie (coin). These laws represented a threat to those, such as Southern planters and coastal merchants, who bought and sold goods on credit and were engaged in trade with Europe. (As we will see in the chapter on contracts, reliance on contract law is especially important when exchange is not simultaneous. Commercial agreements between U.S. and European merchants involved substantial intervals of time and geographic distance.) The debtor relief laws made creditors doubt that they would be fully repaid; consequently there was an increase in the rate of interest, even in the states where these laws had not been enacted, since creditors feared that they would be enacted there in due course. Creditors probably also responded to debtor relief laws by requiring more collateral, making fewer loans, or making smaller loans.

Apart from ceding to the states the important powers described above, the Confederation had other fundamental weaknesses. The federal government lacked the authority to enter into binding commercial treaties with European nations. It could not enlist troops. The potential for chaos that existed when the validity of contracts was uncertain and the central government lacked military power was made clear by Shays' rebellion in western Massachusetts in 1786–87.[10]

The Constitution, whose convention held its last meeting on September 17, 1787, established a much stronger federal government, and ensured that loan agreements could be enforced without interference by the states. Article I, Section 10, prohibited states from coining money, emitting bills of credit, or making "any Thing but gold and silver Coin a Tender in Payment of Debts." This language precluded the state laws concerning paper money and legal tender referred to above, and another clause prohibited states from enacting any laws "impairing the Obligation of Contracts." Moreover, states were prohibited from entering into treaties or alliances. These provisions, by ensuring that loan agreements could be enforced, reduced the cost of providing credit. This caused the supply curve for goods sold on credit to shift to the right, increasing the quantity of goods sold and lowering the equilibrium price. By establishing the legal foundation required for efficient credit markets, the Constitution stimulated investment and economic growth.

As previously noted, the government created by the Constitution had far more power than the Confederation. The extensive powers granted to Congress in Article I, Section 8, were intended to be exclusive, in that states were not allowed to enact their own laws in the areas specified. The military powers granted to the federal government in this section would enable it to quash any domestic insurrections like Shays' rebellion, and thus made such disturbances less likely.

Subsequent research has shown that the dynamics of the political process leading to adoption of the Constitution were considerably more complex and multi-dimensional than the simple conflict between two economic groups depicted by Beard. However his thesis has stimulated research that has greatly improved our understanding of the Constitution. Beard's own contribution was to show that there is often a relationship between an individual's economic interests and his political views, and that many provisions of the Constitution were critically important to the economic development of the emerging nation.

Broadly speaking, there were two major consequences of the Constitution's scheme to transfer power from the states to the central government. First, it was thought necessary to include many provisions that would prevent an undue concentration, or monopoly, of governmental power. Second, to ensure ratification, the framers had to promise to amend the Constitution promptly with a Bill of Rights, to provide individuals guarantees against the arbitrary exercise of power by the federal government. In the next section we will analyze the Constitution as a plan to avoid a monopoly of governmental power.

Provisions that prevent a monopoly of governmental power

As previously noted, Beard argued that it served the economic interests of merchants, traders, and manufacturers for the Constitution to depart from the scheme of the Articles of Confederation, by transferring vast powers from the states to the federal government. At the same time, the founders wanted to ensure that this transfer would not lead to an excessive concentration of power in the central government. Accordingly, many provisions of the

Constitution are specifically designed to prevent that outcome. In this section we examine these "checks and balances."

First, there is a separation of powers between the federal and state governments; second, since the founders were primarily concerned about a concentration of power in the federal government, there is a division of powers among its three branches, executive, legislative, and judicial. The power to enact legislation is further divided, both within the legislative branch, between the House of Representatives and the Senate, and because some of it (the President's veto power) is allocated to the executive branch. The power to conduct foreign policy is shared by the President and Congress. The Judicial branch also shares some power with the President, who has the right to grant reprieves and pardons, and to appoint Supreme Court Justices with the advice and consent of the Senate. Another impediment to monopoly is that officers of government are chosen for different terms – members of the House of Representatives for two years, Senators for six years, the President for four years, and federal judges for life – and by different groups of constituents: Senators by the state legislatures, the President by the electoral college, judges by the President and Senate, etc., so that a suddenly emerging popular majority would not be able to take immediate control of all departments of the federal government.

States are protected against overreaching by the federal government. For example, the Tenth Amendment reserves to the states all powers not expressly granted by the Constitution to the federal government. Within the legislative branch, the Senate provides equal representation to each state, and the Constitution cannot be amended without the consent of three-fourths of the states.

The powers assigned to each branch of government are limited not only by the scope of the powers granted, and by explicit limitations on them, but also by remedies for abuse of power that can be implemented by the other branches. The first ten amendments to the Constitution, known as the Bill of Rights, limit the powers of the federal government only, not the states. However, various other provisions, such as Article I, and the Sixth and Fourteenth Amendments, do restrict the powers of the states. In particular, the Sixth Amendment provides that the federal constitution and laws take precedence over those of the states. Moreover, the Fourteenth Amendment requires states to provide "due process of law" and "equal protection of the laws" to persons under their jurisdiction.

The President, and other members of the executive and the judicial branches, are subject to impeachment for crimes, and the powers of impeachment and trial are divided between the two houses of Congress. While officials can be removed for serious misconduct, other provisions are designed to ensure that under normal conditions, each branch will be capable of acting independently from the others. For example, the Constitutional Convention rejected a proposal that the President be chosen by Congress, on the ground that he would then be too dependent on the legislative branch. Federal judges have life tenure to ensure their independence from the executive and legislative branches, and their compensation cannot be reduced while they are in office. The compensation of the President cannot be either decreased or increased during his term of office. The founders understood that Congress could try to bring pressure on the President, who has a term of only four years, either through the threat of a tax (a reduction in salary), or by the offer of a subsidy (an increase in salary). Given the life tenure of the federal judges, it was necessary to allow for periodic increases in their salary to compensate for inflation; in order for judges to be both well qualified and independent, they would have to earn a reasonable salary.

This elaborate scheme of separation of powers, and checks and balances, could of course be circumvented if the separate branches colluded to form a cartel – a monopoly of governmental power. However a cartel is less likely to be formed, or to be sustainable, the greater the costs of collusion. Normally as these costs increase, the greater the number of parties who must enter the agreement, and the more equal the distribution of power among them. A cartel of political power would require the agreement of the legislative branch, to enact the coercive statute, of the executive branch, to enforce it, and of the judicial branch, to uphold it.

There are additional safeguards. All officials in federal and state governments must take an oath to support the U.S. Constitution (Article VI), but far more importantly, the Judiciary has the power of judicial review – the power to determine whether actions of the legislative or executive branch violate the Constitution. The fundamental importance of maintaining the separation of powers provides the economic rationale for the measures taken to ensure the independence of the judiciary.

The doctrine of selective incorporation

The first ten amendments to the U.S. Constitution, which are known as the Bill of Rights, took effect in 1791. These amendments impose limitations on the powers of the federal government only, not state governments. At the time of the Constitutional Convention the founders were concerned about granting excessive powers to the federal government, and a number of state legislatures had ratified the Constitution with the understanding that it would promptly be amended by the addition of a bill of rights.

It often happens that those challenging a state law as being unconstitutional argue that the law violates one of the provisions of the Bill of Rights. For example, in one case[11] a plaintiff challenged payments made under New Jersey law by local school boards. The payments were for the costs of transportation to and from schools, including private schools. The plaintiff argued that these payments benefited parochial Catholic schools, and were thus unconstitutional, on the grounds that this violated the provision in the First Amendment that "Congress shall make no law respecting an establishment of religion ..." But, one might ask, how can anyone argue that a state law must satisfy the requirements of the Bill of Rights, given that these amendments restrict only the powers of the federal government? It turns out that those who challenge state laws as being unconstitutional are really arguing that these laws violate, not anything in the Bill of Rights, but rather the "due process" clause of the Fourteenth Amendment, which does apply to the states. Some historical background is in order here.

The Fourteenth Amendment was proposed by Congress in 1866, immediately after the Civil War, in order to restrict the powers of the states. The objective of this amendment was to guarantee the civil and political rights of black citizens, and to prevent the southern states from discriminating against them. This amendment states that "[No] State [shall] deprive any person of life, liberty, or property, without due process of law; nor deny to any person ... the equal protection of the laws." Over time, in a series of decisions, The Supreme Court has held that the "due process" and "equal protection" clauses provide constitutional protections of broad scope against state actions for all citizens, not just blacks. The Court has ruled that many of the specific guarantees in the Bill of Rights, such as the First Amendment right to "freedom of speech," or the Sixth Amendment's guarantee to criminal defendants of a "speedy and public trial, by an impartial jury" are "inherent" in the "due process" clause; this is known as the doctrine of "selective incorporation." Thus, for example, the provision of the First Amendment prohibiting an "establishment" of religion applies to state statutes not directly, but indirectly because the "due process" clause of the Fourteenth Amendment is deemed to include this rule. Indeed, most of the protections and safeguards of the first eight amendments of the Bill of Rights now apply to state law through the due process clause. There are a few rights that the Supreme Court has decided are not inherent in due process, such as the Fifth Amendment's provision that "no person shall be held to answer for a … crime, unless on [an] indictment of a Grand Jury," and other rights that the Court has not ruled on one way or the other. This then explains why state laws can be challenged on the grounds that they violate specific provisions of the Bill of Rights, even though the Bill of Rights are nominally limitations on the federal government only.

Now that we have introduced some legal terms, and reviewed some basic features of the legal system, we are prepared to examine the major areas of the common law. In the next chapter we begin with a review of property law.

Bibliography

Beard, Charles A., *An Economic Interpretation of the Constitution of the United States* (1913).

Farrand, Max, *The Records of the Federal Convention of 1787* (1937).

Hannon, Michael, "A Closer Look at Unpublished Opinions in the United States Courts of Appeals," 3 (1) *Journal of Appellate Practice and Process* 199–250 (spring 2001).

Landes, William M., and Richard A. Posner, "Legal Precedent: A Theoretical and Empirical Analysis," 19 *Journal of Law and Economics* 249 (1976).

Spurr, Stephen J., "The Role of Nonbinding Alternative Dispute Resolution in Litigation," 42 (1) *Journal of Economic Behavior and Organization* 75–96 (May 2000).

Tushnet, Mark V., "The Constitution as an Economic Document: Beard Revisited," 56 *George Washington Law Review* 106–113 (1987–1988).

Problems

1.   What theories have been offered to explain why a Supreme Court Justice would vote for certiorari, i.e., vote in favor of a case being reviewed by the Supreme Court?
2.   What is the standard of proof in a criminal case? How and why is it different from the standards of proof in civil cases?

4   Property law

This chapter begins by suggesting an economic justification for the existence of property rights, namely their incentive effects, and provides some illustrations of how property rights are often created informally if they are not recognized by law. We analyze various forms of intellectual property, e.g., patents, copyrights, and trademarks, and how the law seeks to maximize the benefits of creative activity and work of good quality, relative to the costs of establishing these property rights.

We will consider a principle of far-reaching importance that is known as the Coase Theorem, set forth in a 1960 paper by the Nobel Laureate Ronald Coase. The Coase Theorem states that, in the event two or more parties have a conflict, there is no need for outside intervention if certain conditions are met, namely the parties' costs of bargaining are low and property rights are well defined. If these conditions are satisfied, the parties will reach an efficient solution by themselves, through their own negotiations. An understanding of the Coase Theorem requires an understanding of efficiency and important types of transaction costs, such as the holdout and free-rider problems. We also consider the arguments for and against the government's power of eminent domain, which has been defended on the grounds that it is necessary to overcome the holdout problem, a problem of monopoly.

Finally, suppose it is well established that there are private property rights in some type of assets. How does the law determine who is the owner of property? If two or more persons claim to be the owner, how does the law decide this dispute? We will examine different legal rules and two different systems of determining the ownership of valuable assets: a system of title registration, and a recording system.

A property right is the right to the exclusive use of a thing. Before we examine issues involving various types of interests in property, we should consider a question which is very basic, and like other questions that are very basic, very important, namely: is it a good idea to have property rights? Aren't property rights essentially selfish – something that would have no place in an ideal society?

Let us consider a society in which there are no property rights. Suppose a man who lives in an agricultural area decides to grow a field of corn.[1] He proceeds to cultivate the soil, plants the seeds, spreads fertilizer, waters the crop regularly, and sprays it with insecticide. His activity adds to the wealth of society because the value of the harvested corn will exceed the value of all the inputs (his labor, the use of the land, irrigation, fertilizer, and insecticide) used to produce it. In the fall the corn is full-grown and tasseling. Before he can harvest it, however, someone else goes on the land, cuts down the corn and carries it away. The farmer cannot object, since by assumption he has no property right in the corn. Given this turn of events, how likely is it that this individual will continue to do such a conscientious job of growing corn?

The principal justification for property rights is that they give people both the ability and the incentive to carry on productive activities. Sometimes conditions arise where it is important to create incentives, but there are no property rights established by law. In such cases people often create, and abide by, their own informal system of property rights. Occasionally, as in the winter of 1977, there are severe snowstorms in the city of Chicago. Streets cannot be cleared by the city for days or even weeks. During these snow emergencies, it often happens that an individual will shovel snow for half an hour or more to create a parking space. When this person drives away, he often leaves a chair in the space he has cleared, to let the world know that this is "his" parking space.[2] A property right (generally respected, although not recognized by city or state law) has been created to give people incentives to clear away the snow.

Whether an interest in something is a property right is determined by its economic characteristics, not by its formal legal description. Rights to use specific broadcasting frequencies have been granted as licenses by the Federal Communications Commission and its predecessor agency, the Federal Radio Commission, since 1928. They currently (in 2009) have a term of eight years and may be renewed upon good behavior; in fact, they have been revoked rarely and only for serious misconduct. They are exclusive (a competing use will be enjoined) and transferable. Congress specifically provided that these licenses are not property rights, to preclude a claim by an owner for compensation in the event his license was not renewed. However, being exclusive and transferable, they are in fact property rights – indeed, property interests of great value.

Finally, it should be recognized that the benefits of property rights extend well beyond their incentive effects. For example, the fact that cars are private property means that there is no conflict or confusion arising from A and B attempting to use the same car at the same time; A knows he has an exclusive right to use his own car, and so does B. We can summarize the various advantages of property rights with a claim that they take society further in the direction of efficiency than alternative methods of allocating resources.[3] Still, the one attribute that seems to be the most important benefit of property rights, relative to other regimes, is their effects on incentives.

Since we have already referred to the idea of efficiency, but have not yet defined it, we begin with an analysis of that term.

Efficiency

Throughout this chapter and this book we will frequently make references to "efficiency," and will characterize rules of law and behavior as being efficient or inefficient. It is therefore important that we have a precise definition of this word. We can define efficiency in different ways that are all equivalent, as follows: an allocation, i.e., an assignment of resources to economic agents, is efficient or Pareto-optimal[4] if (1) there is no way to make some individual better off without making someone else worse off; or (2) there is no way to make everyone better off; or (3) it is not possible to make any trades which are mutually advantageous. Conversely, if an allocation is not efficient, it is possible to make someone better off without making anyone else worse off. Alternatively, it is possible to make everyone better off.

Suppose there is a tract of land consisting of 1,000 separate parcels, each of which is owned by a different person. Suppose also that each owner values his or her parcel at $8,000. Thus the land has an aggregate value to its owners of $8 million. A city near the land is considering whether to purchase the entire tract, to convert it into a public park, for the use of its 100,000 residents. Assume that the value of the land as a park would be $100 to each of its residents. Thus the aggregate value of the land as a park would be $10 million.

Under these circumstances, it is easy to show the sale of the land by its owners to the city will yield a net gain to society. Suppose, for example, that the land is sold to the city for $8 million. The current owners of the land would have neither a gain nor a loss, since they would be giving up property they value at $8 million, but would receive $8 million in exchange for it. However, the city is certainly better off, since it receives property worth $10 million for only $8 million. Therefore the sale would make someone better off (the city) without making others worse off (the current owners). From the definition of efficiency, we conclude that the current allocation, under which the land is held by the landowners, is not efficient.

Now suppose that the land is purchased by the city for $10 million. In this case the city will be no better off nor worse off, but the landowners will be better off, since they have received property worth $10 million in exchange for property they valued at $8 million. In the definition of efficiency, we noted that if it was possible to make someone better off without making anyone else worse off, then it was also possible to make everyone better off. In this case, suppose the current landowners sold the land to the city for $9 million. Then the city would have a gain of $10 million – $9 million = $1 million, and the landowners would have a gain of $9 million – $8 million = $1 million. The transfer would make everyone better off.

In general, the way to achieve efficiency is to allocate resources to their use of highest value. Assets, like the land in this example, should be assigned to those who value them the most. Consequently it is important that property rights be transferable. If property cannot be transferred, resources can't be reassigned from less valuable to more valuable uses.

Although efficiency is illustrated by the preceding example, a little reflection will show that the literal requirements of Pareto efficiency are very rarely satisfied in the real world. Virtually any transaction is likely to leave someone at least slightly worse off. In our example, the transfer of land to the city for use as a park may be expected to reduce the demand of the city's residents to visit other parks in the surrounding area, which could reduce the volume of business at concession stands in those parks. The owners of those concession stands, and their suppliers, will be worse off. Similarly, the invention of pocket calculators was undoubtedly a great boon to mankind, but was not good news to individuals who owned stock in firms that made slide rules. Since the standard of Pareto efficiency is so difficult to meet, some economists, notably Nicholas Kaldor[5] and J. R. Hicks,[6] have proposed alternative definitions of efficiency.

Kaldor suggested that there is an improvement in social welfare from a change that would enable those who gain from it to compensate those who lose, and still have gains left over. Thus, by the Kaldor criterion, there is an improvement in welfare if those who benefit from a transaction gain enough to fully compensate those who lose, *even if that compensation never occurs*. Consequently a Kaldor improvement is a potential Pareto improvement, but not more than that, unless all losing parties are fully compensated. When people use the term "efficient" or "inefficient" in reference to a specific proposal, it is very likely that they are using the criterion of Kaldor or Hicks rather than the strict definition of Pareto.

Transaction costs

Given that there is a net gain to society from the transfer of the land, the next question is whether it will happen. The answer is that it may or may not, depending on transaction costs.

By transaction costs, we mean all the costs of carrying out an exchange. These costs include the costs of identifying the parties with whom one must negotiate, the costs of getting together with them, the costs of the bargaining process itself (e.g. hiring a lawyer), and the costs of enforcing the resulting agreement.

Transaction costs are generally large when many parties have an interest in the dispute. Consider, for example, a factory polluting Lake Superior with taconite pellets. It may be worth $1 million to the factory to be able to pollute the lake, since it would cost an additional $1 million to dispose of the taconite in some other way. On the other hand, this pollution may reduce the value of the lake for many people who live near the lake or visit it, to the extent of $2 million. However, it would be extremely costly to identify all the individuals who are affected by the pollution, arrange for them to get together, and determine the value they attach to eliminating the pollution.

An example of transaction costs – and how they may be overcome – is provided by the American Society of Composers, Authors, and Publishers (ASCAP) and Broadcast Music Incorporated (BMI), both of which enter into license agreements with businesses to allow them to play music produced by their members, who are authors and publishers. The customers of ASCAP, for example, include all types of businesses that play music – television and radio stations, cable and satellite networks, internet web sites, cellphone ring tones, colleges and universities, night clubs, taverns and restaurants, hotels, shopping centers, retail stores, dance halls, health and fitness clubs, airlines, skating rinks, and many others. Most of ASCAP's license fees are collected from local television and radio stations and from television networks, under "blanket" license agreements, which give a business the right to perform any piece in ASCAP's library.

After deducting operating expenses, ASCAP distributes the revenues that it collects to its members. The amount distributed to each member is based on how often his or her music is played, and how large the audience is when it is played. If there were no organization such as ASCAP, each business owner would have to find and negotiate with all the owners of all the music that he wished to use. Similarly, each composer or publisher would have to monitor the use of the hundreds of thousands of businesses that play music, to learn whether, and how often, their own music was played. These enormous transaction costs are avoided by having one umbrella organization issue blanket licenses to businesses on standard terms.

To determine how the revenues should be distributed among its members, ASCAP must monitor its customers to learn how often each piece is played. All the music on network television, which has a very large audience, is measured exactly, but plays on local television, local radio, wired music, and other venues are estimated by a random sampling scheme.

The collective administration of copyrighted material carried out by ASCAP and BMI creates the potential for monopolistic behavior, and both organizations have been the subject of government and private antitrust lawsuits. The government lawsuits were settled when ASCAP and BMI agreed to certain changes in licensing procedures.

Bilateral monopoly

Another important type of transaction cost arises in a bilateral monopoly, i.e., a negotiation between two parties where neither party has a good alternative to dealing with the other party. For example, suppose A, a buyer who is dissatisfied with the products made for the mass market, hires firm B to make a product tailored to A's specifications. Then, once the product is made, B will know that if A does not find it satisfactory, there will be no good alternative buyers available, and A will know that there are no good alternative products available for his purchase. The lack of substitutes available to either party means that both demand and supply are inelastic, and that both buyer and seller have monopoly power – hence the term "bilateral monopoly."

A well-known historical example (although its accuracy has recently been questioned)[7] is the business relationship between General Motors Corporation and Fisher Body Company. Fisher Body Co. built chassis specifically designed for General Motors vehicles. To illustrate the problem, suppose these two corporations entered into a contract under which Fisher Body agrees to provide 1,000 chassis to GM for $1 million. Assume that if GM does not obtain these chassis from Fisher Body on time, it will cost $5 million to obtain them from an alternative source. On the other hand, if GM rejects the chassis that are tendered by Fisher Body, these chassis, being specifically designed for GM, would be worth no more than $100,000 to anyone else. Under these circumstances there is ample room for opportunistic behavior by either Fisher Body or GM. Once the chassis are built, GM may claim that they do not meet the contract specifications exactly (even if the deviation is trivial), and, knowing that any other firm would pay only $100,000 for the chassis, may offer Fisher Body only, say, $101,000. On the other hand, Fisher Body might claim that some language in the contract, or custom of the industry, supports supplemental payments by GM, on the grounds that GM asked for additional work beyond the original design specifications. Therefore, Fisher Body, knowing that it would cost GM $5 million to obtain chassis from an alternative source, might demand, say, $4,900,000. The parties must bargain over the difference between $100,000 and $5 million. Ultimately, this severe transaction cost problem was solved by a merger: after years of haggling, GM decided to acquire Fisher Body in 1926.

This historical episode illustrates a general principle: assets that are specialized, whether machinery, equipment, land or human capital, are more likely to be owned or directly employed by the firm that uses them than to be hired from outside. Generalized resources, which can be employed outside the firm with little or no loss of productivity, are more likely than specialized assets to be hired for use from third parties.

Let us return to the example of the city that desires to acquire land, to be used as a park for the city's residents. What are the transactions costs that might prevent the sale of this land? One very important potential obstacle is known as the holdout problem. In order for the sale to occur, the purchase price must be at least $8 million (since the landowners will not accept less than the value of the land to them), but cannot exceed $10 million (since the city will not pay more than the value of the land to its residents). We know that the value of each parcel to its owner is only $8,000. Nonetheless, many landowners, knowing that the value of the land to the city is $2 million more than the value to all the current owners, might demand a higher price than $8,000. If too many of them adopt this strategy and hold out for more than $10,000, the total asking price will exceed $10 million, and the deal won't take place.

In addition to the holdout problem, there may also be a problem on the buyers' side – the free-rider problem. The free-rider problem arises when a number of individuals share something of value, like property or an experience, and some of them avoid paying their share of the costs. This problem explains why many restaurants add a 15 percent tip to the bill for large groups. Some in the group are likely to leave less than the cost of the meal plus their share of a reasonable tip, hoping the difference will be made up by others (and knowing that it is often difficult to determine who paid less than his share).

To see how the free-rider problem arises in this case, suppose there is no holdout problem, and that the landowners are willing to sell for $8 million. We know that the value of the land as a park is $100 to each resident of the city. Suppose that, to raise money for the purchase, the city asks each resident to make a contribution equal to the amount that the land would be worth to the resident as a park. Under these circumstances some individuals may contribute less than $100, hoping that enough others will admit to a higher value so that the total contributions will exceed the $8 million required for the purchase. Some may even claim that the park would be of no value to them, hoping thereby to obtain a benefit of $100 for nothing. However, if too many city residents adopt this strategy, the total amount raised from them will be less than $8 million, and again the deal will fall through.

One study analyzed the amount of water consumed by households in Australia when a household had its own water meter, compared to the situation where there was a single water meter for a group of households, ranging in size from two to 222, with an average of thirty-one. When there was a group meter, each household was charged with an equal share of the total water bill. The study found that because of the free-rider problem, individual households consumed more water when they shared a meter with a group than if they had their own meter. The free-rider problem was more severe the larger the number of households sharing the meter. When there were two households in the group A and B, and A uses a great deal of water, B will be charged with one-half the amount used by A, and so has an incentive to exert social pressure on A not to over-consume. When, on the other hand there are 200 households, including households C and D, and C makes excessive use of water, D will be charged with only one-two hundredth of the amount used by C, and has much less incentive to police C's consumption.

How disputes are decided by law

An important article by Calabresi and Melamed (1972) examines how the legal system should resolve a dispute between two parties whose interests are in conflict. The law must decide two issues: (1) When the interests of two parties are in conflict, who should prevail? (2) Once we have decided which party should prevail, how should that party's interest be protected? What remedy should that party have under the legal system? Their article provides an example of two individuals who live next door to each other, Taney and Marshall. Taney likes to make noise, but Marshall prefers silence.

First we must decide who should get the entitlement: is Taney entitled to make noise, or is Marshall entitled to silence? Suppose we decide that Marshall gets the entitlement. Do we protect that entitlement by (1) a property right, (2) a rule of liability, (3) a rule of inalienability, or (4) through government intervention, with a tax, subsidy or some other form of direct regulation?

If Marshall has a property right to silence, he can go to court and obtain an injunction (a court order) prohibiting Taney from making noise. If Taney disobeyed the injunction, he would be in contempt of court and could be thrown in jail. Clearly, in this situation Taney cannot make noise without Marshall's consent. If he wants to make noise, he must buy the right to do so from Marshall, at a price that is acceptable to Marshall. This is the approach of property law.

Alternatively, Marshall's entitlement could be protected only by a rule of liability. In this case, Taney can make noise, but if he does, he must pay Marshall money damages that are determined by an external, objective standard of value. In effect Taney would have the right to take Marshall's entitlement upon payment of compensation.

Finally, the entitlement could be enforced by the government rather than by the party who is directly affected. The government could tax Taney to the extent he caused damage to others by making noise. It could also achieve this objective by a subsidy; instead of taxing Taney for making noise, it could pay him if he agrees not to do so. In this case also Taney would be penalized for making noise, since he would lose the amount of the subsidy. The government could also impose a quota, mandate or some other form of direct regulation.

As indicated above, the government can provide the same incentive to an individual in two different ways: (1) by imposing a tax on an activity, or (2) by providing a subsidy if the individual refrains from the activity. A city government may pay a citizen $100 for shoveling snow from his sidewalk, or charge him $100 if he has not done so; in either case the incentive to shovel, and the cost of not shoveling, is $100. Of course, the individual is $100 richer in one case, and $100 poorer in the other, but this is a secondary issue essentially unrelated to his incentives.[8]

This point may seem trite, but could actually be of practical use to someone who is, or will become, a lawyer. The author was recently asked to review a proposed contract between a township and a nonprofit organization, under which the township agreed, for a payment of $3 million, to construct facilities to provide water and sewer services to the organization. The author noticed that under the contract the township had no incentive to complete the project on schedule, on the proposed completion date of December 31, 2002. Accordingly, he suggested that the township incur a penalty of $500,000 if the project was not completed on schedule, and of $1 million if it were not completed one month later, on January 31, 2003. However, the township supervisor informed the author that this clause had no chance of being approved by the township board of supervisors. There would be a public hearing on the contract, and the citizens would never accept an agreement that could subject the township to penalties.

After some reflection, the author suggested an alternative clause, providing that the township would receive $2 million if the project was completed after January 31, 2003, but in addition, would get a bonus payment of $500,000 if it were completed before that date, and an additional bonus of $500,000 if it were completed by December 31, 2002. The supervisor said that this alternative contract was much better, and would easily be approved at the board meeting!

The Coase Theorem

How then do we decide whether the entitlement should be protected by a property right, a rule of liability, or by direct government intervention? In making this decision, we should consider what has come to be known as the Coase Theorem (Coase 1960). According to the Coase Theorem, if there are no transaction costs and property rights are well defined, the parties will agree on a Pareto-optimal, efficient outcome. They will arrive at an efficient outcome regardless of the way property rights are assigned. The implication is that if transaction costs are zero or relatively small, entitlements should be protected by property rights. Regardless of who has the property right – the entitlement – the parties will arrive at an efficient outcome.

The Coase Theorem can be understood as a response to classical welfare economics, the most prominent representative of which was A. C. Pigou (1877–1959). This area of economics considered problems involving externalities. An externality arises when the actions of one economic agent affect the environment of another in some way other than a change in prices. Important examples of externalities are pollution and congestion.

Consider, for example, the conflicting interests of a cattle rancher and a farmer who have adjacent properties. The larger the herd of cattle raised by the rancher, the more the farmer's crops will be trampled by cattle who wander away from the ranch (assume there is no fence

Figure 4.1 Conflict between the cattle rancher and the farmer.

because both properties are very large, and the costs of building and maintaining a fence would exceed the benefits). This situation is illustrated in Figure 4.1. MC_p represents the private marginal cost of raising cattle to the rancher, and P* represents the market price of beef. If the cattle rancher disregards the damage caused by his cattle, he will raise Q_p cattle, since at this level of output he is maximizing profits; at Q_p his price = marginal revenue = marginal cost.[9] However, this outcome is not efficient, since it ignores an externality – the damage to the farmer's crops.

To achieve efficiency, we must maximize total social benefit minus total social cost. We can do this by setting the size of the herd at the level where the marginal social benefit of cattle equals its marginal social cost. Note that the marginal social benefit equals the market price of beef, since this price – the height of the market demand curve at equilibrium – represents the value of an additional steer to society. MC_s represents the marginal social cost of cattle, which increases with the number of cattle. The vertical distance between MC_p and MC_s equals the damage to the farm, a cost not borne by the rancher. The socially optimal level of cattle production is Q_s, where the marginal social benefit equals marginal social cost.

The solution of the classical economists was to impose on the cattle rancher a "Pigovian tax" of the amount BD. The idea was that this tax would make the cattle rancher bear the full cost of his actions; the social marginal cost curve MC_s becomes his private marginal cost, and he will choose the socially optimal level of output Q_s. The externality has been internalized.

The critique of Coase was that, if there are no transaction costs and property rights are well defined, a Pigovian tax is not necessary, and indeed will drive the parties away from the optimum. Note that at any point between Q_s and Q_p, the vertical distance between MC_p and MC_s – the marginal loss sustained by the farmer – exceeds the distance between P* and MC_p – the marginal gain to the cattle rancher. This means that the farmer can offer the rancher a "bribe" to reduce the size of his herd, of some amount exceeding the rancher's marginal gain. Consider Table 4.1.

Table 4.1 Relation between size of herd, profit of cattle rancher, and damage to crops

No. of steers	0	100	200	300	400	500	600
Profit of rancher (2)	0	200	500	600	900	1,000	800
Damage to farmer's crops (3)	0	100	400	500	600	800	1,000
(2) − (3)	0	100	100	100	300	200	−200

The socially optimal number of steer is the number that maximizes total social benefit minus total social cost, that is, the profit to the cattle rancher minus the damage to the farmer. This will occur when the number of steer equals 400, and the net social benefit equals $300. According to the Coase Theorem, if there are no transactions costs, the parties will arrive at this outcome regardless of who has the entitlement – whether the rancher has the right to allow his cattle to roam, or the farmer has the right to prevent cattle from trespassing.

Suppose first that the cattle rancher had the entitlement, and was prepared to raise 500 steers, to maximize his profit. The farmer could then offer him a bribe of, say, $101, to reduce his herd to 400 steers. This transaction will make the farmer better off, since his damages will be reduced by $200. Moreover, the rancher will accept this offer, since he loses only $100 of profit by doing so. Now suppose the farmer has the property right, and takes the position that the size of the herd should be zero. In this case the rancher could offer him a bribe of, say, $601 to induce him to accept a herd of 400. The rancher would not be able to bribe him to increase the herd size from 400 to 500, since that would increase the farmer's damages by $200, but would increase the rancher's profit by only $100.

Finally, note that if there are substantial costs of negotiation, it does make a difference who has the entitlement. If the rancher has the property right, he will have a herd of 500 cattle for a net social gain of $200. If the farmer has the entitlement, there will be no cattle, and no gain to society. Here again a possible solution is to internalize the externality by a merger. The rancher could acquire the adjacent farm land, and would then take into account the crop damage in determining the size of his herd.

An interesting example of a merger involved the Walt Disney company. The original Disneyland amusement park, in Anaheim, California, was an exceedingly popular tourist attraction. The park was eventually surrounded by many small businesses selling food, souvenirs, gift items, and the like, and the resulting crowding and traffic congestion reduced the quality of the experience of a Disneyland visitor. When the Disney company opened a second amusement park in Florida, it purchased almost an entire county to avoid any problem of crowding. The externality of crowding businesses was internalized by a merger.

The reserve clause: an application of the Coase Theorem

Although transaction costs are clearly important in many cases, it would be a mistake to view the Coase Theorem as a pure abstraction that never applies to the real world. Consider, for example, the reserve clause that was formerly a part of the contract between every player in major league baseball and the club that employed him. Under the reserve clause, a major league baseball club owned the rights to the services of each player it had under contract.[10] Before the reserve clause was abolished, one of the arguments made by the club owners for it was that without the reserve clause, the wealthy clubs would acquire the most talented players, leading to a competitive imbalance that would cause irreparable damage to the sport. However, the Coase Theorem shows that this analysis is incorrect – that the degree of competitive imbalance should not be affected by the abolition of the reserve clause.

If there are no, or minimal, transactions costs, we know from the Coase Theorem that the assignment of players to teams will be efficient, i.e., done in a way that maximizes total social value. The assumption that transactions costs are minimal seems quite reasonable here, since the general manager of one team can simply pick up the telephone to propose a deal to another team, and both parties have extensive information about the abilities of players. Suppose then the reserve clause is in effect, and a player has a contract with club A to play for $30,000. Suppose further that the value of this player's services is $60,000 to club A, but would be $65,000 to club B. Then both clubs would benefit from a sale of the player to club B for some amount between $30,000 and $35,000. If, for example, the player were sold for $33,000, club A would gain $3,000 ($33,000 – $30,000, the value to it of rights to the player), while club B would gain $2,000 ($35,000, the value to it of rights to the player, –$33,000). Now suppose the reserve clause is no longer in effect, and the market for baseball players is competitive. In this case club A would be willing to offer the player at most $60,000, while club B would be willing to offer as much as $65,000. Again the player will end up with club B.

On the other hand, suppose the player has a strong preference for one club over the other. Wouldn't it then make a difference whether or not the reserve clause was in effect, in determining how players are assigned to teams? In fact, as we will see, it would make no difference whatsoever. Suppose the value of a player is $70,000 to club B, but only $60,000 to club A, which currently has him under contract for that amount. Let us also assume that it is worth $15,000 to the player to be with club A rather than club B, because club A is in a city with better weather, better restaurants, and more night life than the city of club B. If there is no reserve clause, this player will not leave club A because, since his salary is $60,000, the value to him of being with club A is $75,000, while the most club B would offer him is $70,000. Finally, suppose the reserve clause is in effect, and the player is under contract with club A for $30,000. Wouldn't the player then be sold by club A to club B? Since by assumption there are no transactions costs, the answer is no. Club B would be willing to offer at most $40,000 for the rights to this player. While the value of the player's contract to club A is only $30,000, the player would offer a side payment of as much as $15,000 to induce club A not to trade him (for example, the player might accept a reduction in salary of this amount). Thus, even if there were a reserve clause the player would remain with club A. The allocation of players to teams will be exactly the same, whether or not the reserve clause is in effect.

We should now return to the question posed above, i.e., whether an entitlement should be protected by a property right, a rule of liability, or by direct government intervention. In the case considered above, involving a city's acquisition of land that would be worth $10 million as a park for its residents, there are substantial transaction costs – problems of holdouts and free-riders. In cases like this, the law often employs a rule of liability, rather than a property right. To get around the holdout problem, a court could determine the value of the land to its current owners, and then award them that amount as compensation. To overcome the free-rider problem, the city could decide the value of the land as a park to each resident, and then assess a tax on residents based on that value. Cities often make assessments on their residents for the cost of municipal improvements, like a new sidewalk, water or sewer system.

It turns out that under the law, the city would probably be able to take the land from its current owners, by exercising a governmental power known as eminent domain. This power is described in the next section.

Eminent domain

The government has a right to take private property for public use, upon payment of its market value.[11] This is the government's power of eminent domain, or condemnation. Thus, although private property is generally protected by a property right, it is protected from the government only by a rule of liability. An economic justification that has been offered for eminent domain is that it is necessary to overcome the holdout problem, which can be viewed as a problem of monopoly, if there are no good substitutes available for the property sought by the government. For example, there may not be good substitutes for land that is directly in the path of an expressway that is being extended.

As previously noted, the owner is entitled to compensation for the property's fair market value. The rationale is that under these conditions, there will be a taking only when it would be efficient, i.e., when the property's value to the government exceeds its value to its owner. There is a danger that the government will make excessive use of a resource if it is not required to pay its full value. In this connection, it should be noted that the government is not required to compensate individuals for time spent in military service, jury duty, filling out tax returns, and the like. Under these circumstances it is more likely that college graduates who are drafted by the army will be assigned to wash dishes, or be otherwise underemployed.

It has been debated whether the power of eminent domain is necessary and if so, how broad its scope should be. Critics point out that private developers, who lack the power of eminent domain, have managed to circumvent the holdout problem by concealing the plans for the properties being acquired and by using contingent contracts. For example, a developer who intends to acquire a large number of individual parcels of land for a shopping center will keep his plans a secret, and have others buy the properties for him, one at a time. In addition, the properties will often be purchased with options, giving the developer the right to rescind in the event that all the properties required for the project cannot be acquired for less than a specified amount. Supporters of eminent domain, however, argue that these techniques for avoiding holdouts may not be suitable for the government; it is usually not feasible (or desirable) for the government to keep plans for major public projects secret. Moreover, in many cases private developers have indirectly taken advantage of the power of eminent domain, by having the government condemn properties so that they can acquire them for development projects.[12]

It is noteworthy that a property owner is entitled to compensation only if there has been a "taking." Many regulatory measures that reduce the value of property do not rise to the level of a taking. Clearly it would be an administrative nightmare to try to compensate everyone whose property values are reduced by regulation, and to tax everyone who benefits from regulation. However, if a regulation reduces the value of property substantially, the owner may bring a lawsuit to have the court declare that there has been a taking, even though the government has not taken possession of the property; this is known as an action for "inverse condemnation." In one case, for example, a court held that allowing airplanes to fly in and out of a county airport at low altitudes substantially reduced the value of adjacent private property, and amounted to a "taking" of the property by the county.[13]

Critics of eminent domain point out that some courts have adopted a very broad definition of public use, the limits of which are unclear. At first the courts typically required that a proposed project be used by a substantial segment of the general public. The concept of public use was subsequently extended to include projects such as municipal civic centers and airport terminals. In one case the Supreme Court held that demolishing slums in order to beautify the urban landscape was a public use.[14] In another controversial case the city of Detroit sought to condemn 465 acres of privately owned land, in order to sell it to General Motors Corporation, which planned to construct an automobile assembly plant on the site.[15] The city argued that there was a public use, since the new plant would create jobs and bring about an economic revitalization of the area. This argument was accepted by the Michigan Supreme Court.[16] Other courts have held that they must defer to the judgment of the legislature in deciding whether a taking serves a public purpose.

As to how eminent domain works in practice, one study[17] found that high-valued properties receive awards exceeding their fair market value, while low-valued properties receive less. The reason is that there are economies of scale in litigation, which have a greater effect on the property owner than on the government, since the government's investment in legal services is prescribed by relatively inflexible regulations. A highly experienced lawyer does not have to invest much more time in a case involving a parcel worth $10 million than he would have to in one involving a parcel worth $100,000. It may be worth while for the claimant to hire such a lawyer only for the $10 million parcel.

Self-assessment

One way to protect property owners from receiving inadequate compensation is to have each owner report the value of his own property. Arnold Harberger (1965) proposed that, to determine property tax, each property owner could declare the value of his property. These declared values would become part of the public record. An owner would then be required to sell his property to any bidder who offered, say, 20 percent more than the declared value. An owner whose property was purchased in this way could hardly complain, since he would be receiving 20 percent more than the amount he had reported as being the value of the property to him.

Harberger anticipated, however, that some people, especially lawyers, would be aghast at the possibility that owners could be "forced" to sell their own property. He therefore suggested an alternative system: a property owner would not be required to declare the value of his property; he could instead accept the assessment made by the tax assessor. If, however, he believed the tax assessor's assessment was too high, he would have the option to declare the property's value himself. However, if he did so, anyone would have a right to purchase his property for an amount 20 percent above the declared value.

The values of properties of course change over time. To avoid the necessity of having owners modify their valuation frequently, their valuation could be adjusted automatically by an appropriate price index.

Saul Levmore (1982) noted that if this kind of self-assessment system were adopted, it would be necessary to prevent property owners from allowing the outside of their residences to deteriorate, in order to discourage prospective buyers. He suggested that the system could require owners to allow periodic property inspections by buyers. The owner could charge a fee for each inspection, as compensation for the inconvenience. Levmore noted that in some European cities, where tax assessments were based on exterior features such as the number of windows, some builders have constructed residences with virtually no windows.

How the entitlement should be protected

When transaction costs are not low, or property rights are not well defined, we may need rules of liability, like eminent domain, to carry out efficient exchanges, like the transfer of land to the city. For example, we use rules of liability for accidents, since it is not feasible for potential accident victims to negotiate with all their potential injurers; putting it differently, the transactions costs of such negotiations are prohibitively high.

It is, however, important to note that rules of liability have their own weaknesses. Suppose, for example, that the value of a particular parcel of land to the city is $10,000, and that recent sale prices of similar parcels have been around $8,000, but that this parcel has special significance to its owner, who values it at $15,000. Under these circumstances a court might easily decide that this parcel should be transferred to the city for compensation of $10,000; however, this transfer would be inefficient. We cannot be sure that the land is going to one who values it more highly than the owner unless both the owner and the purchaser have agreed on the purchase price. Thus a major drawback with rules of liability, as opposed to property rights, is that because of uncertainty about the value of resources to their owners, those resources may not be assigned to their use of highest value. Another weakness is the administrative costs involved in determining the amount of damages.

Finally, as we shall see, another problem with rules of liability is the potential for moral hazard. Moral hazard is the inefficiency that arises when someone does not bear the full cost of his actions. When someone enjoys the full benefit of an action but bears none or only part of the costs, she may pursue that action beyond the point of efficiency, i.e., beyond the point where its net social benefits are maximized.

We want to examine the potential for moral hazard arising from rules of liability. Consider, for example, a railroad whose cars occasionally throw a shower of sparks on the land of a farmer that is adjacent to the tracks. If the railroad is liable for all damage caused by fire, the farmer may not take the trouble to clear away brush that is near the tracks, and might even plant flammable crops there. The most valuable use of his land may be as a means of obtaining compensation from the railroad for fire damage. If, on the other hand, the railroad is not liable for such damage, it may not bother to take measures that reduce the risk of sparks. One possible solution is a merger; the railroad may buy a strip of land adjacent to the tracks. Under these circumstances it has the appropriate incentive to minimize the total cost of taking precautions to reduce sparks and clear the adjacent land.

One of Coase's profound insights was that the optimal solution to an externality problem is one of three alternatives: (1) there may be an "interior solution" involving activity on the part of both parties; (2) the injurer should shut down its operations; or (3) the victim should shut down its operations. Consider, for example, how we should regulate the activities of pet tigers. We might adopt an interior solution – a regulation that anyone with a pet tiger must keep it on a strong leash and take it outside for a walk only between 3:00 A.M. and 5:00 A.M.; or perhaps the optimal solution is not to allow anyone to have a pet tiger.

Consider a conflict between a factory and a laundry whose business is damaged by pollution from the factory. In Figure 4.2, curve Fq_f shows how the marginal profits of the factory vary with output. It is assumed that marginal profits decline with output and equal 0 at q_f. Let us assume the profits of the laundry are a fixed amount π_l but are reduced to the extent of the total pollution damage. 0C represents marginal damages to the laundry, which increase with the factory's output. Note that at q_s the laundry will shut down, since the total damages caused by pollution (the area under the marginal damages curve 0C out to q_s) will exactly equal the laundry's fixed profit π_l and will therefore eliminate all of those profits. Thus if the factory had no output, and therefore caused no pollution damage to the laundry, the laundry would have a profit equal to area $0Cq_s = \pi_l$.

Assuming that both the factory and laundry should stay in business, the efficient outcome will maximize their combined profits, or equivalently, the total profits of the factory minus the total damages to the laundry. Now at any output below q^*, each additional unit of output

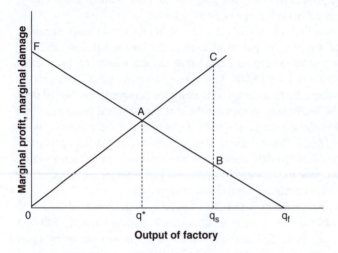

Figure 4.2 Conflict between a factory and a laundry.

increases the profits of the factory more than it reduces the profits of the laundry – the factory's marginal profit is greater than the marginal loss of profits by the laundry. At any output above q*, each unit of output reduces the profits of the laundry more than it increases the profits of the factory. Therefore the optimum is at q*. At this point the total profit of both businesses equals 0FAq*, the profits of the factory, plus ACq_sq^*, the profits of the laundry.

As we have already noted, however, it might not be optimal for both firms to stay in business. Another possibility is that the factory should shut down. In this case the social gain would be area $0Cq_s = \pi_l$, the total fixed profits of the laundry. Finally, there is the possibility that the laundry should disappear. In this case the social gain would be Fq_f0, the total profit of the factory at output q_f. To determine the social optimum, we must compare these three alternatives, and choose the one that yields the largest social gain.

Suppose the optimum is q*. If the laundry has the entitlement, it might have a property right or a claim under tort law. If it has a property right, it could obtain an injunction prohibiting the factory from polluting. If its claim lies in tort law, it would not be able to obtain an injunction, but would be entitled to damages from the factory to the extent its profits are reduced by pollution.

What if the factory has the right to pollute? According to the Coase Theorem, if there are no costs of negotiation and property rights are well defined, the parties will agree on an output of q*; the laundry will be able to bribe the factory to reduce its output to this level. Now, however, there is an additional problem: the possibility of subsequent entry by another factory. Note that at q* the factory has a positive marginal profit; under these circumstances other factories will want to enter the area. This is really a problem of incomplete property rights,[18] since the factory cannot deliver clean air. Accordingly, there is a problem if the polluter has the entitlement; the requirements of the Coase Theorem are not satisfied, since property rights are incomplete. Note that there is no problem if the laundry has the entitlement, since any new factory that entered the area would be liable for damages, or subject to an injunction.

Finally, the government could impose a Pigovian tax on the factory equal to Aq*. Alternatively, it could set a quota on the factory's output equal to 0q*. There is, however, a problem with government intervention; the government may not have good information about the marginal profit and marginal damages functions which determine the location of q*. The parties have this information, but the government will not be able to get it from them. In response to an inquiry by the government, the laundry will exaggerate the pollution damage, while the factory will contend there is no damage.

One ingenious solution that has been employed in certain markets is to create marketable pollution certificates. This solves the problem of incomplete property rights and private or "asymmetric" information at a single stroke. The government could print up these certificates, give them to the laundry, and allow it to sell as many certificates as it wants to the factory. Presumably the laundry would sell just enough certificates so that the factory would operate at q*. This way the parties will arrive at the efficient outcome, even if the government has no knowledge about the extent of damages caused by pollution.

One case[19] provides an interesting example of how the victim of an externality can be the aggressor. It involved a cattle feedlot adjacent to a large residential community in Arizona, called Sun City. Sun City brought an action seeking an injunction against the feedlot on the ground that the flies and the odor of manure resulting from its cattle feeding operation were a nuisance that reduced the quality of life for its residents, and posed health risks to them. The feedlot had been established there first, when the area was distinctly rural, and the first homes of Sun City were built at a distance from the feedlot, and so were unaffected by it. Later, however, the developer built houses closer to the feedlot.

The feedlot relied on a rule of property law "coming to the nuisance," holding that a residential landowner who moves next to industrial or agricultural activities should not be granted an injunction on the ground that those activities are a nuisance. A partial explanation of this doctrine is that the externality arises only when the alleged victim moves next to the nuisance. In this case, there was no nuisance before Sun City chose to locate next to the feedlot. Moreover, it is likely that the developer paid less for the land close to the feedlot because of the unpleasant conditions of that location. That is, the buyer had already been compensated for the externality through a reduction of the purchase price. (This assumes that the purchase price did not reflect the possibility that the buyer could force the feedlot to move.)

The court fashioned an ingenious remedy by issuing the injunction against the feedlot, on the condition that Sun City pay the feedlot the costs of shutting down or moving to another location. The gain to Sun City's residents from removal of the feedlot was probably greater than either the cost of moving the feedlot or the profits of the feedlot lost by having it disappear.

The parties were unable to negotiate a solution via the Coase Theorem because of transaction costs. First, property rights were not well defined because there was uncertainty about the law. Second, this was a case of bilateral monopoly: Sun City had no one to deal with other than the feedlot, and vice versa, and there was probably a large differential between the gain to Sun City resulting from the feedlot's disappearance and the cost of moving the feedlot.

As the preceding case shows, the courts will sometimes decide the issue of an injunction in favor of one party but award damages to the other side. Another case[20] involved an action for an injunction filed against a cement company by neighboring land owners, who alleged injury from vibrations and dust emanating from a cement plant. An injunction would have required the plant to shut down. The court held that it would not grant an injunction, provided the cement company paid money damages to the plaintiffs to compensate them for the nuisance. If the cement company did so, it would acquire a "servitude on the land" of the plaintiff landowners, i.e., a permanent property right to carry on its operations to the extent they affected the plaintiffs' lands.

The trial court found that the cost of the cement plant was over $45 million, and the total damage to all plaintiffs was $185,000. This suggests that the court was correct to choose a remedy that assigned the property right to operate to the cement plant. The Coase Theorem did not apply here, because of the transaction cost of bilateral monopoly. There was an enormous difference between the maximum amount the cement plant would be willing to pay to keep the plant in operation and the minimum amount the plaintiffs would be willing to accept for this outcome, $185,000. There is great potential for holdouts and holdups implicit in this differential.

In the two cases outlined above it seems the court is in effect applying a rule of "private condemnation" for the "taking" involved in that decision – the feedlot in the Sun City case, and the neighbors of the cement company in the second case.

Sometimes the social cost of pollution can be minimized by some means other than adjusting the level of output of the polluter. In this case, it might be optimal either (1) for the polluter to take measures to reduce pollution at its source, or, alternatively, (2) for the victims to take protective measures to reduce the damage to them. Suppose, for example, airplanes flying over a residential area cause noise pollution damage of $1,000 to each of 1,000 homes. Assume these damages could be avoided if either the airlines installed soundproofing equipment on their airplanes, for a total cost of $400,000, or if each homeowner soundproofed her own house, at a cost of $600 each. Suppose the cost to each homeowner of negotiating with the airlines, in terms of time, legal fees, etc., is $800.

Assume first that the airlines are liable for any noise damage. Then clearly the airlines would install the soundproofing equipment, since they would rather incur a cost of $400,000 than be liable for damages of $1 million. Now suppose the airlines were not liable for noise pollution. If there were no transaction costs, the homeowners would join together and arrange to buy the soundproofing equipment and pay to have it installed on the aircraft. If, however, the cost of negotiating were $800 for each homeowner, each homeowner would instead soundproof her own house, for a total social cost of $600,000. This outcome would of course be inefficient. Since the requirements of the Coase Theorem are not satisfied, it is important to place liability on the party who can avoid damages at least cost – in this case the airlines.

How to determine ownership of property

Finally, let us consider another type of conflict, namely a dispute between two or more persons, each of whom claims to be the exclusive owner of some valuable property. How does the law decide who owns the property? We will examine different legal rules, and two different systems of determining the ownership of valuable assets: a system of title registration, and a recording system.

Some time in the middle of the 1960s, a mail clerk at the Guggenheim Museum in New York stole a painting by Marc Chagall entitled "The Cattle Dealer." The museum did not notify law enforcement agencies, museums, galleries, or art organizations of the theft. In 1967 Jules and Rachel Lubell bought the painting from a reputable New York gallery, and put it on display in their home, where it remained for over twenty years. In 1985 the Guggenheim learned of the painting's location and demanded its return. When the Lubells refused, the museum filed a lawsuit.

This case raises the question of who should have priority, the original owner of an asset or someone who bought it in good faith, i.e. without reason to believe it had been stolen. One way to approach this issue is to inquire who could have avoided this conflict, or "accident," at lower cost, the owner or the subsequent purchaser? It could be argued that both of the parties in the case described above bore some responsibility. On the one hand, the museum did not report the theft; on the other hand, the buyers could have easily discovered that the Guggenheim owned the painting by consulting a catalogue of Chagall's work.[21] On appeal, the New York Court of Appeals did not make a decision clearly assigning ownership to either side; instead, the Court sent the case back to the trial court to consider the relative blameworthiness of the parties. (The case was eventually settled.)

The bona fide purchaser rule

One approach that has been taken is to treat the subsequent purchaser as the owner if, at the time of the purchase, he had no reason to suspect the property was stolen; this is known as the bona fide purchaser rule. The alternative approach is the position that the subsequent purchaser could not have acquired title to the property, since the original owner did not sell it; this is known as the original ownership rule.

The bona fide purchaser rule has been criticized on the ground that it encourages theft. Under this rule, an owner is unlikely to be able to recover his property unless he catches the thief in the act of stealing it. Thieves can be confident that there will be a market for articles they steal, since purchasers will be able to acquire title to the property unless they are confronted by evidence that theft was likely. Under this rule purchasers have no incentive to investigate whether the property was stolen; while they would bear the full cost of such an investigation, they would derive no benefit from it. Under the original ownership rule, however, a purchaser has an incentive to determine whether the property was stolen, since in that event they would not acquire title to the property. Thus there will be little demand for property for which the seller cannot provide proof of ownership, and the thief who intends to resell property will have little incentive to steal it.

Registration systems

One way to eliminate, or at least substantially reduce, uncertainty about ownership is to establish a registration system. Under a registration system there is a list that identifies the owners of items of property. Any questions about ownership are resolved easily and instantly by learning who is listed as the owner in the registry. When the property is sold, the sale is reported to the registry and the purchaser is then listed as the new owner. Since ownership is conclusively determined by a registration system, the system promotes the sale of property and deters theft. Sales by the registered owner are facilitated, since a purchaser knows the owner can provide a good title. Thefts are deterred, since the thief will be unable to offer a good title to a prospective purchaser; moreover, the thief runs the risk of being apprehended if the police find him in possession of property registered to another. There are other benefits of a registry: for example, it enables the owner to insure his property, or use it as collateral for a loan.[22]

The benefits of a registry – facilitating the sale of property, deterring theft, and the like – are greater for property that is valuable and durable. On the other hand, the costs of a registry, which are essentially bookkeeping expenses, do not increase much with the value of property. Accordingly we find that, in the real world, registries have been established primarily for valuable durable goods: land, motor vehicles, aircraft, boats of a certain size, and heavy construction equipment. Valuable intangible assets such as patents, copyrights, trademarks, and security interests in property, are also registered.

There may be significant startup costs involved in creating a comprehensive registry of, say, land or valuable art objects, since one must compile a list of all the objects, and determine the ownership (and other legal interests) for each of them. If the deterrence of theft is the principal benefit of a registry, and it is costly to include all existing objects, an alternative is to establish a "theft registry": a registry only for objects that have been stolen, the thefts being reported by their owners. For example, there is an international computerized registry for stolen art objects. Bibas (1993) argues that if a work of art is stolen, the owner should prevail over subsequent purchasers if he promptly notifies the police and the art theft database. In his view, an owner who fails to take these measures should lose to a bona fide purchaser, but not to one with reason to believe the object was stolen.

In most of the United States interests in land are disclosed by a recording system, rather than a registration system. A recording system, unlike a registration system, does not identify anyone as the current owner of property; it merely shows all the transfers of property that have been reported. However, title registration is used for land in a few areas of the United States, in many countries in Europe, and by those of the British Commonwealth. The system of title registration that is used in a few U.S. states, and extensively in British Commonwealth countries, is the Torrens title system. This system was invented by Sir Robert Richard Torrens in the late 1850s, and was first implemented in Australia in 1858. The Torrens system creates an official certificate of ownership that includes all encumbrances (liens, mortgages, judgments, etc.) on the parcel. No interest in land, such as a mortgage, has any legal validity until it is filed with the registrar and listed on the face of the certificate of ownership. As with other systems of title registration, the person named as the owner in the certificate is deemed to be the owner because the law, and the government, declares him to be such. An owner whose land is registered cannot lose his property to someone whose claim is based on a deed obtained before registration, i.e., a registered owner cannot lose his land because of a break in the chain of his title. However, his protection is not absolute: he could lose his property because of a registration mistake in the future.

Recording systems

In contrast to a system of title registration, a recording system for land does not designate anyone as the owner. Consequently a purchaser must make sure that the seller has good title, i.e., that there is no break in the chain of conveyances that begins with the original grantee and ends with the seller. Purchasers normally buy insurance (called title insurance) to insure this risk. That way, if they purchase the property and the seller's title proves to be invalid, they will lose the property but be compensated by the insurance company.

If there is a break in the chain of title that has gone unnoticed for many years, the courts sometimes award full ownership to someone whose title is defective, under the doctrine of adverse possession. Under this doctrine, a person who has been openly in possession of land for a sufficiently long period thereby acquires title to the property, even if his legal claim to the property is otherwise flawed.

Adverse possession

Under the doctrine of adverse possession, someone who occupies another person's land can acquire title to the land without either compensating the owner or obtaining his consent. In order to do so, a party must possess the true owner's land for a period of time specified by statute – which is often seven years. The requirements for adverse possession are that the possessor must be using the property openly rather than surreptitiously, by himself, without the owner's permission, and must do so continuously for the full statutory period. (The corresponding legal jargon is that possession must be "actual, open, notorious, exclusive, hostile, adverse, and continuous" for the required period.) At the end of the period the adverse possessor becomes the new owner.

How can this legal rule possibly be justified? Some say it cannot be: adverse possession has been called a means of obtaining title by theft.

1   The best argument for the rule is to consider what would happen without it. Under a recording system, which is predominant in the United States, anyone who wishes to buy land will want to make sure the seller has a good title. This requires an investigation to ensure that there are no missing links in the chain of title – the chronological sequence of transfers by successive owners ending with the transfer of the property to the seller. If there were no rule of adverse possession, a seller would not have good title if there were a break in his chain of title at any time in the distant past. The older the records of prior land transfers, the less reliable they are, so it would be very difficult (costly) to verify that the chain of title was unbroken. This would create uncertainty about property rights in land. Under the doctrine of adverse possession, it is necessary only to verify that the seller and his predecessors in the chain of title have lived openly and continuously on the land for the period of the statute of limitations. Thus (so goes the argument) adverse possession reduces the risks associated with transfers of title. Indeed in many jurisdictions this purpose is made clear by a legal requirement that adverse possession must be "under color of title," i.e., the person occupying the land must be relying on a document that purports to give him title.

2   Another argument is that without the rule, an owner of property would have no incentive to promptly correct others who encroach on his property by mistake. If A was beginning construction of a high-rise building, and did not notice that the building occupied a corner of B's land, B could wait until construction was completed and then demand that A remove the encroachment, in order to extract a large payment from A. B would have no incentive to interrupt the construction at the outset. Moreover, the requirements that adverse possession be open, exclusive and continuous are designed to give the true owner notice of the situation, and ample opportunity to recover his property prior to investments by the encroaching party.

Argument (1) had more force in the past, when records of land ownership were much less reliable. Boundary mistakes are less likely today with modern surveying equipment, global positioning systems, and computerized records. Moreover, this argument would not apply if there were a registration system for land titles, since the person listed as the registered owner is conclusively deemed to have good title.

Argument (2) overlooks the fact that mistakes are more likely with adverse possession because of moral hazard: people have less of an incentive to avoid mistakes – indeed, one can benefit by mistakenly (or deliberately) occupying someone else's property (this problem is, however, mitigated if the encroaching party knows that the owner is likely to detect his encroachment and demand withdrawal, so that the cost of the mistake is borne by the encroacher). Also, adverse possession has its own costs; it compels owners to monitor their property continuously, to ensure that no one else is occupying it or encroaching on its boundaries. These costs are a pure waste of resources. Under certain conditions they can be large, e.g., if the statutory period of limitations is short, or there are many absentee landowners, or owners are induced to take extra precautions because the property that they could lose is very valuable.

Should we have a rule of adverse possession? The case for adverse possession is strongest when we have a recording system for land. The alternative is a system of title registration. Mistakes can be made under either system.

The American recording system: race, notice, and notice-race statutes

Even if the seller's chain of title is unbroken, problems can arise. A conflict typically arises when the seller, A, sells the property to B, and then subsequently sells the same property to C. In this situation, one must consult the state's recording statute to learn whether the property goes to B or C. There are three different types of recording statutes in the United States: statutes are classified into the categories of "notice," "race," or "notice-race" statutes. Under a "notice" statute, an unrecorded deed is invalid against a subsequent purchaser without notice of the prior conveyance. That is, if the subsequent purchaser made his purchase in good faith before the earlier purchaser's deed was recorded, the subsequent purchaser will prevail. This is consistent with the idea that the problem could have been avoided at lower cost by the original purchaser. If the original purchaser had immediately recorded his deed, the second person could have seen it and would not have made his purchase.

Under a "race" or "pure race" statute, the first purchaser who records his interest is protected; a subsequent purchaser prevails if he is the first to record, *even if he was aware of the previous conveyance at the time of his purchase*. Finally, there is the "notice-race" statute. Under this type of statute, a subsequent purchaser is protected only if he both (1) purchased without knowledge of the previous conveyance and (2) recorded his interest before the earlier purchaser.

Most of the earliest recording statutes were the pure race type; today most are the notice type. The race statute has the appeal of administrative simplicity, since all one must do to determine title is learn who recorded first. However, it also tends to encourage fraud, since it can award title to a purchaser who did not act in good faith, i.e. who knew of a previous conveyance. The notice-type statute provides maximum protection to the bona fide purchaser, and also provides an incentive to any purchaser to record his interest promptly (to cut off the interest of a subsequent purchaser). However it allows for some uncertainty, since there may be a factual issue (1) whether a subsequent purchaser bought the property with or without notice, and (2) whether the subsequent purchase, even if made in good faith, occurred before or after the interest of the first purchaser was recorded. Under the notice-race statute, the only source of uncertainty is whether the subsequent purchase was bona fide, i.e., whether the subsequent purchaser knew of the prior conveyance at the time of his purchase.

Intellectual property

The basic idea underlying patents, copyrights, trademarks, and other forms of intellectual property is to provide incentives for creative activity, for the benefit of society. The U.S.

Constitution provides that "The Congress shall have power ... to promote the progress of science and useful arts, by securing for limited times to authors and inventors the exclusive right to their respective writings and discoveries ..."[23] The first statute to recognize a copyright,[24] enacted by the British parliament in 1710, gave authors a property interest in their literary work, "to encourage ... learned men to compose and write useful books."

Assets that are intellectual property are, for the most part, public goods, in the sense that consumption of them by one person does not in any way preclude the consumption of them by another. This is true, for example, for an idea expressed in an invention, music, or a published article. However, creating the various forms of intellectual property often requires large expenditures of time and resources. Once the asset is created, these costs may be considered fixed, since they do not increase no matter how much or how little the asset is used. Then, making the asset available to users often requires little or nothing in costs. It may cost millions to produce a motion picture, but once made it can now be digitally transferred to customers at essentially zero cost. It may take months, and thousands of dollars to write, arrange and record a song, but once recorded it can be downloaded to someone's personal computer at virtually no cost.

To give people an incentive to create intellectual property, we must ensure that they can be compensated for these fixed costs. We might try to do so by offering a reward, or subsidizing the research and development process (these alternatives are considered below). If we do not do that, the author or inventor must be able to charge his customers a price for use of the asset above the zero marginal cost of distributing it. However, if he sets a price above marginal cost, he invites the entry of competing firms, who will have the same low marginal costs of providing the asset to consumers but do not have to incur the fixed costs incurred by the inventor. Their competition will drive the price down to marginal cost, and the inventor will have a loss. As consequence, the invention will not be created in the first place. The solution of intellectual property law is to grant the inventor a monopoly, which allows him to charge a price above marginal cost and exclude competitors.

Patents

A patent confers an exclusive right to use and sell an invention for a period of twenty years from the date of application for the patent. One must apply for a patent to a specialized government office (in the United States, the U.S. Patent and Trademark Office) that reviews the application to determine whether the requirements of a patent have been met. A patent is awarded to the first person who applies for it, to cover a particular invention. To qualify for a patent, an invention must be useful, novel, and an advance over prior art that is not obvious to persons skilled in the activity. In most countries the patent is awarded to the person who files the first patent application; however in the United States the patent goes to the first one to discover the invention, who may not have been the first to file. The first-to-file standard is much easier (less costly) to administer. In support of the first-to-invent criterion, some have argued that it protects the independent inventor, who may not have the resources or legal knowledge to file his patent application as quickly as the large corporation. On the other hand, it may be quite difficult (costly) to determine who was the first to discover an invention, and it is not clear that the independent inventor has benefited much from the U.S. rule.

It is noteworthy that the approval and issuance of a patent by the U.S. Patent and Trademark Office may be subsequently challenged in court. If the case goes to trial, the court will determine once and for all (subject to appeal) whether the patent is valid. Patent litigation is unusual in that all appeals of patent cases from the U.S. District Courts or Patent and

Trademark Office are heard only in the Court of Appeals for the Federal Circuit, which was created in the belief that a specialized court could provide more expertise and uniformity in patent decisions, and decide cases more quickly, than courts of general jurisdiction.

Relatively few patents are litigated to verdict, but of those that are, a substantial portion are held invalid. Given that a substantial fraction of patents that are fully evaluated by a court are found to be invalid, many have argued that the Patent and Trademark Office should examine patent applications more thoroughly before issuing a patent. Lemley (2001), however, contends that it is rational for the Patent and Trademark Office not to be too conscientious. As it happens, the vast majority of patents evidently have no commercial value; only about 5 percent of patents are either licensed or challenged in litigation. Of those, only about 2 percent are litigated to verdict. Lemley argues that the social cost of litigating a few commercially important patents is likely to be less than the costs of a thorough examination of all patent applications. Of course, patents that have been incorrectly issued may discourage innovation within the scope of the patent, or induce firms to incur costs to avoid use of the patented technology, but this effect is presumably small for patents without commercial value.

The patent is the strongest property right in intellectual property. A patent holder who believes that his patent has been infringed may bring a lawsuit against those who make, use or sell the infringing product. If the court finds in his favor, it may award him an injunction barring further use of the infringing device, damages equal to a reasonable royalty or lost profits, and costs of litigation.

One cost of the patent system is the inefficiency arising from monopoly during the term of the patent. However, the assumption is that this cost is outweighed by the benefit of the increased research and development that is induced by the potential reward of a patent. The patent system is also designed to maximize the social benefit of an invention by requiring publication of the patent, a complete description of the invention. The patent application must also disclose the best (least cost) way to practice the patent.

The economist Gary Becker (1968) has suggested that the patent system could be replaced by a system in which inventors were awarded cash prizes, rather than property rights in their inventions. This system would avoid the inefficiency of monopoly rights granted under the current system. Moreover, there are historical precedents for this method. In 1714 the British government offered a prize to anyone who could determine a ship's longitude precisely; this resulted in a revolutionary tool for navigators, the chronometer. However, in general it might prove to be quite difficult (costly) to determine independently how large an award a particular invention deserves. One advantage of the current system is that the reward for an invention, i.e. the royalties paid for the use of a patent, is determined accurately and objectively by the market.

Another important issue concerns the scope of things that can be patented. One cannot patent an abstract idea, laws of nature or natural phenomena. Once upon a time, mathematical algorithms – step-by-step procedures used to solve complex problems – were considered to be in the category of unpatentable ideas. Moreover, one could not obtain a patent on a method of doing business, such as the practice of assigning each waiter in a restaurant a number and placing the number on the waiter's order slips to prevent fraud. However, more recent court decisions[25] have substantially extended the range of patentable objects to include genetically engineered bacteria, computer programs, and various methods of doing business. Mathematical algorithms can now be patented if they are incorporated into computer software. Under the category of business methods, firms are patenting novel types of financial products, such as insurance policies, bank certificates, methods of collecting and filing patient records, and a method of training janitors by using a sequence of pictures. IBM patented a method for keeping track of the number of people waiting in line for the bathroom. It has even been suggested that techniques used in sports, such as a new type of pitch in baseball, should be patentable.

The extension of patents to business methods has been criticized on the grounds that, historically, many business techniques of great importance – the moving assembly line, the mail-order catalogue, the frequent-flier mile – were adopted without benefit of patent protection. However, this argument misses the point; new business methods of great value will always be adopted. The real issue is whether commercial innovations of less importance, but still of substantial value, would have been implemented, or at least adopted sooner, if the inventor had had the additional incentive of a patent.[26] A businessman considering whether to adopt a new business method might decide not to do so, if he knew that after he had incurred the costs of developing and refining the new technique, other firms could adopt it immediately and eliminate his competitive advantage. This free-rider problem might deter any firm from bearing the costs of developing the new business method.

The counter-argument is that if we reach the point where patents apply to every aspect of everyday life, social welfare will be reduced by all the transaction costs involved in obtaining licenses and in patent litigation. It could, however, be argued that this concern is overblown, since the number of patents issued can be reduced as much as desired by simply raising the standard of the requirements of novelty, usefulness, and nonobviousness.

Copyrights

The protection of a copyright covers written work, choreography, motion pictures, photography, sound recordings, and other art forms. Copyright protection applies to works of creative expression, but not general ideas. The term of copyright protection is now the life of the author plus seventy years. The prerequisite for a copyright is that the creative work meet a "modest threshold of creative activity"[27] and, under many statutes, the work must also be fixed in a tangible form.

Thus the term of a copyright is much longer than a patent, and there are other differences between these two property rights. For example, it is not necessary to apply for a copyright; it arises automatically, without any administrative action. Since a copyright is acquired without an application to the government, there is no official registry of copyrights in a central location. There are, however, some copyright collecting organizations such as the Copyright Clearance Center, a nonprofit organization based in the United States that obtains permission from copyright owners to grant licenses permitting users to photocopy works at fees set by the owners. The royalties paid by users, mainly libraries, corporations, and government agencies, are distributed to the copyright owners. If, however, no copyright collecting organization has been authorized to handle the copyright, those who wish to use the copyrighted work – for example, by producing plays, performing dances, exhibiting photographs, etc. – must bear "tracing costs," the costs of finding the current owner of the copyright and negotiating an agreement for its use. These costs may be substantial if the copyright is old, or has been transferred repeatedly.

Another important difference between a patent and a copyright is that so long as the work is created independently, it will qualify for copyright no matter how similar it is to the previous work of others, indeed, even if it is identical. There could be several valid copyrights to the text of Keats's "Ode on a Grecian Urn" as long as each author, by singular coincidence, created the poem independently.[28] In contrast, under the patent system, if two similar inventions are discovered by two individuals working independently, the inventor who is the first to file (or in the United States, the first to invent) obtains the patent, and the second inventor is liable for infringement if she attempts to exploit her invention. How can this difference between patent and copyright law be explained? Shavell[29] suggests that the difference lies in the fact that the value of work subject to copyright arises from the exact form in which it is expressed. The value of a painting by Vermeer is in the exact way it is done: the colors, the use of light, the composition of the figures in it, etc. If one were to change the colors just slightly, it would not be the same painting – undoubtedly not nearly as good. Moreover, different works that are subject to copyright can each be of great value even though they involve the same subject matter. A painting of the harbor in Gloucester loses none of its value if another painting is done of the same scene; thus the incentive to do the first painting is not diminished.

On the other hand, the value of a patentable invention is not derived from the form in which the idea is expressed. The value of the invention of the vacuum cleaner was not based on the proposed length of its dust bag, the size of its motor, etc., but rather was based on the idea that a fan driven by an electric motor could pump air out of a hose, thereby creating a suction that draws in dust and dirt. A corollary is that the value to mankind of a second discovery that a vacuum can be used to pick up household dirt is zero. If after the original discovery, someone could obtain a patent, or property right in the same idea, just because he thought of it independently, the incentive to make a major discovery would be seriously diluted. This also explains why, given a choice between obtaining a patent and copyright, an inventor will invariably choose a patent. Even though the term of the patent is shorter, the scope of its coverage is much broader than a copyright. Conversely, it is much less troublesome for a copyright to have a long term than it would be for a patent to have one, since a copyright does not inhibit anyone's independent creative activity.

We can summarize one aspect of the difference between copyrights and patents as follows: copyright protects the expression of an idea, but not the idea itself, whereas a patent does protect the idea. Although the scope of a copyright is narrower than that of a patent, the benefits of copyright protection should not be understated. History provides us with what amounts to a controlled experiment concerning the incentive effects of copyright law. Shortly after the French Revolution of 1789, the new National Assembly abolished copyright protection. The consequence was that, after a few years, virtually the only works being published were either pornographic or seditious, i.e., stirring up resistance to the government. (Evidently the motivation for these types of work is sufficiently strong that copyright protection is not needed.) The French government ultimately found it necessary to restore copyright protection, to induce the publication of creative work in other areas.[30]

One of the basic rights of a copyright owner is the right to create a derivative work, that is, a work based on one or more pre-existing works. Examples of such works are a translation, a musical arrangement, and a motion picture adapted from a book. There may be more than one tier of derivative works, as when a toy or t-shirt logo is based on a movie version of a book.

There is a dispute as to the scope of the copyright holder's exclusive right to produce derivative works. One view is that this right should be broad, to maximize the incentive to produce the original work. According to this approach, someone else who creates another work should be held to be infringing the copyright of the original work if there is substantial similarity between the original and the following work. Landes and Posner (1989) argue that if this were not the rule, authors might delay publication so that they could get a head start on the derivative work to gain an advantage over competitors. However, others argue that the author of the original work should have a narrow right to derivative works – that there should be a broad "zone of freedom" for others to produce derivative works to maximize the production of creative variations of the original.

With respect to the rights to derivative works, there is an interesting difference between patent and copyright law. If someone who does not own a patent makes an improvement to the underlying invention, he can patent the improvement, even though he cannot use or sell it without obtaining a license from the patent owner. Neither the owner of the original patent nor the owner of the improvement can use or sell the improved version without a license from the other. This is a classic example of bilateral monopoly. For that reason both patents in this situation are known as "blocking patents." In contrast, as noted above, only the owner of the copyright has the right to produce derivative works; no one else can obtain a property right in such works. Posner (2005) has suggested that the reason for the difference is that improvements in technology are continuous over time, and it is important to provide incentives to those who have ideas for improving a patented invention. However the fine arts do not experience "progress" in the same sense. No one believes that there have been great advances in playwriting over the works of Shakespeare, or improvements in musical composition that render the works of Beethoven obsolete. Thus it is not appropriate to restrict the rights of the copyright owner in derivative works.

To prove that a copyright was infringed, the owner of the copyright must prove that the work was not independently done, i.e. that it was copied. If the defendant denies that she copied the original work, the plaintiff may prove copying by indirect evidence, i.e., that the defendant had access to the original work and that there is "substantial similarity" between the original work and the allegedly infringing work. In determining whether there is substantial similarity, quantity is important – the jury is likely to rule for the plaintiff if two or three pages of a book are identical – but quality can be quite important too – a court may find a song to be infringing if it uses only two chords of the original, if that motif is considered "the heart of the song."

The scope of copyright protection is limited by the doctrine of "fair use," under which persons may use portions of a copyrighted work without obtaining the author's permission. The legal formulation is that the use of the copyrighted work must not "adversely affect the present or potential economic interest of the owner of the copyright." In most cases of fair use, only a small part of the work is used and the author is acknowledged. The fair use doctrine has been applied to a brief quotation from a copyrighted book in an article or book review, or the classroom use of a few pages from a larger work. It is generally considered fair use for a scholar to make one copy of a copyrighted work so that he can study it in connection with his research.

An economic justification for the fair use doctrine is that, without it, this kind of use would often be precluded by transaction costs. Suppose, for example, students were not allowed to photocopy one or two pages of a book for use in a course without the author's agreement. The transaction costs involved in contacting the author, agreeing on a payment, and monitoring the subsequent use, would often exceed the value to the class, so that the author's work would not be used at all – an inefficient outcome.

The common-law applications of the fair use privilege suggest that the courts have carefully weighed costs and benefits. For example, a parody is an established category of fair use, and the courts understand that it may have to quote extensively from the original work to be recognized as a parody. They also understand that a parody has social benefits in terms of entertainment and criticism, and that the transaction costs of the parodist's reaching an agreement with the author may be prohibitive, since the author may wish to avoid being humiliated by a mockery of his work. It is quite possible that the fair use doctrine could benefit the author as well as the users; for example, quoting someone's work in an article will often enhance the author's reputation and increase interest in his work. Without the fair use doctrine, an author could, of course, waive his right to compensation, but this involves a transaction cost that would often prevent use of his work.

Of course, the applicability of the fair use doctrine depends on the value of the benefits relative to transaction costs and the costs to the author. Reprinting an out-of-print book would usually not adversely affect the economic interests of the owner of its copyright, and thus should be considered fair use. At the other extreme, we noted in our discussion of ASCAP that the playing of all music on network television, which has a vast audience, is measured exactly. The use of a few bars of a song in a Super Bowl commercial could yield a great deal of income to the copyright holder.

A literature considers how high the standard should be for awarding a patent, what the period of the patent should be, and how broad it should be. Clearly a patent will be more valuable the longer its term and the broader its scope. The more valuable a patent is, the more incentives there are for research and development activity. On the other hand, the broader the scope of a patent, the more that subsequent research and development in that area may be deterred, since the invention it leads to could fall within the scope of the existing patent. On the other hand, the more narrow patents are, the greater the total cost of the patent system, and the more patent licenses an entrepreneur must obtain in order to exploit a technology that uses a given range of patented knowledge.

Another issue is whether the owner of a patent or copyright should be protected by a property right or a rule of liability.[31] It could be argued that a rule of liability is necessary here, because of transaction costs involved in negotiating with the patent owner to obtain a license. Since the patent owner has a monopoly, a mandatory license may be necessary to avoid the holdout problem. Indeed, many copyright statutes provide for compulsory licenses to be granted at a stated or reasonable royalty payment, a rule of liability. The U.S. Copyright Act provides for mandatory licenses with license fees determined by statute for some uses, such as the retransmission of broadcast signals by cable television systems. It may happen that a firm needs access to patented technology to enable it to comply with provisions of the Clean Air Act. In such a case, a statute provides that the federal government can compel the owner of the patented technology to grant the firm a patent license for a "reasonable royalty." Were it not for this provision, the owner of the patent would be able to extract from the firm the entire value of its business, since it would have to shut down if it could not comply with the Clean Air Act.

Several European countries have enacted mandatory licenses for taping broadcast programs off-air, other forms of home recording, and photocopying, where the license fees are collected through taxes on blank recording machinery or other media. Here, of course, the objective is to extract payment from the user, rather than compel the producer of the program to sell it to the user. Copyright owners in the United States have unsuccessfully tried to have similar taxes imposed to compensate for potential revenue lost from persons recording programs at home.

Another issue is whether the owner of a patent or copyright should be required to pay periodic fees to maintain it. In some countries the owner of a patent is required to pay fees every few years to prevent it from expiring prematurely. One argument in favor of this requirement is that a patent or copyright inhibits creative activity within the scope of its coverage; consequently if it does not provide any rewards to its owner, through commercial exploitation or otherwise, it should expire (if it did provide rewards to its owner, he would be willing to pay small fees to keep it in effect). An incidental benefit of this type of requirement is that, if it applied to copyrights, it would eliminate the tracing costs referred to above, since the identity of the party paying the fee would be known.

Trade secrets

An invention may also be protected as a trade secret; an example is the formula for Coca-Cola. Some inventors prefer to keep their invention a trade secret rather than patent it. One reason is the cost and delay involved in obtaining a patent; another is that the inventor might be able to profit from a trade secret for a longer period, since, unlike a patent, there is no limit on the duration of a trade secret. However, once a trade secret has been discovered by others, it is no longer protected. Thus the inventor must incur costs to prevent its discovery, for example by building high fences around his research facility, or limiting the number of employees who have access to the trade secret. Under trade secret law, an inventor is required to take only reasonable measures to maintain its secrecy. If he does so, he will have strong legal remedies against employees or others who have been given access to the trade secret on condition that they not reveal it to outsiders.

Trade secrets have substantial social costs, which is an argument in support of patent protection: if inventors could not obtain patents, there would be many more trade secrets. The largest cost is that the protected knowledge does not enter the public domain so long as it is maintained as a trade secret; other firms cannot exploit the trade secret, or make improvements to the technology it covers. There are also inefficiencies arising from use of the trade secret by the firm that has it. A firm with a trade secret may manufacture a product itself, even though another firm could manufacture it at lower cost, because of a fear that the secret would be revealed to outsiders if the firm attempted to hire the low-cost firm to manufacture the good.

Trademarks

A trademark or trade name is a property right in a name, word, symbol or design that is used to identify the product of a particular firm and distinguish it from competing products. The scope of this property right is determined by the product to which it refers.

For example, one firm has a long-established right in the name "Ford" as applied to automobiles, trucks, and related products, while another firm has a right in this name as applied to a commercial modeling agency. The owner of a trademark or trade name has an exclusive right to use the symbol or name in conjunction with the associated product, and can be protected from an infringing use. Trademark protection applies to those who were the first to use a distinctive mark in commerce. A business that uses the mark first to identify its product to consumers can prevent later firms from using the mark for their similar products.

In the United States. trademarks are protected by the Federal Trademark Act of 1946 (the Lanham Act), which provides a method to register trademarks with the federal government.[32] The Trademark Office will register a trademark only if it determines that the mark is "distinctive" and not so similar to existing trademarks as to cause confusion; thus, the basic requirement is that the mark must identify the product of a particular seller. By registering a mark with the Trademark Office, one becomes entitled to certain privileges, one of which is the right to place next to the trademark a circled R that indicates that the mark is officially registered.

Trademarks have two important economic functions: (1) they provide consumers with information about the characteristics and quality of products – information that would otherwise be costly to acquire – and (2) they give firms an incentive to make products of high quality. The two functions of trademarks were described in the legislative history of the Lanham Act:

> One is to protect the public so it may be confident that, in purchasing a trademark which it favorably knows, it will get the product which it asks for and wants to get. Secondly, where the owner of a trademark has spent energy, time and money in presenting to the public the product, he is protected in his investment from its misappropriation by pirates and cheats. This is the well established rule of law protecting both the public and the trademark owner.[33]

Sellers usually know more about the characteristics of their goods than buyers. Often the value of a good to the buyer depends on characteristics that the buyer cannot observe before purchase; consider, for example, a can of tuna fish. If there were no trademarks or trade names to indicate who made the product, consumers would often be unable to differentiate between products of high and low quality. In this situation, firms, which would be unable to inform consumers about the positive unobservable characteristics of their goods, would tend to produce goods with the cheapest possible unobservable characteristics. Trademarks make it possible for consumers to learn the unobservable qualities of a product before they purchase it. It is therefore important to prevent infringement of a trademark, to prevent firms from deceiving consumers and free-riding on the reputation of a trademark owner by selling goods of lower quality.[34]

Since the economic benefits of trademarks – providing information about product quality to consumers, and giving firms an incentive to produce goods of high quality – continue undiminished over time, there is no limit on the duration of trademarks, unlike patents and copyrights. Since trademarks indicate the type and quality of a good, manufacturers often choose not to use the same trademark for goods that meet different standards of quality. For example, Honda uses the name Acura, and Toyota the name Lexus, for their top-of-the-line models.

Almost all the specific doctrines of trademark law are based on the principles of providing information to consumers about quality and giving firms incentives to maintain quality. For example, a trademark is forfeited if the trademark is sold "in gross," i.e., without the machinery, equipment, and personnel used to make the trademarked good. Kraft Foods, the owner of the "Grey Poupon," brand of Dijon mustard, could not sell the name to label the mustard of another firm if it retained the assets and facilities that are used to produce it. Bausch & Lomb could not sell another firm the right to use its name on microscopes if it did not simultaneously transfer the assets it used to make them. The rationale is that the consumer cannot be assured that the quality of the trademarked product will be maintained if the assets previously used to make the product are no longer so used.

Another example is the doctrine that "functional" marks cannot be protected as trademarks. A mark is functional if it achieves an objective beyond identifying the firm manufacturing the good, and thus, if reserved for the exclusive use of the firm with the trademark, would put competitors at a significant competitive disadvantage. Thus a black color cannot be part of the trademark for an outboard motor, since that color coordinates best with a variety of boat colors. Awarding the right to use the color black as part of a trademark would put competing outboard motor manufacturers at a disadvantage, and is not necessary to identify the manufacturer. Similarly, one case held that the orange flavor of a drug could not be registered as a trademark because it masked the drug's bad taste; awarding it trademark status would leave competitors with bad-tasting drugs.

One cannot obtain a trademark on a word or expression in common use, since that would prevent other businesses from using it, and would therefore make it more difficult (costly) for them to communicate with potential customers. For example, a restaurant cannot obtain a trademark on the phrase "We serve good food" since that would make it more costly for other restaurants to describe their characteristics to consumers.[35] From time to time the trade name of a product with a dominant market share comes to be used by the public as a general or "generic" name for a product of that kind made by any firm. Some examples of trademarks that became generic are aspirin, cellophane, escalator, shredded wheat, thermos, and yo-yo. If and when a trade name becomes a generic term, the owner loses the property right in that name. The economic justification for this is that the name no longer serves the purpose of indicating the product of a specific firm, and maintaining the trademark would increase the costs of other firms. If not for this rule, a manufacturer who wished to compete with the yo-yo would have to advertise his product as "a toy consisting of a flattened spool wound with string that is spun down from and reeled up to the hand by motions of the wrist." Allowing a firm to keep its trademark after it had become a generic term would increase the cost to competing firms of providing information to consumers. Some firms, such as Xerox and Lego, have spent large sums on advertising campaigns to urge the public not to use their trade names as nouns, to prevent the names from becoming common terms for copying machines and interlocking building blocks, respectively.

Bibliography

Becker, Gary, "Crime and Punishment: An Economic Approach," 76 (2) *Journal of Political Economy* 169–217 (1968).

Besen, Stanley M., and Leo J. Raskind, "An Introduction to the Law and Economics of Intellectual Property," 5 (1) *Journal of Economic Perspectives* 3–27 (winter 1991).

Bibas, Steven A., "The Case against Statutes of Limitations for Stolen Art," 103 *Yale Law Journal* 2437–2469 (1993–1994).

Biblowit, C., "International Law and the Allocation of Property Rights in Common Resources," 4 *New York International Law Review* 273–292 (1991).

Calabresi, G., and A. D. Melamed, "Property Rights, Liability Rules and Inalienability: One View of the Cathedral," 85 *Harvard Law Review* 1089 (1972).

Casadesus-Masanell, Ramon, and Daniel F. Spulber, "The Fable of Fisher Body," 43 (1) *Journal of Law and Economics* 67–104 (April 2000).

Coase, Ronald, "The Problem of Social Cost," *Journal of Law and Economics* (October 1960).

Dales, John Harkness, *Pollution, Property and Prices: An Essay in Policy-making and Economics* (Toronto: University of Toronto Press, 1968).

Eckert, R. D., *The Enclosure of Ocean Resources: Economics and the Law of the Sea* (Stanford, CA: Hoover Institution, 1979).

Economides, Nicholas, entry "Trademarks," in Peter K. Newman, ed., *The New Palgrave Dictionary of Economics and the Law* (London: Macmillan, 2001).

Goldner, Barry, "The Torrens System of Title Registration: A New Proposal for Effective Implementation," 29 (3) *UCLA Law Review* 661–710 (February 1982).

Griffin, James M., "OPEC Behavior: A Test of Alternative Hypotheses," 75 *American Economic Review* 954–963 (December 1985).

Grossman, Philip J., Marco Pirozzi, and Jeff Pope, "An Empirical Test of Free-rider Behavior," *Australian Economic Papers* 152–160 (June 1993).

Harberger, Arnold, "Issues of Tax Reform for Latin America," in *Joint Tax Program, OAS/IBD/ECLA* (Baltimore, MD: Johns Hopkins University Press, 1965).

Hicks, J. R., "The Valuation of the Social Income," 7 *Economica* 105–124 (May 1940).

Howlett, Debbie, "To Chicagoans, Parking is Property," *Detroit News*, January 8, 1999.

Kaldor, Nicholas, "Welfare Propositions of Economics and Interpersonal Comparisons of Utility," 49 *Economic Journal* 549–551 (September 1939).

Kaplow, Louis, and Steven Shavell, "Economic Analysis of Law," in Alan J. Auerbach and Martin Feldstein, eds., *Handbook of Public Economics*, Vol. 3 (Amsterdam: Elsevier, 2002).

Klein, Benjamin, "Fisher–General Motors and the Nature of the Firm," 43 (1) *Journal of Law and Economics* 105–139 (April 2000).

Lemley, Mark A., "Rational Ignorance at the Patent Office," 95 *Northwestern University Law Review* 1495–1532 (2001).

Levmore, Saul, "Self-assessed Valuation Systems for Tort and Other Law," 68 *Virginia Law Review* 771 (1982).

Lipsey, R. G., and K. J. Lancaster, "The General Theory of the Second Best," 24 *Review of Economic Studies* 11–32 (1956–57).

Munch, Patricia, "An Economic Analysis of Eminent Domain," 84 *Journal of Political Economy* 473 (1976).

Polinsky, A. Mitchell, "Controlling Externalities and Protecting Entitlements: Property Right, Liability Rule, and Tax: Subsidy Approaches," *Journal of Legal Studies* (January 1979).

Posner, Richard A., "Intellectual Property: The Law and Economics Approach," 19 (2) *Journal of Economic Perspectives* 57–73 (spring 2005).

Raskind, Leo J., entry "Copyright," in Peter K. Newman, ed., *The New Palgrave Dictionary of Economics and the Law* (London: Macmillan, 2001).

Shavell, Steven, *Foundations of Economic Analysis of Law* (Cambridge, MA : Harvard University Press, 2003).

Sweat, Ray E., "Race, Race-Notice and Notice Statutes: The American Recording System," 3 (3) *Probate and Property* 27–31 (May/June 1989).

Turvey, Ralph, "On Divergences between Social Cost and Private Cost," 30 *Economica* 309–313 (August 1963).

Varian, Hal R., "Economic Scene," *New York Times*, July 27, 2000, at C2.

Problems

1.   (a) What is the economic justification for the government's power of eminent domain?
     (b) Persons who wish to acquire a large area of land for some project like a shopping mall or amusement park face the same kinds of problems the government does when it acquires land for an expressway; however, unlike the government, they do not have the power of eminent domain. How do they deal with these problems?

2.   Mr. X has owned and operated a tattoo parlor in Harper Woods for ten years. The city then passes an ordinance making tattooing illegal. Does Mr. X have a possible remedy under the law of eminent domain? Discuss.

3.   Why is there no limit on the duration of a trademark, unlike patents and copyrights? Also, why do many manufacturers use several different trademarks for different products that they make?

4.   Explain the difference between the bona fide purchaser rule and the original ownership rule. How might these rules differ in their effect on theft?

5 Problems of incomplete property rights

According to the Coase Theorem, in the event of a conflict the parties will arrive at the efficient outcome through their own negotiations, provided that transaction costs are low and property rights are well defined. This chapter examines the kinds of problems that arise when property rights are nonexistent or incomplete. For example, property rights can be incomplete if the good is not transferable, thus lacking a basic characteristic of property, or if property is held under common ownership, whether the ownership rights are divided horizontally, as between joint tenants, or vertically over time, as between a life tenant and remainderman.

Finally, we examine why the law is surely justified in imposing some limits on the vertical dimension of property rights. Here we consider the problem of the "dead hand," i.e., situations in which enforcing the conditions of the donor or testator long after her death would lead to an inefficient or illegal use of resources.

Inalienability

As we saw earlier, there are some things that are subject to a rule of inalienability, i.e., the law prohibits their sale under any circumstances. Examples include legal claims, human beings, certain drugs, voting rights, and sexual services. Now when objects can be traded, they tend to be transferred to those who value them the most. A rule of inalienability means that in general, objects will not be assigned to those to whom they are most valuable. In this section we consider two cases in which the rule of inalienability is quite well established, so that a proposal to depart from it may seem bizarre and even disturbing. However, a close analysis of these cases may raise substantial doubts as to whether the prohibition of trade should be maintained. The cases in question are transplantable human organs, and human babies.

The market for human organs

Human organs are an important example of inalienable goods. The first successful solid organ transplant – which involved a kidney – was performed on December 23, 1954.[1] Since then there have been dramatic advances in transplant surgery, and in the rates of success of transplants of many different organs – kidneys, hearts, lungs, heart–lung combinations, pancreata, livers, corneas, pituitary glands, and ear bone tissue. In 1993 about 95 percent of kidneys were functioning one year after transplantation, compared with 62–65 percent in 1979. The most important breakthroughs came with the development of immunosuppressive drugs such as Cyclosporine, which was introduced in the United States in 1979. These drugs inhibit the body's tendency to reject foreign matter such as a transplanted organ.

Over the last two decades there has been an enormous increase in demand for organs, primarily because of the improvement in the quality of this good (viz., the higher success rate of transplants), but also because the share of older people in the population has increased, and the income of this group has also increased. While demand has increased, the supply of organs has steadily decreased. Until recently[2] the majority of organ donors were victims of fatal accidents, and there is a trend of decline in the rate of fatal accidents; for example there was a decline of 16 percent between 1978 and 1988. Motor vehicle accidents have been reduced by more stringent regulation of drunk driving, the increase in the minimum drinking age to twenty-one, and by various highway safety measures such as the 55 m.p.h. speed limit, motorcycle helmet laws, seat belts, airbags, anti-lock brakes, electronic stability controls, and restricted driver's licenses for young drivers. Other factors that have contributed to the reduction in supply of organs are a decline in the homicide rate, and major improvements in the equipment and technology used in emergency rescue operations.

By far the most important factor restricting the supply of organs is the law: specifically, federal and State laws that make it illegal to use incentives to promote the donation of organs. Under the National Organ Transplant Act, enacted in 1984, it is illegal to encourage the donation of organs by offering to pay the hospital, funeral or burial expenses of the prospective donor. Thus the law imposes a price ceiling of zero on human organs. As shown in Figure 5.1, the consequence is that there is a shortage of organs equal to CF, the difference between 0F, the amount demanded at a price of zero, and 0C, the amount supplied at that price. This shortage has been exacerbated by the factors described above, which have caused the demand curve to shift to the right and the supply curve to shift left. In 2001 it was estimated that only 25 percent of some 78,000 organ transplants sought would occur in time to save a life.[3]

In Figure 5.1, 0C organs are provided to recipients under the current regime. This diagram indicates that in a free market, 0E organs would be provided. The value to recipients of the additional CE organs would be area ABEC. It is estimated that in 1984 less than 17 percent of those who died and were potential donors actually became donors. Allowing the use of

Figure 5.1 The market for transplant organs.

incentives to increase donations would increase social welfare by the area ABC. Moreover, this analysis is conservative: note that we have assumed that all the organs supplied under the current regime, 0C, are going to those patients to whom the organs are most valuable. However, the system now being used might not assign organs to the patients to whom the organs are most valuable, that is, to those on the highest portion of the market demand curve AD. If we assume instead that organs are assigned randomly to recipients in terms of their valuation of organs, i.e. their willingness to pay, then the organs would be assigned randomly to all patients on the demand curve DF. In this case, the value and consumer surplus to recipients of the 0C organs provided under the current system would be DC0. In contrast, under a free market the transplant recipients would have a consumer surplus of DBC0. Therefore, assuming the assignment of organs to patients under the current regime is random, the net social gain from changing to a market system would be DCB.

Since in Figure 5.1 there is excess demand for organs CF, the question arises how it is decided who gets the organs under the current system. Organs are now rationed by waiting in line; there are waiting lists for organs administered by the United Network for Organ Sharing, a nonprofit corporation that has been assigned this responsibility by the federal government.

A commonly heard objection to allowing a market is that "the rich would get all the organs." This is ironic, in view of the considerable advantages for high-income individuals under the current system. A patient will not be placed on a waiting list unless a source of payment for the transplant operation has been identified. Generally the individual must have personal wealth or private health insurance that will cover the cost of the operation, which can be substantial. For example, the cost of a liver transplant was $216,000 in 1990. Moreover, wealthy patients can often increase their chances of obtaining an organ through certain kinds of strategic behavior, such as getting on multiple waiting lists, i.e., joining the waiting lists of several different transplant centers and organ procurement organizations.

As with other goods that are subject to a price ceiling, buyers (in this case patients) will take extraordinary measures to obtain the good that is rationed (organs). This is known as "rent-seeking" behavior, i.e., competitive efforts to obtain something of value that is not subject to price competition. There is an international black market in kidneys, which are procured from both living donors and cadavers. Sometimes families of patients have made appeals to the public through the news or entertainment media, or through politicians, who have access to these media. These appeals ask that an organ be donated directly to a specified patient, bypassing the waiting lists. Another consequence of the increasing shortage is an increase in social pressure on relatives and friends of patients to make "voluntary" donations of organs.

Given the strong opposition to the use of market incentives, two economists[4] have proposed alternatives to their use: presumed consent or mandated choice. Under a system of presumed consent, the government would simply assume that people want to donate their organs in the event of a fatal accident unless they have explicitly stated that they do not wish to do so. There is evidence that under a system of presumed consent, many more people would be determined to be organ donors. In a 2003 study, only 42 percent of people chose to be organ donors when their donation required an affirmative decision, but only 18 percent chose to opt out when their consent was presumed.

Under a system of mandated choice, people would be forced to make a decision on whether they wished to donate their organs. For example, a person might be required to state whether she was willing to donate her organs, in order to obtain a driver's license. She could say yes or no, but would not be able to obtain a license without answering the question one way or the other. The State of Illinois has adopted this requirement for driver's licenses, and in 2009 had a 60 percent signup rate for organ donation, compared to a national rate of 38 percent.[5]

With regard to these proposals, recall that any behavior that can be achieved by a tax can also be achieved by a subsidy, and vice versa. With a system of presumed consent or mandated choice, instead of subsidizing the donation of organs, or allowing a market to provide incentives, the State has effectively imposed a cost (a tax) on a refusal to donate organs – namely the potential embarrassment (if any) that someone may feel by making an explicit statement that she would not donate her organs.

With regard to the proposed market for organs, a number of commentators have urged that the law prohibiting the use of incentives be repealed. The stakes are high: the United Network for Organ Sharing reported in 2001 that every day fifteen people die while waiting for an organ transplant.[6]

The market for babies

Another area in which there is a well-established prohibition of trade and property rights involves human beings. A proposal to allow the sale of babies is even more controversial than allowing the use of incentives to increase the supply of organs. However, the stakes involved argue for serious consideration of proposals that may seem far-fetched, if they offer promise of improvement of the health and welfare of children. Landes and Posner (1978) have made compelling arguments for allowing such a market, under certain restrictions designed to prevent abuse. They contend that the shortage of babies available for adoption is a consequence of government regulation that makes it illegal to offer compensation for them.

The demand for babies comes primarily from married couples who are unable to have children.[7] The majority of babies supplied for adoption were the unintended consequence of sexual intercourse, although some have been removed by the State from the custody of their natural parents for reasons such as death, abuse or extreme poverty. In recent years the supply of babies has declined, partly because of the increased availability of contraception and abortion. Another factor is that mothers of children born out of wedlock are more likely to keep them now than in previous years. Landes and Posner suggest that the reason for this change, and for the lessening of the stigma of having an illegitimate child, is that women now have greater economic opportunities; they no longer need a male partner to be able to support a child.

Aside from adoptions by relatives, such as a stepfather, most adoptions are arranged through adoption agencies, although a small share of them[8] are done as independent adoptions. The fees that are charged by adoption agencies are well below the price that would equilibrate supply and demand. In Figure 5.2, the free market price would be P*, and the quantity of babies supplied for adoption would be Q*. However the actual price – the fee charged by adoption agencies – is Pc. At this price the quantity supplied (found from the supply curve) is only Qc, and there is excess demand of AB that must be rationed. To ration the excess demand for their babies, adoption agencies use various criteria to determine whether applicants are "fit"; there is usually a minimum standard based on the applicants' income or employment history, and some agencies may require that the adoptive parents have the same religion as the birth mother. However, the primary method used to ration the excess demand is waiting in line – once approved by the agency, prospective parents may have to wait for a child between three and seven years.

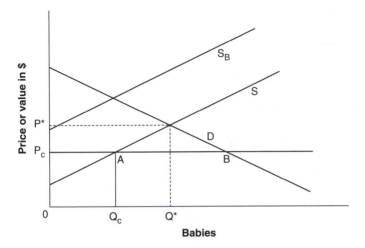

Figure 5.2 The market for babies.

In an independent adoption, the only costs that may be paid by the buyer are compensation to the natural mother for her medical expenses and some maintenance, and to the obstetrician and the lawyer for their medical and legal services, respectively. It is not legal to pay for the baby, or to compensate the lawyer or other intermediary for his services in finding a match between the natural mother and the adopting parents. However, it is difficult (costly) to enforce the requirement that all of the payments made by the adoptive parents to the natural parents or middlemen are made only for out-of-pocket expenses and professional services; thus there are "black market" transactions in which part of the compensation is for the value of the baby. There are persistent reports of prices on this market as high as $40,000.

Note that in Figure 5.2, S_B, the black market supply curve, is higher than the free-market supply curve would be. The costs are substantially higher for suppliers on the black market; they must carry out their transactions in secret and bear the costs of expected punishment, such as criminal penalties and the potential loss of professional licenses. While the supply curve is higher, the demand curve may be somewhat lower than what it would be in a free market, since a buyer cannot obtain a warranty or other guarantee of the health or ancestry of the baby, and reports indicate that the characteristics of babies are often misrepresented. Nonetheless, because of the increased costs of suppliers, the equilibrium price of babies on the black market is probably much higher than it would be in a free market.

What would be the consequences of a free market? First, there would no longer be a shortage of babies; supply would equal demand. Second, the total number of babies adopted would be likely to increase, because of increases in both supply and demand. The supply would increase, since some women would provide their babies to the adoption market rather than undergo an abortion, while others would do so rather than keep them. In the latter case, custody of the baby would be transferred to parents who valued the child more highly than the natural mother. Another reason for an increase in supply is that some women might take fewer precautions against becoming pregnant, since, with a free market, the alternative to the options of abortion and keeping the child is to receive compensation for the costs of pregnancy and childbirth. To a certain extent demand would also increase since, unlike the situation in a black market, adopting parents would be able to obtain and enforce guarantees of the health and other characteristics of the babies. Another consequence of a free market is that many couples would choose to adopt a child rather than make massive, often futile, investments in fertility treatments.

One objection that might be made to this proposal is that "the rich people would get all the babies." If this were true, of course, it might not be a bad thing, from the standpoint of the babies; yet it is quite possible that low-income applicants would have a better chance of obtaining a child under a free market than under the current system. The objection is based on the assumption that a couple want more children, the higher their family income, but a couple that want two children if their family income is $50,000 would not necessarily want more if their income were $100,000; they might choose instead to make a greater investment in the two children, in the form of piano lessons, clothes, vacations, and the like. It should be noted that the cost of children is higher for high-income parents: children require large investments of time, and the cost of time is greater for high-income individuals. Under the current system, applicants whose income falls below a given standard are screened out by adoption agencies. The prospects for such applicants might be considerably better under a free market because of an increase in the supply of babies.

In the next section we analyze various problems that arise when property rights are not well defined and complete. First we consider situations in which property rights either do not exist or are incomplete; here we examine the fisheries problem. Then we consider cases in which property is under common ownership. These cases can be subdivided into (1) those in which property rights are divided horizontally, e.g. between joint tenants, between author and publisher, between lessor and developer under an oil lease, among owners of adjacent parcels of land above an oilfield, between landowners on either side of a fence or party wall; (2) those in which property rights are divided vertically over time, e.g. between life tenant and remainderman; and (3) those in which property rights are divided both horizontally and vertically, e.g. between landlord and tenant.

Problems when there are no property rights

The fisheries problem

We first consider a case in which there are no property rights. Until quite recently, wild animals, including most fish, were not regarded as anyone's property until they were killed or captured. This was true of oysters, among other species. Historically, most oysters harvested in the United States have grown in areas to which fishermen have unlimited access. The consequence has been overfishing. Figure 5.3 shows the demand for oysters, which represents their marginal social benefit. The demand curve is downward-sloping but elastic, since reasonably good substitutes for oysters are available (e.g., clams, mussels, shrimp, scallops, etc.) The supply curve, MC_p, represents the marginal private cost to fishermen, which includes the cost of their supplies and equipment, the use of their boats, and the value of their time. MC_s, the curve of marginal social cost, lies above MC_p, because it includes all the costs in MC_p plus an additional cost not borne exclusively by the fishermen: the cost of reduction of the oyster population. This is an example of moral hazard, since the fishermen do not bear the full cost of their activity.

Social welfare would be maximized by maximizing the net social benefit, i.e., total social benefit minus total social cost. This would be achieved at Q^*, where marginal social benefit

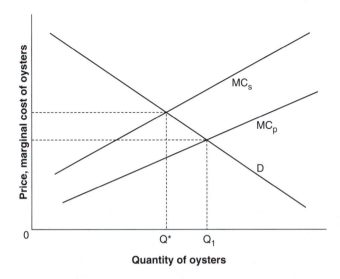

Figure 5.3 The problem of overfishing.

equals marginal social cost. Let P equal the price of oysters to consumers, and let Q equal the amount of oysters sold annually, in millions of bushels. Suppose the equation for the demand curve is:

$$P = 14 - Q \tag{1}$$

the marginal social cost is:

$$MC_s = 2 + 3Q \tag{2}$$

and the marginal private cost is:

$$MC_p = 2 + 2Q \tag{3}$$

Then Q* can be determined by setting $P = MC_s$. By solving this equation, we find that Q* equals 3 million bushels of oysters. If we then substitute this value of Q into either (1) or (2), we obtain a value for P of $11 a bushel.

The problem of overfishing arises because the effective supply curve is MC_p. The market equilibrium will occur where supply equals demand, or $MC_p = P$. Solving this equation, we find that Q now equals 4 million bushels of oysters. We will call this amount Q_1. If we substitute this value of Q into either (1) or (3), we find that P now equals $10 a bushel. Since Q_1 is greater than Q*, the efficient level of fishing, there is overfishing, which will cause a decline of the oyster population.

Note that this problem arises because the oysters are not owned by anyone – they are a common property resource. If someone owned an oyster bed, he would charge the fishermen a fee equal to the marginal cost of depleting the oyster population (the vertical distance between MC_p and MC_s),[9] so that the new MC_p would be identical to MC_s, and fishing would then occur at the efficient level Q*.This analysis of course applies not only to oysters, but to all other animals, plants, or indeed any resources that are not owned by anyone.

In Maryland, for example, the annual harvest of oysters has declined from 3.2 million bushels in 1973 to 124,000 bushels in 1993; there was a similar trend in other areas.[10] After a serious decline in the oyster population in important fisheries such as Chesapeake Bay, an increasing share of the annual catch has come from leased oyster beds and privately owned oyster farms, in which fishermen either pay a fee for the right to harvest an oyster bed or raise the oysters themselves, thus internalizing the cost of reducing the oyster population. As a consequence, there has been in recent years a substantial recovery and indeed growth in the amount of oysters harvested each year.

Property rights and elephants

In some cases, the best way to protect an endangered species of animal is to allow it to be hunted! This paradox is explained by the effect of creating property rights in the animal when there were none before.

Consider the recent history of African elephants. There has been a sharp decline in the population of these animals since 1979.The elephant population in Africa declined from 1.3 million in 1979, to 600,000 in 1989, to 543,000 in 1994.[11]

The reasons for this trend are easily identified. The ivory of the tusks and the hide of the elephant have great commercial value; tusks have been sold for $2,000 or more. Consequently, although it is generally illegal to kill an elephant, poaching is widespread. Poachers have been tolerated or even encouraged by the peasants in African villages, because the elephant was regarded as a pest. Elephants trample or consume crops, kill domestic animals, and compete with the peasants and their livestock for water, which is scarce in most of Africa. Accordingly villagers are not often inclined to assist in the prosecution of poachers.

Two countries, Kenya and Zimbabwe, have responded to this crisis in different ways. In Kenya the sale of ivory is illegal, and the hunting of elephants has been banned for decades. Despite these laws, the elephant population of Kenya declined from 65,000 to 19,000 from 1979 to 1989. In Zimbabwe, however, the government decided to give the villages ownership rights to the elephants in their vicinity. When they have property rights in the elephants, villagers can obtain revenue from hunting safaris, photographic safaris, or from the sale of elephant products such as tusks, meat, and hides. The peasants have the right to hunt a certain number of elephants each year, and may sell these rights to others. Some villages have obtained as much as $5 million from the sale of these hunting rights to safari operators. Poaching is not a major problem in Zimbabwe, since poachers are shot on sight! In Zimbabwe the elephant population has grown from 30,000 in 1979, to 52,000 in 1989, to 81,855 in 1994. The peasants, who now have property rights in the elephants, have a powerful incentive to protect and maintain them.[12]

While property rights provide an incentive to people to protect animals from poachers, they can also be protected by modifying the incentives of poachers. There is evidence – impressive although anecdotal – that the opportunity cost of natives, e.g., the earnings in their best alternative to poaching, is important. Between 1986 and 2007 people working on conservation projects taught rural Zambians how to farm more efficiently and carry on other profitable activities. During this period the poaching of elephants in Zambia's North Luanga National Park, which previously (during the 1980s) had reduced the population from 17,000 to 1300, declined to almost nothing.[13]

Problems when property rights are divided

The conflict among joint tenants

Under both a tenancy in common and a joint tenancy, all the tenants (owners) have the right to use and possession of the entire property. The property in question may be land, tangible personal property like an automobile, or intangible personal property like stocks, bonds, or bank accounts. Thus the joint tenant of a savings account has the right to withdraw the entire balance. The difference between the joint tenancy and the tenancy in common is that under the joint tenancy there is a "right of survivorship," i.e., if one joint tenant dies, his interest expires and the property is owned entirely by the surviving joint tenants. Under the tenancy in common, there is no right of survivorship, so the heirs of a deceased tenant succeed to his interest. In about half the States there is an estate known as tenancy by the entireties, which is simply a joint tenancy between a husband and wife.

Suppose land is owned by two joint tenants A and B, and that A spends his money to make substantial improvements to the property. Since each joint tenant has the right to use the entire property, B will share equally in the value of the improvements. Thus there is a free rider problem, which will deter A from making efficient improvements. This problem is aggravated the more joint tenants there are. If there are n joint tenants, each tenant must bear the full cost of any improvements he wishes to make, but might be viewed as enjoying only $1/n$ of the benefits. The common law deals with this problem by allowing any joint tenant to obtain a partition of the property into separate, individually owned parcels. In addition, in the event the property is sold, a joint tenant is given credit for any improvements he has made, to the extent they have increased the value of the property.

A similar rule applies to fences and party walls. Suppose owners of adjacent townhouses share a party wall that is badly in need of repair. If they cannot reach an agreement on how to divide the cost of repair, one owner can simply replace the wall and recover one-half the cost from his neighbor. This law enables the parties to overcome the transaction costs of bilateral monopoly (each owner has no alternative to dealing with his neighbor) and the free rider problem.

The conflict between author and publisher

Next we consider whether there is a conflict of interest between the interests of an author and the publisher of the author's book. Under the typical contract between author and publisher, the author receives a royalty equal to a fixed percentage of the publisher's gross revenue, for example 10 percent of total revenue. Once the book has been written, all the costs of printing, binding, distribution, promotion, and sale may be borne by the publisher. Since there is only one seller of a particular book, we can apply the theory of monopoly.

The question is whether there will be a difference of opinion between author and publisher, as to what the retail price of the book should be. Since the author receives a percentage of revenues, he will simply want to maximize total revenue. Putting it differently, since the author's marginal cost is zero, he will maximize profit at the point where marginal revenue is zero. In Figure 5.4, the author would like to choose the level of output q_a, where total revenue (the area under the marginal revenue curve Eq_a0) is maximized. At this point the price of the book, obtained from the demand curve, would be P_a, and the author's profit would be Aq_aE. The publisher, on the other hand, wants to produce at the level where its marginal revenue

Figure 5.4 Conflict between author and publisher.

equals marginal cost. Since the publisher gets 90 percent of total revenue, it would like to choose the level of output q_p, where $(0.9 \times$ marginal revenue$)$ = marginal cost. Here the price will be P_p, and the publisher's profit will be area ABC. Thus it is in the publisher's interest to set a higher price (implying a smaller number of books sold) than the price that would be chosen by the author. Finally, it is important to note that the efficient level of output, where the parties' combined profits will be maximized, is the intermediate point q^*, at which total marginal revenue = marginal cost. At q^* the price is P^*, and the total profit would be area EFC, which could then be divided between the parties.

It should be noted that this conflict of interest is muted by the fact that the parties often expect to have a continuing relationship. A publisher that wishes to obtain subsequent manuscripts from the author will not be inclined to set the price too much above P^*. Note also that there would be no conflict if the author had to bear 10 percent of the costs of publication. In this case the individual profit-maximizing condition for both publisher and author is to set marginal revenue equal to marginal cost, and choose the price P^*. This would maximize the profits of the author, since the point where MR = MC is also the point where $0.10\text{MR} = 0.10\text{MC}$. Many recent publishing contracts have required authors to assist the publisher in promotion of the book, through appearances at bookstores, on radio and television programs, in internet sessions, and in other venues. This trend might be explained in part as an attempt to align the incentives of the parties.

Oil leases

Under the usual terms of an oil lease, the landowner (lessor) receives a fixed royalty for each barrel of oil extracted, while the oil company or developer which is the lessee bears the full cost of drilling wells and extracting the oil and gas. If the market for oil is competitive, the demand curve facing the developer will be horizontal, as in Figure 5.5. If P is the competitive price of oil, and r is the fraction of total revenue paid to the lessor, the developer's marginal and average revenue will be $(P \times (1-r))$. The developer would maximize profit by extracting the amount of oil q_d, where its own marginal revenue equals marginal cost. However, in order to

Figure 5.5 Conflict between lessor and developer.

maximize the parties' joint profit, the developer should extract the larger amount q*.Thus there is a conflict; the landowner will want a greater investment in drilling, e.g., more wells, than the developer. For this reason, most lease agreements for oil and gas contain a "development" clause that requires the lessee to drill a "reasonable," i.e., cost-justified, number of wells.

Now if the landowner had to bear a fraction r of the costs, the developer would receive a share $1 - r$ of the profits, and would have an incentive to maximize total profits by producing q* barrels. The developer would maximize its profits at q* because at this level of output $P = MC$ and $P(1 - r) = MC(1 - r)$. Since this outcome would be efficient, it is natural to ask why the great majority of oil lease agreements give the lessor a share of total revenues, rather than a share of total profits.

Profits equal total revenues minus total costs, which can be divided into total variable costs and total fixed costs. The developer will have many fixed costs that are not allocable to any given oil field – the cost of its corporate headquarters, the salaries of top management, insurance, etc. The share of fixed costs that is assigned to any specific project is a completely arbitrary decision. Moreover, the developer has much better information about both its variable and fixed costs than the lessor. For these reasons, if the lessor is entitled to a share of net profits, the developer will be inclined to minimize its payment to the lessor by overstating the costs that are attributable to this lease. This kind of manipulation is less likely when the payment to the lessor is based on total revenues, which are much easier to measure.

In the production of films, actors, directors, or writers are sometimes promised a percentage of net profits. These agreements often end up in litigation. For example, the actor James Garner was assigned a share of profits of the hit television series *The Rockford Files*, which was on NBC from 1974 to 1980 and then went into off-network sales. Although the show's total revenues from syndication, foreign and other markets exceeded $120 million, the accountant for Universal Studios informed Garner that profits were less than $1 million, and Garner's share was less than $250,000.Garner sued and eventually settled for a reported $5 million.[14] In 1992, the executive producers of the film *Batman* sued the movie studios Polygram and Warner Brothers, alleging that they had received nothing for their 13 percent of net profit points. At the time Batman was the sixth highest-grossing film of all time, with worldwide sales in excess of $600 million. The plaintiffs' lawyer stated that the studios' position was that the film was about \$20 million in the red.[15] There is an old adage that in Hollywood the most creative people are the accountants.

Because of the potential for financial chicanery, compensation is often based on total revenues, rather than profits, notwithstanding the problem of underinvestment by the party who bears the costs. If this problem seems too serious, the parties may base compensation on profits, but define costs in great detail in the contract, so they can be more readily measured and verified. However, this strategy has its own risks. First, there are substantial costs involved in specifying the various costs, and subsequently collecting data on them. Experience may indicate a need for expenditures different from those anticipated at the outset. Some costs (those most difficult to measure) will be ignored or underrepresented, and the operator will be inclined to make excessive (and inefficient) expenditures on expenses that are easily measured and verified.

Compulsory unitization statutes

Most States in which there are substantial reserves of oil and gas have "compulsory unitization" statutes. Under these statutes, owners of separate parcels of land above an oil field can vote to operate the field as under common ownership, upon approval by a substantial majority of the owners, usually two-thirds. Any dissenting owners are bound by this decision. If the field were not unitized, the owners would compete among themselves to extract oil from the common field as rapidly as possible.[16] This competition would lower the fluid pressure, which would reduce the total yield of oil and gas from the field.

If a unanimous vote were required, there would be a problem with holdouts. The compulsory unitization statutes allow the majority owners to achieve a merger.

The conflict between life tenant and remainderman

In the United States and other countries in which the law is based on English common law, outright ownership of land is called ownership in fee simple absolute. It was once common to have ownership divided over time between a life estate and a remainder interest. The owner of a life estate, who is called the life tenant, has the right to exclusive use and possession of the property during his lifetime; upon his death the holder of the remainder interest, known as the remainderman, succeeds to full ownership, that is, he acquires a fee simple absolute. This division of property created a potential conflict between life tenant and remainderman. Suppose, for example, there was timber on the property. A life tenant of advanced years, knowing that he and his heirs would lose all interest in the property upon his death, would have an incentive to cut the timber before it reached mature growth. This was inefficient, in that the value of the property would be maximized by harvesting later.

To make this point more precisely, consider the general problem of when a growing thing, whether plant or animal, should be harvested to maximize the profits of the business. In Appendix 5.1, at the end of this chapter, we show that, for example, a tree should be harvested when the percentage rate of growth in value of the tree equals the prevailing rate of interest. Similarly, a hog should be butchered when its rate of growth equals the rate of interest.

The rate of growth of any living thing declines gradually over time. A tree should be allowed to grow as long as it is growing at a rate greater than the interest rate. Once its growth rate falls below the interest rate, it should be harvested. Intuitively, one maximizes wealth by investing it wherever it yields the highest rate of return. When the tree is growing

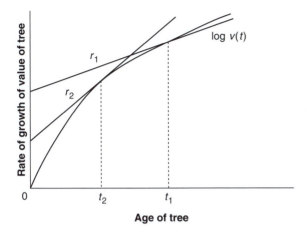

Figure 5.6 When to chop a tree down.

more rapidly than money in a savings account, the owner's wealth should be invested in the form of timber. When the growth rate of the tree falls below the rate of interest, the wealth should be converted from timber into cash, and placed in a savings account. In Figure 5.6, the horizontal axis shows the age of the tree t, while the vertical axis shows the natural logarithm of the value of the tree $v(t)$ at each age. The slope of the line segment r_1 is the rate of interest. The tree should be chopped down at time t_1, when the slope of r_1 equals the slope of log $v(t)$, the rate of growth of the tree. Waiting longer than t_1 to cut the tree down will yield less lumber than cutting it down and planting new trees, which will grow faster than a tree t_1 years old and faster than the interest rate. Note also that if the interest rate increased to r_2, it would be optimal to cut down the tree earlier, at t_2.

Under the common law the rights of life tenant and remainderman were governed by the law of waste, under which the life tenant was limited to a "reasonable" use of the property. Essentially the life tenant was not allowed to reduce the property's market value. For example, the life tenant could operate a mine already on the property, but could not construct a new mine. The specific restrictions imposed on the life tenant varied with the environment and economic conditions. In the United States, where timber was abundant in most parts until the twentieth century, the life tenant was allowed to clear timber, since that would be considered an improvement that would increase the value of the land. In England, however, where timber had become scarce, it would reduce the value of the land, and was accordingly prohibited as waste.

In light of the Coase Theorem, one might ask whether the parties could negotiate a plan for the optimal development of the property. There are some substantial transaction costs, however. Some of the parties may not be identified; the identity of the remaindermen might not be known, or they may be children, who lack the legal capacity to enter into contracts. Even if the life tenant and remainderman are known, the situation is one of bilateral monopoly, and the costs of negotiation may be large.

In modern times the law of waste has been largely superseded by the trust. Under this arrangement the legal title to the property is held by a trustee, who has a fiduciary responsibility to maximize the value of the property for the beneficiaries, who may have life estate and remainder interests. The Uniform Principal and Income Act provides rules to guide trustees in determining whether additions to the trust, such as stock dividends and capital gains, are principal, which goes to the remainderman, or income, which goes to the life tenant. The trust achieves a merger that enables the trustee to manage the property efficiently as a single unit.

Landlord and tenant

A potential conflict like the one between life tenant and remainderman, but more acute, arises in the relationships between the landlord and tenant of real property, or between the owner and renter of personal property. For example, people are not as careful with automobiles they rent as they are with those they own. This is, of course, a case of moral hazard, since the renter, who has the vehicle for only a short time, does not bear the full cost of the wear and tear resulting from his use. Rental companies attempt to minimize this problem by charging fees based on mileage (a rough measure of intensity of use), refusing to rent to drivers who are more likely than others to cause damage (e.g., the young or the very old), requiring a security deposit, and inspecting the vehicles when they are returned. However, these measures do not completely eliminate the problem of substandard care resulting from moral hazard.

In rentals of real property, the tenant does not have the incentive to maintain and improve the property that he would if he were the owner, since the value of any improvements he might make would be lost on the expiration of the lease.[17] Since tenants generally do not maintain a residence as well as an owner would, the premiums for homeowner's insurance on a dwelling, covering risks of fire, theft, storm damage, etc., typically increase when an owner converts his residence to rental property.

The problem of underinvestment by tenants is less serious the longer the term of the lease. Posner (1986) has suggested that for this reason, there is a system of customary tenant rights in Ireland that makes it difficult (costly) for landlords to evict tenants. Economists have a saying that "no one in the history of the world has ever washed a rented car," but cars that are leased for a year or more are often washed.

Landlords generally require a security deposit, to ensure that their property does not depreciate too much during the lease. This practice deters opportunistic behavior on the part of the tenant, but also makes it possible for the landlord, who could refuse to return the deposit by citing trivial flaws even when the property is returned to him in good condition. A tenant who anticipated this type of advantage-taking behavior could hold back his final payment of rent, knowing that the landlord would probably be unable to evict him before the lease expired.

Moral hazard is also relevant to the question whether a tenant has the right to sublet the premises. Often the lease does not allow a tenant to sublet, or to do so only with the landlord's consent, since the tenant would not bear the cost if, for example, the subtenant was noisy and disturbed his neighbors.

Problems when property rights are uncertain

A property rights explanation of increasing oil prices

A clever argument based on the idea of uncertain property rights, and a divergence of interests like that between a life tenant and remainderman, has been made to question the claim that the Organization of Petroleum Exporting Countries (OPEC) was an effective cartel during the 1970s. On January 1, 1973, the price of Saudi Arabian crude oil was $2.12 a barrel.

One year later, the price had increased to $7.61 a barrel, and one year after that, the price was around $10.50. This trend was generally believed to be attributable to the success of a cartel, OPEC, that raised prices by restricting the output of its member countries. However, another explanation was offered by A. D. Johany. Johany (1978) argued that over a period extending from the 1950s to 1973, the international oil companies operating in Middle Eastern countries became increasingly uncertain how long they would be allowed to remain there, and therefore extracted oil far more rapidly than they would have if their property rights had been secure. In the event it turned out that the concerns of the oil companies were well founded; by the end of 1973 they had been taken over or displaced by firms owned and controlled by the host countries. The successor firms had secure property rights, and consequently reduced the rate of extraction to a level consistent with long-run competition. The price level that resulted from this decline in production was naturally higher than the artificially low prices prevailing before 1973, resulting from the much higher rate of extraction by the predecessor oil companies. While this explanation of the change in oil prices during the 1970s is ingenious and elegant, it does not seem to have found much empirical support. Most researchers have concluded that the evidence indicates some sort of market-sharing cartel.[18]

Limits on the disposition of property at death

The cy pres doctrine

A charitable trust is administered in accordance with the wishes of the settlor, and may have perpetual life. Since the use of assets is determined by the specific instructions of an individual who may have died long ago, it often happens that the settlor's "dead hand" requires activity that is no longer legal, practical or efficient because of changed circumstances.

In one case[19] a woman's will left a bequest to the city of Detroit, Michigan, to create a "playfield for white children." The court had to decide whether to modify her gift, to create a playfield for the use of children of all races, or to rule that her gift had failed, so that the bequest would go to her heirs under the will's residuary clause. Under the cy pres doctrine a court may under certain conditions revise the specific terms of a gift that would be illegal or inefficient, to achieve a charitable purpose that falls within the general charitable purpose of the settlor. The term "cy pres" is derived from the French phrase *cy pres comme possible*, meaning "as near as possible."

The basic issue is whether the intentions of the settlor are served better by failure of the gift, or by a modification within the scope of his general intent, that is as near as possible to his expressed wishes. The paramount importance of the settlor's intent is reflected in two rules:

1   The gift will fail if there is a "gift over," i.e., a gift to an alternative recipient, in the event the specific terms of the trust cannot be carried out, or if there is a reverter, i.e., a clause providing that the assets revert to the settlor.
2   The courts will modify the gift, rather than allow it to fail, only if there is evidence of a general charitable purpose on the part of the settlor.

In the Detroit playground case the cy pres doctrine was not applied, and the gift failed. However, many other courts have applied cy pres to remove trust restrictions based on race, religion or sex.[20] For example, the trust under which Rice University was established provided for the instruction of the "white inhabitants of the city of Houston." The court, however, held that the university's trustees should admit all qualified students without regard to race, on the grounds that discrimination on the basis of race would make it impossible for the school to become a university of the first class.[21]

Another case[22] illustrates how cy pres may be applied when the opportunity cost greatly exceeds the benefits of carrying out the specific terms of the trust. There the testator's residuary estate was bequeathed to three Michigan colleges. The will provided that the political science courses taught in these colleges should give primary emphasis to certain specified political and economic theories, and that two books, including *The History of Building the Constitution of the United States*, a political science primer written by the testator, should be distributed to all the students. Testimony by professors of political science at these colleges showed that the obligations that would be imposed on them by the will would infringe on their academic freedom, since the testator's books were poorly written and out of date, presented a philosophy that was viewed with disfavor, and could not be used as textbooks. The court subsequently approved plans proposed by the colleges to use the trust funds differently, but in accordance with the testator's general purpose of promoting education in political science.

Any policy that involved frequent deviation from the specific wishes of the testator would discourage the creation of charitable trusts, and would also promote litigation (rent-seeking behavior) by parties competing for the use of assets of the trust. On the other hand, it is often illegal or inefficient to carry out the instructions of the settlor literally because of changed circumstances. Unless the testator indicates otherwise, by a gift over or reverter, it is reasonable to assume that he would anticipate that his original design might be thwarted by changes in social and economic conditions, and would accept modifications that minimize deviations from the original plan, but still achieve his basic purpose.

The rule against perpetuities

The problem of the "dead hand" arises in another context when a grantor divides his property in a way that allows the property rights of his grantees to be uncertain and subject to contingencies for too long. The common-law rule against perpetuities prevents property rights from being uncertain for an indefinite period. The rule provides that "no interest is valid unless it must vest within twenty-one years after a life in being when the interest was created." Consider a conveyance of land by will "to A, but if liquor is ever served on the premises, then to B or his descendants." If this were upheld, there would be no time limit on the encumbrance in favor of B. The estate might be in A's family for a thousand years, but there would always be in the background the possibility that it would go to B in the event that liquor was served on the property. It is inefficient to have this kind of perpetual uncertainty about property rights, so the conveyance is invalid under the rule against perpetuities.

Suppose the testator instead provided that the property would go to B in the event liquor was served on the premises at any time before a period of 21 years plus the lifetime of the youngest beneficiary of his will. This conveyance would not violate the Rule.

The destructibility of contingent remainders

The same policy against uncertainty about property rights is illustrated by the common-law doctrine of the destructibility of contingent remainders. Under this doctrine, every remainder must vest at or before the termination of the preceding estate, or it will be destroyed. Suppose there is a conveyance from A to B for life, with a remainder to C if C completes his Ph.D. in economics. C has a contingent remainder. If C completes his Ph.D. before B dies, he will have a vested remainder, and upon B's death will take the estate in fee simple. If, however, C is still in graduate school when B dies, the property would revert to A; C's contingent interest would be destroyed under the doctrine of destructibility. If not for this doctrine, the interest could spring back to C whenever he completed his degree, which would make A's property interest very uncertain.

Again the objective is to eliminate excessive uncertainty about property rights. Interests in property that are complete, and not subject to contingencies, can be relied upon and transferred more easily than those that are uncertain.

Ensuring the transferability of land

The rule in Shelley's case

It has been argued that much of the historical development of the English law of real property can be explained by a desire to increase the transferability of property. The law was especially hostile to arrangements that made it impossible for anyone to transfer property, even for a finite period of time. This propensity is illustrated by two rules of property law: the rule in Shelley's case, and the doctrine of worthier title.

The rule in Shelley's case applied if a grantor gave a life estate in real property to A, with a remainder interest to A's heirs. Under the rule, this assignment of interests was invalid; instead A took a fee simple absolute. The problem with the proposed conveyance is that it would not be possible to identify A's heirs until his death; consequently his heirs could not transfer the remainder interest until then. Since at the time of the conveyance no one but A acquired any interest in the property, the common law simply gave A the fee simple, to enable him to transfer the entire property. If not for the rule in Shelley's case, A would be able to convey only a life estate, and the remainder interest would not be transferable until his death.

The doctrine of worthier title

The same principle explains the doctrine of worthier title. This rule applied if a grantor gave a life estate to A, with a remainder to the grantor's heirs. In this case, under the doctrine of worthier title, the grantor, rather than his heirs, owned the remainder and could therefore sell it. Again this rule made the remainder interest transferable; without the rule it would not be possible for anyone to transfer the remainder interest before the death of the grantor.

The widow's forced share

In the States governed by common law, the basic principle concerning marital property rights is that each spouse has separate property, and owns all that he or she earns.[23] In practice, of course, many married couples hold most of their property – real estate, bank accounts, securities, automobiles, and the like – in joint tenancy. In those marriages where property is owned separately, however, there is a possibility that the spouse who owns most of the property could disinherit the other.

Many States therefore have statutes, known as "forced share" statutes, providing that widow cannot be completely disinherited by her husband. The origins of these statutes are t! rights of dower and curtesy recognized by the English common law. Widows were protect from disinheritance by dower, which gave them a life estate in one-third of the husband's inheritable lands. A widower had a corresponding right of curtesy if a child was born of the marriage. Curtesy was a life estate in all of the wife's inheritable land. Dower provided an effective guarantee of financial security for many widows when the most important industry was agriculture, and most wealth was in the form of land. Eventually, however, dower came into disfavor for interfering with the transferability of land. The doctrine was largely abolished by legislation in England in 1833.[24]

In the United States, while dower and curtesy originally became part of the common law of many States, these doctrines were often replaced by statutes providing for a widow's forced share. Under a typical forced-share statute, the surviving spouse was entitled to claim a one-third share of the decedent's entire estate. The rationale behind these statutes, and the common-law right of dower, is that a widow has usually provided valuable household services by raising the children, cooking, doing laundry, etc., and has thereby enabled the husband to acquire his estate. Some portion of the property that has been acquired by her husband over the course of the marriage should be considered to be her contribution.

A number of commentators have called for abolition or revision of forced-share statutes.[25] One criticism is that the widow's right to a fixed share is independent of the duration of the marriage; a spouse of five days clearly has not made the same contribution to the marriage as one of five decades, but has the same forced share. This problem is more serious in modern times, since people now live longer than before and often have more than one marriage. Much of the litigation concerning forced shares involves a dispute between a wife whom the decedent married late in life and children that he had from a previous marriage. One response to this argument is that a spouse may waive her right to a forced share by contract, either during the marriage or by a prenuptial agreement. However, this option may not be exercised because of substantial transaction costs: it is usually necessary to hire a lawyer to draft the waiver, and the husband may be reluctant to raise the issue for fear of offending his wife. Under one reform proposal, the amount the spouse is entitled to would increase during each year of the marriage, up to a maximum of one-half of the husband's estate.

It should also be noted that there are eight States,[26] known as "community property" States, in which the law is derived from the Spanish legal system, rather than from the common law. There are no forced share statutes in these States, since there is no problem of widows being disinherited. In these community property States, each spouse acquires an immediate one-half interest in amounts that the other spouse earns during the marriage.

Finally, it should be noted that, notwithstanding forced-share statutes, there is far more testamentary freedom in the United States than in other major industrial nations. In the major European countries, for example, the children of the decedent have the right to a forced share. In England and the principal nations of the British Commonwealth (the Canadian provinces, the Australian states, New Zealand), there is a statutory scheme known as testator's family maintenance. Under this legislation a chancery judge has broad discretion to modify the decedent's disposition of his property, to provide for his relatives and other dependants.

Appendix 5.1 When should a tree be harvested?

This mathematical appendix will show that, to maximize profits, a farmer should harvest a growing animal or plant at the time when it is growing in value at the rate of interest.

Suppose a tree is planted at time $t = 0$, and grows in value over time. Let $g(t)$ be its value at time t. We will assume that $g'(t) > 0$, i.e., the value of the tree increases over time, and

$g''(t) < 0$, i.e., the rate of growth decreases over time. We want to determine when the farmer should cut down the tree to maximize profits. That is, when should the farmer cut down the tree to maximize the present value of its timber?

If the interest rate, now and in the future, equals r, we can express the discounted present value of the tree, $P(t)$, as follows:

$$P(t) = g(t)e^{-rt}$$

(The reader who is puzzled why we use the expression e^{-rt} should consult Appendix 2.1, which explains how to discount future payments to their present value when compounding is continuous.)

To maximize present value, we take the derivative of $P(t)$ with respect to t, and set it equal to 0.

$$\frac{dp}{dt} = -rg(t)e^{-rt} + e^{-rt}g'(t) = 0$$

$$\Rightarrow -rg(t) + g'(t) = 0$$

$$\Rightarrow \frac{g'(t)}{g(t)} = r$$

The expression on the left-hand side is the percentage rate of growth of the value of the tree at time t. r, the rate of interest, represents the opportunity cost to the farmer of leaving his investment in the form of timber rather than cutting down the tree, selling the wood, and depositing the proceeds in a savings account where it would earn the rate of interest. To maximize profits, the tree should be cut down when the percentage rate of growth of the tree equals the opportunity cost of capital, equal to the rate of interest.

Bibliography

"A.M.A. Debates Plan for Organ Donors," *New York Times*, December 3, 2001, p. A14.

Annotation, "Validity and Effect of Gift for Charitable Purposes which Excludes Otherwise Qualified Beneficiaries because of their Race or Religion," 25 ALR 3d 736.

Blair, Roger D., and David L. Kaserman, "The Economics and Ethics of Alternative Cadaveric Organ Procurement Policies," 8 (2) *Yale Journal on Regulation* 403–452 (summer 1991).

Cones, John W., *How the Movie Wars were Won* (Los Angeles: Rivas Canyon Press, 1977).

Curnutte, Scott A., "Preventing Spousal Disinheritance: An Equitable Solution," 92 *West Virginia Law Review* 441–458 (winter 1989).

Griffin, James M., "OPEC Behavior: A Test of Alternative Hypotheses," 75 (5) *American Economic Review* 954–963 (December 1985).

Johany, Ali D., "OPEC is Not a Cartel: A Property Rights Explanation of the Rise in Crude Oil Prices," unpublished doctoral dissertation, University of California, Santa Barbara (June 1978).

Landes, Elisabeth M., and Richard A. Posner, "The Economics of the Baby Shortage," 7 *Journal of Legal Studies* 323–348 (1978).

Langbein, John H., and Lawrence W. Waggoner, "Redesigning the Spouse's Forced Share," 22 *Real Property, Probate and Trust Journal* 303–321 (1987).

McPherson, Michael A., and Michael L. Nieswiadomy, "African Elephants: The Effect of Property Rights and Political Stability," 18 (1) *Contemporary Economic Policy* 14–26 (January 2000).

Perloff, Jeffrey M., *Microeconomics* (2nd ed., Boston, MA: Addison-Wesley, 2001).

Simmons, Randy T., and Urs P. Kreuter, "Herd Mentality: Banning Ivory Sales is no Way to Save the Elephant," *Policy Review*, fall 1989, pp. 46–49.

Spurr, Stephen J., "The Shortage of Transplantable Organs: An Analysis and a Proposal," 15 (4) *Law and Policy* 355–395 (1993).

Strom, Stephanie, "Giving of Yourself, Literally, to People You've Never Met," *New York Times*, July 27, 2003, p. 3, Sec. 4.

Sunstein, Cass R., and Richard H. Thaler, *Nudge: Improving Decisions about Health, Wealth and Happiness* (New York: Caravan Books, 2008).

Thaler, Richard H., "Opting In vs. Opting Out," *New York Times*, September 27, 2009, p. 6, Sec. 4.

Wines, Michael, "Saving Wildlife in Zambia, and Raising Human Prospects," *New York Times*, June 30, 2007, p. A4.

Problems

1. Most crawfish in Louisiana are on public lands, which are open to anyone who wants to catch crawfish. Show, with a diagram, why there has been overfishing of crawfish in Louisiana. Label and explain each curve in the diagram.
2. What is the justification for statutes providing that a widow is entitled to a forced share upon the death of her spouse? Why have these statutes been criticized?
3. Under the law of waste, a life tenant was not allowed to cut timber before it had achieved mature growth. What is the efficient, value-maximizing rule one should follow in deciding when to cut timber, or when to butcher a hog? Explain why there was a potential conflict between a life tenant and a remainderman.
4. Under the usual contract, the publisher of a book pays all costs of production, and the author receives a percentage of total sales revenues. Would you expect the author to have an opinion different from the publisher on the question of what the price of the book should be? Explain why in detail.
5. Draw a diagram showing the supply and demand of babies for adoption in the United States. Explain why the supply curve has shifted to the left since 1950 (think of all the possible reasons for this shift), and why there is a shortage of babies. How is it decided which couples get the babies that are provided to the adoption agencies?
6. What would be the consequences of allowing a mother to sell an unwanted baby at birth under regulation that would ensure that babies were not purchased for illegal purposes? Compare this scenario to the situation under current law.
7. What factors have brought about the recent increase in the "shortage" or excess demand for transplantable human organs? What methods are used to compete for organs under the current law?
8. People who are opposed to allowing a market for organs often argue that, if there were such a market, "the rich would get all the organs." How could those who support the proposed market for organs answer this argument?

6 Informal creation of property rights

At the beginning of Chapter 4 we encountered an example of a property right created entirely outside the legal system: in Chicago, people who had shoveled snow from a parking place claimed a property right in the space by placing a chair there. In situations where there is no formal law of property, and it becomes apparent that the benefits of having property rights would greatly exceed the costs, it often happens that people create their own informal system of property rights.

For most of recorded history there was no law recognizing property rights in fish, because there was no need for it: the supply of fish in the ocean seemed inexhaustible. In modern times, however, because of increased numbers of fishermen and changes in the technology of fishing, the stock of many species has been seriously depleted. One response to this development has been that many countries have claimed property rights in fish in waters adjacent to their borders.[1] In this section we examine other cases in which people have created property rights and other rules governing their activities.

The Gold Rush

In a study of the California Gold Rush, John Umbeck (1978) has shown how a society can create an efficient system of property rights when no formal body of law is applicable. Before 1846 the land that is now California was governed by Mexican law. From 1846 to 1848 the United States was engaged in a war with Mexico, which was concluded by the signing of a peace treaty on January 31, 1848. Gold was discovered near Sacramento nine days before the peace treaty was signed. Upon execution of the treaty, all the land that was not privately owned legally belonged to the U.S. government; there was no law concerning the right to mine on federally owned land. In any case, there were not enough soldiers in the gold-mining territory to enforce any rules of property law, had there been any. Despite the absence of both law and law enforcement, incidents of physical violence were rare in the goldfields. The miners created and enforced their own system of property rights.

After gold was discovered there was an enormous migration into the gold-mining areas, the population of which grew from about 800 in May 1848 to 264,000 in 1851. The early mining took the gold that was easily available, from the banks of rivers and streams. Later the beds of the rivers were mined. Mining was originally done with a pan. The prospector would wash away the sand and dirt, leaving the much heavier gold ore in the bottom of the pan. In 1848 the cradle was invented. It was a rectangular wooden box set on rockers. After the miner deposited dirt in it, the cradle was simultaneously rocked and washed with water, so that the dirt flowed through while the heavier gold was trapped by cleats or riffles on the bottom.

With the arrival of hundreds of newcomers each week, the miners found it expedient to form groups that would each claim an area of land, called a mining district. Individuals who were not in the group were excluded from mining in this area. Within each group the miners entered into an agreement that specified how the work would be done, and how the gold would be divided among the members. Two general types of agreement were used: the sharing contract and the land allotment contract.

Under the sharing contract, each miner in the group agreed to work a certain number of hours per day. At the end of each day, all the gold collected by the members was deposited into a common pool. It was then measured, and divided among the members of the group according to a specified formula, usually an equal share for each member.

Under the land allotment contract, however, each individual in the group was assigned a separate parcel of land within the mining district. Each miner got to keep all the gold he extracted from his own parcel. This contract had certain standard features that enabled the land to be used efficiently: the parcel allotted to a member could be sold, and would be forfeited to the group if it were not mined for a specified period, usually five days.

It is instructive to compare the costs and benefits of each type of contract. The costs of a sharing contract include the costs of reaching an agreement, the costs of enforcing the work requirements of the members, and of measuring and distributing the gold. The benefits of a sharing contract include the gain to the group from cooperation in the mining enterprise and the sharing of risk. With respect to the benefits of cooperation, members often built a dam and diverted the river to a ditch parallel to the river, so that the river bed could be mined more effectively. This type of cooperation was less likely to occur under the land allotment contract.

The invention of the cradle reduced the costs of enforcing the sharing contract. All other activities of the group were halted while the cradle was being emptied. All the miners washed dirt from the gold with a pan, so it was easy for each miner to watch the others, to ensure that the gold was divided in accordance with the agreement.

Under the land allotment contract, there is no cost of enforcing a work requirement, since each miner has no interest in the level of effort made by others in the group. On the other hand, the risk of mining is not shared with others in the group.

It is important to note that the costs of enforcing the sharing contract increase with the size of the group. As the group becomes larger, each miner has a greater incentive to shirk his work responsibilities and to cheat the group. Suppose the value to the individual of taking a day off from work is $50, and that, on average, a full day of work will yield gold worth $200. If the group has two members, the cost to the individual miner of taking a day off is $(1/2) \times 200 - 50 = \$50$. If, however, the group has twenty members, the cost to him is $(1/20) \times 200 - 50 = -40$, i.e., there is a net benefit to him of $40. In addition, if the group has two members, and a miner finds a gold nugget worth $100, the benefit of concealing his discovery from his partner is $\$100 - (1/2) \times 100 = \$50$. If, however, the group has twenty members, the benefit of concealing it is $\$100 - (1/20) \times 100 = \$95$. The greater benefit of shirking and cheating under the sharing contract when the size of the group increases makes it necessary to monitor individuals more closely.

With thousands of new prospectors arriving each week, the miners already in the gold-mining territory found it necessary to increase the size of their groups, so that the group would be large enough to keep outsiders off its land. Historically, the first contracts were virtually all sharing contracts, with groups ranging in size from two to eight members. These groups later expanded to a size of about sixteen. It appears that this was about the maximum feasible number for a group with a sharing contract. Evidence of this limitation is provided in records indicating that along one river there were nine different groups with sharing contracts, each of which constructed a separate dam and separate ditch. Despite the obvious economies of scale, these groups did not merge into one large group, to build one dam and one long ditch.

Eventually, with the enormous population influx, it became necessary for a group to have more than sixteen members. The sharing contract was then replaced by the land allotment contract.

Sharecropping contracts

Umbeck's analysis of contracts used in the gold rush is in many ways similar to a classic study by Steven Cheung of agricultural contracts used in China and Southeast Asia. Three different types of contracts were made between the landowners and tenant farmers: the fixed-rent contract, the wage contract, and the sharecropping contract, under which the landowner received a specified proportion of the crop grown by the tenant. Cheung observed that of the three contract types, the costs of negotiation were highest for the sharecropping contract, since the parties had to agree on matters such as the land to be cultivated, the materials to be supplied by the tenant and the owner, and many other details. The share contract was also the most costly to enforce, since the landowner had to learn the amount of the crop harvested by the tenant before he could determine the amount he was entitled to.

Given that the share contract involves greater transactions costs than the other two contracts, the question arises why it was used at all. Cheung noted that there is considerable variability of output in agriculture because of unpredictable factors like weather and the infestation of pests. Under a fixed-rent contract, the tenant bears almost all the risk of this variation of output. Under a wage contract, the landowner bears almost all the risk. Under a share contract, however, the risk is divided between landowner and tenant. This feature could be valuable to the parties if each of them were risk-averse. Cheung concluded that a sharecropping contract would be chosen if the higher transactions costs of this type of contract were outweighed by the benefits of risk sharing by the landlord and tenant. Cheung's analysis is supported by empirical evidence from Taiwan indicating that sharecropping is more prevalent in wheat farming than in rice, given that there is much greater variability in wheat than in rice.

Whaling customs

Robert Ellickson (1989) has argued that people are more likely to develop norms or customs that are wealth-maximizing when they live in a close-knit community. He supports this hypothesis with a close analysis of rules concerning property rights in whales, developed in the U.S. and British whaling industries between 1750 and 1870. Whalers were a close-knit social group. American whalers were concentrated in a few ports in southern New England, especially Nantucket and New Bedford. The rules developed by whalers actually became law; in all the reported judicial decisions involving a dispute over ownership of a whale, the court decided the case by applying the whalers' local custom.

Ellickson examines the two major rules prevailing during that period: the "fast fish" rule and the rule that "the iron holds the whale." Under the fast-fish rule, a claimant owned a whale, whether it was dead or alive, so long as it was fastened by a line to the claimant's boat. If the whale happened to break free from the line, it was considered a loose fish that was fair game for all takers. This rule, which was applied by British whaling vessels operating in the Greenland fishery, was well suited to the right whale, which was the most important commercial species in that region. Right whales are relatively slow and mild-mannered, and were not likely to break loose from a harpoon line. The fast-fish rule was a clear, unambiguous rule that was optimal for these conditions.

The alternative rule, the-iron-holds-the-whale, gave exclusive ownership to the first whaling vessel that affixed a harpoon or other whaling craft to the whale. This rule differed from the fast-fish rule in that the iron did not have to remain fastened to the boat that had fixed it in the whale as long as that boat remained in fresh pursuit. The rule was applied to whales who had been harpooned with a line with a drogue at the end. The drogue, a device originally used by Native Americans, was a wooden float attached to the trailing end of a line connected to a harpoon. After the whale was harpooned, the drogue was thrown overboard by the crew. The drogue served both to mark the position of the whale, and to tire it out as the whale dragged it around.

The iron-holds-the-whale rule, which was applied in New England waters, was well suited to sperm whales, the most important species in that region. Sperm whales swim faster, dive deeper, and resist capture much more violently than right whales. If a whaling boat attempted to hold a line to a sperm whale, the whale was likely to capsize the boat, or break the line by force or by sounding to a great depth. Since the boat that first struck the whale was not likely to be able to hold it, application of the fast-fish rule would have substantially reduced the incentive to make the first strike. The iron-holds-the-whale rule provided an incentive to whalers to take this action, which was the most important step toward capturing the whale. Moreover, sperm whales often travelled in schools, and the iron-holds-the-whale rule gave boats an incentive to kill or mortally wound as many whales as possible without stopping to attach their carcasses to the boat. The iron-holds-the-whale rule was efficient in that it enabled whalers to maximize the total catch. This rule was more ambiguous than the fast-fish rule, since it might require a determination of whether a boat had remained in fresh pursuit or had abandoned the chase. However the greater administrative costs of the rule were outweighed by its benefit of facilitating the efficient harvesting of the whales.

In some situations whaling customs called for a division of the whale between the boat that made the first strike and the ultimate taker. Ellickson cites an English decision holding that a sperm whale taken in a fishery around the Galapagos Islands should be divided, in accordance with the local custom, equally between the boat that first harpooned it and the boat that subsequently recovered the carcass. On the other hand, a decision involving a finback whale, citing a custom in eastern Cape Cod, held that a beached whale recovered by a stranger should be awarded to the boat that had struck the whale with a bomb-lance, on condition that the stranger be paid "reasonable salvage." Compared with the fifty–fifty split, this rule had the virtue of providing better incentives, by rewarding claimants according to their relative marginal product, but had the disadvantage of requiring a case-by-case determination of the contributions made by each party.

The division of profits in law firms

A similar tradeoff between transaction costs and the incentive effect of basing rewards on productivity arises in large law firms. Gilson and Mnookin (1985) found that there were two alternative methods of dividing profits among partners in large New York City and Washington law firms. One method was essentially an equal division of profits. After *n* years as a partner, each individual received the same percentage share of profits (a "full share"). Before reaching that point, a partner's share increased each year, but was determined entirely by the number of years he had been a partner; thus there was a lockstep progression toward a full share.

The other method was to divide profits among partners according to their individual productivity. However, measuring lawyer productivity involves substantial transaction costs, since it requires consideration of the number of hours worked, the lawyer's generation of clients, and his participation in firm management. Many firms try to simplify the process by using formulas, but formulas give lawyers an incentive to maximize the factors used in the formula, rather than maximizing their own productivity. For example, a formula based only on the number of hours billed ignores the fact that some lawyers complete tasks more quickly than others, without any sacrifice in quality. Thus a lawyer who does work more efficiently than others is in effect penalized for his efficiency. Moreover, measuring productivity solely by the number of hours billed would provide no rewards for a partner's efforts to attract clients to the law firm, or for time spent managing the firm. Clearly, however, these activities are vital to the firm's prosperity.

Suppose, then, the law firm gives the partner who brings in a client a one-time bonus at the time the client first retains the firm. The problem with this arrangement is that it gives the partner no incentive to keep the client satisfied in the future, or to obtain additional business from that client. The law firm could avoid this problem by making periodic payments to the lawyer who brings the client in, determined by the volume of work provided by the client. This scheme has its own pitfalls, however. Suppose another partner begins to work for the client, and the client, pleased by his services, provides more business to the law firm. The issue then arises as to who should get credit for this business – the partner who originally brought the client in, or the partner whose good work induced the client to provide the additional business. It is noteworthy that in law firms that reward partners for generating business, there are often complaints that partners "hoard" to themselves the clients they bring in, rather than allowing other partners to work for them.[2]

A similar problem arises in universities, when a department's budget, and the number of faculty members it is allowed to hire, are determined primarily by the number of students enrolled in courses offered by the department. Under these conditions faculty members have an incentive to encourage students to take courses in their department, rather than cognate courses in other departments. For example, a political science department might steer its majors toward additional courses in political science rather than courses in economics which could be quite useful in analyzing issues in political science.

Given the perverse incentives that may result from a formula designed to measure a lawyer's productivity, the equal division of profits, or the lockstep progression toward a full share, does not look so bad. The great virtue of this method is its administrative simplicity. The disadvantage is its deviation from productivity: it does not penalize shirking, and a partner who is much more productive than average might become dissatisfied and leave the firm. The advantage of the alternative approach, using a formula based on marginal productivity, is that the compensation scheme, in principle, should provide a better incentive. The disadvantage is the associated transaction costs: either there are distortions in behavior resulting from use of a rigid formula, or costs of haggling involved in arriving at individualized determinations of productivity, and potential ill will generated by that process. The fact that both these methods have been used by major law firms indicates that the administrative convenience of the first method is approximately offset by its dilution of incentives.

The Shakers

Another example of the problems arising from equal distribution of profits is afforded by the history of an American religious sect, the Shakers.[3] The Shakers were a communal religious group that held property in common, provided food, clothing, and shelter to their members in equal shares, and practiced celibacy. Members of the early Shaker communities, who called themselves "Believers," were highly literate, productive, and prosperous. During the period from 1774 to about 1850, they had considerable commercial success with products such as garden seeds, patent medicines, baskets, bonnets, and chairs. During this same period the Society grew from 12 Believers to almost 4,000 in 1850, despite their practice of celibacy. However, after the middle of the nineteenth century the membership of this sect began to decline, and one Shaker community after another disbanded. Today there is one remaining Shaker community, in Maine.

The conventional wisdom was that their numbers declined because of celibacy and the general decline of evangelical religious groups in the postbellum United States. However Murray (1995) shows that their attrition cannot be explained by such factors, and that it was in fact attributable to the free-rider problem and adverse selection. Since a Shaker received the average product of the Shaker community, rather than his own marginal product, joining the sect yielded an economic benefit to those with relatively little human capital, i.e., those who were relatively unproductive, with few outside opportunities.

From Shaker documents Murray was able to determine the number of literate members in a community by whether an individual signed his name or instead left a mark. A member's literacy was a reasonably good indication of his educational level and the extent of his human capital. Murray found that after the period of the Shakers' initial prosperity, an increasing proportion of those who joined the sect were illiterate, with little human capital or material wealth; these entrants were sometimes derided as "winter Shakers" or "bread and butter" Shakers, and their religious commitment was questioned. However, the Shakers did not turn away these applicants, since their religious objective was to offer potential salvation to as many people as possible. An additional, and related, problem was that those who chose to leave the sect tended increasingly to be from the ranks of the literate, highly productive members. Eventually Shaker communities became less literate than the surrounding population. These trends inevitably led to a drastic decline in the overall membership of the Shakers.

Bibliography

Becker, Gary, "Crime and Punishment: An Economic Approach," 76 (2) *Journal of Political Economy* 169–217 (1968).

Biblowit, C., "International Law and the Allocation of Property Rights in Common Resources," 4 *New York International Law Review* 273–292 (1991).

Cheung, Steven N. S., "Transaction Costs, Risk Aversion, and the Choice of Contractual Arrangements," 12 *Journal of Law and Economics* 23 (1969).

Cheung, Steven N. S., *The Theory of Share Tenancy* (Chicago: University of Chicago Press, 1969).

Dales, John Harkness, *Pollution, Property and Prices: An Essay in Policy-making and Economics* (Toronto: University of Toronto Press, 1968).

Eckert, R. D., *The Enclosure of Ocean Resources: Economics and the Law of the Sea* (Stanford, CA: Hoover Institution, 1979).

Ellickson, Robert C., "A Hypothesis of Wealth-maximizing Norms: Evidence from the Whaling Industry," 5 (1) *Journal of Law, Economics and Organization* 83–97 (spring 1989).

Gilson, Ronald J., and Robert H. Mnookin, "Sharing among the Human Capitalists: An Economic Inquiry into the Corporate Law Firm and how Partners Split Profits," 37 *Stanford Law Review* 313–397 (January 1985).

Griffin, James M., "OPEC Behavior: A Test of Alternative Hypotheses," 75 *American Economic Review* 954–963 (December 1985).

Kaplow, Louis, and Steven Shavell, "Economic Analysis of Law," in Alan J. Auerbach and Martin Feldstein, eds., *Handbook of Public Economics*, Vol. 3 (Amsterdam: Elsevier, 2002).

Lipsey, R. G., and K. J. Lancaster, "The General Theory of the Second Best," 24 *Review of Economic Studies* 11–32 (1956–57).

Murray, John E., "Human Capital in Religious Communes: Literacy and Selection of Nineteenth Century Shakers," 32 *Explorations in Economic History* 217–235 (1995).

Umbeck, John, "A Theory of Contract Choice and the California Gold Rush," 20 *Journal of Law and Economics* 421 (1978).

Problems

1. What are the two leading rules concerning the ownership of harvested whales that were followed in the whaling industry during the period from 1750 to 1870? How well suited was each rule to the hunting of (*a*) sperm whales, or (*b*) right whales? Consider also the two main alternative methods used to divide profits among the partners in large law firms. What are the advantages and disadvantages of each method?

2. The Shakers were a communal religious group that held property in common, distributed goods to their members in equal shares, and practiced celibacy. Explain why the numbers of the Shakers declined during the period from 1850 to the present.

7   The law of contracts

What exactly is a contract? One attempt at a definition is "a contract is a promise enforceable at law directly or indirectly." This definition is, however, flawed, since a contract may, and usually does, involve more than one promise; generally there are many interrelated and conditional promises in a contract. Another proposed definition is "a contract is an agreement enforceable at law." This is, however, too narrow, since the term "agreement" doesn't really fit unilateral contracts, like a reward for a lost dog.

Arthur L. Corbin, whose entire life was devoted to the study of contracts, stated that the word "contract" is used to mean three different things: "(1) the series of operative acts of the parties expressing their assent, (2) a physical document executed by the parties, and (3) the legal relations resulting from the operative acts of the parties." Finally, the Uniform Commercial Code states that "'contract' means the total obligation in law which results from the parties' agreement as affected by this Act and any other applicable rules of law."

Of course, none of these definitions tells us what kinds of actions by the parties will create legally binding rights and duties. We will consider this issue in the first part of this chapter, which concerns the formation of contracts. This part considers the economic function of the rule that a promise, to be enforceable, must be supported by "consideration"; the requirement that there be an "offer" and an "acceptance"; whether there is a contract when there has been a unilateral or mutual mistake; unilateral contracts such as rewards; and implied contracts.

The next section of this chapter considers various issues concerning the validity and enforceability of contracts: procedural and substantive unconscionability; the economic function of the "holder in due course" rule, a rule that has been challenged as unconscionable; the controversy concerning the widespread use of standard form contracts; issues concerning allocation of risk; and the doctrines of impossibility and frustration of purpose.

The last part of the chapter considers issues arising when a party has not kept the promises it made in the contract; this is known as a "breach" of contract. We examine the remedies for breach available to the injured party, money damages, and specific performance. We review the alternative measures of money damages, i.e., the expectation, reliance, and restitution measures; the rule that the breaching party is liable only for foreseeable consequences of the breach; that the plaintiff must mitigate his damages; appropriate damages for lost profits and the problem of the "expansible seller"; the prohibition of penalties, and the distinction between a penalty and liquidated damages.

The economic functions of the law of contracts

The basic purpose of the law of contracts is to maximize the net benefits of exchange. Contract law allows us to make binding, and therefore credible, legal commitments. Consider what would happen if there were no law of contracts. A may wish to hire B, a contractor, to construct an office building, a job that will take several months and require the use of materials and labor costing millions of dollars. If there were no law of contracts, there is the possibility that once B's work was completed, A would simply refuse the pay him the amount that was agreed upon. Consequently B may decide not to take the job, an outcome that is inefficient, since the value to A of the office building would greatly exceed the cost of materials and labor that would be incurred by B. If, however, there is a law of contracts, B will accept the job, knowing that he can rely on an enforceable legal claim against A.

Another important function of the law of contracts is to provide normal or "default" terms for an incomplete agreement. Mr. A may buy milk at the local grocery without saying a word to any of the store's employees; he may simply take the milk to the counter, and pay the clerk when he learns the price. When he performs this action, however, whether he knows it or not, he has entered into a contract with the grocery that has exceedingly detailed rules for any conceivable contingency, all provided by the law of contracts. For example, this body of law will specify the remedies available to him if on returning home, he learns the milk is spoiled. The precise terms of the complete contract made between Mr. A and the grocery, if put in written form, would require thousands of pages. The law of contracts expedites efficient transactions, by enabling the parties to avoid the costs of negotiating all the myriad terms of a complete agreement.

An optimal law of contracts will maximize the net benefits of exchange. Suppose, for example, A agrees to buy B's house for a given price. Two days before B is to deliver possession of the house to A, the house burns down. If the contract between A and B does not specify who shall bear the loss, it will be borne by B. It is efficient to assign the risk of loss to B, since before A gains possession B can prevent this loss at a lower cost than A could. Thus the law of contracts promotes efficient behavior, and the efficient use of resources.

As a final example, consider the Statute of Frauds. This statute, which was enacted by the English parliament in 1677, is the basis of modern state statutes of the same name which require that certain kinds of agreements must be in writing to be enforceable. While these statutes vary somewhat from state to state, many of them require a written agreement for (1) contracts to sell real property, (2) contracts for the sale of goods for $500 or more, (3) contracts to assume the obligation of another, (4) contracts not to be performed within the lifetime of the promisor, and (5) contracts that will not be performed within one year from the time the contract is made. If these types of agreements were not required to be in writing, there would be a high probability of either fraud or disagreement about the terms of the contract, resulting from an original misunderstanding or different recollections of what was agreed to. Since these contracts generally involve property of substantial value, there is little harm in compelling parties to invest the time required to commit their agreement to writing; few transactions will be discouraged by this requirement.

The benefits of the Statute of Frauds – reduction of fraud, conflict, and litigation – outweigh the costs – the time cost required to write things down, and the risk that, occasionally, verbal agreements that were made by the parties in good faith will not be enforced. Moreover, contract law seeks to minimize even these costs by accepting a writing that is minimal, and by exempting oral agreements from the Statute of Frauds when there is independent evidence that there was a valid agreement. Thus, for example, an oral contract that would otherwise be subject to the statute will be enforced if there has been partial performance, or when one of the parties admits that a contract was made. Still, one consequence of the Statute of Frauds is that some people will be able to renege on promises they made in a valid agreement. The law accepts this cost, because it is believed to be less than the benefits of the statute – avoiding fraud, or disagreement about the terms of the contract resulting from the lack of a written document that can be consulted.

General rules of contract law

The requirement of consideration

One rule is that a promise is not enforceable as a contract unless the party to whom the promise was made has provided some "consideration," i.e., something of value. The effect of the requirement of consideration is to deny that there is an enforceable contract in two types of cases:

1   Cases in which the parties intended to reach an agreement, but the contract is seriously incomplete, or too vague to be enforced. For example, suppose A has agreed in principle to sell his house to B, but A and B have not yet agreed on a price. In such a case the court will find that there is no "consideration," and therefore no enforceable contract. This is appropriate, since otherwise the court itself would have to decide on a price, a task for which it is not well suited. The courts do not have enough information to determine a price that exceeds the value of the house to the owner, and is also less than the value of the house to the prospective buyer. Since the courts are at an informational disadvantage compared to the parties, they should not attempt to make decisions for the parties.
2   Cases where there is only a "gratuitous promise" to confer a benefit on someone. Suppose A, a wealthy individual, offers to send B to an expensive college. Later, after he suffers unexpected financial reverses, A reneges on his promise. A's offer is likely to be considered a "gratuitous promise" that is not supported by consideration and is therefore not enforceable. If people who made spontaneous, gratuitous offers of assistance were always compelled to make good on their promises, they would be less inclined to offer assistance, or would always have to state that they did not intend their offer to be legally binding.

There is an exception to rule 2 when there has been "detrimental reliance" by the person to whom the promise was made. Suppose B, relying on A's promise, quit his job and took several summer school courses to prepare for college. The court might well view B's actions as detrimental reliance which can supply consideration, and make A's promise legally binding. In this case A's promise induced detrimental reliance by B, so that B would incur a large cost if A did not make good on his promise.

   With regard to the issue of consideration, it should be noted that courts decide only whether there is consideration (in which case there is an enforceable contract), not whether the consideration is valuable enough for there to be a valid contract. Otherwise the courts would have to delve into all the terms of the contract to decide whether it is "fair" or "reasonable." This is something the court should not do, since it has less information than the parties about the value of the agreement to each party.

The requirement of offer and acceptance

Another general rule is that there is no valid contract unless there is both an offer and an acceptance that matches the terms of the offer. If A offers to sell his car to B for $20,000, there is no contract unless B accepts that offer. If B responds by offering to buy the car for

$19,000, that response would be considered a counter-offer rather than an acceptance. A could then respond either by accepting B's counter-offer, or by making another counter-offer, e.g., offering to sell the car for $19,500. We will see, however, that these formal rules are not especially useful in predicting whether there is a valid contract. We will examine several cases which show that the courts have in effect used a cost–benefit analysis that promotes efficiency, in deciding whether an agreement is an enforceable contract.

The question whether there has been an acceptance arises when there is a unilateral contract. Suppose A offers a reward of $50 for the return of his lost dog. When B returns the dog, is he legally entitled to the reward? Here there has been no explicit acceptance of A's offer. However, if B knows of the reward his performance in accordance with its terms would generally be treated as an acceptance. Most courts would require that B know about the offer to be able to claim the reward; the formal justification is that one must have knowledge of an offer in order to accept it. The economic rationale for treating the finder's performance as an acceptance is that it is not feasible (i.e., it is too costly) for the dog's owner to negotiate with every person who might possibly find the dog. An enforceable contract provides a method of overcoming these costs of negotiating with potential finders. It may be reasonable to require that the finder have knowledge of the reward, since otherwise the reward cannot have any incentive effect.

Implied contracts

Another way that transactions costs are overcome is with the doctrine of "implied contract." Suppose a customer in a restaurant begins to choke on a chicken bone, and a physician who was sitting at the next table performs an emergency tracheotomy to save the customer's life. Under the doctrine of implied contract the physician has an enforceable right to be compensated by the customer for his professional services. Under the circumstances it was not feasible for the parties to enter into an agreement, via an offer and acceptance, before the services were performed. Since there is a great benefit from having a contract in this situation, the law provides one.

On the other hand, suppose that without any previous communication, A Co. mails B a set of personalized return address labels, with B's name and address. B is delighted to receive them, and subsequently attaches these labels to many letters he mails. B is, however, not liable for any payment to A Co. In this case there are costs of imputing a contract – the costs of determining appropriate terms of the agreement, the cost of the risk that the payment decided on exceeds the value of the performance to the party who is held liable – but in contrast to the previous example, there are no offsetting benefits to doing so, so the courts will not impose a contract on the parties.

Unilateral mistake and the duty of disclosure

In some instances the courts will hold that a contract has been made even though the acceptance does not exactly match the offer. These cases involve the issue of whether there has been "mutual assent" when there is a mistake by only one party – a "unilateral mistake." Suppose A offers to buy B's car for $5,000, but the secretary who types A's letter makes a clerical error, so there is an apparent offer of $6,000. Here the parties might not have reached an agreement at all if their communications had been accurate; the car might have been worth $5,500 to B, but only $5,000 to A. Nonetheless the court may decide to enforce this contract of sale for $6,000. A misunderstanding is like an accident.

When there is a misunderstanding, the question is which party could have avoided it at a lower cost; that party should bear the loss. Here A, the buyer, could have avoided the misunderstanding at a lower cost, by proofreading his own letter. If A is held liable, he will be more careful to avoid such mistakes in the future. Courts are generally reluctant to excuse a promisor who has made a mistake, since he is generally in a better position than the other party to prevent his own error. A subsidiary theme is that someone who changed his mind could always claim that his secretary made a clerical error, so that his offer was invalid. One important function of contract law is to hold people to their promises.

Suppose, however, that A's secretary had inadvertently typed an additional zero, so that A's letter offered to buy the car for $50,000. In this case it should be apparent to B that A's letter contains a clerical error. Consequently, it is likely that A would be permitted to withdraw his offer. Again the issue is which party can avoid (or correct) the mistake at lower cost. Here at first A, the bidder, could avoid the mistake at less cost by being more careful. Later, however, B can prevent the misunderstanding at lower cost because he knows that there has been a mistake. Consequently the loss should be imposed on B, i.e., A should be allowed to rescind his offer. The rule of these cases, therefore, bears a striking resemblance to the rule of last clear chance in the law of negligence.

It is instructive to compare cases on unilateral mistake with those concerning fraud and the duty of disclosure. The fraud cases differ from the cases on unilateral mistake because in the fraud cases, one party knows that the other party is uninformed or mistaken about something, and does not give that party the accurate information. The issue then is whether the party who entered into the contract without the correct information can avoid the contract on the ground that he was owed a duty of disclosure. It turns out that the uninformed party is released from the contract in some cases, but not in others.

The case of Laidlaw v. Organ[1] involved a contract for the sale of tobacco. Organ, the buyer, knew that a peace treaty ending the War of 1812 had been signed, an event that caused the market price of tobacco in Louisiana to increase by approximately 50 percent. (The end of hostilities made it possible for sellers to reach many consumers to whom they did not previously have access, in effect causing the demand curve to shift up and to the right.) Organ did not inform Laidlaw that the war had ended, and in those days, before the invention of the telegraph, telephone, and broadcast media, it could take considerable time for such news to be disseminated. The U.S. Supreme Court stated, in dictum, that Organ was not obliged to disclose this information, since it was equally available to both the parties. Anthony Kronman has suggested a distinction based on whether the individual who has the vital information has obtained it by a deliberate, methodical search, or instead has acquired it casually or accidentally. If the buyer in the Laidlaw case learned of the treaty through a costly process of research, a disclosure requirement would deprive him of the benefit of that information, and deter him from making similar investments in the future. A seller would also have little incentive to do research, since he could obtain the information from the buyer without cost. Putting it differently, the seller would find it advantageous to free ride off the buyer's costly search. The net effect is that no one would have an incentive to do research. This is inefficient since this type of information is socially valuable; it enables the economy to respond quickly to changes in the value of resources. Farmers who learn about the peace agreement can adapt quickly by planting tobacco instead of another crop; this will lower the price to smokers.

We may conclude that disclosure should not be required in situations where it is likely that the information is generated at a cost, rather than casually discovered. We will see that the same analysis applies to the rule protecting attorney work product and to takeovers of corporations. Finally, note that there is no social cost when someone who acquires information accidentally is required to disclose it; this will not discourage investments in information. For example, when there is an obvious clerical error in a buyer's bid, the seller's knowledge of the error is not the fruit of a deliberate search. Accordingly there is no compelling reason to allow the seller to benefit from that information.

Mutual mistake

Sometimes both the parties are mistaken about the subject matter of the contract. Such cases fall under the heading of "mutual mistake." Sherwood v. Walker[2] involved the sale of a cow. Both the buyer and seller believed the cow was barren. In fact the cow was pregnant, and therefore was worth roughly ten times the price specified in the contract. The seller discovered the cow's condition before delivering the cow to the buyer, and then refused to perform. The court upheld the cancellation of the sale.

Contracts often fail to specify how to deal with various contingencies that may arise. As a general rule, the loss should be borne by the party who could have avoided it at lower cost. When there is a mutual mistake involving the sale of property, the owner is usually in a better position than the buyer to know the characteristics of what he is selling. Accordingly, it is usually reasonable to impose the loss on the seller. Thus if a contract for the sale of a house does not specify who is liable for a defect, the seller is liable so long as the defect is "latent," i.e., not obvious.

Suppose the cow was worth $4,000 as beef, but was sold for $5,000. In this case the courts are apt to uphold the sale on the ground that the premium appears to reflect the expected value of a low probability event, namely that the cow is pregnant. A pregnant cow might be worth an additional $20,000, but the probability of this contingency might be only five percent, for an expected value of $1,000. Clearly the buyer has paid for this possibility.

Suppose that the unexpected event is not an increase in value of the property, but rather a decrease. For example, in the sale of a cow both parties believe it is fertile, but it later turns out to be barren. Here again the loss should normally be imposed on the seller; that will be achieved by allowing the buyer to rescind.

Impossibility and related doctrines

Sometimes the parties learn that it will be impossible to perform a contract. In that case, who should bear the resulting loss? In many situations in contract or tort law a loss can be avoided – that is, the cost of preventing or avoiding the loss is small compared to the loss itself. In other situations, however, the loss cannot be prevented – that is, the cost of avoiding or preventing the loss is so large that it exceeds the loss itself. Nonetheless, in these cases, the loss can still be insured. When there is a loss resulting from nonperformance of a contract, the contract may specify who is to bear the loss. If, however, the contract is silent or unclear on this point, the matter is resolved by the doctrines of impossibility, impracticability, and frustration of purpose.

The general principle underlying these doctrines is that the loss should be imposed on the party who can insure at lower cost. To decide this issue, we must consider:

1   *Measurement costs*: each party's ability to estimate both the probability of loss, and the amount of any loss that occurs.
2   *Transaction costs*: a party's ability to pool the risk of loss with other risks, to reduce or eliminate that risk.

Generally, a party is excused from performance in the event of death; that is, the party's estate will not be liable for breach of contract. Thus a singer who has an engagement to perform is not liable to the concert hall if she dies before the concert. In this case both parties have the same ability to predict the event that causes the loss (death), but the concert hall can probably insure more cheaply, since it has a better idea of the amount of the loss if the singer cannot perform. If, however, the singer knew that she had a terminal illness, but did not inform the concert hall, her estate would be liable, since then she would have an advantage in estimating the probability of loss, i.e., a lower measurement cost.

Suppose a firm enters into a contract to drill a well for water on someone's land, and the cost of drilling turns out to be prohibitive because of soil conditions. If the contract does not specify who is liable, the contractor would be. He can probably insure at lower cost than the landowner for two reasons: (1) he has an advantage in terms of measurement costs, since he knows better the likelihood that he will encounter adverse soil conditions; and (2) he has lower transaction costs. He is in a better position to self-insure, since he has contracts to drill wells in many different areas.

Sometimes performance of the contract becomes impossible for legal reasons, rather than because of physical conditions. Before the United States entered World War II, a railroad had entered into a contract to carry copra (dried coconut meat, which is the source of coconut oil) that was intended for export to the government of Norway. After Japan attacked Pearl Harbor, the U.S. government ordered the railroad to carry wood instead of copra. A court held that the railroad was excused from the contract.[3] In this case the railroad had no advantage over the promisee in terms of ability to predict the occurrence of war, or the amount of the loss to the promisee.

In some situations performance of the contract is physically possible, but would no longer serve its essential purpose. Cases of this kind fall under the heading of "frustration of purpose." In London a parade was planned for June 1902 in connection with the coronation of Edward VII. Many property owners along the parade route rented rooms for the day to persons who wanted to observe the parade. It turned out, however, that the parade was postponed because of illness in the royal family. Many of those who had rented rooms refused to pay, and some of the property owners brought an action to enforce the contract. The court held that these contracts could not be enforced because their purpose had been destroyed by postponement of the parade.[4] Here it is likely that neither party to the contract – property owner or renter – was in a better position to predict that the parade would be postponed, but the property owner was probably better able to insure the loss, since he could pool this kind of risk, by renting his rooms out for many other events throughout the rest of the year.

It is important to bear in mind that the doctrines of impossibility, impracticability, and frustration of purpose come into play only when the contract does not make an explicit assignment of risk to one of the parties. During the late 1960s and early 1970s Westinghouse Electric Company sold nuclear reactors and fuel systems to various electric utilities. Many of these customers were concerned as to whether uranium fuel for these reactors would be available in the future. Accordingly Westinghouse offered to supply uranium to its customers at a fixed base price which allowed for some escalation. By 1975, however, Westinghouse found that its commitments to supply uranium greatly exceeded its capacity to do so. As of January 1, 1975, Westinghouse was short of some 40,000 tons of uranium, at a time when the total world supply was about 13,000 tons per year. In September 1975 the corporation announced that it would not be able to honor fixed-price contracts under which it was obliged to deliver about 70 million pounds of uranium. Westinghouse claimed it should be excused from performance under the Uniform Commercial Code on the grounds of "commercial impracticability."

Under the UCC this defense required Westinghouse to show that its failure to be able to honor its contracts was "unforeseeable" at the time the contracts were made. The economist Paul Joskow (1976) argued that even if Westinghouse had not carefully analyzed the possible future behavior of uranium prices, it should not be allowed to avoid the contract on grounds that the price increase was unforeseeable. To hold otherwise would encourage the neglect of available information. Under another provision of the UCC, a party could not be excused from its obligation if it had assumed the risk of failure to perform directly or indirectly. In this situation it was clear that the contracts between Westinghouse and its customers had assigned the risk of a change in the price of uranium to Westinghouse. Therefore there was no occasion to even consider the doctrines of impossibility or impracticability. A ruling that the increase in price was unforeseeable by Westinghouse would reward a deliberate effort to avoid information, and make it virtually impossible for anyone to assume this type of risk in the future. In the event all the lawsuits against Westinghouse were settled out of court.

The common law of slavery

Let us consider some applications of contract law in a context that may be jarring to the reader, since it involves a troubling period of American history. Specifically, we will examine some issues concerning allocation of risk in cases involving slaves in the American south before the Civil War. Jenny B. Wahl (1993, 1996) found that in some of these cases a slave had been hired out by his owner to another firm, and was either injured or had escaped; in either case, the owner incurred a substantial loss. In some instances the court found an allocation of risk in the contract. For example, if the slaveowner was being paid a premium above the standard wage, the courts generally inferred that he was being compensated for an unusual risk of injury or escape. Since the master had assumed the risk of loss, he could not recover.

In other cases a slave who was being transported on a common carrier either escaped or was injured. When the contract between the slaveowner and the common carrier did not specify who would bear the loss, the courts assigned it to the party who could avoid it at lower cost. One such case involved a slave who escaped from a steamboat. The court held that the steamboat company was liable to the slave's owner, since it was in a better position to prevent the escape. In cases involving personal injury on a common carrier, if the court found that the slave's injuries were caused by his own carelessness, the slaveowner could not recover. Since the slaveowner was more familiar with the slave's behavior than the common carrier, he could have avoided the loss at a lower cost.

The controversy concerning standard form contracts

When two large firms negotiate a new contract, every clause is reviewed carefully by a lawyer for each party, and the contract language proposed by either side is often revised during the negotiations. In contrast, the contracts that are used in most consumer transactions – a purchase of a car from an automobile dealer, or a mortgage loan made to a home buyer – are typically standard form contracts, with much "fine print" or "boilerplate" that the consumer never reads. When someone buys a car, he usually negotiates the price with the salesman, but does not negotiate on the contract clauses that specify the right of the lender to repossess the vehicle if payments are delinquent, or the lender's right to sell his promissory note to a third party. In fact, if a customer proposed a change in the standard contract language on these matters, he would be informed that these matters were not open to negotiation.

Victor Goldberg (1974) has argued that the widespread use of standard contracts in consumer transactions may lead to inefficiency. Even in a competitive industry, there is a tendency to gravitate toward contract clauses that benefit the seller at the expense of the buyer. Competition among sellers will not protect the buyer, since very few buyers would notice any differences in the terms of the contracts offered by different sellers. Since the cost to consumers of reading and understanding the detailed terms of the contract is much greater than it is for the price terms, there is a movement in the direction of low prices and harsh contract terms.

An example is the contract between a parking garage and a customer. Customers are frequently handed a receipt stating that the parking garage is not liable if the car is damaged or stolen.[5] It could, however, be argued that it is inefficient to relieve a parking garage staffed by an attendant from liability when a customer's car is stolen. The parking garage can usually prevent the loss of the car at lower cost than the customer. Suppose, for example, that the garage could prevent the theft of vehicles by making expenditures on security that cost $2 per parked car. Assume that if the garage did not take these precautions, the probability of a theft and total loss of the car would be 1 in 10,000, and the amount of the loss would be $30,000. Thus the expected loss to a customer from theft would be $3. Clearly under these assumptions it would be efficient for the contract to place the risk of liability for theft on the garage: if the garage is not liable, it will not take the precautions, and there is an expected social cost of $3; if, on the other hand, the garage is liable, it will make the expenditures on security, and the social cost is $2.

Nonetheless, the point of Goldberg's critique is that the contract might not assign liability for theft to the garage since there is a transaction cost – a lack of information on the part of the consumer. The consumer is unable to distinguish between different contracts offered by different parking lots. There is therefore a "race to the bottom" like the one which, according to Ralph Nader, leads states to adopt suboptimal rules of corporation law (see the discussion in chapter 11). If customers had perfect information and there were no costs of negotiation, the Coase Theorem would apply, and customers would flock to the parking garage that assumed liability for theft and charged $2 more for parking. Since, however, customers do not read their contract, they are blind to everything but the price, so there is an inefficient equilibrium in which no garage will assume such liability. Goldberg suggests that the solution is for the government to intervene on behalf of consumers, and require that the contract include certain standardized terms that promote efficiency.

Ronald Coase (1974) strongly disagrees with this analysis, however. Coase contends that a firm that offers more favorable contract terms than its competitors has an incentive to inform consumers about it. An automobile manufacturer that offers a better warranty than its competitors (i.e., a warranty covering more parts, or effective for a longer period) is likely to advertise that feature to potential buyers. In the case of the parking garage, a garage that makes expenditures on security could post a sign stating that "we insure against theft and damage to your vehicle, unlike our competitors." Coase argues that because of competition, firms will not want to include in their standard contract a clause that reduces the value of its product to consumers more than it reduces costs. Government regulation is likely to make consumers worse off, since it can enable firms to enforce cartel arrangements. As an example, Coase cites a study by Sam Peltzman of banking regulation which showed that the regulation reduced the number of banks below the number that would have existed without it. Moreover, other economists have pointed out that there can be effective competition between firms on the basis of contract terms even if many consumers are uninformed, so long as some have good information. Those consumers who are aware of important differences in contract terms will shift their demand to the firm offering favorable terms; thus the market will reward that firm and punish the firm offering unfavorable terms, thereby protecting even uninformed consumers.[6]

Neoclassical economists such as Coase and Posner would concede that firms are not willing to negotiate the terms of a standard form contract with consumers. They would, however, not infer from this fact that the firms have monopoly power, or that competition requires them to impose harsh terms on consumers. Rather, they would point out that employees who deal with customers are generally not trained in the law. Therefore it would be far too costly to allow every customer to negotiate all the detailed terms of a contract.

Unconscionability

In this section we examine the doctrine of unconscionability. This doctrine is not easily defined, but is generally applied by the courts to conduct, or to terms of a contract that seem so unfair as to "shock the conscience" of the court. Under the Uniform Commercial Code, if a court determines that a clause in a contract is unconscionable, it may decide not to enforce the entire contract, or may instead enforce the remainder of the contract without the offending clause.

Michael Trebilcock (1976) has proposed a distinction between procedural unconscionability, i.e. unconscionability in the process of contract formation, and substantive unconscionability, i.e. substantive unfairness in the terms of the contract. To many scholars the idea of procedural unconscionability is less controversial, so we consider it first.

Richard Epstein (1975) has pointed out that because of the risk of fraud or duress, a number of legal rules declare certain types of contracts to be invalid, even though some of these contracts would otherwise be perfectly legitimate agreements. For example, the Statute of Frauds requires that certain kinds of agreements, such as a sale of real property (land) must be in writing. An oral agreement to purchase land will not be enforced, even if both parties fully intended to enter into a binding contract. Similarly, the parol evidence rule prohibits the use of oral or written evidence to vary or contradict the terms of an "integrated" written contract. This rule would prevent someone from testifying, for example, that a deed was really intended to be a mortgage, so that the apparent seller actually retained ownership of the property. Also, in many states there is a "cooling off" period, which is often three days, in which a consumer who has signed a contract can rescind it. The inevitable consequence of these rules is that some legitimate contracts will not be enforced. In the case of each of these rules, the risk that there would be fraudulent or ill-advised transactions without the rule outweighs the risk that some valid agreements will be nullified by the rule.

Epstein argues that procedural unconscionability is another such doctrine, which can protect against duress, fraud, and incompetence without requiring specific proof of any of these conditions. He cites a case in which application of this doctrine seems appropriate: prisoners of war in Vietnam, shortly after returning to the United States, were approached by experienced salesmen who persuaded them to buy municipal bonds of dubious value. These individuals were especially vulnerable because of their circumstances – a long captivity, after which they were suddenly given control of substantial funds representing their back pay. Here the doctrine would provide relief to a narrowly defined group.

Let us now turn to cases involving the issue of substantive unconscionability. In Macaulay v. Schroeder Publishing Co.[7] the plaintiff had entered into a contract with the defendant, a music publisher, when he began his career as an unknown writer of popular songs. Under this contract the plaintiff was required to write songs exclusively for the defendant, and would receive 50 per cent of net royalties. The initial term of the agreement was for five years, but it was renewable automatically for another five years if the plaintiff's royalties during the first term exceeded £5,000 sterling. The defendant could terminate the agreement at any time, but the plaintiff had no right to terminate. After several years the plaintiff had become well known as a songwriter, and now sought to be released from his contract with the music publisher.

The court held unanimously that the contract was unconscionable, and therefore void, on the ground that its provisions gave the publisher the right to terminate at any time, but the songwriter could not terminate even if the publisher chose not to publish his songs. The court ruled the contract was unenforceable because of this perceived imbalance in contractual rights. Michael Trebilcock argued that this decision ignored the fact that the terms of the contract simply reflected the economics of the music publishing business. The reality is that very few unknown songwriters ever become known. Publishers enter into contracts with many aspiring songwriters, and make substantial investments in them, in the hope that at least some of them will write songs that are commercially successful. The profits generated for the publisher from the few who succeed offset the losses incurred by the publisher on the many who fail. If a songwriter would be allowed to withdraw from his agreement as soon as he has gained a following, a publisher would be left with unrecovered losses on contracts with all the songwriters who do not achieve success.

Trebilcock noted that the rule of this decision, if upheld and followed by other courts, could have far-reaching consequences for the music publishing industry. The rule is likely to increase the costs of the industry, since it would no longer be feasible for publishers to make investments in unknown songwriters and "carry" them for years while they develop their talents. The increase in the costs of songwriters – an important factor of production in this industry – would have both scale and substitution effects. If the music publishing industry is competitive, a rule that increases the costs of the industry would cause its output to contract, and would therefore reduce the industry's demand for intermediate inputs such as songwriters. One would therefore expect the prices of these inputs to fall. In this case we would expect that the royalty rates of songwriters would be reduced, or that publishers would substitute away from unknown songwriters toward the established ones.

A number of cases on unconscionability involve installment sales of goods to consumers. One example is a sale of a consumer good for credit, in which a clause of the contract provides that the seller may sell the buyer's promissory note to a third party (the third party is usually someone who has expertise at collecting on debt obligations, e.g., a finance company). In Figure 7.1, a consumer buys a high-definition television set for credit from Best Buy, which then sells her promissory note to a finance company. Under the "holder in due course" doctrine, the finance company can compel the consumer to pay the full purchase price even if, for example, the television is defective, so that the consumer would have been able to avoid payment if she had been sued by Best Buy rather than by the finance company. Since the finance company is a holder in due course, it can enforce the note free from most defenses that the consumer might have raised if the lawsuit had been brought by Best Buy. (It should, however, be noted that the consumer would still have a valid claim against Best Buy for breach of warranty.)

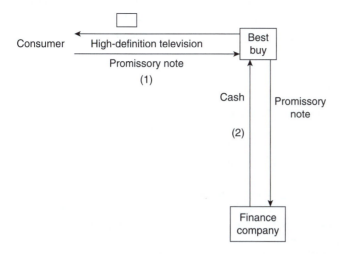

Figure 7.1 The sale of a buyer's note to a holder in due course.

If this doctrine seems unfair, one should recognize that it actually benefits the consumer by making her promise more liquid – more like cash. If the consumer had paid cash for the good, she would be in the same position as she is under the holder in due course doctrine. This rule reduces the cost of financing installment sales by making suits for collection less costly and more likely to succeed. If the holder in due course rule was held invalid on the ground that it is unconscionable, the cost of making sales for credit would increase. Sellers would then either charge a higher rate of interest, or impose higher standards on buyers who wished to buy on credit.

Another provision that has often been challenged is the add-on clause. Suppose a consumer makes separate purchases of a television set, a sofa, a bed, and finally a toaster from the same department store. If there is an add-on clause in the installment sale contract, the seller has a security interest covering all of these goods until the entire debt has been paid. All the goods previously purchased are "added on" as collateral for the last good purchased, the toaster. Consequently, if the consumer pays for the television, sofa, and bed, but is delinquent in making payments on the toaster, the store could repossess all of the goods.[8]

The economic justification for the add-on clause is that the value of consumer goods often declines more rapidly than the amount that is owed for them. Thus after a while the outstanding debt often exceeds the value of the goods. The add-on clause provides the creditor with assurance that there will be sufficient collateral to ensure repayment of the debt. If the use of this clause were prohibited, businesses that frequently sell goods for credit would either charge a higher rate of interest, or become more selective in screening applicants who wish to buy on credit. Which of these responses dominates will depend on how difficult (costly) it is to determine which applicants are most likely to default on their obligations. If it is very difficult to predict which applicants will be delinquent, the dominant effect will be a general increase in interest rates.

The preceding analysis of obstacles to enforcement of consumer loan agreements applies to other types of loans. In some states a bank that seeks to foreclose on a mortgage faces substantial legal hurdles in the courts. Such legal rules simply increase the cost of making mortgage loans. The foreseeable consequence is that banks will respond by either (1) requiring that customers meet a higher standard of creditworthiness, i.e. that they have a higher income, or more wealth, or (2) requiring a higher down payment, or (3) charging a higher rate of interest.

Remedies for breach of contract[9]

In general the remedies potentially available to the victim of a breach of contract, whom we will call the aggrieved or nonbreaching party, can be classified into two categories: (1) money damages, the usual "default" remedy, and (2) specific performance. In this section we consider the award of money damages; in a subsequent section we will examine the remedy of specific performance.

Within the general category of money damages, there are several alternative measures of damages. Depending on the particular facts and circumstances of the case, the aggrieved party may be entitled to damages based on only one of these measures, or he may be allowed to choose between more than one measure. The basic, default measure of damages – the measure that is most widely applied – is the expectation measure. Expectation damages award the aggrieved party an amount that puts him in as good a position as he would have been in if the contract had been performed. An alternative measure is reliance damages, which restores the injured party to the position he would have been in if he had never entered into the contract. Finally, there are also restitution damages, which equal the value of any benefits the aggrieved party has previously conferred on the breaching party.

An important question is whether the remedies available for breach are determined entirely by law outside the contract, or instead may be specified by the parties in the contract itself. A provision in the contract that specifies the damages to be paid upon breach is known as a "liquidated damages" clause. The courts have generally been inclined to uphold such agreements, especially when the amount of damages is uncertain and difficult to estimate, viz., a breach of a promise to marry, or a specified payment for each day's delay in completing construction of a building. Today a liquidated damages clause will be enforced unless the court finds it to be a "penalty," i.e., a provision that imposes substantially more damages than the expectation measure.

Suppose a woodcarver C and a buyer B1 enter into a contract, under which C will carve a totem pole for B1 for $300. B1 pays the purchase price to C in advance. Assume the value of the totem pole to B1 is $400. Since B1 plans to put the totem pole in the living room of his house, he spends $50 to raise a portion of his roof high enough to accommodate the totem pole. We will assume that this expenditure has no value to B1 unless he obtains the totem pole. After C has finished carving the totem pole but before he has delivered it to B1, C is approached by another potential buyer B2. Let us assume that the value of the totem pole to B2 is either $325, $375, or $450, and that, whichever value applies, B2 will offer exactly that amount to C.

The effect of damages on the decision to breach

Let us consider, first, the amount that would be awarded to B1 in the event that C breaches the contract and sells the totem pole to B2. Then we must consider how the prospect of being liable for damages might affect C's decision whether to breach the contract. Finally, we will take into account that under certain circumstances, it will be efficient for C to breach. Therefore, we investigate whether each measure of damages will lead to an "efficient breach," i.e., whether the amount of damages will induce C to breach when, and only when, it is efficient for him to do so.

First let us consider damages to be awarded under the expectation measure. If the contract had been completed, B1 would have received a value of $400. His overall gain from the transaction would be $400 − 300 − 50 = $50. Since B1 has already paid the purchase price of $300, and made a reliance expenditure of $50, his damages under the expectation measure should be equal to the value of the totem pole he did not receive, $400. Now, since C knows that he would have to pay damages of $400 upon breach, he will breach if B2 offers him $450, but not if he offers $375 or $325. Efficiency would require C to breach if, and only if, the value of the pole to B2 exceeds its value to B1. But this is exactly what happens under the expectation measure.

Now consider the damages for which C would be liable under the reliance measure. What amount would restore B1 to the position he would have been in if he had never entered into the contract? To achieve this objective, B1 must be compensated both for the $300 purchase price he paid in advance and his reliance expenditure of $50. Therefore if the reliance measure is in effect, C knows that upon breach he would be liable for damages of $350. Therefore C will breach if B2 offers him either $375 or $450, but not if B2 offers only $325. Note, however, that if the value of the pole to B2 is only $375, it would be inefficient for C to breach, since the value of the pole to B2 would then be less than its value to B1, $400. Thus we see that the reliance measure, unlike the expectation measure, may lead to an inefficient breach.

Finally, the restitution measure of damages would award B1 an amount equal to the benefits he has conferred upon C. Here the only benefit obtained by C was the receipt of the purchase price of $300. Therefore C will breach when the offer made by B2 is $325 or $375. In either of these cases breach would be inefficient, given that the value of the pole to B1 is $400.

Summing up these results, we conclude that both the reliance and restitution measure may lead to an inefficient breach, but the restitution measure is more likely to do so, since damages under this rule do not include the buyer's reliance expenditure, which normally would not benefit the seller.

Informational requirements

Another important consideration is the amount of information that is required to calculate damages for each measure. The expectation measure requires a determination of the value that performance of the contract would have had for the aggrieved party. This will often be hard to do. Suppose, for example, that X Co. has agreed to build a computerized neon sign to be used in outdoor advertising by Y Co. If X Co. does not make the sign, how would the court determine how much walk-in business Y Co. would have obtained from the sign? The difficulty of determining the value of performance to the nonbreaching party is a factor weighed by the courts in deciding whether to grant the remedy of specific performance.

To compute reliance damages, the court must know the amount of payments made under the contract and the reliance expenditures made by the nonbreaching party. While it is harder to verify reliance expenditures than payments of the purchase price, at least these expenditures are made before the court must decide the amount of damages.

For the restitution remedy, the court need only determine the value of benefits that were conferred on the breaching party, e.g. the purchase price. It is easier to evaluate these benefits than reliance expenditures, since both parties are familiar with them. To summarize, the remedy that seems easiest (least costly) to implement is the restitution measure, and the next easiest is the reliance measure. The one that, because of the informational requirements, is most difficult to implement is the expectation measure.

The requirement of foreseeability

As noted previously, the basic, default measure of damages for breach of contract is the expectation measure. The objective of this measure is to put the aggrieved party in the position he would have been in if the contract had been completed. The scope of the expectation measure is, however, limited by a requirement that the damages sustained by the plaintiff must have been "foreseeable" by the defendant.

The requirement of foreseeability was set forth in the English case of Hadley v. Baxendale (1854),[10] which is probably the most famous and most cited case in the law of contracts. The plaintiffs in this case owned a mill, which was forced to shut down when the crankshaft broke. The defendants were hired by the mill's owners to transport the broken shaft to Greenwich, so it could be used as a model for a new shaft that would be made to replace it. The defendants delayed transporting the broken shaft; consequently it took longer than it would have otherwise to construct the new shaft and deliver it to the mill. The plaintiffs sued the defendants for lost profits.

The court held that expectation damages were limited by a requirement that they be foreseeable by the breaching party. To be foreseeable, damages had to be either (1) those which would generally arise from a breach of contract, i.e. those which are reasonably expected, or (2) those which the breaching party was notified about in advance. In this case, the court found that the defendants had no reason to expect that the delay in transporting the crankshaft would cause the mill to lose profits. For example, the defendants may have assumed that the mill had a spare crankshaft that would enable it to remain in operation. Alternatively, they may have thought that even if the new shaft was delivered promptly, other machinery or equipment was broken that would prevent the mill from working. Accordingly the plaintiff was not entitled to lost profits.

Under the rule of Hadley v. Baxendale, the breaching party is liable only for consequences of its breach that are foreseeable. If the risk of loss is known only by the aggrieved party, the breaching party is not liable. The basic idea is that the risk of loss should be borne by the party who can avoid the loss at a lower cost. Consider a professional photographer who goes on an expensive trip to Africa to take pictures of wildlife for a travel magazine. Upon his return to the United States, he gives the photographs to a drugstore to have them developed. The drugstore accidentally destroys the negatives. Under the rule of Hadley v. Baxendale, the drugstore is not liable for the cost of the trip to Africa unless the photographer had informed the drugstore of the importance of the photographs. Of course, if the drugstore had been informed, it probably would have taken extra precautions, and have charged a higher price. It is clearly less costly for the photographer to provide this information to the drugstore than it is for the drugstore to take the precautions that are appropriate for valuable professional photographs with all the photos that it receives.

The duty to mitigate damages

When the contract is breached, the injured party has a duty to "mitigate" damages. The injured party cannot recover for damages that could have been avoided by a reasonable effort. Suppose A is building custom-made goods for B, and is notified that B is terminating the contract. A cannot subsequently recover for any costs he incurs after notice of termination.

Suppose A has chartered a ship owned by B. If A breaches, the damages that B can recover are reduced by the amount the ship could earn in service to others. The duty to mitigate damages is clearly efficient in that it promotes the full employment of resources.

An employee who is wrongfully discharged must take another job if it becomes available to him.[11] The original common-law rule was that the employee could recover his full wages from the employer, provided he remained ready and willing to return to work. In time this rule was recognized as inefficient and abandoned. The employee who is wrongfully terminated may also recover expenditures reasonably incurred in searching for another job, even if the search is unsuccessful.

When a defendant breached its contract to sponsor a television program, the network's damages were reduced by the amounts it received from resale of the television time. In another case, however, an advertiser cancelled its contract for space in a magazine. There the court held that the magazine's publisher was entitled to the full contract price, minus the cost of setting up the ad; damages were not reduced even though the specific space the defendant was to use was sold to another advertiser. The court noted that the magazine had ample room to accommodate any additional advertising that the publisher could obtain. These two cases raise the general question whether a seller's damages for breach of contract should be reduced when the good or service is resold to a subsequent buyer. This issue is considered in the next section.

The lost-volume or expansible seller

This section considers a well-known problem in the law of contracts: the problem of the lost-volume or "expansible" seller. This issue arises when the contract does not have a "liquidated damages" provision explaining how the seller's damages should be computed if the buyer reneges. Suppose Ms. B, a consumer, enters into a contract with Mr. A, an automobile dealer, to purchase a new automobile for $20,000. The cost of the vehicle to A is $16,000. Subsequently B reneges. A then arranges to sell the vehicle to C, another customer, for $19,000, and sues B for breach of contract. Let us assume that the court wishes to apply the expectation measure of damages; thus the objective is to put the injured party A in as good a position as he would have occupied if the contract had been performed. B will argue that A is entitled to damages of only $1,000. A, however, will argue that if B had completed her purchase, he could have sold C an identical vehicle on the same terms. Thus if the contract had been carried out, A would have had a total gain of $7,000: $4,000, the profit from the sale to B, plus $3,000, the profit from the sale to C. Given that B breached, A realized a gain of only $3,000; consequently he argues that he is entitled to damages of $4,000 under the expectation measure. Here A should prevail, since the sale to C would probably have been made even if B had completed her purchase.

In general, the amount of the seller's loss resulting from the buyer's breach is the contract price minus the cost of performing that particular contract. In certain circumstances this cost may be quite low. For the hotel whose room reservation is cancelled at the last minute – too late to find another customer – virtually the only cost of performance is that of having the maid clean the room for the next occupant. In other situations, however, the cost of performance includes the lost opportunity of a sale to a subsequent buyer. In these situations the consequence of nonperformance is loss of the original contract price, but a gain of the price paid upon the subsequent resale, minus any additional selling costs incurred to make the resale.

Suppose a tenant defaults, and the landlord rents her apartment to another for the remainder of the lease. The question is whether the rental paid by the new tenant must be deducted from damages. The issue here is what the successor tenant would have done if the original tenant had not breached. If not all the other apartments in the building are occupied, the successor tenant might have rented another apartment even if the first tenant had stayed. On the other hand, it could be that the leased apartment was substantially different from the other vacant apartments in the landlord's building (perhaps because it had an additional bedroom or a full kitchen). In this case, or if all the other apartments were occupied, the second tenant presumably would not have rented another of the landlord's apartments; thus the gain of this tenant's rental was made possible by the breach of the first tenant, and the damages should be offset. Note that if all the remaining apartments were occupied, the landlord is deemed not to have lost volume because, ordinarily, the total number of apartments she can provide is "fixed," i.e., the marginal cost of constructing an additional apartment at short notice is prohibitively large.

In the case of what the courts call a "specific" good, such as a painting by Rembrandt, the resale price is deducted from the price of the original contract. Here again, the real issue is what the second buyer would have done if the first buyer had not breached. If a contract to purchase a Rembrandt from an art dealer is breached, it is at least possible that the subsequent buyer would have bought another old master from the dealer. One complication, however, is that one can no longer assume that the terms of this hypothetical alternative transaction would be identical to those of the actual sale. Allowing a court to speculate about this counterfactual transaction could introduce substantial uncertainty into the law; this is an important consideration in favor of the rule of thumb for specific goods.

If the court decides that the seller should receive damages for lost profits, it must determine the cost of performing the contract. The costs to be deducted are the marginal costs of production, at the level of output chosen by the seller. Selling costs should not be deducted, since these are costs of obtaining the contract, rather than costs of performing. Putting it differently, selling costs are not costs of performance since they do not increase as a result of performance.

Costs can be classified into two categories: fixed and variable. Fixed costs are those which do not vary with the level of production. Such costs would typically include rent, insurance, interest on long-term debt, and perhaps a minimal number of employees. Since, by definition, these costs do not increase with the level of production, they are not part of the marginal cost of production. All costs which are not fixed are variable. Variable costs generally include expenses of wages, salaries, and raw materials, to the extent these costs increase with the level of output. In computing the seller's damages, only variable costs of production should be subtracted from the contract price.

A question that frequently arises is whether "overhead" expenses can be deducted. This simply depends on whether the expenses in question are fixed or variable costs. Note that costs may be variable and therefore "marginal" even if they are not specifically attributable to any particular units of output. For example, operating ten taxicabs may require two dispatchers, while five taxicabs may require only one. Therefore the marginal cost of one unit of taxicab service would include one-fifth of a dispatcher's time.

Finally, it should be noted that the contract could have a provision for liquidated damages. In the case of consumer goods, this is the nonrefundable deposit. In general, the contract could either provide that damages will equal the contract price minus the amount recovered by the seller upon resale, or alternatively, that damages equal a specified amount that approximates the contract price minus the marginal cost of production.

Specific performance

The normal, default remedy for breach of contract is an award of money damages. This is a rule of liability, since a party can refuse to perform on condition of being liable for damages, determined under an objective standard applied by the courts. In certain situations, however, the court may grant a remedy known as specific performance; that is, the court may issue an injunction ordering the breaching party to complete performance.[12] This remedy is a rule of property, since a promisor who wishes not to perform must obtain the consent of the promisee. A court will grant an aggrieved party specific performance when an award of money damages is deemed to be inadequate. The courts often state that specific performance is allowed when "the subject matter of a contract is unique in character and cannot be duplicated."

The kinds of cases in which specific performance is granted involve contracts for the sale of land (all land is considered unique), contracts for the sale of heirlooms, antiques, licenses and patent rights; contracts for the sale of a majority of shares of a corporation; machinery and equipment specially designed for a particular business; and long-term output and requirements contracts. A common characteristic of these cases is that it is difficult (costly) to determine damages accurately, since there is a dearth of objective evidence of value of these goods. Family heirlooms, for example, typically have great value to a few family members, but little or no value to others. In one case in which the defendant had agreed to erect and maintain an advertising sign for the plaintiff's business, the court granted specific performance since the injury to the business resulting from not having the sign could not be accurately measured. If, on the other hand, a replacement for a good is readily available, the courts will not grant specific performance.

Specific performance can be justified as an alternative to money damages. Anthony Kronman notes that when a court calculates damages, there is always a risk that it will under- or overcompensate the injured party. However the extent of this risk is determined by the amount and quality of available information about the value of the subject matter. The risk is minimal when the good is a homogeneous commodity traded in large volume on an established market. The risk is substantial when there is no market, or only a few isolated transactions.

One consideration that argues for restraint in the use of specific performance is the administrative costs of this remedy. When a court makes an award of money damages, the case is over, although the plaintiff may later file an action to enforce the judgment. In contrast, when a court grants specific performance, it must usually keep the case on its docket until performance is completed. It will often be costly to monitor the parties' actions or verify that performance has occurred in employment or construction contracts, for example (on the other hand, if it were sufficiently important to the parties to have a right of specific performance, they could provide for compensation of the court's administrative costs, so those costs should not rule out this remedy automatically).

Another question is whether a contract can give a party a right to specific performance, if he would not qualify for this remedy under the uniqueness standard. Kronman suggests that there may be legitimate economic reasons to do so. For example, a firm without an established reputation may agree to give a buyer a right to specific performance, in order to signal its confidence in its ability to perform. However, the courts are generally not likely to allow parties to create a private right to specific performance, on the ground that it imposes substantial administrative costs on the judicial system.

An application: rings and promises

The following material may strike some readers, especially women, as boorish and offensive; we are sorry if that is the case. However, we would also point out that we are summarizing important research done by a woman, and that one of her key findings is that since World War II there has been a sea change in the role of women in society and the economy: the increase in their productivity has led to their economic and social independence.

The research we refer to is by Margaret Brinig, who has provided an interesting explanation of the economic function of a diamond ring, given by a man to a woman as an engagement present. Brinig notes that before the Depression of 1929–1933 it was not customary for a woman to receive a diamond ring when she became engaged. During this period it was important for a woman to marry, in order to gain social status and financial security. People would assume that an "old maid" was too unattractive to find a husband; in addition, she was likely to be financially insecure in later years. Consider then the plight of a woman who became engaged, had sexual relations with her fiancé, but is subsequently discarded by him before marriage. A woman in these circumstances could not present herself as a virgin to other suitors, a fact that in those times tended to reduce her market value.

There was, however, a legal remedy available: the woman could sue her former fiancé for breach of promise to marry. Centuries ago this action was within the jurisdiction of the English ecclesiastical courts. In many cases a consequence of the filing of this action was specific performance of the marriage contract, since the man was often anxious to avoid liability for damages.

The action for breach of promise eventually came into disfavor, for several reasons. Many were scandalized by the court proceedings, in which women would prove damages by introducing evidence of their sexual relations with their former fiancé. To mitigate damages, a defendant might attempt to show that his fiancée had been sexually intimate with others. Moreover people came to believe it was not advisable to allow men to be coerced into marriage by the threat of a lawsuit. Consequently, beginning in 1935, the states began, one by one, to abolish the breach of promise action by statute. By 1945 sixteen states had done so.

As the breach of promise action faded from the scene, a new custom came into fashion, whereby a man would propose to a woman by giving her a diamond ring. Brinig found statistical evidence that this custom was practiced more widely in states where the breach of promise action had been abolished than in states where the action survived. She inferred that the diamond was in effect a bond or pledge replacing the breach of promise action. If the man broke the engagement, the woman was compensated by being able to keep the ring. The ring was a form of liquidated damages.

There is evidence that in recent years the use of diamond rings for engagements has declined. Since 1980, engagement rings have not exceeded 20 percent of total sales of diamond jewelry. Brinig argues that this trend is consistent with her interpretation. Sexual activity outside of marriage is not uncommon now, since the link between sex and children has been broken by the availability of contraceptive methods and abortion. Virginity is no longer prized (nor expected), and marriage is no longer the key to financial security for women, who now have many career options. Thus, since a woman who is jilted no longer suffers serious financial damage (as opposed to emotional costs), there is no longer a need for a diamond to serve as liquidated damages. Accordingly it is not surprising that the gift of a diamond is no longer a prerequisite for premarital intimacy.

Liquidated damages and penalties

As previously noted, a liquidated damages clause in a contract will not be enforced if the court finds it to be a "penalty," i.e., a provision that imposes substantially more damages than the expectation measure. The courts have often justified the penalty rule on either of two grounds: (1) it is against public policy to enforce a contract in the nature of a gamble, or (2), it is unjust to give a plaintiff more than his actual (expectation) damages. These arguments are, however, rejected by a number of scholars, who contend that it is inefficient for a court to rewrite a contract that was entered into by parties who had far better information about the subject matter and the damages that would result from breach.

Goetz and Scott give an example of a deeply loyal fan of a college basketball team. After many years of being mired in mediocrity, the fan's team advances to the Conference Championship game at the end of the season. The fan charters a bus to transport him, and twenty-four friends who are equally rabid fans of the team, to the Championship game. The fan does not want to worry about the possibility that the bus will not arrive at the game on time. Assume that in this situation damages for a late arrival are normally $1,000, but that the emotional and psychic cost to this fan of missing the Championship game would be at least $10,000. However it would be difficult and very costly to prove these damages in court. The fan is willing to pay the bus company $500 in addition to the normal fare if, in return, the bus company would agree to pay damages of $10,000 upon failure of performance. However, this arrangement would be considered an unenforceable penalty.

An alternative would be for the fan to insure against breach with an insurance company. The problem with this solution is that it is inefficient, since the bus company can provide insurance at a lower cost. The insurance company might, for example, hire an empty bus to follow the chartered bus, so that it could pick up the passengers in the event of a breakdown. However, it would have to charge a premium much higher than $500 for this service. The bus company would take the appropriate, socially optimal level of precautions if it were fully liable for the damages of $10,000 that would result if it missed the game. If the bus company is not liable for the full amount of damages, the precautions it will take will be inadequate. This is, of course, a straightforward example of moral hazard, the inefficiency that arises when someone (in this case the bus company) does not bear the full social cost of his actions. Here the parties do not arrive at an efficient outcome because of a transaction cost, namely a law which prohibits penalty clauses.

Bibliography

Brinig, Margaret F., "Rings and Promises," 6 *Journal of Law Economics and Organization* 203 (1990).

Coase, Ronald H., "The Choice of the Institutional Framework: A Comment," 17 *Journal of Law and Economics* 493–496 (1974).

Cooter, Robert D., and Thomas S. Ulen, *Law and Economics* (3rd. ed., Reading, MA: Addison-Wesley, 2000).

Epstein, Richard A., "Unconscionability: A Critical Reappraisal," 18 *Journal of Law and Economics* 293–311 (1975).

Goetz, Charles J., and Robert E. Scott, "Liquidated Damages, Penalties and the Just Compensation Principle: Some Notes on an Enforcement Model and a Theory of Efficient Breach," 77 *Columbia Law Review* 554–594 (1977).

Goldberg, Victor P., "Institutional Change and the Quasi-invisible Hand," 17 *Journal of Law and Economics* 461–490 (1974).

Joskow, Paul L., "Commercial Impossibility, the Uranium Market and the Westinghouse Case," 6 *Journal of Legal Studies* 119 (1976).

Kronman, Anthony, "Specific Performance," 45 *University of Chicago Law Review* 351–375 (1978).

Peltzman, Sam, "Bank Stock Prices and the Effects of Regulation of the Banking Structure," 41 *Journal of Business* 413 (1968).

Polinsky, A. Mitchell, *An Introduction to Law and Economics* (Boston, MA: Little Brown, 1983).

Schwarz, Alan and Louis Wilde, "Imperfect Information in Markets for Contract Terms," 69 *Virginia Law Review* 1387 (1983).

Shavell, Steven, "Damage Measures for Breach of Contract," 11 *Bell Journal of Economics* 466 (1980).

Shavell, "The Design of Contracts and Remedies for Breach," 98 *Quarterly Journal of Economics* 121 (1984).

Trebilcock, Michael J., "The Doctrine of Inequality of Bargaining Power: Post-Benthamite Economics in the House of Lords," 26 *University of Toronto Law Journal* 359 (1976).

Wahl, Jenny Bourne, "The Bondsman's Burden: An Economic Analysis of the Jurisprudence of Slaves and Common Carriers," 53 (3) *Journal of Economic History* 495–526 (September 1993).

Wahl, Jenny Bourne, "The Jurisprudence of American Slave Sales," 56 (1) *Journal of Economic History* 143–169 (March 1996).

Problems

1. The case of Laidlaw v. Organ involved the question of whether a contract for the purchase of tobacco was valid when the buyer had failed to inform the seller about an event which affected the value of the tobacco (the treaty ending the War of 1812). Discuss the economic significance of this case.

2. The Miami Seaquarium enters into a contract with Mr. Q whereby Mr. Q promises to deliver two healthy full-grown California gray whales to the Seaquarium by January 1, 1992. Shortly after the contract is entered into, an epidemic among whales causes California gray whales to become extinct. Is Mr. Q liable for failure to deliver the whales to the Seaquarium? Would it matter if Mr. Q were (*a*) an individual commercial fisherman or (*b*) a large corporation in the business of providing hundreds of species of rare animals to zoos?

3. Some courts have held that the "holder in due course" doctrine is unconscionable. Could this doctrine be efficient? What are the likely consequences to consumers if the courts succeed in abolishing it?

4. Customers who repeatedly buy on credit often sign agreements which contain an "add-on" clause. Under this type of clause, all goods previously purchased by the customer from the seller are "security" for the price of the goods which were purchased last. What is the purpose of this kind of clause? Suppose the courts held that this type of clause was "unconscionable." What might be the effects of this ruling in the market for credit sales of consumer goods?

5. Mr. X enters into a contract with Mr. Z under which Mr. Z agrees to build a customized telescope for X for $500. The value of the completed telescope to X will be $600. Expecting that the telescope will be delivered on schedule, X pays the purchase price to Z, and drills a hole in his roof at a cost of $300. However, before Z delivers the telescope, Ms. Y, another amateur astronomer, offers to buy it from Z for $550. Would Z breach his contract with Mr. X if the measure of damages were (*a*) the expectation interest, (*b*) the restitution measure, or (*c*) the reliance measure? Explain why in detail.

6. Mr. M enters into a contract with Mr. R, under which Mr. R agrees to build a model railroad for $200. The value of the model railroad to Mr. M is $300. Expecting that the model railroad will be delivered, Mr. M spends $40 remodeling his basement to make room for it. Before Mr. R has received any payment from Mr. M, another model railroad enthusiast, Ms. J, offers to buy the model railroad from Mr. R for $250, which is also the value of the model railroad to Ms. J. If Mr. R were to breach his contract with Mr. M by selling the model railroad to Ms. J, how much would he have to pay Mr. M under (*a*) an expectation measure of damages, (*b*) a restitution measure of damages, or (*c*) a reliance measure of damages? In answering this question, explain the objective of each of these alternative measures of damages. Would Mr. R breach under any of these damage measures? Would it be efficient for Mr. R to breach? Explain why or why not.

7. Mr. D is a professional basketball player who orders some shoes through the mail. The mail order house promises all customers delivery within thirty days of receiving the order. Mr. D's shoes do not get delivered to him on time; as a result he has to wear ill fitting, uncomfortable shoes in the NBA championship game. Since his feet hurt him, he does not perform well, and his team loses the game. Can he sue the mail order house for the $10 million in endorsements he loses by not having the right pair of shoes?

8. A. Nimzovitch, a top-ranked chess player, hired a taxicab to pick him up at his hotel and take him to a chess match, the winner of which was to receive $1 million. Before the match Nimzovitch was favored to win easily. Unfortunately the taxi broke down, making Nimzovitch late for the match, which he therefore lost by forfeit. Subsequently Nimzovitch sues the taxicab company for breach of contract, asking $1 million in damages. Under the law of contracts will he get it?

9. Mrs. Wilson enters into a contract to buy an automobile for $20,000 from Z Co., a dealer. Mrs. Wilson subsequently backs out of the contract. Z Co. then sells the vehicle to Mr. Thompson for $19,000. Z Co. sues Mrs. Wilson for breach of contract. During the trial, an accountant reports that the "cost" of the vehicle to Z Co. was $16,000. However, on cross-examination this witness testifies that, of the $16,000, $2,000 are fixed costs, i.e. costs which must be paid by the dealer regardless of how many vehicles it sells. What is the amount of damages that Z Co. should recover from Mrs. Wilson? Suppose alternatively that: (*a*) the evidence shows clearly that Mr. Thompson would have bought another similar vehicle from Z Co. if the vehicle which Mrs. Wilson agreed to buy had not been available; (*b*) the vehicle was a one-of-a-kind gullwing Mercedes. If Z Co. had not had this car available, Mr. Thompson would not have purchased anything.

10. X Co. is a retail dealer of garden tractors. Mr. Y signs a contract to buy a garden tractor for $400 but later backs out of the agreement. The tractor that Mr. Y agreed to buy is subsequently sold to Mr. Z for $380. The average cost of a garden tractor to X Co. is $260, and the average variable cost is $220. The marginal cost to X Co. of supplying an additional tractor to a customer is $300. X Co. sues Mr. Y for breach of contract. How much damages should be awarded to X Co? You must explain your answer to get any credit.

11. Mr. X is a retailer of snow blowers. Mr. Y signs a contract to buy a snow blower from Mr. X but then decides he does not want it. The snow blower that Mr. Y agreed to buy is subsequently sold to Mr. Z for $225. The average variable cost of a snow blower to Mr. X is $180. The marginal cost to Mr. X of supplying an additional snow blower

to a customer is $200. X sues Y for breach of contract. How much damages should be awarded to X? You must explain your answer to get any credit.

12. Margaret Brinig found that there was a large increase in the use of diamond rings for engagements in states after the abolition of the action for breach of promise to marry. What is her explanation of this? How does she explain the decline in demand for diamond engagement rings since about 1980?

13. Until 1834 slaves were used in the Turks and Caicos Islands to produce salt. The slaves occasionally managed to escape from the islands at night on ships moored in the harbor. Regulations in effect in 1767 provided that if the owner of a sail boat left its sails on at night, and the sailboat was used by slaves to escape, the sail boat's owner was liable to the owner of the slaves for their loss. If, however, the sail boat had no sails left on it, but was still used to escape, the slaves' owners were liable to the sailboat owner for his loss. What is the economic rationale for this law?

14. While A reclines on a bench in the park, B approaches him and then, without being asked, sings a medley of Broadway show tunes. A thoroughly enjoys the performance, but declines an invitation to throw coins into B's cup. Does A have an obligation to compensate B? Explain why or why not.

8 Torts

In this chapter we provide an economic analysis of some of the most important rules of tort law. What is a tort? A tort is a cause of action, that is, it provides the grounds for a lawsuit for damages. One definition is that a tort is a wrong, other than a breach of contract, that subjects the wrongdoer to civil liability.[1] To be subject to tort liability, the defendant's conduct must fall within one of the established common-law categories that has come to be recognized as a tort, some of which are trespass, nuisance, negligence, strict liability in tort, libel, slander, intentional infliction of emotional harm, assault, battery, conversion, and fraud. It has been suggested that in general, tort liability is based on conduct that is socially unreasonable, or on an unreasonable interference with the interests of others. However these generalizations are not very useful, since conduct that is harmful to others is not a basis for tort liability unless it falls within the definition of a recognized tort.[2] By far the most important torts, in terms of their share of total actions filed, or total payments for common-law tort liability, are negligence and strict liability in tort.

Economic analysis can articulate the principles of efficiency underlying much of tort law, and suggest how the law might be amended when it deviates from those principles. For torts that involve accidents, the law should minimize the total social cost of accidents, which includes both the direct cost of accidents, e.g., personal injury, property damage, and the disruption of productive activity, and the costs of avoiding or preventing accidents. In general, it will be efficient to impose liability on the party who can avoid the accident at least cost.[3] This is implicit in innumerable laws and regulations. For example, sailboats have the right of way over power boats (unless the power boat is in a channel), because it is more difficult, i.e., more costly, for the sailboat to maneuver to avoid a collision. On the other hand, a power boat in a narrow channel may well have more difficulty avoiding a collision than a sailboat. A vehicle that collides with the rear end of another vehicle is presumed to be negligent, and therefore liable. It is easier (less costly) for the rear vehicle to stay a safe distance behind other vehicles, than it is for a vehicle to stay clear of vehicles behind it.

Negligence

We will first examine the elements of negligence, its defenses and related doctrines as set forth by the courts and traditional legal scholarship. We will then consider the Learned Hand[4] rule, a very simple formulation. We will find that the Learned Hand rule is far more powerful in explaining the outcomes of judicial decisions than the traditional ad hoc justifications of the various common-law rules associated with negligence.

At common law there were four elements, or requirements, for there to be a cause of action for negligence:

1   A duty or obligation, requiring a person to conform to a standard of conduct to protect others against unreasonable risks.
2   A failure to conform to the standard.
3   A reasonably close causal connection between the conduct and the resulting injury (this is sometimes known as the requirement of "proximate cause").
4   Actual loss or damage to another (the threat of future harm, not yet realized, is not enough).

We will consider two affirmative defenses to negligence: contributory negligence and assumption of risk. They are called affirmative defenses because the defendant has the burden of proof to establish them.[5]

Contributory negligence is conduct on the part of the plaintiff that contributes as a cause to the harm he suffered, and that falls below the standard he is required to conform to for his own protection. Again the requirement of causation should be noted. For an example of contributory negligence, consider a passenger riding in an automobile at high speed with a drunken driver. If the driver stops for gas, so the passenger has an opportunity to leave the vehicle, but if he failed to do so, he would be contributorily negligent.

The scope of this defense is limited to some extent by the doctrine of "last clear chance." Under this doctrine, the defendant is liable if, even though the plaintiff was negligent, the defendant could still have prevented an injury to the plaintiff by the exercise of reasonable care. In one case the plaintiff left a donkey in the highway and the defendant drove into it. The court held that the plaintiff could recover for negligence if the defendant could have avoided injuring the animal by proper care. Here the plaintiff was contributorily negligent, in leaving the donkey in the path of highway traffic, but the defendant was still liable, since in the moments before the accident he had a clear opportunity to avoid the collision by exercising reasonable care.

The other defense we consider is assumption of risk. A plaintiff may not recover for negligence if he has assumed the risk of injury, either by express agreement, i.e., a waiver of liability, or by an implied acceptance of the risk. For example, someone who goes to a baseball game, and sits in an unscreened seat, assumes the risk of being hit by a foul ball. An individual who goes to a hockey game accepts the risk of being injured by a flying puck. Below we show an example of an express waiver of liability, used by a resort in the Bahamas that offers visitors an opportunity to see sharks on a scuba dive.

Strict liability

Another basis of tort liability, distinct from negligence, is strict liability in tort. There is strict liability for injuries resulting from inherently dangerous things and activities; the use of explosives, fire, inflammable liquids, sewage, insecticides, and damage done by dangerous animals. Strict liability also applies to products liability, i.e., the liability of manufacturers for injuries caused by their products. Someone who sells a product "in a defective condition unreasonably dangerous to the user … is subject to liability for physical harm thereby caused to the … user."[6] Products liability is essentially based on three subsidiary doctrines.[7] First, under the design defect doctrine, a firm can be liable for injuries caused by its product if its design was defective, meaning that the injury could have been avoided by a different design that was not overly expensive. Second, under the manufacturing defect doctrine, a firm can be held liable if the product that caused the injury was not manufactured in accordance with its intended design. Third, under the failure to warn doctrine, a firm can be held liable if it fails to provide a reasonable warning about the hazard involved in the use of its product.

Box 8.1 Stuart Cove's Dive Bahamas Nassau Bahamas

Shark Dive Assumption of Risk and Complete Release of Liability

I, _____, hereby request that Stuart Cove's Dive Bahamas, Nassau Undersea Adventures Ltd., its employees, its agents, and its boats (whether owned, operated, leased or chartered) hereby referred to as "Stuart Cove's," allow me to pay for and participate in a "Shark Dive" organized and supervised by Stuart Cove's. I understand that I am requesting to participate in a scuba dive that is intended to be done in the presence of wild and unpredictable sharks. I understand that Stuart Cove's will intentionally attract these sharks to the immediate area of this dive and that I will be swimming unprotected within ten feet or less of these sharks. By my signature on this Assumption of Risk and Complete Release of Liability, I acknowledge that I am making this request to dive with these sharks with the full knowledge of the dangers involved with swimming with sharks. I have not been promised nor told anything to the contrary from what is stated in this Release and Waiver Agreement.

In consideration for allowing me to participate in this shark dive, with knowledge of the danger involved in such a dive, I hereby voluntarily release, discharge, waive, and relinquish any and all actions or causes of action for my personal injury, property damage or wrongful death occurring to me, which injury, property damage or wrongful death occurring to me, which injury, property damage or wrongful death arises as a result of engaging in this shark dive and any activities incidental to such shark dive wherever, whenever or however such may occur … By signing this document, I acknowledge that I assume the risk of personal injury, property damage, or wrongful death upon myself during this shark dive.

The undersigned acknowledges that he has read the foregoing paragraphs and fully understands the legal rights that he is giving up by signing this document. He further warrants that he has been fully and completely advised of the potential hazard and dangers incidental to engaging in a shark dive.

NAME: _____   DATE: _____

SIGNATURE: _____   WITNESS: _____

Yet another basis of strict liability is the doctrine of respondeat superior or vicarious liability. Under this principle an employer is strictly liable for any torts committed by its employees within the scope of their employment. (*Respondeat superior* is Latin for "Let the superior be answerable.")[8] It should be noted that in a claim for strict liability, the defendant has no defense of contributory negligence; there is, however, a defense of assumption of risk.

The rules of evidence of the common law governing claims of negligence and strict liability reveal an understanding of the importance of incentives. Under the "subsequent repair" doctrine, plaintiffs are not allowed to introduce evidence that after an accident, the defendant made repairs that might have prevented the accident, or made changes in the design of a product to make it safer. The rationale is that allowing such information to be used as evidence that the defendant was negligent, or that its product was defective, would tend to discourage such safety improvements from being made, or at least delay them – an undesirable outcome that outweighed the potential gain in accuracy in the determination of the defendant's liability.

The Learned Hand rule

In this section we will consider a useful analytical tool known as the Learned Hand rule. It should be clearly understood that the Learned Hand rule is not a rule of law; rather it is an economic rationale for the decisions made by judges in negligence cases, and it also provides a standard as to how cases should be decided. We will see that the Learned Hand rule provides a much better way to understand the law of negligence than the hodgepodge of rules, exceptions, and legal fictions that are the traditional legal principles.

Under the Learned Hand rule, the defendant is liable for negligence if the amount of the loss, multiplied by the probability of the accident occurring when the defendant does not exercise due care, exceeds the cost of care, i.e., the cost of preventing the accident. Let B = the cost of care, p = the probability of the accident, and L = the amount of the loss if there is an accident. Then the defendant is liable if $B < pL$.

Suppose the amount of the loss is \$3,000, the probability of an accident when there is no care is one in five, and the cost to the defendant of preventing the accident is \$400. Then if the accident occurs, the defendant is liable for \$3,000 under the Learned Hand rule.

An English case[9] involved water pipes that were buried underground on the plaintiff's property. During winter there was an unusually severe frost, which made the pipes freeze and burst, causing damage to the plaintiff's home. The plaintiff claimed the water company was negligent for not burying the pipes deeper underground, so that they would not have frozen. The court, however, held that the water company was not negligent, since the probability of such a severe frost was very low. In this case $pL < B$, since p was quite small.

Let us return to the example in which L = \$3,000, $p = 1/5$ and B, the cost of care to the defendant, = \$400. Now suppose the plaintiff could also have avoided the accident, but at a cost of \$300. Suppose further that neither the plaintiff nor the defendant exercised care, so the accident occurs. In this case, the plaintiff is contributorily negligent, since the plaintiff's cost of care B_p = \$300 < pL = \$600. Of course the defendant's cost of care, \$400, is also less than \$600, but \$300 is less than \$400. Since the cost of the accident should be imposed on the party who can avoid it at least cost, it is efficient to impose liability on the plaintiff, that is, to prevent any recovery by the plaintiff.

For another application of the Learned Hand rule, consider the doctrine of foreseeability set forth in Palsgraf v. Long Island Railroad.[10] This case involved a passenger who arrived late at a railroad station, and was running to catch the defendant's train. The railroad's employees, who were trying to assist the passenger to board the train, dislodged a package she was holding, which fell on the rails. The package, which contained fireworks, then exploded, and the concussion overturned some scales, which fell upon the plaintiff and injured her. The court found that the railroad had not been negligent, since negligence requires foreseeability of harm to the person who is injured. There was no duty to the unforeseeable plaintiff, and therefore no negligence.

Rather than invent a new legal doctrine (the doctrine of foreseeability), we could simply apply the Learned Hand rule. Under this rule, there is no negligence, since $B > pL$.

The expected accident cost pL is small, since p, the probability of this chain of events, is very low. If the cost of taking precautions B is substantial, the defendant should not be liable.[11]

This analysis also provides a rationale for the doctrine of last clear chance. In Ploof v. Putnam[12] the plaintiff was boating on a lake. A storm approached, and the plaintiff sought to moor his boat at the dock of the defendant. However, an employee of the defendant shoved the boat away, and it was wrecked by the storm. Here the probability of an accident was large, as was the expected accident cost, and B, the cost to the defendant of preventing it, was small. Although the plaintiff, as a trespasser, was in a compromised position legally,[13] the defendant is liable under the Learned Hand rule.

Consider also a man who uses a railroad track as a footpath, and is therefore of course trespassing.[14] If the crew of an approaching train see him, they are obliged to blow the whistle and take other reasonable (i.e., cost-justified) measures to avoid hitting him. How quickly the brakes should be applied depends on the situation, since braking too suddenly might cause injuries to the train's passengers. Here again $B < pL$, since the probability of injury and the expected loss are large, and the cost of reasonable avoidance measures is small.

The law of rescue

Under Anglo-American common law there is no duty to rescue.[15] An obligation to rescue may, of course, be imposed by contract on, for example, a lifeguard, the crew of a cruise ship, or a teacher, but unless there is a contract or some kind of "special relationship" there is no duty.[16] A bystander is not required to call out to warn someone about to step into an open manhole. A passer-by with a cellular phone, who sees injured persons lying in the middle of an expressway after an accident, has no obligation to call the police. An expert swimmer on a dock, with a rope and a boat nearby, need not throw a line to someone who is drowning.

It seems difficult to reconcile the common-law rule with the Learned Hand rule. While in some cases a rescue attempt could involve a substantial risk to the rescuers, e.g. diving in to assist a drowning person, in many situations the cost of a rescue – a verbal warning or a telephone call to 911 – is much less than the expected accident cost. The common-law rule is often criticized for this reason. However, the rule has also been defended. It has been argued, for example, that a duty to rescue would create an unmanageable standard. If there are hundreds of people on a beach, but no lifeguard, which of them is obliged to help a swimmer in distress? Also, if the law required one to attempt a rescue only if it would not be hazardous to do so, it might be difficult in a split second to determine whether a rescue attempt involved such a risk. Another argument for the common-law rule is that if someone were liable for a failure to rescue, he would not be able to prove that a rescue he made was altruistic. A possible consequence, arguably, would be fewer rescues.

Liability for failure to rescue is, of course, a tax, and we know that anything that can be achieved by a tax can also be done by a subsidy – so why not give the rescuer a reward, instead of imposing liability for failure to rescue? It happens that in some cases, the law does exactly that. As we saw in the chapter on contracts, a physician who renders assistance in an emergency is entitled to a fee for his services (at a competitive rate), under the doctrine of "implied contract." The issue also arises under admiralty law, when a ship on the high seas is rescued by another. Under the law of salvage, the vessel that performs the rescue is entitled to a competitive price for the service, taking into account the danger involved, the level of skill required, the risk of failure, and the like. These implied contracts enable the parties to overcome the transaction costs of bargaining, in situations where it is not feasible (it is too costly) for the parties to negotiate the terms of a rescue. However, there is no general right to compensation outside of rescues performed by health professionals and other special cases.[17] The law of rescue may well be an example of an inefficient rule of tort law.

The collateral source rule

A plaintiff who has been injured by tortious conduct often receives benefits from a "collateral source." The source is called "collateral" because it's someone other than the injurer. For example, the victim may receive a payment from a policy of accident or workers' compensation insurance, or his medical expenses may be covered under his employer's health plan, or his salary may be paid during his disability by insurance sponsored by his employer. Under the collateral source rule of the common law, the defendant's damages are not reduced by the amount of benefits the plaintiff receives from sources other than the wrongdoer. To do so would violate the basic principle of tort law that the wrongdoer should bear the full social cost of his actions.

Suppose the victim's loss from an accident is $100,000, but he has an accident insurance policy for $40,000. The damages owed by the defendant would be only $60,000 if reduced by the amount of this policy. Suppose p, the probability that the accident will occur in the absence of care, is $1/1,000$, and B, the cost of care to the defendant, is $80. Since $B < pL$, it is efficient for the defendant to take care in this situation, and he will do so if liable for the full damages of $100,000. If, however, he knows he would be liable for only $60,000, his expected liability will be only $60 = 1/1,000 \times \$60,000$, and he would not have an incentive to exercise proper care.

Some courts have made a distinction based on whether collateral benefits are "gratuitous," i.e., benefits that the plaintiff has not paid for, and have deducted them from damages if they meet this requirement. However, this would still violate the principle of tort law cited above. Moreover, most benefits that have been classified as gratuitous have been paid for by the victim directly or indirectly. A plaintiff who obtains health insurance benefits from his employer receives those benefits in exchange for his labor, and his salary would be higher if the employer did not provide them.

Comparative negligence

In many jurisdictions common law negligence has been replaced, at least for certain types of cases, by an alternative regime known as comparative negligence. Under comparative negligence, responsibility for the accident is apportioned between plaintiff and defendant, and the plaintiff's damages are then reduced by his share of responsibility. Suppose, for example, that the plaintiff's damages are $1 million, but the court determines that he bears 20 percent of responsibility for the accident, while the defendant is 80 percent responsible. In this case the plaintiff is entitled to a recovery of only $800,000.

There is more than one type of comparative negligence. Under "pure" comparative negligence, a plaintiff may recover even if his share of responsibility is greater than the defendant's, or in the case of multiple defendants, more than that of all defendants combined.[18] In contrast, under modified comparative negligence, a plaintiff is barred from recovery if his share of responsibility exceeds a specified fraction. In some jurisdictions the plaintiff's share of fault must be less than one-half; in others it must not exceed one-half.

This modified form of comparative negligence can lead to some bizarre results. Suppose, for example, a plaintiff suffers damages of $1 million in an automobile accident. Assume the plaintiff was negligent, but the defendant had the last clear chance to avoid the collision. If the jury finds that the plaintiff was 40 percent negligent (but not contributory negligent since her share of negligence is less than 50 percent), she will recover $600,000 under the rules of comparative negligence. However, suppose instead that the plaintiff is found to be 60 percent negligent. The plaintiff is thus contributorily negligent, but will recover $1 million under the doctrine of last clear chance.[19] For being 20 percent more negligent, the plaintiff receives additional compensation of $400,000!

More on strict liability

Let us recall the hypothetical situation above, where the amount of the loss $L = \$3,000$, the probability of an accident when there is no care, p, is 1/5, B_d, the cost to the defendant of avoiding the accident, is $400, and B_p, the cost to the plaintiff of avoiding the accident, is $300. Recall that if the tort applicable to this situation is negligence, our analysis was as follows: if neither party takes care, and the accident occurs, the defendant would be negligent, but the plaintiff would be contributorily negligent and would therefore obtain no recovery. Knowing this, the plaintiff will make the expenditure of $300 to avoid an expected loss of $600. The defendant, knowing that she will not be liable if the accident occurs, will not make the expenditure of $400. This equilibrium is efficient; the social cost of accidents is minimized by the plaintiff's expenditure.

Now suppose that the tort applicable to these facts is strict liability rather than negligence. In this case if the accident occurs the defendant is liable, since there is no defense of contributory negligence. The victim, knowing that the defendant would be fully liable in the event of an accident, will not exercise care. The defendant, knowing that the victim will not make the expenditure, will make the expenditure of $400 to avoid an expected liability of $600. This equilibrium is of course inefficient, since the social cost would be lower if the victim, rather than the defendant, exercised due care.

If there were no transaction costs, we know from the Coase Theorem that the parties would reach an efficient outcome. The defendant would offer the victim an amount between $300 and $400 to sign a waiver of liability, in which the victim would waive his right to recover from the defendant in the event of an accident. The victim would then make his expenditure of $300 to avoid an expected liability of $600. In the real world, however, there may well be transaction costs that would prevent this efficient assignment of liability. For example, the courts often refuse to uphold waivers, on the ground that there was "inequality of bargaining power" between the parties, or that the waiver was a "contract of adhesion."

The inference to be drawn from the preceding analysis is that it is important to have conduct covered by negligence rather than strict liability in cases where the cost of avoiding the accident is lower for the victim. And, on reflection, it seems clear that in most cases the cost of avoiding injury will be lower for the party who is strictly liable than it would be for the victim. This certainly seems to be true for inherently dangerous things and activities; it is easier for those planting dynamite charges to warn bystanders than it is for bystanders to infer that blasting is being done.

Recall also that under the doctrine of respondeat superior, an employer is strictly liable for torts committed by its employees within the scope of their employment. In general, the cost of avoiding injury should be lower for the employer than for the victim, since the employer is the one who decides whom to hire, what tasks are assigned to the employee, how much training he must have, what safeguards he must use, and the like. Note, however, that under the fellow-servant rule the employer was not liable when one employee committed a tort against another. This rule was justified on two grounds: (1) this risk is known by employees, and is compensated by an increase in the wage; thus the risk is assumed by employees as part of the employment contract; and (2) the rule gives workers, who are in the best position to avoid injury, an incentive to take care, to avoid being injured by their coworkers. Note also that the fellow-servant rule did not apply if the employer knew that the tort would occur; in this case, of course, the cost of avoiding injury is lower for the employer.

Products liability

During the twentieth century the law of products liability in the United States was gradually transformed from negligence into strict liability. Landes and Posner (1987) have suggested that this development can be explained by a change in the cost to victims of avoiding injury. In the nineteenth century, especially in rural areas, many products purchased by consumers were made by farmers and individual craftsmen. The purchasers of these products often understood how they were made and how they worked as well as those who constructed them. Over the course of the twentieth century, however, products became more and more complex. With increasing specialization and division of labor, consumers were often unfamiliar with the products they bought, outside the range of their own area of business. As consumers became more helpless to avoid injuries, i.e., as the cost to consumers of avoiding injury increased, it made sense to avoid a pointless inquiry into contributory negligence, and to simply impose strict liability on the manufacturer.

On the other hand, strict liability may lead to the disappearance of valuable products. Newer children's playgrounds in the United States generally do not have see-saws or "monkey bars," sacrificing some enjoyment by the children and future benefits from learning how to deal with the risks inherent in exercise.

An argument often made for strict liability, as opposed to negligence, is that it provides an incentive for research and development in safety innovations. Suppose that $L = \$3,000$, $p = 1/5$, but B_d, the cost to the defendant of avoiding the accident, is \$800. Under the Learned Hand rule, the defendant would not be liable for negligence. Now suppose there is a promising idea for a potential safety improvement, which if successfully developed, would prevent the accident, but would cost \$400 to implement. A firm operating under a negligence regime would have no interest in sponsoring research and development of this safety improvement, given that its arrival would actually increase the firm's costs by \$400. A firm that was strictly liable would, however, be interested, since this innovation would enable it to reduce its costs from \$600 (its expected liability) to \$400.

Finally, it is interesting to note that the balancing of costs underlying the Learned Hand rule is reflected in the common law of strict liability. For example, there is a defense of "mishandling" that is similar to contributory negligence. And, even if there was mishandling, a firm will be strictly liable if there was "foreseeable misuse" of its product. Thus a manufacturer of a plastic garment bag must anticipate that bags may be left within the reach of children who, while playing with the bags, may suffocate. A manufacturer who fails to warn of this danger will be liable. Similarly, a tire manufacturer could be liable if its tire explodes at 85 m.p.h, since it should foresee that its tires may be used at speeds beyond the legal limit. In these cases, while the injury results from misuse or carelessness of the consumer, the accident could have been prevented by the manufacturer at a small cost. This idea, of course, bears more than a passing resemblance to the doctrine of last clear chance in negligence law.

Polinsky and Shavell (2010) argue that the law of products liability may be inefficient. A principal objective of products liability is to induce firms to make their products safer. They contend that even without products liability, firms have a strong incentive to ensure that their products are safe, because their sales and profits will fall if consumers learn that their products are unsafe, and they are likely to learn about product hazards, at least for products that are widely sold, because they will be informed of such hazards by various media – print media such as newspapers and magazines, radio, television, the internet, and informal word of mouth. Moreover, there is extensive safety regulation that requires firms to reduce the risks of injury from many products, such as pharmaceuticals, food, automobiles, and household appliances. Thus market forces and regulation already provide strong incentives to firms to make their products safe, and it seems unlikely that the potential of products liability will give them much additional incentive to do so.

Polinsky and Shavell also point out that products liability in effect forces consumers to buy insurance for injuries resulting from use of a product, since the expected cost to the firm of liability to customers for accidents is incorporated into the product price. Suppose the price of a bicycle would be $100 without consideration of products liability. Assume also there is no liability for defective products. In this case, if the customer were injured while riding the bicycle because of a defect in its design, he would have no "insurance" in the form of a claim for products liability against the manufacturer, although he might have insurance from other sources in the form of explicit policies of life, disability or health insurance. Now suppose there is products liability. If there was a 1 in 100,000 chance of an accident resulting in a liability of $1 million to the bicycle manufacturer, an expected cost of $10 would be added to the bicycle's price, but in the event the accident happened the customer would now effectively be insured in the form of a claim for $1 million. However, this example assumes that the customer would recover the entire amount that the bicycle manufacturer would be required to pay. In fact studies show that plaintiffs in tort litigation cases receive less than half of the total cost incurred by defendants; defendants also make substantial payments for lawyers and other costs of litigation. Thus this "insurance" for customers has very high "overheads." In other words, the reality is that if there were an accident, the bicycle manufacturer would spend at least $2 million as a defendant in the products liability case, so the bicycle's price would actually increase by an expected cost of $20, to $120. The effects on the price can actually be much larger than this example suggests. Manning (1996) studied the effect of products liability lawsuits on the diphtheria, pertussis, and tetanus vaccine. He found that this liability increased the price of the vaccine twentyfold, with the result that one million fewer children were vaccinated. Moreover, the litigation apparently did not cause an improvement in the safety of the vaccine.

One point in favor of products liability is that if products are indeed harmful to consumers, plaintiffs' lawyers have a powerful incentive to find out about it. Regulators may become captives of the industries they regulate; they are also susceptible to corruption, or may simply shirk their responsibilities to monitor product safety. With regard to market forces, the media will report on injuries that are obviously attributable to products, but in many cases a determination of whether an injury was caused by a product requires costly research. The media may not be inclined to make a large investment into potential hazards of a product in situations where it would be worth while for plaintiffs' lawyers to do so. In addition, injuries resulting from the use of products are less likely to be reported if the product is not widely used, and it is even possible that firms manufacturing the product will spread disinformation, as the tobacco companies did.

Medical malpractice

A claim of "medical malpractice" is actually a claim of negligence. The issue is whether the physician's treatment complied with the customary standards of his area of practice, where "area" refers both to geographic location and area of specialization. The idea that conduct is not negligent if it is the custom of the industry applies only to claims involving the performance of professional services. It has been justified on the ground that there is a contract between the plaintiff and defendant, which requires the defendant to exercise care that is customary in the profession.

Many have argued that the costs of medical malpractice liability exceed its benefits. The expected benefits are the improvements in the practice of medicine resulting from imposing liability on careless physicians. However, critics contend that the judicial system often makes mistakes, both in determining whether there was negligence and in assessing the extent of injury resulting from it. If the link between liability and care quality is uncertain, the deterrent effect of tort liability is diluted. Of course, if tort liability were completely random, it would give physicians no additional incentive to be careful. It is argued that one cost of the system is the practice of "defensive medicine," e.g., giving unnecessary tests and doing procedures that are not cost-justified, such as caesarean rather than natural delivery. One must add to this cost the costs of the court system itself – all the resources used in litigation, including the value of the time of lawyers, court personnel, and the parties.

These criticisms have prompted proposals to replace tort liability with a no-fault system like those used for workers' compensation and no-fault automobile insurance. In two states, Florida and Virginia, the no-fault principle has been implemented to provide compensation for neurological injuries to infants.[20] Epstein (1976) has suggested that medical malpractice law, like products liability law, has been evolving from negligence toward strict liability. In the next section we examine recent trends in medical malpractice liability: a cycle of growth, followed by contraction. This pattern is typical of other types of tort liability.

Changes in medical malpractice litigation

During a period that varied from state to state, but in one typical state, Michigan, extended from roughly 1974 to 1986, there were substantial increases in the frequency and severity of medical malpractice claims,[21] rapid growth of insurance premiums, and a withdrawal of many insurers from the market. Perception of a medical malpractice "crisis" led to the enactment of tort reform legislation in most states. Various factors that have been found to be important in causing the growth of medical malpractice litigation are described below.

1   There was substantial erosion or abolition of the locality rule, which provided that a physician was not negligent if his treatment met the standard of care customary in the location of his practice. The principal effect of this rule had been to limit the pool of doctors who were qualified to testify whether the defendant's performance met the standard of care. If, say, the defendant was a South Dakota physician, one could argue that the only experts who could testify on the issue of negligence would be other physicians from South Dakota. A specialist whose practice was dependent on referrals from other physicians might find it advisable not to testify for the plaintiff. This was the alleged "conspiracy of silence."

Over time, many courts decided to adopt a national standard of care, which reduced the cost to the plaintiff of obtaining expert testimony. Courts also began to allow medical textbooks to provide evidence of customary practice.

2   There was expanded use of the doctrine of "res ipsa loquitur" (the thing speaks for itself). Under this doctrine, certain circumstances are deemed sufficient to support a finding of negligence, e.g., sponges left in the patient by a surgeon. Some courts have given the rule an additional procedural effect, by having the burden of proof shift to the defendant.

3   Courts applied the doctrine of respondeat superior to make hospitals liable for the actions of their employees.

4   Many states, by statute or judicial decision, abolished charitable and sovereign immunity, i.e. the common-law immunity of charitable institutions and government from tort liability. This made it possible to sue voluntary (nonprofit) and government hospitals for medical malpractice.

5   Under the doctrine of informed consent, a patient who was not fully informed of the risks of a procedure could sue for negligence.[22] The courts determined that a physician has a duty to disclose to the patient all information that a reasonable person would want to know under the circumstances.

The response to the growth of such litigation was a nationwide wave of tort reform legislation. Some of the most important types of legislative responses were as follows:

1   Many states reinstated some form of the locality rule, or limited the scope of the doctrine of res ipsa loquitur.

2   Some states reduced the period of the statute of limitations applicable to medical malpractice. Sometimes the law was changed to have the period of limitations run from the date of the injury, rather than from the (later) date on which the injury or negligence was discovered.

3   Many states repealed the collateral benefits rule, allowing damages to be reduced by collateral payments such as the plaintiff's insurance coverage. Some of these statutes allowed evidence of such payments to be introduced at trial, and some required that court awards be reduced by the amount of these payments. These statutes, of course, violated the basic principle underlying the collateral benefits rule, that the wrongdoer should bear the full social cost of his actions.

4   As of 1991 at least twenty-five states had imposed limitations on medical malpractice awards.

5   Certain states, such as California, limited the percentage that could be paid to lawyers working on a contingent fee basis (i.e., all lawyers who represented plaintiffs). Some research has found that these caps on contingent fees reduced the severity of malpractice awards.

6   Another innovation was the creation of state patient compensation funds.[23] The purpose of these funds was to relieve physicians or hospitals from liability above some threshold level, typically $100,000 for a physician. The state fund was liable for awards in excess of this amount, usually up to a ceiling such as $1 million. The fund was financed by imposing surcharges on the malpractice insurance policies of physicians – for example, 25 percent of the premium. These funds in effect required low-risk physicians to subsidize those of high risk, like the "assigned risk" plans often used in automobile insurance.

7   Finally, a number of states provided for mediation, arbitration, or pretrial screening panels. Some states required the plaintiff to file a physician's affidavit that the case had merit, or to post a bond. The primary motivation for most of this legislation was a desire to weed out claims lacking legal merit. However, these initiatives were based on a misunderstanding of the economics of personal injury litigation. The most

effective screening device is undoubtedly the plaintiff's lawyer. Since the lawyer's fee is contingent on the recovery, it is in his interest to decline a client who has a frivolous claim.

Another proposal for malpractice law reform is to enact laws that authorize regulatory agencies to publish "practice parameters," which are detailed guidelines of practice for various medical specialties such as emergency room medicine, obstetrics and gynecology, anesthesiology, and radiology. These statutes would allow a physician to raise an affirmative defense against a charge of malpractice if he can show he has followed the practice protocols; however, they would bar plaintiffs from introducing a practice parameter into evidence to show that a physician who did not follow it provided substandard care.

There is a substantial question as to how practice parameters would affect the quality of medical care, and also whether they would reduce or increase the practice of "defensive medicine." Hospitals might find it optimal to inoculate themselves against liability by having their physicians follow all the directives of the practice parameters, even if some of the prescribed procedures were not cost-effective. Moreover, tests that were medically appropriate, but not required by the practice parameters, might not be done.

As a general proposition, it is more costly to regulate behavior through detailed rules rather than through a general standard such as "customary standards of the physician's area of practice." Substantial costs would be incurred both in formulating practice parameters initially, and then in revising them periodically to keep them abreast of advances in technology and medical knowledge. Unless the rules were quite specific, the physician would not be able to show conclusively that he satisfied their requirements; but the more specific the rules, the more complex they would have to be, and the more often they would have to be revised. For the foregoing reasons, most commentators believe that the introduction of practice parameters would actually increase the cost of medical care.

Effects of malpractice liability on physician behavior

What are the consequences of a substantial increase in medical malpractice liability? A number of possible responses on the supply side can be identified. We would expect changes on both the intensive and extensive margins of medical practice.[24] On the intensive margin, surgeons may reduce the number of operations they perform, or may decide not to do high-risk procedures. Some have argued that the quality of medical practice improves as physicians become more inclined to refer to specialists cases for which they are only marginally qualified (the counterargument is that such referrals may be unwarranted, and simply increase the cost of medical practice by adding a transaction cost).

On the extensive margin, physicians may withdraw entirely from a high-risk area of practice, or may decide to retire sooner than they would have otherwise. Moreover, medical students may choose not to enter areas of specialization with a high rate of malpractice liability. There is also a spatial extensive margin: physicians who are completing their education may choose not to enter states with high malpractice exposure, and physicians in such states may eventually choose to relocate. Of course, whether individuals make these decisions depends on the costs of doing so, and on the extent and expected duration of unusual levels of liability. We would expect the least costly types of adjustments, e.g. doing fewer risky procedures, to be made more often than those of high cost, e.g. moving one's practice to another state.

In medical malpractice cases the plaintiff's lawyer typically sues a number of different defendants directly or indirectly involved in the patient's care: the attending physician, nurses, the hospital, manufacturers of medical equipment, and others. If the plaintiff succeeds in obtaining a recovery against several named defendants, the question arises as to how the liability is apportioned among them. This issue applies not only to medical malpractice cases, but to any tort claim made against multiple defendants. This subject is considered in the next section, which examines the doctrine of joint and several liability and rules concerning contribution among joint tortfeasors.

Contribution

At common law, if two or more persons were liable for harm done to a third person, their liability was "joint and several." If, for example, a plaintiff obtained a recovery against five co-defendants for $1 million, he could collect the entire amount from any one of the defendants, or could collect a different amount from each defendant in any combination of amounts, so long as the total amount collected equaled $1 million. Now suppose the plaintiff elected to collect the entire $1 million from one of the defendants. Could that defendant then recover a pro rata portion of the recovery, $200,000, from each of the other four defendants? In legal parlance, the issue is whether there is a "right of contribution" among joint tortfeasors. Under American common law, there was no right of contribution. However, in many states the common-law rule of no contribution has been overruled, at least to some extent, by statute or judicial decision. As we shall see, a rule of no contribution helps plaintiffs and encourages settlement, relative to a rule allowing contribution.[25]

Suppose the plaintiff, A, has been injured by a violation of tort law involving n defendants. Let p be the probability that the plaintiff will win at trial, and let X equal the amount the plaintiff recovers if he wins. If none of the defendants settles, the expected liability of each defendant is pX/n. Therefore any defendant would be willing to settle with the plaintiff for an amount less than pX/n. Also, the plaintiff would want to settle with a defendant for any positive amount, until all but one of the defendants has settled. This is so because, by settling with a defendant, the plaintiff is exchanging uncertain dollars for certain dollars. We can prove this as follows.

When no contribution is allowed

If the plaintiff does not settle with any defendant, and goes to trial, his expected recovery is pX. Now suppose instead he settles with one of the defendants for some amount S. His expected recovery then becomes:

$$S + p(X - S) = S + pX - pS = pX + S(1 - p)$$

which is clearly greater than pX since p is less than 1.

If the plaintiff settles with one defendant after another, until there is only one remaining defendant who has not settled, the expected liability of the remaining defendant is:

$$p\left[X - \sum_{i=1}^{n-1} S_i\right]$$

where S_i is the amount of the settlement payment from defendant i. We can imagine that there will be a competition among the defendants, in which a defendant who offers the plaintiff a low settlement payment will be outbid by another offering a higher payment, until the amount offered in settlement just equals the expected liability of a defendant who does not settle. For simplicity, let us assume that the outcome of this competition is an equilibrium in which all of the defendants but one settle, and the settlement payment of each settling defendant is the same amount S (recall that in an equilibrium each party is doing the best he can, and no one has an incentive to change his position). Then the expected liability of the sole nonsettling defendant, which we will call V, equals $p[X - (n - 1)S]$, and by the assumption above $V = S$. Therefore:

$$S = p[X - (n-1)S] \Rightarrow S = pX - pS(n-1) \Rightarrow S[1 + p(n-1)] = pX \Rightarrow S = \frac{pX}{1 + p(n-1)}$$

Now the total expected recovery of the plaintiff will be n times this amount, or:

$$nS = \frac{npX}{1 + p(n-1)}$$

This is greater than pX, the plaintiff's expected recovery if none of the defendants settles, so long as $p < 1$. Thus a rule of no contribution enables a plaintiff to do better than he would if none of the defendants settled. They will settle (all but one of them) because it is to their advantage to do so.

Note also that if n is a very large number, the plaintiff's total expected recovery approaches X. If we consider p to be a measure of the quality of the plaintiff's claim, where for a worthless claim $p = 0$, and for an incontestable claim $p = 1$, then we see that as n, the number of defendants, becomes very large, the competition among the defendants enables the plaintiff's expected recovery to approach X regardless of the merits of the claim p. This occurs because the plaintiff can "whipsaw" the defendants with the threat of suing them for the residual liability if they do not settle.

The defendants would do better if they could agree among themselves that none of them would enter into a separate settlement agreement with the plaintiff. They could agree that no one would settle unless the plaintiff agreed to settle with all the defendants for a total payment of pX. The share of each defendant would then be pX/n. This is less than the expected liability when defendants do settle separately:

$$\frac{pX}{1 + p(n-1)}$$

The problem is, of course, that the plaintiff is likely to be able to induce a defendant to breach such an agreement by offering to settle with him for less than pX/n.

When contribution is allowed

If, on the other hand, contribution is allowed, there is no incentive for a defendant to settle with the plaintiff. Indeed, a defendant who settles with the plaintiff would actually increase his expected liability. This can be seen as follows. Recall that if none of the defendants settles, a defendant's expected liability is pX/n. Now suppose a defendant settles for some amount S. His expected liability now is:

$$S + p\left(\frac{X}{n} - S\right) = S - pS + \frac{pX}{n} = \frac{pX}{n} + S(1-p)$$

which is larger than pX/n. The defendant is always worse off if he settles, since he is trading certain dollars (in the settlement payment) for uncertain dollars. Consequently a rule allowing contribution has been compared to government enforcement of a cartel agreement among defendants not to settle.[26] When contribution is allowed, defendants are less likely to settle and plaintiffs are unambiguously worse off.

Damages

There are four components of damages for a nonfatal injury: medical expenses, lost earnings, the lost value of household services, and pain and suffering. When there is a long period of disability resulting from the injury, the expert witness who is asked to calculate damages must predict the amounts of the losses in future years and then compute the discounted present value of the stream of losses. Damages are normally paid in a lump sum rather than as periodic payments. One reason for this practice is moral hazard. Since the objective is to compensate the individual for the time during which his earnings are reduced by disability, one could argue that he should be paid his earnings every year until he is able to return to work full-time. The problem with this arrangement is that it gives the individual an incentive to remain disabled; consequently damages are paid in a lump sum.

Lost earnings

If the victim was employed, the expert will examine the time path of earnings for an individual in that occupation. If, for example, the victim was a twenty-five-year-old physical therapist, the expert will forecast future earnings from cross-sectional data on earnings of physical therapists of different ages, and will use an expected work life for a person of the victim's characteristics, such as sex, age, and level of education. When the victim is a child, one usually does not know what occupation the child would have chosen. Here the expert might predict the level of education the child would have completed, given relevant variables such as the parents' educational level and income, and then use the median earnings and expected work life for an individual with those characteristics (e.g., imputed level of education, age, and gender).

In determining expected work life, a worker's educational level has both an income effect and a substitution effect. A worker with more human capital than average has a higher salary and therefore a higher opportunity cost of retirement; this substitution or price effect tends to increase the age of retirement: since leisure time costs more, the individual is inclined to "purchase" less of it. On the other hand, a highly educated worker also has a higher income and greater wealth than the average worker; his greater income leads him to "purchase" more normal goods, including leisure time. Accordingly this income effect will tend to reduce the age of retirement. It is not clear a priori which of these effects will dominate, but it is clear that the level of education is important in predicting retirement age.

The expert's report will take into account that earnings would change in future years not only because of changes in age and experience, but also from expected promotions or possible layoffs. In addition, earnings will change because of inflation and increases in productivity. Increases resulting from these two factors are often forecast from a time series such as the Employment Cost Index maintained by the Bureau of Labor Statistics, which shows how the combined value of wages and fringe benefits for workers has increased over the years, for different occupations and industry groups.

Another factor that should be considered is that damages are generally nontaxable, while the earnings they replace would have been subject to federal, state, and perhaps city income tax (the fringe benefits, however, would not have been taxed).[27] Under some statutes, such as the Federal Employers' Liability Act, damages are therefore based on after-tax rather than pre-tax earnings.[28]

The interest rates that should be used to convert future losses into present value are those on U.S. government treasury securities.[29] Since interest rates vary, depending on time to maturity, ideally one would discount damages for each future year by the current interest rate applicable to that year, derived from a treasury bond. It is important to use Treasury securities rather than, say, corporate bonds, since interest rates on nongovernmental obligations are higher, to compensate for the risk of default. It is more likely that a corporation would fail to pay its debt than that the U.S. government would.

To recapitulate, the victim's future nominal (money) earnings are forecast by adjusting his current earnings for the effects of inflation and increases in the productivity of labor.[30] These future amounts are then reduced to present value by discounting at the nominal rate of interest, which equals the real rate of interest plus the expected rate of inflation. Note that the expected rate of inflation is included in both the upward and downward adjustments. These two adjustments do not necessarily cancel each other out, however, because the rate of increase in labor productivity may not equal the real rate of interest.

Lost value of household services

An element of damages that is increasingly important is the lost value of household services. In actions for personal injury or wrongful death, and divorce cases, it is often necessary to assign a value to activity that is economically productive, but done outside the labor market, e.g., cooking, cleaning, doing laundry, child care, gardening, painting, and home maintenance. Two alternative methods have been used to determine the value of such services.[31]

One approach is to use replacement cost, i.e., the cost of services of outside professionals, by adding the wages of a short-order cook to the cost of maid service, day care, and the like. A basic problem with this approach is that these services were not in fact purchased in the market; thus the family was not willing to pay the market price for such services, or, putting it differently, the value of these services to the family was less than the market price. Consequently this method of valuation may overstate the value of these services to the family. Another problem is that hiring professionals to provide these services would involve many transaction costs, reflected in the market price, that do not arise when all of them are performed by one person.

The other approach is based on opportunity cost, i.e., valuing an hour of household work by estimating what the individual would have been able to earn, after all taxes (but including incremental fringe benefits), if she had worked an additional hour rather than stay home. However, there are difficulties with this approach if the individual did not do any work outside the home. In this case there are two problems: (1) if there is no recent activity in the labor market, we don't know what the individual would have earned, if she had worked; and (2) even if we did know that, we know the individual valued her time doing household work more than her outside wage, since, after all, she did choose to stay home. Thus the opportunity cost approach would tend to understate the value of her household services. Notwithstanding these difficulties, the value of household work is now a well-established category of damages in personal injury cases, and a basis for division of property in divorce cases.

Damages for a fatal injury

Damages for a fatal injury include two of the components for a nonfatal injury, medical expenses and pain and suffering, and an additional component representing the financial loss to the victim's survivors: the victim's lost earnings, and the lost value of his household services, minus the income and household services he would have consumed if he had lived. The idea is that since the victim has died, his family has lost his earnings, but it is no longer necessary to pay for his living expenses (as it would be if he had been permanently disabled). Thus, rather than increase damages by the total present value of the deceased victim's lost earnings, one should deduct the present value of the share of *household* income that would have been consumed each year by the victim. Similarly, rather than increase damages by the total present value of the victim's lost household services, one should offset the present value of the additional household services that would have been provided (whether by the victim or by others in his household) because of his being there, if he had lived. In other words, one should deduct from damages the marginal cost to the family of the victim's being there, had he survived. Because of indivisibilities and economies of scale, the marginal cost of certain household expenditures might be zero; for example, the cost of keeping the lawn mowed will be the same whether there are three or four people in the household.

This conventional measure of damages has been criticized on the ground that it does not accurately measure the social cost of the victim's death. According to this view, it would be better to use a market measure of the value of the victim's life, where value is determined (as it always is in economics) by willingness to pay. That is, we may consider the value of A's life to be equal to the total amount that A, his family, friends, and others are willing to pay for it. In practice, this is done by attempting to determine the individual's valuation of his own life. The assumption is that the individual will incorporate into his own valuation the valuation of his life by relatives and friends, and there is some evidence that this is the case. One study (DeLeire and Levy 2004) found that married women with children worked in jobs with a lower risk of death than married women without children, but that single mothers, whose death would leave their children without a parent, chose to work in even safer jobs. Men who were single parents also worked in safer jobs than married men.

The worker's valuation of his life is inferred from market data, such as the wage premium that is paid to workers in occupations that are physically hazardous. Suppose, for example, that a policeman with the usual responsibilities has a salary of $30,000. Suppose also that work on an undercover narcotics unit requires the same skills and the same commitment of time, but involves a risk of death that is 1 percent higher than routine police work. Assume that the salary required to fill this position is $40,000. It appears, then, that a policeman who joins the narcotics unit is willing to accept a 1 percent increase in risk of death for $10,000.

There are obviously a number of critical assumptions behind this conclusion. We are assuming, for example, that from the policeman's standpoint there is no difference between the two positions aside from the difference in risk. We are also ignoring the fact that on the narcotics unit there may be a greater risk of nonfatal injury, as well as a greater risk of death. Finally, we are assuming that the individual has perfect information about the risks of each position.

How then do we use this information to arrive at a value of life? We could argue as follows. If a 1 percent increase in risk of death is valued at $10,000, then perhaps a 100 percent probability of death is valued at $1 million. This is of course a gross oversimplification of the econometric methods used to calculate a value of life. One problem with this example is that the value of safety to an individual may not be – indeed, surely is not – a proportional or linear function of risk. That is, many people might accept a 1 percent increase in risk for $10,000, but very, very few of them would be willing to die for a payment of $1 million. Note that even if we ignore this problem, the preceding calculation assumes that the individual is risk-neutral. If the individual were risk-averse, the value of life to him would be less than $1 million, since he would demand more than an actuarially fair amount to accept the additional 1 percent risk.

Another problem comes under the heading of selectivity bias. Individuals who take risky jobs, and whose earnings are used to estimate the value of life, may be more willing to accept risk than most people. Returning to the example of the narcotics unit, suppose the great majority of officers in the precinct would demand $20,000 as compensation for the additional risk, but that a few individuals would demand only $9,000. Then the individuals working in the narcotics unit will be atypical of the general population, since they would all be drawn from the group with an unusual tolerance for risk. The economist would infer from the data that the value of life is $1 million when the value for the vast majority of the population is $2 million. There are econometric methods that are designed to address these and other issues arising in value-of-life calculations, but they are beyond the scope of this book.

The value of life has also been calculated from various transactions outside the labor market that reveal the amount people are willing to pay to avoid risk. Different studies have analyzed data on whether people buy smoke detectors, whether they buckle a seatbelt, their choice of highway speed, the decision to smoke cigarettes, the effect of air pollution on property values, and how the fatality rate for a specific automobile model affects its purchase price.[32] Obtaining similar estimates of the value of life from different sources enhances one's confidence in the feasibility of this approach.

Punitive damages

In some cases a defendant may be held liable for damages beyond the amount required to compensate victims for their loss. Damages beyond the compensatory amount are known as punitive damages. Court decisions and the legal literature have provided little guidance as to when punitive damages should be awarded, and if so, how much they should be; the courts have only stated in general terms that the goals of punitive damages are deterrence and punishment.[33] Some commentators have criticized the uncertainty about the appropriate amount of punitive damages, and their resulting unpredictability, and there have been occasional, albeit rare, instances of very large awards, even though these are usually reduced substantially on appeal. For example, a purchaser of a new BMW sued when he learned that part of his car had been repainted because of damage before the car was shipped to the dealer. A jury awarded him $4,000 in compensatory damages and $4 million in punitive damages. After appeals the punitive damages were reduced to $50,000[34] (see the discussion of *remittitur* below). In another case, the *Exxon Valdez*, a supertanker, ran aground on a reef, spilling 11 million gallons of oil and polluting over 1,000 miles of Alaska coastline. The plaintiffs, fishermen and Alaskan natives, obtained a recovery of several hundred million dollars in compensatory damages and $5 billion in punitive damages. The Ninth Circuit Court of Appeals ruled that the award of punitive damages was excessive.[35] The U.S. Supreme Court agreed to hear the case, and decided that the punitive damages could not exceed the compensatory damages that the company had already paid for the victims' economic losses, \$507.5 million.[36] Publicity about cases like these (the BMW case more than the *Exxon Valdez* case) has prompted many proposals to limit the amount of punitive damages, and ceilings have been imposed in many states.

Much if not all the uncertainty surrounding punitive damages could be eliminated if they were determined in a way suggested by certain researchers.[37] Their proposal is that punitive damages be awarded only when the wrongdoer will sometimes be able to avoid liability for the harm he causes. According to this view, it is not appropriate to award punitive damages in situations where it is virtually certain that the wrongdoer will be held liable for his actions.

Suppose the ship of a cruise line routinely dumps waste oil into the ocean, and falsifies its log books to conceal its activities. Let us assume that the social cost of each act of pollution is \$100,000, and the probability the ship will be caught on any given occasion is 10 percent, or 0.10. Under general principles of tort law, a wrongdoer should be held liable for the full amount of damages resulting from its actions. Here the cruise line causes on average $10 \times \$100,000 = \$1$ million of total damage for every time it is caught. Therefore each time it is caught the cruise line should be held liable for \$1 million, not just the \$100,000 of damage it caused on the occasion in question. Every time the cruise line is caught dumping oil, it should be liable for \$100,000 of compensatory damages and \$900,000 of punitive damages. In general, if X is the average amount of damages resulting from each violation and p is the probability the wrongdoer will be apprehended, the wrongdoer should be required to pay damages of $(1/p)X$ each time it is apprehended. The justification for this amount is as follows: if we follow this rule, then with probability p, the wrongdoer will be caught and have to pay damages of X/p, and with probability $1 - p$ the wrongdoer will not be caught and will pay damages of 0. Therefore its expected damages for each wrongful act are:

$$p \cdot \frac{X}{p} + (1-p) \cdot 0 = X$$

which is what they should be, since the actual damages of the act are X. Thus the wrongdoer should pay total damages of $(1/p)X$ each time it is apprehended. These damages will have a compensatory component of X and a punitive component of:

$$\frac{1}{p}X - X = X\left(\frac{1}{p} - 1\right)$$

Punitive damages will generally be appropriate when there has been an attempt to conceal wrongful conduct, since by definition this makes it likely that the conduct will not be discovered. Conversely, punitive damages are not appropriate when it is for all practical purposes certain that the wrongdoer will be sued for damages, e.g., when there has been an airplane crash, or a collapse of a defectively designed building. With regard to the two cases referred to above, it has been argued that punitive damages were appropriate in the BMW case, since it is likely that many purchasers whose cars were repainted were not aware of that fact and did not bring a lawsuit. Polinsky and Shavell contend that punitive damages were not appropriate in the *Exxon Valdez* case, since it is virtually certain that a lawsuit would be brought against a supertanker running aground and polluting 1,000 miles of coastline.

(However, they note that punitive damages should be awarded in a case where a cruise ship covertly dumps oil into the ocean.)

In some states part of punitive damages is paid to the state, rather than the plaintiffs. For example, in Iowa the plaintiff receives only 25 percent of punitive damages under certain circumstances. In general this "decoupling" of the amount paid by defendants from the amount received by plaintiffs should not reduce the deterrent effect of damages; expected damages will have the same deterrent effect whether defendants must pay them to the plaintiffs or the state. But what if the plaintiffs stood to receive none, or a very small share, of punitive damages? In this case we might expect the parties to settle the case, with the defendant agreeing to increase its payment of compensatory damages in return for the plaintiff's agreement to relinquish its claim for punitive damages.[38]

Box 8.2 Additur and remittitur

The principal procedure used to correct trial awards that deviate substantially from the expected outcome is review by additur or remittitur. If a defendant believes that the damages awarded by the jury or judge are excessive, he can file with the trial court a request for a new trial on the issue of damages. The court can then order that the defendant's request be granted unless the plaintiff agrees to a reduction of the award by a specified amount; this procedure is called *remittitur* (from the Latin word *remittere*, to abate, release, or return). For example, if the defendant requests a new trial on the ground that a jury's award of $1 million is excessive, and the trial judge agrees, she may offer the plaintiff the option of agreeing to a reduction of the award to $600,000 in lieu of a new trial. It is almost always in the plaintiff's interest to accept the proposed reduction, since a new trial would have substantial costs (legal expenses and the risk of a lower award) and no expected benefit, since it is implicit in the court's use of remittitur that it would be applied again if the second trial yielded another large award.

Additur is the corresponding remedy for a plaintiff who believes that the award of damages was too low. If, for example, a plaintiff files a request for a new trial on the issue of damages on the ground that an award of $250,000 was too low, and the judge agrees, she might offer the defendant the option of agreeing to an increase of the award to $500,000 as an alternative to a new trial.

Litigants often appeal decisions by the trial court on additur or remittitur, and it is not uncommon for appellate courts to modify awards made by trial courts, most often by reducing them. Both additur and remittitur are employed in state courts, although the use of remittitur is more common. While remittitur is applied in federal courts, additur is not, since the Supreme Court has held that it denies a defendant its Seventh Amendment right to a jury trial in civil cases.

Whether dangerous conduct should be controlled by tort law or regulation

Another major issue is whether certain types of dangerous conduct, in particular those that may cause catastrophic injuries, should be controlled by tort law or regulation, i.e. by victim enforcement or government enforcement. Some commentators contend that tort law is ill suited to control actions that may injure many persons, for three reasons:

1   When there are many victims the total damages may exceed the wrongdoer's total value.
2   In certain cases, e.g., the burial of hazardous waste in defective containers, a long period of time may elapse between the defendant's actions and the discovery of the victims' injuries. In these cases it may be difficult to prove the victims' injuries were caused by the defendant because of lost records, uncertain memories, lost or unavailable witnesses, and the like.
3   For other reasons, e.g. multiple possible injurers, it may be impossible to determine which defendant is responsible for the injury to a particular victim.

The first objection overlooks the point that the objective of the tort system is to provide deterrence rather than compensation. A potential injurer will have an incentive to take precautions as long as the cost of doing so is less than the expected loss of the injurer's net worth if the precautions are not taken. In any case, regulation could require a firm wishing to enter into a dangerous activity to post a bond or obtain insurance to provide for full compensation to potential victims. If no one could provide such insurance then presumably no one should be allowed to enter into that activity.

With regard to points 2 and 3, let us consider an example of the difficulty of proving causation. Suppose there is an accident involving a nuclear reactor that increases the probability that everyone within a fifty-mile radius of the reactor will get cancer by 25 percent. Any person within this area who subsequently got cancer would not know whether he got it because of the nuclear accident, or would have gotten it anyway.

Landes and Posner (1984), and Oi (1984) have analyzed different ways of dealing with this problem. If the defendant in this example were not held liable for any damages there would be no deterrence of dangerous conduct; on the other hand, if the defendant were liable for full damages of all cancer cases there would be overdeterrence, in violation of the Learned Hand rule. Suppose the damages incurred by a victim of cancer were X. One option is to hold the defendant liable to each person who eventually gets cancer for the proportion of total damages attributable to the increased risk. In the example cited above this would be a liability to each person who gets cancer of:

$$\frac{0.25}{1.0 + 0.25} \bullet X = 0.20X$$

Another option is to redefine the injury as the increase in the risk of getting cancer, rather than cancer itself. Suppose normally only 20 percent of the population in the surrounding area would get cancer, but because of the nuclear accident 25 percent would. In this case the defendant could be held liable to every person in the affected population for an amount representing the increase in expected damages resulting from the increased probability of cancer. In this example this would be a liability of $(0.25X - 0.20X) = 0.05X$ to each person in the surrounding area. This approach would be especially useful in cases where there is a long period of latency between exposure to the hazard and the onset of the disease; under this proposal the claims of all potential victims could be resolved quickly after the accident. However this would require a substantial modification of tort law: a claim based on strict liability or negligence normally requires actual damages, not just a fear of injury.

Difficulties in proving causation are also likely to arise when there are multiple injurers. If C worked for A and B, two firms that each had asbestos in the workplace, and subsequently became ill from an asbestos-related disease, we would not know which of the firms was responsible.

In cases like this, where there are multiple injurers and it is impossible to determine who caused a specific injury, the courts have sometimes apportioned damages based on each defendant's share of the market. For example, the issue of causation arose in litigation involving the drug DES (diethylstilbestrol), which was given to millions of pregnant women between 1941 and 1971. DES was originally believed to prevent miscarriages and improve the health of newborn babies, but was later found to cause cancer and birth defects. Since the harmful effects of DES sometimes did not appear for twenty or more years after it was taken, the plaintiffs were usually unable to identify the pharmaceutical company that had manufactured the drug they took. The solution that was adopted by some courts was to apportion liability among all the companies that sold DES according to their respective shares of the market.

Some commentators have argued that in these situations it is better to control the dangerous conduct by direct regulation rather than modify the traditional requirements of tort law. However, a full analysis must consider the administrative costs of each regime. The objective, as noted by Walter Oi, is to choose the regime that minimizes the sum of (1) the costs of accidents, (2) the costs of avoiding accidents, and (3) the administrative costs of the legal system.

Under tort law, the cost of litigation is greater for claims based on negligence than those for strict liability, since the former involve the additional issue of negligence. On the other hand, under strict liability more claims may be filed, since the plaintiff is not required to prove negligence. Under either tort the costs of litigation can be substantial, even if all individual claims are combined into one action to exploit economies of scale in litigation. However, the alternative of direct regulation has its own costs: there are costs of formulating the regulation, and costs of enforcing it.

As we noted in our discussion of practice parameters for physicians, it is more costly to regulate behavior with detailed rules than with a general standard. The use of specific rules entails greater costs both in formulating the rules initially, and revising them periodically to keep abreast of changing conditions. A set of detailed rules becomes outmoded more quickly than a general standard. On the other hand, a general standard of conduct creates more uncertainty; it is more likely to inhibit activities that were not meant to be proscribed. The more general the regulation is, the more difficult it is to be sure that one is not in violation of it.

We must also consider the costs of enforcement. Tort law is enforced vigorously by the victims of torts, who have an incentive to sue, and usually have more information than anyone else about the extent of their injuries. In contrast, when it comes to the enforcement of regulations, public officials often have much less to gain from enforcement than the regulated parties stand to lose, and this disparity is reflected in the quality of enforcement.[39] Consider the example of antitrust law: those who violate certain antitrust laws are subject to both criminal prosecution and civil damages. The plaintiffs in civil actions can recover treble damages, an amount equal to three times their actual damages. It is well known that, to those considering business arrangements that may violate antitrust laws, the prospect of treble damage actions has a much greater deterrent effect than the threat of criminal prosecution.

All of the factors referred to above must be considered in determining what kinds of conduct should be controlled by tort law, regulation, or both. In the next section we examine another alternative to tort law: a system that would provide compensation for injuries without regard to fault.

No-fault automobile insurance

Criticism of the tort system has led many states to adopt no-fault automobile insurance. Under the typical no-fault statute, an accident victim can recover medical expenses and lost earnings from his own insurer regardless of the circumstances, e.g., even if no other vehicle was involved, or the victim himself was negligent, or another driver was involved but was not negligent. Collateral benefits are often deducted from the victim's recovery, and there is no compensation for pain and suffering. However, in most jurisdictions tort liability is preserved for serious accidents. Generally a victim may sue in tort if his damages, other than pain and suffering, exceed a prescribed threshold. Colorado, for example, allows an individual to sue for negligence if his accident results in medical expenses exceeding $500, or a loss in earnings for more than a year.[40] Michigan allows a tort action if the injury is "serious impairment of body function, or permanent serious disfigurement."

The case for no-fault is generally based on two alternative grounds: (1) the tort system provides inadequate compensation to accident victims; and (2) if the major objective of tort law is to deter careless driving, the costs of the system exceed the benefits. Critics argue that the only real deterrent to careless driving is the fear of physical injury – of being killed or maimed. According to this view, the prospect of tort liability provides no additional deterrence, especially since it is usually covered by insurance.

With respect to the argument based on inadequate compensation, it is true that under the negligence system a person injured in a driving accident receives no compensation in a number of different situations: when no other vehicle was involved, when the defendant is uninsured and insolvent, when the defendant cannot be identified, e.g., because he is a hit-and-run driver, when the defendant was not negligent, or when the victim himself was negligent. However the basic justification for the law of negligence is deterrence, not compensation. Individuals can purchase insurance to cover losses not compensated under tort law. Indeed, in many states no-fault insurance is viewed as a supplement to compensation obtained through the tort system, rather than a replacement for it.[41]

The second argument is that the only real deterrent to careless driving is the driver's instinct for self-preservation. This argument seems plausible, but does not survive close scrutiny. The basic problem with a no-fault scheme that displaces tort liability is that it separates an action from its consequences; that is, it opens the door to moral hazard. Careless driving may involve social costs apart from physical injury to the occupants of the driver's vehicle. Driving that involves little risk to the driver may cause injuries to pedestrians, or persons on bicycles, motorcycles or other vehicles, as well as property damage. Such careless driving activity may be deterred by imposing its costs on the driver, whether through civil liability, criminal penalties, or both.

Tort liability may be a substantial deterrent even if it is covered by insurance. First, the insurance policy may not cover all the damages, or there may be a deductible or copayment. Second, a careless driver is likely to be in a number of accidents, which are likely to increase his premiums. Thirdly, one must consider deterrence on the extensive as well as the intensive margin. Since firms that employ drivers of trucks, taxicabs, buses, and limousines have vicarious liability for tort damages, they will not be inclined to hire individuals with a poor driving record. Moreover, persons whose insurance premiums are very high may decide not to drive at all, or if they do drive illegally without insurance, are likely to do a minimal amount with great care.

The amount of deterrence of course depends on the link between careless driving and liability, and it can be argued that this link is weak. This is true, but it is largely a consequence of regulation that prevents insurance companies from using all statistically significant variables to set rates. For example, many states require insurance companies doing business in their state to participate in "assigned risk pools." Under these regulations, the state assigns the most dangerous drivers, who would normally pay very high rates or be unable to buy insurance, to insurance companies, and requires the companies to provide these drivers insurance at rates only slightly above average. This arrangement basically forces low-risk drivers to subsidize high-risk driving. In addition regulators often do not allow use of various criteria, e.g., age, sex, race, ethnic origin, religion, or exact geographic location, that may be useful in predicting accident rates.

There is some empirical evidence that liability for negligence deters careless driving. A number of studies have found that the fatal accident rate increases when a jurisdiction changes from a system of tort liability to a no-fault regime in which insurance premiums are unrelated to risk characteristics.[42]

Bibliography

Bovbjerg, Randall R., Frank A. Sloan, and Peter J. Rankin, "Administrative Performance of 'No-fault' Compensation for Medical Injury," 60 (2) *Law and Contemporary Problems* 71–115 (spring 1997).

Calabresi, Guido, *The Costs of Accidents: A Legal and Economic Analysis* (New Haven, CT: Yale University Press, 1970).

DeLeire, Thomas and Helen Levy, "Worker Sorting and the Risk of Death on the Job," 22 *Journal of Labor Economics* 925–953 (October 2004).

Devlin, Rose Anne, "Liability versus No-fault Automobile Insurance Regimes: An Analysis of the Experience in Quebec," in G. Dionne (ed.) *Contributions to Insurance Economics* (Norwell, MA: Kluwer 1991), 499–520.

Easterbrook, Frank, William M. Landes, and Richard A. Posner, "Contribution among Antitrust Defendants: A Legal and Economic Analysis," 23 *Journal of Law and Economics* 331 (1980).

Epstein, Richard A., "Medical Malpractice: The Case for Contract," 1 *American Bar Foundation Research Journal* 87 (1976).

Gaudry, Mark, "The Effects on Road Safety of the Compulsory Insurance, Flat Premium Rating and No-fault Features of the 1978 Quebec Automobile Act," appendix to *Report of the Inquiry into Motor Vehicle Accident Compensation in Ontario* (Toronto: Queen's Printer, 1988).

Harper, Fowler V., Fleming James, Jr., and Oscar S. Gray, *The Law of Torts* (2nd ed., Boston, MA: Little Brown, 1986).

Hylton, Keith N., "Punitive Damages and the Economic Theory of Penalties," 87 (2) *Georgetown Law Review* 421–467 (November 1998).

Landes, William M., and Richard A. Posner, *The Economic Structure of Tort Law* (Cambridge, MA: Harvard University Press, 1987).

Landes, William M., and Richard A. Posner, "Tort Law as a Regulatory Regime for Catastrophic Personal Injuries," 13 *Journal of Legal Studies* 417–434 (August 1984).

Manning, Richard L., "Is the Insurance Aspect of Producer Liability valued by Consumers? Liability Changes and Childhood Vaccine Consumption," 13 *Journal of Risk and Uncertainty* 37 (1996).

O'Connell, Jeffrey, and Robert H. Joost, "Giving Motorists a Choice between Fault and No-fault Insurance," 72 *Virginia Law Review* 61 (1986).

Oi, Walter Y., "Tort Law as a Regulatory Regime: A Comment on Landes and Posner," 13 *Journal of Legal Studies* 435–440 (August 1984).

Polinsky, A. Mitchell, and Steven Shavell, "Punitive Damages: An Economic Analysis," 111 (4) *Harvard Law Review* 869–962 (February 1998).

Polinsky, A. Mitchell, and Steven Shavell, "The Uneasy Case for Products Liability," working paper, Harvard University (2010).

Posner, James R., "Trends in Medical Malpractice Insurance," 49 *Law and Contemporary Problems* 37–56 (1986).

Silver, Jay, "The Duty to Rescue: A Reexamination and Proposal," 26 *William and Mary Law Review* 423 (1985).

Sloan, Frank A., Kathryn Whetten-Goldstein, Stephen S. Entman, Elizabeth D. Kulas, and Emily M. Stout, "The Road from Medical Injury to Claims Resolution: How No-fault and Tort Differ," 60 (2) *Law and Contemporary Problems* 35–70 (spring 1997).

Viscusi, W. Kip, "The Value of Risks to Life and Health," 31 *Journal of Economic Literature* 1912–1946 (December 1993).

White, Christopher H., "No Good Deed Goes Unpunished: The Case for Reform of the Rescue Doctrine," 97(1) *Northwestern University Law Review* 507–545 (fall 2002).

Problems

1. A group of hikers decide to lie down and rest on some railroad tracks. The engineer of an oncoming train sees the hikers and blows the whistle but makes no effort to stop, reasoning that the train has the right of way. Is the railroad liable for the death of the hikers? Explain the common-law rule. Is it efficient?

2. A tractor pulling a group of college students on a "hay ride" turns on to a busy four-lane highway at night. (This action was negligent, since (*a*) the wagon carrying the hay had no tail lights, as required by law; and (*b*) it is generally illegal for this type of vehicle to travel on four-lane highways.) An automobile collided into the back of the hay wagon, causing injuries to the college students. The driver of the automobile could have avoided the hay wagon if he had not been distracted by the intense conversation he was having on his cellular phone. Is the driver of the automobile liable under negligence for the injuries to the college students? Explain why in detail.

3. Mr. A, while attempting to inflate the tube of his bicycle tire, causes the tube to burst loudly, which startles a neighbor, Ms. C, who was restraining her dog on a leash to prevent it from chasing a squirrel. After Ms. C lets go of the leash, the dog dashes across the street towards the squirrel, causing a motor cycle to swerve to avoid the dog. The motor cycle hits B, injuring him. Is Mr. A liable to Mr. B for negligence? Give a general economic explanation for the rule of tort law that applies here.

4. What is the economic justification for the rule of foreseeability in negligence law, i.e., the rule that there is no negligence unless it was foreseeable that the defendant's action would result in an injury to the plaintiff? (Hint: consider the Learned Hand rule.)

5. Discuss whether the common law of rescue is efficient.

6. Mr. A through negligence causes an injury to Mrs. B, resulting in damages of $30,000 to her, part of which is medical expenses. The health insurance provided at no cost to Mrs. B by her employer pays for $10,000 of her expenses. Is Mr. A liable to Mrs. B for $30,000 or only $20,000? Explain what the rule is under the common law, and then indicate whether that rule is or is not efficient.

7. A negligence case involved a young boy who was seriously injured when he sat on a vacuum drain at the bottom of a swimming pool. Suppose actual damages to the boy were $3 million. As a result of the accident the family was paid $1 million under a family accident insurance policy, which was provided to the boy's father at no cost by his employer. Is the manufacturer of the vacuum drain liable for $3 million or $2 million? What is the applicable legal rule? Is it efficient?

8. Under what circumstances is it important to have conduct covered by the law of negligence rather than strict liability?

9. What are the economic arguments that have been made against the current system of liability for medical malpractice, i.e., the arguments which suggest that the system is inefficient?

10. How could the activities of physicians change if there were a substantial increase in medical malpractice liability in their area of medical practice? Try to think of all the possibilities.

11. Suppose the owner of a paint factory is caught dumping toxic waste in a public landfill and is sued in a civil action under pollution laws. Assume the probability he is detected when he does this is 10 percent, and the average social cost of each violation is $200,000. Should he be liable for punitive in addition to compensatory damages? If so, for how much?

9   The economics of litigation

An optimal judicial system

In the chapter on tort law we examined the Learned Hand rule. According to this rule, a defendant should be liable for negligence if an accident occurs which could have been avoided if the defendant had taken precautions, in a situation where the cost of taking such precautions, B, is less than the expected damages resulting from an accident, pL. Implicit in our discussion was an assumption that the courts are perfectly accurate in determining whether B is less than pL. In reality, of course, the courts do make mistakes from time to time. Courts find defendants liable when they were not negligent, and find them not liable when they were in fact negligent. These mistakes have a social cost, since they dilute the deterrent effect of tort law. Individuals and firms are more apt to be negligent the less likely it is that they will be held accountable for damage resulting from their negligence. The question therefore arises as to how many resources should be invested to improve the accuracy of the legal system. In general, the legal system will be more accurate the more resources are committed to making it so. For example, if the salaries of judges are increased, it will be possible to fill judicial positions with brighter, more conscientious persons who are less likely to make mistakes. Also, judges will be less susceptible to corruption, since they will have more to lose (see the section "Factors affecting the quality of law enforcement" in Chapter 10).

One way to analyze this issue is to view it as a problem of minimizing the total costs of a judicial system. According to this view, there are two types of cost: the cost of judicial errors, and the direct costs of operating the judicial system. Suppose that 10 percent of the time, the courts fail to hold a defendant liable when he has in fact been negligent. Assume that B, the cost of care, is \$94,000, p, the probability that the accident will occur if the precautions are not taken, is 10 percent, and L, the damage resulting from an accident, is \$1 million. Since $B < pL$, it is efficient for a potential defendant to incur these costs. If, however, the courts fail to hold a defendant liable 10 percent of the time an accident results from his negligence, the potential defendant who does not take care has an expected liability of $0.90 \times 0.10 \times \$1$ million $= \$90,000$. Since the cost of care, \$94,000, exceeds this amount, the potential defendant will not take the precautions. Now suppose the rate of error of the courts could be reduced from 10 percent to 5 percent for an additional cost of \$8,000. Should this additional expenditure be made? If it were made, the potential defendant's expected liability would increase to $0.95 \times 0.10 \times \$1$ million $= \$95,000$. Since this amount exceeds the cost of care, the defendant will now take the appropriate (efficient) precautions. Note, however, that under the previous system, the social cost of having an inaccurate system was only \$6,000 – the difference between B, \$94,000, and the expected damages of \$100,000 which occur when the precautions are not taken. Clearly it is not worth while to invest $8,000 to eliminate this cost. The general point is that we should invest resources to improve the accuracy of the judicial system only so long as the benefits of greater accuracy exceed its costs.

The standard of proof for a preliminary injunction

In Chapter 2 we learned that the standard of proof is different in different types of cases: in most civil cases the standard is a "preponderance of the evidence," but in some civil cases it is "clear and convincing evidence," and in criminal cases guilt must be proved "beyond a reasonable doubt." We also determined that these differences in the standard of proof might be explained by differences in the costs of error.

Another interesting question concerns the burden of proof that should be satisfied by a litigant who requests a preliminary injunction. A plaintiff may ask the court to grant an injunction before the trial, to remain in effect pending the outcome of the litigation. In these situations the judge is being asked to make a decision quickly, generally without good information about the merits of the case. John Leubsdorf has suggested that a judge should grant a request by a plaintiff for a preliminary injunction only if the expected loss – the expected "irreparable harm" – from an injunction is less than the expected loss from a failure to grant the injunction. Suppose H_D is the irreparable harm the defendant will suffer if the injunction is granted, and H_P is the irreparable harm the plaintiff will suffer if the injunction is not granted. Let P be the probability that the plaintiff will win at trial. Then, according to Leubsdorf, the preliminary injunction should be granted if and only if:

$$P \cdot H_P > (1 - P) \cdot H_D$$

This proposal raises the question as to what sort of injuries should qualify as "irreparable harm." Suppose, for example, that unless the injunction is issued the defendant may become insolvent before the end of the trial. Alternatively, suppose that without the injunction the defendant will take some action which will injure the plaintiff in a way which is very difficult (i.e., costly) to quantify. For example, the defendant might demolish a building of great historic significance.

The economic model of litigation

Let us consider the choice between settlement and litigation, in a case where there is a single plaintiff and a single defendant. From a social point of view, the question whether a case is settled or tried to verdict is important, because litigation, like war, is almost entirely a waste of resources (the qualification is necessary because litigation may have incidental byproducts of minor value: a trial may provide some entertainment or instruction for spectators in the courtroom, or may occasionally lead to a precedent, as described in a section below). For the most part, however, the resources used in litigation are a deadweight loss.

Returning to our analysis, we will represent the plaintiff as A, and the defendant as B. Both parties are assumed to be risk-neutral. We will use the following notation: X is the amount of damages A will recover if there is a trial and A wins. P_A is A's estimate of the probability that he will win in the event of a trial; P_B is B's estimate of the probability that A will win. C_A and C_B are the costs of litigation to A and B, respectively. V_A is the expected gain to the plaintiff from litigation, while V_B is the expected loss to the defendant from litigation.

First, note that V_A is the minimum amount that A would accept to settle his claim out of court. But $V_A = (P_A X) - C_A$. Next note that the defendant would be willing to settle for any amount less than V_B. But we know that $V_B = (P_B X) + C_B$. Note that here costs of litigation are added, not subtracted, since these expenses increase the defendant's loss. Now there will be a settlement if $V_B > V_A$. Since in this case both parties can be made better off by a settlement amount S, such that $V_A \leq S \leq V_B$. S cannot exceed V_B, since the defendant will not be willing to pay more than V_B, and it cannot be less than V_A, since the plaintiff will not accept less than V_A in settlement. The condition for a settlement, $V_B > V_A$, can be rewritten as follows:

$$V_B - V_A > 0 \implies (P_B X + C_B) - (P_A X - C_A) > 0 \implies X(P_B - P_A) + C_B + C_A > 0 \quad (1)$$

We may note some immediate implications of this simple model:

1 If both parties have the same opinion of the probable outcome of the trial, so that $P_A = P_B$, there will be a settlement, since inequality (1) will be satisfied.
2 Holding other things constant, a settlement is more likely to occur the larger the costs of litigation C_A and C_B, since it is then more likely that inequality (1) is satisfied.
3 If the parties are pessimistic about their own chances at trial, so that $P_A < P_B$, there will be an out-of-court settlement. If, on the other hand, the parties are optimistic, so that $P_A > P_B$, there may or may not be a settlement, depending on whether (1) is satisfied. Other things equal, a trial is more likely the larger the amount at stake X. In fact there is considerable empirical evidence that the probability of a trial increases with the amount at stake in the controversy.

Pre-trial discovery

Mechanisms for "pre-trial discovery" will influence the decision of the parties whether to settle or litigate. In Chapter 3 we learned that during the discovery process, each party obtains information from the other side by various means, such as interrogatories (written questions); oral depositions, in which witnesses are required to testify under oath; and the discovery of documents and things (physical evidence). When the health or fitness of an injured person is an issue in a case, the person can be compelled to submit to an examination by a physician hired by the opposing side. These methods of discovery enable both sides to become fully informed about the merits of a case at a minimum cost. This should increase the likelihood of settlement, since if both sides have accurate information, P_B will converge toward P_A.

Procedural rules which make litigation more efficient

The purpose of many procedural rules is to increase the productivity of resources used in litigation, or alternatively, to reduce the expected costs of error for a given expenditure of resources in litigation. For example, according to the doctrine of "judicial notice," facts that are obviously true do not have to be proved by the introduction of evidence. Thus the judge can consider as established uncontroversial historical facts, geography, and the like.

An important limitation on the scope of pretrial discovery was established by the Supreme Court in the case of Hickman v. Taylor.[1] A lawsuit was brought against the owners of a tugboat, based on the death of a member of the crew who drowned when the tugboat sank.

After the accident, the lawyer for the defendants interviewed witnesses and took statements from them. These witnesses were still available to be questioned by the plaintiff's lawyers. The plaintiff's lawyer submitted an interrogatory which sought the statements previously taken from these witnesses by the defendant's lawyer. The Supreme Court held that this information was "work product" of the lawyer which was not subject to discovery. This work product included the lawyer's notes and memoranda and anything which reflected his "mental impressions, conclusions, opinions, or legal theories."

The Court's opinion shows a clear understanding of the consequences of moral hazard. If the work product of attorneys were not protected, lawyers would have little incentive to prepare thoroughly for trial, since the opposing side could simply wait until the eve of trial and then request all the documents reflecting the lawyer's theories, in effect taking a free ride on the lawyer's preparation. The net effect, then, would be inadequate investment of resources in preparation for trial by both sides. This is like the problem involving joint ownership, in which an owner will decide not to make needed improvements because part of the benefit of the improvements will be gained by another.

Agency problems

An attorney acts as an agent of the client he or she represents. The relationship between the attorney and the client is a specific example of a principal–agent relationship. In this case the agent is the attorney, who acts on behalf of his client, the principal. The client naturally expects the attorney to act in the client's best interests. However, problems can arise in any principal–client relationship if the agent has an incentive to act in a way that does not best serve the client's interests. Such problems tend to arise frequently in situations where the principal does not have very good information as to what the agent is doing. In the next two sections we will consider two examples of a potential conflict between the interests of the client and those of the attorney. The first example concerns the use of the contingent legal fee as the method for compensating the lawyer. The second example involves the behavior of an attorney who represents a class of persons in a class action.

Contingent fees

The contingent fee is the universal method of compensating the lawyer in certain types of cases, and is almost never used for other types. Lawyers who represent plaintiffs in personal injury actions, eminent domain matters, and collection cases are invariably compensated on a contingent fee basis. Thus if the lawyer's agreement provides that he is entitled to one-third of the amount recovered, and he succeeds in obtaining a net recovery of $300,000 for his client, his fee will be $100,000. A lawyer could be paid on an hourly basis, according to the number of hours worked, or on a contingent fee basis. One problem with paying the lawyer on an hourly basis is the problem of "shirking." The lawyer might be tempted to "run up the bill" by spending an excessive amount of time on the case, or could even charge for more time than he actually spent working.

The contingent fee performs several important economic functions:

1   *Monitoring the effort of the lawyer.* Since the lawyer's earnings are determined by the amount recovered for the client, the contingent fee gives the lawyer a powerful incentive to maximize that recovery. However, we shall see that the lawyer's incentives are not quite ideal, from the client's point of view.

2   *Shifting risk to the party who can bear it at a lower cost.* If the client obtains no recovery, the lawyer receives no fee. If the lawyer were being paid on an hourly basis and there was no recovery, the client would have a loss, equal to the total amount paid to the lawyer. Under a contingent fee arrangement the risk of this loss is transferred from client to lawyer. If the lawyer obtains nothing for his client, he receives no compensation for his investment of time and effort. It is efficient for this risk to be transferred from the client to the lawyer, since the lawyer can bear the risk at a lower cost. The lawyer is generally handling a large number of claims, some of which will bear fruit and some of which will not. He is thus able to pool the risks of all these claims.

3   *The contingent fee enables the client to purchase legal services on credit.* Clients who have been injured, many of whom have a low income, might not have enough money to pay the lawyer in advance, on an hourly basis. The contingent fee enables such persons to borrow the services of the lawyer. Parenthetically, a victim would not be able to borrow from a bank, using his claim as collateral, since most legal claims are not assignable as a matter of law. It is efficient for the lawyer to operate as a lender in this situation, since he is most knowledgeable about the value of the claim.

The lawyers for defendants in personal injury actions are almost always compensated on an hourly basis. One might ask why the contingent fee is not useful for a defendant, if it is for the plaintiff. It turns out that the defendants in these cases are almost invariably insurance companies. We shall see that the contingent fee arrangement does not provide the perfect incentive to the lawyer, from the client's standpoint, and for insurance companies, the advantages 1–3 described above are not sufficient to overcome this deficiency.

Advantage 2 is not worth while, since an insurance company can pool risks better than a lawyer – indeed, it specializes in the assumption of risks. Advantage 3 is not useful, since insurance companies have large cash reserves from the accumulation of premiums they receive; they are lenders, rather than borrowers. Finally, 1 is not useful, since the cost of monitoring the effort of the lawyer is much lower for the insurance company than it would be for an individual client. An insurance company has business to give out to lawyers year after year. If a lawyer hired by the insurance company does a poor job, it may decide not to assign any more cases to him – a severe penalty which the lawyer will do his best to avoid. (In contrast, an individual client who is a personal injury victim generally will not have any "repeat business" for the lawyer to be concerned about.) Thus it is understandable that the contingent fee is not used by the defendants in these cases.

It remains to be shown why the contingent fee arrangement does not provide the perfect incentive for the lawyer. To analyze this issue, let us first consider the amount of work the lawyer would do if he did have the correct incentive. Suppose the client (the plaintiff) could perfectly observe the amount of time invested by his lawyer on the client's behalf. Let L be the number of hours worked by the lawyer, R be the amount of the recovery, and w the cost of the lawyer's time. The plaintiff would hire the lawyer at his wage w, and purchase the level of the lawyer's time L which would maximize his net recovery: maximize $R(L) - wL$ with respect to L,

$$\implies \frac{dR}{dL} = w = 0$$

The client would hire the lawyer to work up to the point where the lawyer's marginal product, i.e., the increase in the amount of the recovery resulting from an additional hour of work, is just equal to the wage. Of course, in reality it is too costly for the client to attempt to monitor the work effort of his lawyer.

Suppose then the lawyer is hired on a contingent fee basis, and will receive a share α of the recovery. The lawyer will be inclined to choose the level of L which will maximize his own profit: maximize $\alpha R(L) - wL$ with respect to L,

$$\Longrightarrow \alpha \frac{dR}{dL} - w = 0$$

The lawyer works only up to the point where his share of the marginal product, i.e., the share of the increase in the recovery he will obtain, is equal to the wage. As shown in Figure 9.1, the lawyer would work only L_{cf} hours, less than the efficient amount L^*, i.e., less than the number of hours he would work if his effort could be monitored costlessly.

This principal-agent problem applies to any worker whose compensation is contingent. Consider, for example, a real estate agent who receives a commission of 6 percent of the sale price of a house. Suppose the agent could sell the house immediately for $200,000, but with additional effort – more advertising, two additional Sunday "open houses," etc., could sell it for $210,000. Suppose further that the total cost of this additional effort, including the opportunity cost of the agent's time, is $1,000. Clearly it is efficient, i.e., value-maximizing, for the agent to make this additional effort, since there would be a net gain of $9,000 which could be divided between the agent and the owner of the house. However, the agent will not make this effort since she would have to incur a cost of $1,000 to obtain a benefit of $600 (6 percent of the additional $10,000).[2]

It has, however, been suggested that market arrangements can alleviate this problem. Suppose lawyers competed with each other in terms of the net recovery they offered to a potential client, $R(1 - \alpha)$. This bidding competition among the lawyers would maximize the expected net recovery for the client, subject to the constraint that the attorney's expected compensation must at least cover the opportunity cost of his time: $\alpha R \geq wL$. The bidding

Figure 9.1 Underinvestment of time by a lawyer on a contingent fee.

competition would maximize $R(L) \cdot (1 - \alpha) + \lambda \cdot (\alpha R(L) - wL)$ with respect to L, α, and λ. The first-order condition for L is that:

$$(1 - \alpha)\frac{dR}{dL} + \lambda(\alpha\frac{dR}{dL} - w) = 0 \tag{2}$$

The first-order condition for α is:

$$-R + \lambda R = 0 \Longrightarrow \lambda = 1 \tag{3}$$

Finally, the first-order condition for λ is that:

$$\alpha R(L) - wL = 0 \tag{4}$$

Combining (2) and (3), we obtain the result that:

$$(1 - \alpha)\frac{dR}{dL} + (\alpha\frac{dR}{dL} - w) = 0 \Longrightarrow \frac{dR}{dL} = w$$

Thus the competition among lawyers will lead to an outcome in which the lawyer who wins the auction will invest the optimal amount of time in the case. The lawyer makes the same effort that he would if he were paid on an hourly basis and the client could observe him perfectly. This argument for market efficiency raises an important issue. In order for an auction to be feasible, there must be a guarantee that bidders will pay the amount they bid. There is an obvious problem if a lawyer could make the highest bid, win the right to represent the client, and then "cheat" by investing only the amount of time which maximizes his own profit, thereby obtaining a recovery less than the amount promised. If the lawyer were not penalized for failing to deliver the promised recovery, the auction would not work, and would be abandoned. What then is the enforcement mechanism that ensures that the lawyer will honor his commitment?

Patricia Danzon argues that this type of auction occurs in the market for real estate, where agents bid for the right to sell the property by suggesting a listing price as well as a commission percentage. In this case both the initial listing price and the final sale price are public information. If the sale price obtained by a real estate agent frequently falls below the initial listing price, or her properties often do not sell for a long time (a consequence of a disparity between the listing price and market value), the reputation of the agent may suffer, so that she will have difficulty obtaining clients in the future. With regard to lawyers, cases which are handled on a contingent fee basis are often referred by one lawyer to another.[3] The lawyer who refers the case receives a fraction of the recovery. If the attorney who receives the case by referral does not obtain the recovery he promised the referring lawyer, he might not obtain referrals from that source in the future.

Thus the task of monitoring the performance of lawyers doing personal injury litigation is to a large extent delegated to other lawyers who refer cases to them. Accordingly market forces may alleviate much of the "conflict of interest" which arises in these situations.

There is of course uncertainty as to the amount of the recovery. We can incorporate uncertainty into our model by replacing R with PX, where, as before, P represents the probability that the plaintiff will win and X is the amount the plaintiff will recover if he wins. Equation (3), the condition that the lawyer's expected compensation must equal the opportunity cost of his time, can then be rewritten as follows:

$$\alpha PX = wL \Longrightarrow \alpha X = \frac{wL}{P}$$

Thus if for medical malpractice claims the probability of winning at trial is about 0.6, the lawyer who wins should receive $1/0.6 = 1.66$ times his hourly wage, a premium of two-thirds his normal wage.

Those who observe that a real estate agent or lawyer is occasionally paid several thousand dollars "for a few hours' work" overlook the fact that in a market where success is highly uncertain the worker must obtain a premium when he succeeds which compensates for the many failures he experiences.

Class actions

Individuals who have a small claim often would not find it worth while to bring a lawsuit, since the fixed costs of doing so may often exceed the amount to be recovered. Thus wrongdoers would have no incentive to refrain from conduct that inflicts a small cost on a large number of people – like a failure to pay a $50 rebate promised to millions of computer purchasers. This problem is solved by the class action.

The class action is a single action filed on behalf of numerous individual plaintiffs who have similar claims against the same defendant or defendants. Indeed, one of the requirements for a lawsuit to become a class action is that "there are questions of law or fact common to the class." The plaintiffs named in the case are deemed to represent the interests of others who are similarly situated. Thus the great majority of plaintiffs are not named individually, but rather are described in terms of their eligibility to participate: for example, all retail purchasers of a specified brand of steel-belted radial tires purchased new at retail and installed on a vehicle in the United States between January 1, 1985, and January 6, 2002.

The class action combines many small claims into one that is large enough to justify the costs of a lawsuit; it is based on the idea that there are economies of scale in litigation. A critically important feature of the class action is that the outcome of the litigation is binding on all members of the class, whether or not they participate in the litigation or even know about it. This feature makes the class action radically different from traditional litigation, in which the outcome is binding only on the parties, who are individually named and know that they are involved in a lawsuit. (They know it either because they have filed the lawsuit or have been served with a summons and complaint.)

The rights of absent class members are supposed to be adequately protected by (1) a requirement that the parties who bring the action can be relied on to represent the interests of all class members (the "representativeness" requirement), and (2) a rule that potential class members have the right to exclude themselves from the action (or "opt out") and, if they wish, pursue individual lawsuits on their own. In order to inform potential class members of their right to opt out, the law requires that they receive some sort of notice of the pending class action. However, the potential class members are often not notified personally; the "notice" may be, for example, published in a newspaper or broadcast over the radio. Finally (3) any proposed settlement of the class action must be approved by the judge; this requirement is designed to ensure that the representative plaintiffs do not enter into agreements with the defendant that would benefit them at the expense of absent class members. If the judge is satisfied that a lawsuit meets all the requirements of a class action, i.e, large numbers of parties (the "numerosity" requirement), common issues of law or fact, plaintiffs who can adequately represent the class and whose claims are typical of the class, he will grant it class action status, or, in legal jargon, certify the class. The decision by a court whether to certify a class (and how broadly to define a class) is generally a moment of truth in the litigation: certification is a severe blow to defendants, and makes the negotiating position of plaintiffs many times stronger. Conversely, a decision that the action does not qualify as a class action is a crippling blow for the plaintiffs' side.

However, the invention of the class action gives rise to some unique problems of judicial administration. One such problem is, if there is a recovery against the defendant, to whom should it be paid? The class may consist of millions of individuals, almost all of whom have not been identified. Since each member of the class is often entitled to a very small amount, perhaps a few dollars, the costs of identifying all the members of the class, and mailing them a check, may well exceed the total recovery. Some courts have decided that unclaimed settlement funds should be treated as abandoned property and escheat (revert) to the state in which the class members reside; other courts have simply decided to distribute them to charitable organizations. In a settlement of a class action in the 1970s charging pharmaceutical companies with price-fixing of antibiotics, the court ordered the companies either to reduce the cost of the drugs in the future, or make contributions to State funds that would help disabled, elderly, or unemployed workers pay their pharmacy bills.

Another problem is that of the lawyer "selling out the class." The lawyer's profit from the litigation is determined by the legal fee he receives rather than by the size of the award. Thus there will be a temptation for the lawyer to collude with the defendant to settle for a small judgment but a relatively large legal fee.

Suppose, for example, the defendant's actions have caused damages of $100,000. The lawyer for the class could press for a recovery of $100,000, out of which a legal fee of $30,000 would be paid. However, both the lawyer and the defendant could benefit by agreeing instead on a recovery of $60,000, from which a legal fee of $40,000 would be paid. In many cases settlements proposed by the class action lawyer and the defendant would not even award cash to class members. For example, in a class action based on a claim that the fuel tanks of pick-up trucks were defective, the original settlement called for class counsel to receive attorneys' fees of $9.5 million, and for class members to receive no more than a certificate of $1,000 to be used toward the purchase of a General Motors truck.[4] Evidence that coupons like this have little value is provided by the fact that most class members don't bother to redeem them.

Class members are supposed to be protected by the requirement that the settlement agreement and lawyers' fees must be approved by the judge. However, the parties will generally have more information than the judge concerning damages to the class members and the effort made by the lawyers for the class. One study[5] found that when courts are more congested, judges are likely to approve higher fees for class action lawyers. The study's authors argued that when a judge's case load increased, he would be inclined to dispose of some cases more rapidly (and less thoroughly) to prevent an increase in the queue of unresolved cases. When a judge must decide what kinds of issues he can decide without thorough consideration, without subjecting himself to criticism and possible reversal, a decision on a request for attorneys' fees is an excellent choice, because the chances he will be second-guessed on this issue are exceedingly small. Accordingly the larger the judge's case load, the larger the class attorney fees that will be approved by the judge.

The problem of the lawyer selling out the class is a problem from a social point of view, because it results in inadequate deterrence. The problem arises since all the members of the class will be apathetic about the outcome of the litigation, since the stakes to each member are trivial; for all practical purposes, there is no real client.

Another, related, problem is that it is often unclear who the lawyer for the class is. Since there is no real client, there is no one to turn to, to ask whom they have hired as the lawyer. What happens in practice is that after the action has been filed, a large number of lawyers will appear claiming to represent the class, or various subgroups of it.

Generally the judge will designate one or a few lawyers as "lead counsel." By virtue of this designation, these lawyers are given the most responsibility, and are therefore entitled to receive the largest share of the compensation. Before the judge makes this determination, one may observe dozens of lawyers attending a routine hearing on a motion, all jockeying for position in hopes of being chosen by the judge. The judge's decision as to who is lead counsel solves the problem of an undefined property right – the right to serve as the lawyer for the class.

Sometimes the defendant will in effect attempt to choose the lead counsel for the court. This is the phenomenon of the "reverse auction" or "plaintiff shopping" by the defendant. There are often multiple class actions filed against the defendant, so the defendant will seek out a counsel whose ability to recover damages is relatively weak, propose to him a settlement with small damages and a large attorney's fee, and then join with him to propose to the court that this settlement be the template for a "global class settlement" covering all the other class actions, further prosecution of which would be enjoined by the court. (Later in this chapter the reader will find a discussion of a similar type of plaintiff shopping by defendants that occurs in the context of collateral estoppel.)

It should be clear that it is efficient for the court to designate lead counsel early in the proceeding, and to specify the formula for counsel's compensation at the beginning of the litigation rather than at the end. Choosing lead counsel, and specifying the formula for compensation at the outset, avoids rent-seeking behavior on the part of those vying for the position of lead counsel, and provides incentives to obtain maximum recovery for the class net of attorney fees.

Some judges have decided that the right to be lead counsel should be decided by an auction, in which bids are made by competing law firms. The term "auction" is actually misleading, because the award is not necessarily made to the firm that offers to charge the lowest attorney fees. In their bids the law firms provide the judge with a profile of the firm, their experience in class actions, their prediction of the recovery, and alternative fee proposals. The judge, acting as agent for the class, then chooses the firm that he believes will provide the maximum net recovery for the class.

What then should be the formula for the compensation of the law firm or lawyer? One possible solution is to have the lawyer receive the entire amount of the recovery. This would certainly solve the problem of underinvestment of the lawyer's effort, and provide the appropriate incentive to maximize the damages collected from the defendant. In one case where the government had already established the liability of the defendant via criminal proceedings, the judge knew it would be easy to recover the first few hundred million of damages, so he ordered that any bid specify a minimum amount that would go entirely to the class; the lawyer would receive 25 percent of any amount recovered above that base amount.[6] Bidders were prohibited from revealing their bids to other bidders. The winning bidder specified a base amount of $405 million, and subsequently settled the case for $512 million. An empirical study found that the amount recovered by the class was the most important determinant of the award of attorney's fees, and that the fees increased with the amount of risk assumed by the lawyer.[7]

Understanding the various problems (costs) that may arise with class actions should not lead one to overlook their potential expected benefits. A truly remarkable example of the potential social benefits of a class action is afforded by the case of Authors Guild v. Google. The guild sued Google in 2005 after Google had entered into agreements with the libraries of Michigan, Stanford, Harvard, and other university libraries to scan and copy millions of books in their collections, to make them available to anyone on the internet. While the copyright had expired on some of these books, many were still protected by copyright. The Authors Guild sued Google for violations of copyright, which seemed indisputable, even though Google contended that its scanning of the books was "fair use." A number of publishers joined the Authors Guild in the class action.

After extensive negotiations the case was settled, under an agreement by which Google was allowed to make the books available on the internet under certain conditions: in particular, 63 percent of revenues obtained from the books covered by copyright (through advertising, online purchase, per-page printing at computer terminals, etc.) would be paid to a new entity, the Book Rights Registry, on behalf of the authors or other copyright holders, and 37 percent would be retained by Google. Colleges, universities, and other organizations would be able to obtain access to Google's vast database by paying for an "institutional license." The new Registry would be the equivalent of ASCAP or BMI for writers and would make payments to them based on the extent their books were used. Many of the books covered by copyright would not be made available in Google's data base unless the copyright owner chose to include them. Google would also make books that are in the public domain available to users to read, download, and print, free of charge.

The settlement of this class action will yield enormous, incalculable benefits for readers, authors or other copyright owners, and Google (although, because of concern about potential monopoly power, Google was not given an exclusive right to use the books). Readers will be able to browse through a collection of books many orders of magnitude greater in size than that of any library in the world, and can buy full online access to most of them. Many of the books made available online were out of print, even if protected by copyright, and were therefore invisible to almost all readers, so making them available on the internet to anyone with access to a computer was a revolutionary development. The device of the class action enabled the parties to avoid the (prohibitive) costs of identifying all the potential plaintiffs (all copyright owners), and the (equally prohibitive) costs of getting together with them and obtaining their agreement.

Some have expressed concern that Google may charge monopoly prices to customers in the future, especially to institutional subscribers such as colleges and universities. However, under the proposed settlement agreement the Book Rights Registry, representing the copyright owners, has the power to change the subscription prices charged by Google, and the owners, whose marginal costs of distribution would be zero, would presumably want to maximize revenues by charging a price at which marginal revenue equals zero. This should be an effective way of maintaining a relatively low price.

The English rule

Apart from class actions, another way to make it feasible for people to pursue small claims in court is to adopt a rule that the losing party must reimburse the winning party for all his legal expenses (i.e. attorney fees, witness fees, court costs, etc.) This is in fact the prevailing rule in England and Europe, but not in the United States. However, there are some federal statutes, e.g. the Civil Rights Act and Clean Air Act, that have adopted the rule.[8]

One important issue is how the rule of indemnity, which is often called the English rule, compares to American practice in terms of its effect on the parties' decision whether to settle the case or litigate. That is, is settlement more likely under the English or under the American rule? To analyze this issue, let us return to the economic model of litigation. Recall that X is the amount at stake, and C_A and C_B are the costs of litigation for the plaintiff and defendant, respectively. P_A is the probability that the plaintiff will win at trial, in the plaintiff's opinion, and P_B is what the defendant thinks about this probability. V_A again is the plaintiff's expected gain from trial, and V_B is the defendant's expected loss.

Now under the English rule, if the plaintiff wins, he recovers X, while if he loses, his (negative) gain is $-C_A - C_B$. On the other hand, if the defendant wins, his loss is 0, while if he loses, his loss is $X + C_A + C_B$. The plaintiff's expected gain from litigation, V_A, is now:

$$V_A = P_A \cdot X + (1 - P_A) \cdot (-C_A - C_B)$$

while V_B, the defendant's expected loss, is now:

$$V_B = P_B \cdot (X + C_A + C_B) + (1 - P_B) \cdot 0$$

As before, the parties will settle the case, rather than litigate, if V_B, the maximum amount the defendant will offer to settle the case, exceeds V_A, the minimum amount the plaintiff would accept. Thus the parties will settle if $V_B > V_A$, or:

$$P_B \cdot (X + C_A + C_B) > P_A X + (1 - P_A)(-C_A - C_B) \tag{5}$$

This can be rewritten as:

$$X(P_B - P_A) + C_A(1 - P_A + P_B) + C_B(1 - P_A + P_B) > 0 \tag{5a}$$

Since our objective is to compare the English rule to the American rule, we want to compare (1a) with the condition for settlement under the American rule:

$$X(P_B - P_A) + C_A + C_B > 0 \tag{6}$$

Recall that under the American rule, the case will be settled if $P_B > P_A$, since then $P_B - P_A > 0$ and condition (2) will be satisfied. Since condition (5a) would also be satisfied, there will be a settlement under either rule if $P_B > P_A$. Thus we need consider only the case where $P_B < P_A$.

A comparison of conditions (5a) and (6) shows that settlement will be less likely under the English rule if $1 - P_A + P_B < 1$. But then $P_B < P_A$. We conclude that if the parties are risk-neutral, litigation is more likely to occur under the English rule than under the American rule.

Table 9.1 shows, in column 3, the difference between winning and losing for each party, under the American rule and the English rule. But what if the parties are risk-averse instead of risk-neutral? Note that under the English rule, the difference between winning and losing is greater for each party by the amount of the total costs of litigation $C_A + C_B$. Since the risk of litigation is greater under the English rule, it can be proved that if the parties are risk-averse, litigation is less likely under this rule.

Table 9.1 Comparison of the English rule and the American rule

	Rule	If plaintiff wins	If plaintiff loses	Difference between winning and losing
Gain of plaintiff	American	$X - C_A$	$-C_A$	X
	English	X	$-C_A - C_B$	$X + C_A + C_B$
Loss of defendant	American	$X + C_B$	C_B	X
	English	$X + C_A + C_B$	0	$X + C_A + C_B$

As we noted at the beginning of this section, the English rule might be expected to increase litigation, since it makes it feasible for people to file actions based on small claims. Nonetheless, it has been suggested that the English rule tends to reduce litigation, for two reasons:

1 The preceding analysis assumes that P_A and P_B, the parties' beliefs about the probability the plaintiff will win, would be the same under the English rule and the American rule. However, the cost to each party of unwarranted optimism is greater under the English rule, since the loss will be increased by the amount of the other party's legal expenses. If the cost of unwarranted optimism increases, we would expect that less of it will be consumed. Under the English rule the parties will evaluate their legal position more closely, so the difference between P_A and P_B should shrink, making it more likely that the case will be settled.

2 The English rule should discourage the filing of nuisance claims, i.e. claims that have little or no legal merit, more than the American rule. Under the rule of indemnity, the cost of litigating a frivolous claim to verdict is greater for the plaintiff, and less for the defendant, by C_B. It should be noted that in most U.S. jurisdictions the court may order a plaintiff to pay the defendant's legal expenses if it determines that the lawsuit was frivolous. However, in practice there is a vast difference between a rule that applies automatically and one applied at the court's discretion; moreover it is quite rare for U.S. courts to award costs under these circumstances.

Court delay

In *Bleak House*, by Charles Dickens, the story is centered around the litigation of a probate matter, Jarndyce v. Jarndyce, involving the distribution of an estate. The case proceeds along at a glacial pace for decades, growing ever more complicated and drawing in more and more parties, lawyers, and Chancellors. "Innumerable children have been born into the cause … innumerable old people have died out of it." Finally the dispute is resolved by the accidental discovery of a will. By this time, however, the entire fortune at stake has been consumed by legal expenses.[9] It is not clear that things have improved much since Dickens's time. One study of closed claims for medical malpractice found that the average time between the injury and the resolution of the claim was five years.[10]

The problem of court congestion and delay has been examined by two groups of scholars, who have completely different views about the effectiveness of measures taken to reduce delay. First, there is the literature on court administration and jury system management, which is unqualifiedly optimistic about the effect of court reform on the duration of cases. The premise underlying these studies is that the time to settlement or time to trial can be substantially reduced if the court takes certain measures to expedite the processing of cases. Second, there is the critique of court reform by Posner (1972) and Priest (1989). Posner compares the problem of court congestion to traffic congestion on an expressway. Traffic engineers have learned that adding lanes to an existing expressway may not do much to relieve traffic congestion in the long run, because the volume of traffic on the expressway does not remain the same after the improvement. Drivers who were previously traveling on other routes will switch to the expressway; this process will continue until there is enough additional traffic so that travel time for commuters on the expanded expressway is about the same as it is on alternative routes. Travel time could be reduced substantially only if there were essentially no alternative routes.

According to Posner and Priest, the same principle applies to changes in court administration that reduce the time to trial. Suppose, for example, the time to trial in court A is cut in half by an overnight increase in the number of judges. This lowers the cost of trial for litigants in cases pending in court A, and also makes court A a more attractive forum relative to other courts, or other alternatives to litigation such as alternative dispute resolution. Consequently, one might expect an increase in the rate at which cases in court A go to trial (a change on the intensive margin) and an increase in the number of cases filed in court A (a change on the extensive margin). Both these responses will add to the docket in court A, until a new equilibrium is reached in which the time to trial in court A is about the same as it is in other forums. Our discussion of traffic congestion suggests that measures to reduce court delay may be more successful if there are no good alternatives to the court, because, for example, it has exclusive jurisdiction over certain types of cases or is highly specialized.

Priest used the economic model of litigation to show that court delay would encourage the parties to settle their case rather than go to trial. Let P_P be the probability that the plaintiff will win at trial, in the plaintiff's opinion, and let P_D be the probability the plaintiff will win, in the defendant's opinion. X is the amount the plaintiff will recover if he wins. Finally, let C_P and C_D be the costs of trial for the plaintiff and defendant, respectively, and let S_P and S_D be their respective costs for settling the case. Then the plaintiff will be willing to accept a settlement payment M if his expected gain from settling the case exceeds his expected gain from trial, or:

$$M - S_P \geq P_P X - C_P \Longrightarrow M \geq P_P X - C_P + S_P$$

The defendant will be willing to settle for some amount M if his expected cost of settlement is less than his expected loss from trial, i.e.:

$$M + S_D \leq P_D X + C_D \Longrightarrow M \leq P_D X + C_D - S_D$$

The case will not be settled, and will go to trial, if the minimum amount that the plaintiff would accept to settle the case exceeds the maximum amount the defendant would be willing to offer, i.e., if:

$$P_P X - C_P + S_P > P_D X + C_D - S_D \Longrightarrow X(P_P - P_D) > C_D + C_P - (S_P + S_D) \tag{7}$$

Thus the probability of trial increases the larger is $(P_P - P_D)$, the parties' difference of opinion on whether the plaintiff will win, and the larger the costs of settlement are relative to the costs of trial.

In order to adapt this model to analyze the issue of delay, Priest made some additional assumptions, namely that (a) all expenses incurred by the parties for either trial or settlement are made currently; (b) if the plaintiff wins at trial, he would obtain the recovery X at a time t years in the future; and (c) there is no provision for prejudgment interest. (If the law provides for prejudgment interest, interest accumulates on the plaintiff's recovery at a specified rate, from either the date of the injury or the date the complaint is filed.) Under these conditions, inequality (1) would be replaced by another condition, namely that the case would go to trial if:

$$\frac{X}{(1+r)^t}(P_P - P_D) > C_D + C_P - (S_P + S_D) \tag{8}$$

Inequality (8) indicates that delay will reduce the likelihood of trial. The larger t is, the smaller the left-hand side of (8) is, and the less likely it is that the condition for trial will be satisfied. Priest also noted that if the law provides for prejudgment interest at a rate i, the term $X/(1+r)^t$ must be replaced by $X/(1+r-i)^t$. Note that if i exceeds r, an increase in delay t would actually increase the probability of trial, since it would increase the present value of the amount at stake in the case.

Of course there are other reasons for delay not captured by the preceding model. Delay may be attributable to factors other than court congestion – for example, it may result from the actions of the litigants. Other things equal, if the legal rate of prejudgment interest exceeds the market rate of interest, the plaintiff has an incentive to delay, while if it is less than the market rate (or zero), the defendant has an incentive to delay. Thus the incentives of the parties to delay will be minimized if the rate of prejudgment interest is equal, or very close to, the market interest rate. The incentives of the lawyers may also be important. Shepherd (1995) found that attorneys who were paid an hourly rate carried out approximately six more days of pretrial discovery than attorneys working under a contingent fee arrangement.

Does the evidence support the bright, optimistic view of the possibilities of court reform or the "dark side" of the Posner-Priest hypothesis? So far the empirical studies are inconclusive. Spurr (1997) examined the effect of a delay reduction program in Wayne County, Michigan, under which a judge intervened early in each case and imposed a rigid time schedule on the main events of the litigation. Spurr found no evidence of an increase in the trial rate, but did find an increase in the number of cases filed annually in that court system. During the period covered by his data the legal rate of prejudgment interest was far above the nominal interest rate for some years, but this differential was later reduced by a change in State law. He found that the duration of cases declined after this change, presumably because plaintiffs' attorneys had less incentive to delay. In another study Spurr (2000) found that the time to settlement increased with the amount at stake in the case, but was sharply reduced when the case was referred to a specialist in personal injury litigation. These results are consistent with the economic model of litigation: when the plaintiff's lawyer is experienced and knowledgeable about the case, the parties are less likely to have different views about the outcome of trial, and are therefore likely to settle earlier.

Expert witnesses

Expert witnesses are allowed to testify on matters within their area of expertise "in the form of an opinion." Those who do not qualify as experts are generally not allowed to express opinions, only to testify about what they observed; the reasoning is that the multiple members of the jury should draw their own inferences about what happened from the facts, and, given their numbers and diversity, their collective conclusion is likely to be more reliable than that of a single non-expert witness.

There is much criticism of expert witnesses along the lines that they are "hired guns" whose testimony is tailored to suit the needs of their clients rather than the truth. Richard Posner, however, has argued that expert witnesses have a strong incentive to be objective, because they are "repeat players." The idea is that their credibility depends on whether they have a reputation for honest testimony, and an expert with substantial credibility is more valuable to his prospective clients. An expert whose opinion is generally perceived to be determined by the client's desires is of no value to anyone. Posner also points out that an expert witness whose testimony is not believable is likely to be criticized by the judge, either in court or in a published opinion, and that such criticism is devastating to the expert's market value, since it can be used to cross-examine him in subsequent cases.

Expert witnesses may be unreliable either on the intensive or on the extensive margin. On the intensive margin, their testimony may be questioned if they have an incentive to deviate from the truth. For this reason, the law prohibits expert witnesses from being compensated on a contingent fee basis. On the extensive margin, the parties might hire experts with views that, although sincerely held, are well outside the mainstream of science. It is not clear that the reputation effect described by Judge Posner is strong enough to ensure that most experts will be impartial. The judge may not have sufficient knowledge to determine whether an expert's testimony is biased or in conflict with the mainstream scientific literature. Moreover, it is costly to determine whether an expert's testimony in a given case is inconsistent with his published work or his testimony in prior cases, and if such an inconsistency can be found, it is often difficult (costly) to explain it to a judge or jury.

The trial judge is assigned the task of "gatekeeping," or excluding proffered expert testimony that is not based on "scientific knowledge." In a 1923 case[11] a federal appellate court, rejecting evidence derived from a precursor to the polygraph machine, stated that the admissibility of testimony depends on whether it has "gained general acceptance in the particular field in which it belongs." However in a 1993 case, Daubert v. Merrell Dow Pharmaceuticals,[12] the U.S. Supreme Court held that the "general acceptance" criterion was too restrictive. However, the court also held that the trial judge should ensure that the testimony is not just relevant, but also reliable, and suggested some factors to consider in determining whether expert testimony is admissible.

The court stated that the theory must ordinarily be falsifiable; that is, it must be capable of being tested and thus being either refuted or confirmed by data. Another consideration, pertinent but not conclusive, is whether the theory or technique has been subjected to peer review or publication. (In some cases unpublished theories may be helpful because some propositions are too new, or of too limited interest, to have been published.) Submitting an article to the scrutiny of the scientific community increases the likelihood that flaws in methodology will be exposed. In regard to the use of a scientific technique, such as voice identification through spectrographic methods, the court should consider the standards controlling the use of the technique and the potential rate of error. Finally, the trial judge should consider the extent to which the theory or technique is accepted by the scientific community.

According to one study, after the Daubert decision, the proportion of expert testimony by scientists that was excluded by the judge increased substantially. This increase is likely to have contributed to a doubling in the rate of successful motions for summary judgment,

90 percent of which were decided against plaintiffs. The exclusion of expert testimony from civil cases tends to adversely affect plaintiffs much more than defendants, because it may prevent plaintiffs from meeting their required burden of proof. Some commentators contend that the Daubert case has shifted the balance in favor of defendants in civil cases. Others have argued that previously the scales were tipped too far in the direction of plaintiffs and the Daubert decision has helped to restore them to their rightful place.

Determining the quality of a judge (or court)

Because judges are obliged to follow precedent, the rate at which a judge's decisions are reversed by a higher court is sometimes used as a measure of the judge's quality. It can also be used to measure the quality of a court that consists of a number of judges.

Richard Posner (2000) used rates of reversal to evaluate the performance of the Ninth Circuit Court of Appeals. His hypothesis was that the quality of the Ninth Circuit's decisions might be compromised by its size; the Ninth Circuit, with twenty-eight judges, was by far the largest Circuit Court. As to why the court's size was relevant, Posner noted that federal judges do not have the incentives to work that most people do, since their compensation is entirely unrelated to their productivity. All judges at the same level of the federal bench have exactly the same salary, regardless of their years of service, case load and the like, and they all have life tenure. Accordingly the only real sanction they face for shirking is the disapproval of their colleagues, and Posner argued that informal norms of work responsibility are enforced more effectively the smaller the group.[13] One might therefore expect that the quality of the judges' performance would deteriorate as the size of the court increased, and that, among the federal Circuit Courts, the problem of shirking would be most serious for the Ninth Circuit, with its twenty-eight judges.

With regard to measuring the quality of the court's output, there are two ways in which the Supreme Court can reverse the decision of a Circuit Court. The more common way is when the Court grants certiorari, and schedules the case for a full briefing and oral argument, followed by a decision. Alternatively, the Court may grant certiorari and reverse without briefing or argument, that is, summarily. This second type of reversal may be viewed as a rebuke to the lower court; the implication is that the lower court's decision is so clearly wrong that there is no need for the Court to consider the legal arguments on each side, via a full briefing and oral argument.

Posner compared the rate of reversal of the Ninth Circuit to those of the other eleven regional circuits.[14] He found that the Ninth Circuit had the highest rate of summary reversal. He also examined the nonsummary reversals by the Supreme Court that were unanimous. The idea here was that reversals that are unanimous are less likely than others to be based on ideological or philosophical differences between the Supreme Court and the lower court, and more likely to be based on a misunderstanding of the law by the lower court. He found that the Ninth Circuit was also the leader in this category of reversals. For another measure of quality, Posner considered how frequently the opinions of each circuit were cited in decisions of the other Circuit Courts. The premise here is that since the judges of one circuit are not obliged to follow the decisions of another circuit, they will be inclined to cite them only if they find their reasoning persuasive. The Ninth Circuit fared poorly by this measure as well. Based on his statistical analysis, Posner found the performance of the Ninth Circuit to be substantially below par, and that this situation was attributable, at least in part, to the size of the court.

Whether the common law is efficient

Several legal scholars have argued that the common law, i.e. law created by judges in the process of deciding cases, is likely to be dominated by efficient legal rules. The basic idea behind this approach is as follows: to the extent there are inefficient rules of law, such rules are more apt to lead to accidents than efficient rules. Consider, for example, a rule that would give power boats the right of way over sail boats. This rule would be inefficient, since liability should be imposed on the party who can avoid the accident at least cost. If there is a collision between a power boat and sail boat, the power boat should normally be liable, as it is under current law, since it could have avoided the collision more easily, i.e. at lower cost, than the sail boat. A rule which imposes liability on the sail boat would be expected to lead to more boating accidents.

Accidents frequently lead to litigation. Since more accidents occur when rules are inefficient than when they are efficient, there will be more litigation of inefficient rules than of efficient rules. Now the more often there is litigation of any legal rule, the more likely it is that some court will decide to overrule that rule of law, and replace it with a different rule. Consequently inefficient rules are more likely to be overturned than efficient rules, and the common law as a whole will move inexorably in the direction of efficiency.

Paul Rubin has proposed a model in which accidents occur even though the party who will be liable for damages incurs costs to prevent the accident. Thus if B would be liable for damages resulting from any accidents, he will spend S_B to avoid accidents, but N_B accidents will occur anyway per unit of time. Suppose X is the social cost of each accident, and B will be liable for damages of X each time there is an accident. The total costs imposed on B, T_B, are then $S_B + N_B X$. If liability were imposed on A instead of B, A would spend S_A to avoid accidents, and N_A accidents would occur per unit of time. The total costs imposed on A, T_A, would then be $S_A + N_A X$. Note that in this framework both parties, A and B, expect to be involved in accidents repeatedly in the future; that is, they each have a continuing interest in litigation.

We will assume that $T_B > T_A$, which means that a rule imposing liability on B would be inefficient. Suppose that the law currently in effect does impose liability on B. Then when an accident occurs A, as the plaintiff, will sue B as the defendant. We will make one additional assumption about the litigation process, which we have not made previously. Assume that if there is a litigation, whoever wins the case – plaintiff or defendant – will also have the rule of law established in his favor as precedent. Thus if B wins the case in which he is a defendant, he will not only avoid liability for damages of X, but also the rule of law will change by imposing liability on A for all accidents occurring thereafter. Let P be the probability that the plaintiff A will win, and that the rule of law making B liable for accidents will not be overruled.

Once the accident has occurred, the parties must decide whether to settle the case or litigate. If C_B is the cost of litigation to B, the expected cost to B of litigation, rather than settlement, is:

$$V_B = PX - (1-P)T_B + C_B$$

The second term on the right-hand side equals the probability that B will win the litigation, $1 - P$, multiplied by $-T_B$, the present value of the costs B will save in the future if he is exempted from liability by a change in the rule of law. This potential expected gain from litigation, $(1 - P)T_B$, reduces the cost of litigation to B. Similarly, the expected gain to A of litigation rather than settlement, is:

$$V_A = PX - (1 - P)T_A - C_A$$

if C_A is the cost of litigation to A. The second term on the right-hand side represents an expected cost of litigation to A: if A should lose the case, an event with probability $1 - P$, he will lose T_A, the present value of the costs of accidents which will be imposed on him in the future.

As before, we know the parties will settle if, and only if, $V_B > V_A$. That is, they will settle if:

$$PX - (1 - P)T_B + C_B > PX - (1 - P)T_A - C_A \Longrightarrow (1 - P)(T_B - T_A) < C_A + C_B$$

so that litigation will occur if:

$$(1 - P)(T_B - T_A) > C_A + C_B \tag{9}$$

Note that $T_B - T_A$ will be larger the greater is the inefficiency in the current rule of law imposing liability on B. Thus, the greater the inefficiency, the more likely it is there will be litigation.

Note also that if the current rule were efficient, so that $T_B < T_A$, there would be no litigation, since the left-hand side of (9) would be negative and the total court costs on the right-hand side would be positive. In general, litigation will be less likely the larger the court costs C_A and C_B. If the left-hand side of equation (9) exceeds the right-hand side, B will litigate rather than settle every time there is an accident. B will continue to litigate until the current rule is overruled. Thereafter A, who will then be liable for damages, will not find it worth while to litigate. Instead he will spend S_A to avoid accidents and bear the full cost $N_A X$ of any accidents which may occur.

Rubin concludes that precedents will evolve toward efficiency if both parties have a substantial interest in precedent, as they would if they were repeatedly involved in accidents, on one side or the other. (In the model set forth above it was assumed that both parties had such a continuing interest in accidents.) However, if only one party had a substantial interest in precedent, the rule of law would eventually be established in favor of that party, whether or not such a rule was efficient.

George Priest has argued that the tendency of the common law to move toward efficiency is more general than is implied by Rubin's analysis. He begins with the proposition that inefficient assignments of liability impose greater costs on the parties subject to them than efficient assignments would. He then points out that if the cost of any commodity increases, people will buy less of it. Safety, or accident avoidance, is like any other commodity: if the cost of avoiding the accident is greater, the amount of accident avoidance purchased will be less. Therefore, imposing liability on the party who has the larger cost of avoiding an accident will lead to more accidents, or more serious accidents, than there would be if liability were imposed on the party who can avoid the accident at lower cost. Inefficient rules are more likely to become involved in litigation than efficient rules because, in comparison with efficient rules, they lead to a greater number of accidents and more severe accidents. Also, the more serious the accident, the greater is X, the amount at stake in the case.

We have already learned that litigation is more likely the greater is the amount at stake. Consequently, efficient rules are less apt to be the subject of litigation, and are less likely to be overruled. It should be noted that both Rubin and Priest allow for the possibility that there are some inefficient rules in the common law. Rubin would argue that the law may be inefficient in disputes where only one party, or neither party, is interested in the effect of a case as precedent. Priest suggests that efficient rules are likely to be more dominant in areas of the law where the issues, or typical disputes, have not changed much over time, e.g. areas such as admiralty law, sales law, or civil procedure.

The claim that the common law evolves toward efficiency has been challenged. For example, Tullock (1997) cites examples of inefficient common-law rules and argues for the superiority of the codes of civil law.[15] However, another line of research has found benefits in a common-law tradition, apart from the quality of legal rules. La Porta et al. (1998) find that on average there is better protection of investors under the common law than under alternative legal regimes. Others have found that countries that provide a high level of protection for investors have more developed financial markets and more rapid economic growth.[16]

Mahoney (2000) finds that common-law countries experienced a significantly higher rate of economic growth than civil law countries during the period from 1960 to 1992. He argues that the divergence is explained by the fact that governments operating under a civil law system tend to intervene in private economic activity more than those constrained by the institutions of the common-law. In common-law countries judges are more independent, and more restrictions are placed on executive action by law, custom, and tradition. It is therefore more difficult (costly) for the government to alter property and contract rights in common-law countries. Since citizens in common-law countries have greater confidence in their property rights, conditions for economic growth are more favorable.

Other economists have argued that a crucial factor in determining the rate of economic growth is the extent to which the society encourages productive activities or instead "rent-seeking" behavior. According to this view, some activities, which we might call "entrepreneurial," increase the wealth of society through innovation or by finding methods to use resources more efficiently, while other activities, which we might call "rent-seeking," simply redistribute wealth from one group to another. Entrepreneurial activities increase the size of the pie, while rent-seeking activities only change the manner in which the pie is divided. Murphy et al. (1991) classified engineering as an entrepreneurial occupation, and deemed law, financial trading, and lobbying for protectionist measures to be primarily redistributive or rent-seeking occupations. They found some empirical evidence that countries with a large portion of the labor force in engineering had a high rate of growth, while those with a large population of lawyers had a lower rate of growth. Yet we know that there are certain conditions that are conducive to economic growth: property rights should be clearly defined; patents, copyrights, and other intellectual property should be protected; contracts should be respected, criminal law should be enforced; and we also know that these legal safeguards are provided and enforced by lawyers. It therefore seems that the link between a nation's economic growth and the size of its legal profession is not a simple one.

Rules of collateral estoppel

A number of legal rules have the objective of ensuring that the property rights of parties involved in litigation are well defined.

Statutes of limitations, for example, are justified on the ground that there is a "need for repose"; it is important to limit the economic uncertainty for persons who may become involved in a lawsuit.

Under the doctrine of res judicata, courts will not allow the same claim to be litigated again between the same parties. The rationale is that the judgments of a court should have "stability and certainty," i.e., uncertainty of property rights should be minimized.

The rules of collateral estoppel determine whether a decision made on issues arising in one case will be binding when the same issues arise in another case when at least one party[17] is involved in both litigations. The rules and requirements of collateral estoppel seem designed to promote efficiency by making the appropriate choice between conflicting objectives of judicial economy and the reduction of judicial error. The goal of judicial economy argues for application of collateral estoppel; once issues have been decided in one case, it seems wasteful for them to be reconsidered in a subsequent case. On the other hand, if a decision made in one litigation has collateral impact on other cases, the stakes of the litigation are increased. If one party has more at stake than the other, it will be inclined to invest more resources in the lawsuit, so there will be a greater probability of judicial error. The manner in which the balance is struck between competing interests depends on the sequence of events:

1. Suppose A sues B and wins, and then sues C on a similar claim. An issue which was decided in A's favor in the first action also arises in his lawsuit with C. A wants to use collateral estoppel against C to have this issue decided automatically in his favor. Some have argued that A should be allowed to do so, so long as C's position was defended adequately by B in the prior lawsuit. Others have opposed this proposal, pointing out that it would increase the stakes of the first litigation for A. This could have two consequences: (a) A might spend much more than B in an effort to win the first lawsuit, and (b) A might choose as his first defendant B someone who would not defend the lawsuit vigorously, perhaps because its liability was small. The courts have not applied collateral estoppel here, on the ground that C has not had "his day in court."

2. Now suppose A sues B and loses. B then wants to use collateral estoppel to preclude C, another plaintiff, from bringing a claim against B. Some have argued that collateral estoppel should be allowed here, as long as C's side was "adequately represented" in the first action. Others have pointed out that this would give the defendant B an incentive to invest a disproportionate amount in the first litigation. There may also be a concern about possible collusion between A and B. The question whether the plaintiff's side was adequately represented by A in the first action is similar to the concern about a "reverse auction" by defendants being sued in multiple class actions, whereby the defendant seeks out a counsel with a weak claim, proposes to him a settlement with small damages and a large attorney's fee, and then joins with him to propose to the court that this settlement be the template for a global class settlement covering all other class actions. In any case, the courts have not applied collateral estoppel here since C has not had his day in court.

3. Suppose A sues B and loses; then A sues C for a similar claim. In this case A has had his day in court, and C is allowed to use collateral estoppel to prevent A from reopening the issue.

4. Finally, suppose A sues B and wins. D then brings a similar action against B, and seeks to use A's judgement to prevent B from relitigating any common issues. The U.S. Supreme Court has held that D could apply collateral estoppel against B, who has had his day in court.

Now consider the combined effect of the rules applied in situations 2 and 4. Professor Currie has pointed out a problem arising from the application of these rules against a single defendant subject to multiple claims. Suppose fifty passengers who were injured in a railroad collision bring separate lawsuits against the railroad. The railroad wins the first twenty-five lawsuits, but loses the twenty-sixth. Currie argued that it was anomalous to apply rule 4 at this juncture, and permit plaintiffs No. 27 through No. 50 to recover by relying on the victory of plaintiff No. 26. This would certainly seem to stack the deck in favor of the plaintiff. The Supreme Court found this argument persuasive, and subsequently indicated that collateral estoppel would not be applied against a defendant when there was a prior inconsistent judgment in favor of the defendant. Note, however, that this modification of rule 4 greatly increases the stakes of the first action for the defendant. Returning to the railroad example, if the railroad loses the first case, collateral estoppel applies and it is precluded from raising a similar defense against the next forty-nine plaintiffs. If, on the other hand, it wins the first case, it need not worry about collateral estoppel being applied against it thereafter, since it has a prior inconsistent judgment. Under these circumstances the railroad could be expected to make an extraordinary effort to win the first case!

The jury

The historical evolution of the jury's role

Jurors were originally drawn from the community where the events in controversy occurred, on the theory that it was best to have the matter decided by persons who were already well informed about it. Thus trial by jury originally had the character of a trial by witnesses. Accordingly jurors have always been put under oath to tell the truth or render a true verdict. At the time when jurors were viewed as being more like witnesses than judges, an incorrect verdict was considered to be something like perjury. If the jurors' original verdict was subsequently found to be false, the verdict was reversed and the jurors were severely punished. Over the course of time it came to be understood that this possibility was a disincentive to serve on a jury, so this procedure, which was known as the writ of attaint, was eventually discarded.[18] An important turning point was the trial of William Penn in London in 1670. Penn, who advocated both the Quaker faith and freedom of religion, was charged with violating a law forbidding religious worship outside the Church of England. The jury, led by Edward Bushel, refused to return a verdict of guilty, whereupon they were fined and imprisoned. Subsequently, however, a higher court ordered their release, and the "Bushel case" in effect established the autonomy of the jury in England.

Although jurors were originally chosen because of their presumed familiarity with the events at issue, from the earliest days they were not restricted to their own personal knowledge; they were allowed to confer with each other, examine evidence, and listen to arguments made by the parties. Over time the jury departed further and further from their role as witnesses, and gradually came to assume the role of deciding issues of fact on the basis of evidence presented at the trial. In England, the responsibility for providing such evidence for the jury was assumed by the parties and their counsel, rather than by the judge. (In continental Europe, on the other hand, this responsibility was assumed by the judge.) Eventually there came to be a clear division of labor: the jury was to decide questions of fact, while the judge would decide questions of law.[19]

Historically the jury has had an important political function; in a sense juries have always represented the people, while judges have tended to represent the prevailing government. The refusal of a New York jury to convict John Peter Zenger of sedition for printing criticism of British colonial officials went far to establish freedom of the press before the American Revolution. Juries have refused to convict for violations of the fugitive slave laws, or of Prohibition laws, or for violations of Selective Service laws during the Vietnam era.

Many procedural rules and devices have evolved from the history of conflict between judge and jury. The Bill of Rights, which was designed to limit the powers of the federal government, guarantees the right to trial by jury in criminal cases and civil cases in the federal courts.[20]

Issues concerning the composition of the jury

The optimal size of the jury

Issues concerning the jury may be divided into those involving the composition of the jury and those concerning the manner in which the jury makes its decision. With regard to the composition of the jury, one issue is the optimal size of the jury; another is how jurors should be chosen. Increasing the size of the jury will reduce the likelihood of error, since the larger the jury, the more likely it is that at least some jurors will be highly intelligent, or have experience which will assist them in arriving at the truth. There would be a high probability of error by a jury consisting of one person, especially if that person were chosen from the population at random. On the other hand, a larger jury is more costly, since the time of more jurors is required, and it may take longer for the jury to reach a decision. In general the costs of reaching a collective decision will increase with the number of participants.

The U.S. Supreme Court originally held that a "jury" must have twelve persons. The Court's reasoning was that if there could be fewer than twelve, there could be eleven, or ten, or even one – but the word "jury" implies that there is more than one! However, in 1970 the Court abandoned this position, indicating that a twelve-member jury may not be necessary even in some federal criminal cases. The Court has also ruled that the use of six-member juries is permissible in state criminal cases and federal civil cases.[21] Moreover, the U.S. Constitution does not require the states to provide "trial by jury" in civil cases, and some states provide for juries of fewer than twelve in such cases. In 1970 the Court stated that it could detect "no discernible difference" between the results reached by six- and twelve-person juries,[22] a claim which was severely criticized by scholars.

Parenthetically, a "jury" should not be confused with a "grand jury," which is an informing or accusing body rather than a judicial tribunal. A grand jury may "indict" persons who are suspected of having committed a crime. An "indictment" is a written accusation or charge of crime made against a person. Without an accusation there can be no valid criminal prosecution. In some states there may be one-man grand juries in some cases.[23]

How jurors should be chosen

Another question is the manner in which we should obtain jurors. Under the present system, jurors are chosen at random from a group deemed to be reasonably representative of the population; generally this is the list of those who have registered to vote. However, perhaps partly because of a concern that this practice might discourage voting, some jurisdictions have expanded the pool of potential jurors by using a more nearly universal database, e.g., by going from voter registration rolls to a combination of this source with others such as drivers' licenses and State income tax records. There are, however, a number of positions and occupations which are exempted from jury duty. (The value of time tends to be high for many of the persons covered by these exemptions.)

The fees which are paid are far less than the time costs of many persons who serve on juries. It has been argued that this system inevitably leads to excessive use of juries. This is the same as the argument made previously for requiring the government to pay the fair market value of land taken under eminent domain; if the government is not required to make such payment, it will not bear the full social cost of its actions, and the consequence will be inefficient overuse of land for governmental purposes. As an alternative to the current system, one could offer to hire all comers, and set the jury fee at a level such that the supply of jurors just equals the demand.

Under this proposal, however, there would be a serious problem of adverse selection: juries would be dominated by individuals with low incomes, or those for whom the value of time is low. If, on the other hand, the jury fee was set high enough to attract individuals with high incomes, the demand for jury positions would exceed the supply, and some form of rationing would be required. If the rationing were done according to some criterion of ability, say, or level of education, the jury would lose the politically desirable characteristic of being a random sample of the population.

Peremptory challenges and challenges for cause

When a case is ready to be heard, potential jurors are examined to determine whether they are suitable for jury duty. The process of questioning persons, to decide which of them will serve on the jury, is known as the "voir dire" phase of the case. *Voir dire* is a French phrase meaning "to speak the truth." Potential jurors may be excused from a case "for cause" or by a "peremptory challenge." A person is excused for cause if the circumstances raise a question about his ability to hear the case impartially. For example, a person would be excused for cause if he were a close relative of the defendant, the victim, or one of the lawyers, or if he already had a firm opinion concerning the guilt of the defendant. The law also gives each side a specified number of peremptory challenges, by which the defense or prosecution can eliminate potential jurors without being required to give an explanation.[24] The number of peremptory challenges allocated to each side varies among the States, and within each State the number of challenges generally increases with the seriousness of the crime. For example, in California each side is given twenty challenges when the offense is punishable by the death penalty or life imprisonment. In other criminal cases, each side is given ten challenges, unless the offense is punishable by no more than ninety days of imprisonment, in which case each side has only six peremptory challenges. While many States, like California, give each side the same number of challenges, other States and the federal system give the defendant more than the prosecution. For example, Georgia gives the defendant twice as many challenges as the State. In federal criminal cases the defense is allowed ten peremptory challenges and the prosecution six.[25] Any lawyer who wishes to exclude a potential juror would certainly prefer to have the person excused for cause rather than through the use of one of his scarce peremptory challenges. There is no cost in having a person excused for cause, since an unlimited number of persons may be excluded in this way.

There is an ongoing debate among legal scholars as to whether the system of peremptory challenges should be preserved, abolished or modified. One argument made for peremptory challenges is that they enable lawyers to remove jurors who are likely to be biased but whose bias does not fit within one of the categories covered by challenges for cause. For example, they enable a lawyer to remove a juror when he previously challenged the juror for cause but was unsuccessful; in this situation the juror may well resent being challenged, and be inclined to vote against the lawyer's position. It has also been argued that peremptory challenges are an important safeguard for defendants from minority groups. Neilson and Winter (2000) found that when the general population is biased against a minority group, it may be optimal to give the minority defendant more peremptory challenges than the prosecution.

As previously noted, some scholars contend that peremptory challenges should be abolished. They argue that if there are juror biases not currently covered by challenges for cause, the solution is to expand the grounds for such challenges. Nonetheless, every jurisdiction in the United States still provides for peremptory challenges in serious criminal cases.

How the jury makes its decision

As to the manner in which the jury makes its decision, one question is what should be the majority required to reach a verdict – a simple majority, unanimous agreement or something in between? Another issue is the standard of proof, which may range from "a preponderance of the evidence" to "beyond a reasonable doubt." A requirement that the verdict be unanimous will be more costly than majority rule, since it will generally take longer to achieve unanimous agreement, and there will be a positive probability of a "hung jury" and therefore a retrial of the same cause. On the other hand, the quality of the jury's deliberations will increase because of the need to convert those opposed to the will of the majority.

In 1967, England, from which the United States had taken the rule of a unanimous verdict, allowed criminal juries to return a guilty verdict by a margin as low as ten to two, as long as the jury had deliberated for at least two hours. Currently in England a conviction can be voted by ten of an eleven- or twelve-man jury, or by nine of a ten-man jury. The U.S. Supreme Court originally held that a jury must reach a unanimous verdict. However, in 1972 the Court held that state laws that allowed criminal defendants to be convicted by ten out of twelve jurors, or nine out of twelve, were constitutional (nonetheless the Court later overturned a state law allowing a criminal conviction by five of a six-man jury).[26]

As noted previously, the states are not required to provide trial by jury in civil cases, and some states authorize a verdict by as few as eight of a twelve-man jury. This difference in treatment between civil and criminal cases is consistent with the notion that the cost of an incorrect verdict for the plaintiff in a civil case is much less than the cost of an erroneous criminal conviction.

Klevorick and Rothschild (1979) used a theoretical model to examine the consequences of replacing a rule of unanimity with a rule allowing the jury to reach a verdict with a majority of ten out of twelve. Comparing these two rules, they found that there would be no significant difference in the decision made by the jury on the merits of a case, but that on average the jury under the ten-person majority rule would take much less time to arrive at a decision – between 25 percent and 100 percent of the time required by a unanimous jury. Their results suggest that a change from a requirement of unanimity to a majority of ten out of twelve would achieve substantial cost savings without adversely affecting the quality of justice.

Juries in death penalty cases

Joseph Kadane has argued that the criteria which are used to excuse potential jurors for cause in cases subject to capital punishment tend to yield juries biased in favor of the prosecution. Generally in capital cases the same jury decides both (1) whether the defendant is guilty and (2) if the defendant is found guilty of a capital offense, whether he will receive the death penalty.[27] Under a Supreme Court ruling[28] there are two categories of persons who are excused for cause in these cases: (1) those who state that they would automatically vote against the death penalty in every case, regardless of the evidence, and (2) those who state that they could not be fair and impartial in deciding the guilt or innocence of the defendant. In addition, in a number of states potential jurors are excused for cause if they state that they would automatically vote for the death penalty in every capital case in which the jury made the requisite finding of guilt.

Thus under current practice two groups – those who would never vote for the death penalty, and those who would always vote for it – are excluded from the determination of guilt or innocence, even though such persons state that they could be fair and impartial in making that determination. The issue is whether this practice has an adverse effect on the prospects of a defendant in a capital case. The population of potential jurors can be divided into four groups:

a1   Those who state that they could not be fair and impartial.
a2   Those who state that they could be fair and impartial, but would always vote for the death penalty.
a3   Those who state that they could be fair and impartial, but would never vote for the death penalty.
a4   Those who state that they could be fair and impartial, and might or might not vote for the death penalty, depending on the evidence.

Kadane's approach was to compare the expected outcome for the defendant if the jury were drawn from groups a2Ua3Ua4 to the expected outcome if the jury were drawn only from group a4, which was the existing practice. To make this comparison, one need only compare group a2Ua3 to group a4. It turns out that group a2Ua3 is dominated by individuals from group a3, since this group is a much larger share of the population than group a2.[29]

Kadane's method was to use statistical analysis to show that a juror drawn randomly from group a2Ua3 was more inclined to favor the defendant on various issues relating to guilt or innocence than a juror drawn randomly from group a4. For this purpose, Kadane used a survey designed to reveal the extent of bias of potential jurors. For example, one question on the survey was whether "failure to testify indicates guilt." The respondent had to answer by choosing among "agree strongly," "agree somewhat," "disagree somewhat," and "disagree strongly." This survey also inquired whether the respondent was in group a3 (those who would never vote for the death penalty). From these data, it was possible to estimate the probability that a juror drawn randomly from group a2Ua3 would take a position on these questions less favorable to the defense than a person from group a4. Kadane found that for most of these questions this probability was quite low, and inferred from these and other data that there was a substantial bias against the defense resulting from the current practice.

Since under the current practice the same jury decides both whether the defendant is guilty and whether the death penalty shall be imposed, one might question how the jury could possibly include persons who would not vote for the death penalty. There are a number of ways to deal with this problem. One solution would be to impanel two juries, one to determine guilt and the other to make the decision regarding the death penalty.

In cases involving capital punishment, State laws and procedures are frequently challenged on the grounds that they violate specific provisions of the Bill of Rights. For example, in the litigation concerning the grounds for peremptory challenges of prospective jurors, lawyers for the defendants argued that the State laws violated the provision of the Sixth Amendment that "in all criminal prosecutions, the accused shall enjoy the right to a speedy and public trial, by an impartial jury … " The argument was that the exclusion of potential jurors who are opposed to the death penalty results in a jury which is not "impartial," since it is biased in favor of the prosecution. In many cases it has been argued that the death penalty violates the Eighth Amendment's prohibition of "cruel and unusual punishments."

Recall from the discussion in Chapter 3 that although the Bill of Rights restricts only the federal government, a state statute may be challenged as violating the "due process" clause of the Fourteenth Amendment, which applies to State laws, and the due process clause is deemed to include many of the specific protections of the Bill of Rights under the doctrine of "selective incorporation." The Supreme Court has ruled that both the Sixth Amendment's guarantee of an impartial jury and the Eighth Amendment's prohibition of cruel and unusual punishments are inherent in the due process clause of the Fourteenth Amendment.

Bibliography

Danzon, Patricia M., "Contingent Fees for Personal Injury Litigation," 14 *Bell Journal of Economics* 213 (1983).

Dickens, Charles, *Bleak House* (New York: Dodd, Mead, 1951).

Dixon, L., and B. Gill, *Changes in the Standards for Admitting Expert Evidence in Federal Civil Cases since the Daubert Decision* (Santa Monica, CA: RAND Institute for Civil Justice, 2002).

Eisenberg, Theodore, and Geoffrey P. Miller, "Attorney Fees in Class Action Settlements: An Empirical Study," 1 (1) *Journal of Empirical Legal Studies* 27–78 (March 2004).

Helland, Eric, and Jonathan Klick, "The Effect of Judicial Expedience on Attorney Fees in Class Actions," 36 *Journal of Legal Studies* 171–187 (January 2007).

James, Fleming Jr., *Civil Procedure* (Boston, MA: Little Brown, 1965).

Kadane, Joseph B., "Juries Hearing Death Penalty Cases: Statistical Analysis of a Legal Procedure,"78 *Journal of the American Statistical Association* 544–552 (1983).

Kadane, Joseph B., "A Note on Taking Account of the Automatic Death Penalty Jurors," 8 *Law and Human Behavior* 115–120 (1984).

Klevorick, Alvin, and Michael Rothschild, "A Model of the Jury Decision Process," 8 *Journal of Legal Studies* 141 (1979).

Landes, William M., and Richard A. Posner, "Legal Precedent: A Theoretical and Empirical Analysis," 19 *Journal of Law and Economics* 249 (1976).

La Porta, Rafael, Florencio Lopez-de-Silanes, Andrei Schleifer, and Robert W. Vishny, "Legal Determinants of External Finance," 52 *Journal of Finance* 1131–1150 (1997).

La Porta, Rafael, Florencio Lopez-de-Silanes, Andrei Schleifer, and Robert W. Vishny, "Law and Finance," 106 *Journal of Political Economy* 1113–1155 (1998).

Leubsdorf, John, "The Standard for Preliminary Injunctions," 91 (3) *Harvard Law Review* 525–566 (January 1978).

Levine, Ross, "Law, Finance and Economic Growth," 8 *Journal of Financial Intermediation* 8–35 (1999).

Levine, Ross, Norman Loayza, and Thorsten Beck, "Financial Intermediation and Growth: Causality and Causes," working paper (1999).

Levitt, Steven D., and Chad Syverson, "Market Distortions when Agents are Better Informed: A Theoretical and Empirical Exploration of the Value of Information in Real Estate Transactions," working paper, University of Chicago (June 2002).

Mahoney, Paul G., "The Common Law and Economic Growth: Hayek might be Right," 30(2) *Journal of Legal Studies* 503–525 (June 2001).

Murphy, Kevin M., Andrei Shleifer, and Robert W. Vishny, "The Allocation of Talent: Implications for Growth," 106 *Quarterly Journal of Economics* 503–530 (May 1991).

Neilson, William S., and Harold Winter, "Bias and the Economics of Jury Selection," 20 *International Review of Law and Economics* 223–250 (2000).

Posner, Richard A., "An Economic Approach to Legal Procedure and Judicial Administration," 2 *Journal of Legal Studies* 399 (1972).

Posner, Richard A., *Economic Analysis of Law* (3rd ed., Riverwoods, IL: Aspen Publishers, 1986), chapter 18.

Posner, Richard A., "Is the Ninth Circuit Too Large? A Statistical Study of Judicial Quality," 29 *Journal of Legal Studies* 711 (June 2000).

Priest, George L., "The Common Law Process and the Selection of Efficient Rules," 6 *Journal of Legal Studies* 65–82 (January 1977).

Priest, George L., "Private Litigants and the Court Congestion Problem," 69 *Boston University Law Review* 527–559 (1989).

Rubin, Paul H., "Why is the Common Law Efficient?," 6 *Journal of Legal Studies* 51–63 (January 1977).

Rubin, Paul H., "Common Law and Statute Law," 11 *Journal of Legal Studies* 205–223 (1982).

Shepherd, George B., "The Economics of Pretrial Discovery: An Empirical Study," working paper, Emory University School of Law (1995).

Spurr, Stephen J., "An Economic Analysis of Collateral Estoppel," 11 *International Review of Law and Economics* 47 (1991).

Spurr, Stephen J., "The Duration of Litigation," 19 (3) *Law and Policy* 285–315 (July 1997).

Spurr, Stephen J., "The Duration of Personal Injury Litigation," 19 *Research in Law and Economics* 223–246 (Greenwich, CT: JAI/Elsevier, 2000).

Studdert, David M., et al., "Claims, Errors and Compensation Payments in Medical Malpractice Litigation," 354 *New England Journal of Medicine* 2024 (2006).

Tullock, Gordon, *The Case against the Common Law* (Durham, NC: Carolina Academic Press, 1997).

Problems

1. Suppose Mr. Smith plans to sue X Co. for $200,000. Both Mr. Smith and X Co. believe that if the case goes to trial, there is a 50 percent chance that Mr. Smith will win. For each party the costs of litigation would be $10,000. Will the case be litigated or settled out of court?

2. (a) Suppose Mr. Green plans to sue Mr. Blue for $100,000. Mr. Green believes that if the case goes to trial, there is a 75 percent chance that he will win. However, Mr. Blue believes that the probability of Mr. Green's winning is only 50 percent. The costs of a trial would be $5,000 for Mr. Green, and $15,000 for Mr. Blue. Will this case be litigated or settled out of court? If you think the case will be settled, indicate the possible range of the amount for which it will be settled.

    (b) Assume the facts are the same as in (a), except that Mr. Blue now believes the probability of Mr. Green's winning is 75 percent. Again, indicate whether the case will be litigated or settled; if you think the case will be settled, indicate the possible range of the settlement amount.

3. Is an attorney for one party entitled to obtain copies of the notes and legal memoranda written by the lawyer for the other side? Explain the rule of law, and provide an economic explanation for the rule.

4. What functions are performed by the contingent legal fee? Why is it not universally used, for all types of legal cases, and by all types of legal clients?

5. Suppose the value of the time of Mr. Jones, a lawyer, is $100 per hour. Mrs. Smith will hire Mr. Jones to represent her in a personal injury case in which she is suing to recover damages. The amount of damages which will be recovered for her depends on

the amount of time invested in the case by Mr. Jones, as in Table 9.2. (*a*) What will be the amount of the recovery if Mr. Jones is hired under a contingent fee arrangement, whereby his fee is one-third of the recovery? (Assume Mr. Jones is interested only in maximizing his own profit.) Hint: consider the marginal effect of each additional hour of work. (*b*) What would be the efficient number of hours for Mr. Jones to work? (In other words, how many hours would Mr. Jones work to maximize the total gain for him and Mrs. Smith?)

Table 9.2 Relation between hours of lawyer's time and the amount recovered

No. of hours of effort	Amount recovered ($)
6	1,400
7	1,800
8	2,160
9	2,280
10	2,370
11	2,450

6.   "Doubling the number of judges in Wayne County courts should reduce the time to trial by approximately one-half." Comment on this statement.

7.   Explain whether collateral estoppel would be applied in the following situations: (*a*) A sues B, A loses; then E sues B. B wants to apply collateral estoppel against E, to avoid being sued again on the issues which were involved in the first lawsuit. (*b*) After a catastrophic hotel fire, the hotel is sued for negligence in separate lawsuits by the victims or their survivors. Victim A sues the hotel and wins. Victim B then sues the hotel, and wants to apply collateral estoppel against the hotel, to avoid relitigation of the issues involved in victim A's case.

8.   Suppose a cruise ship sank, resulting in the deaths of many passengers. The cruise line is then sued for negligence in 100 separate lawsuits by the victims or their survivors. What would be the collateral estoppel effect of the outcome of the first litigation? Consider both possibilities: (*a*) the plaintiff wins the first lawsuit; (*b*) the defendant cruise line wins.

9.   Students A and B are taking a course in economic analysis of law. Student A has attended every class, read all the assigned materials, taken careful and comprehensive notes, and revised them. Student B has skipped most classes and done none of the reading. A week before the final exam, student B approaches student A and asks to copy all her notes. Compare this scenario to the rationale behind the doctrine of attorney work product.

10 Criminal law

The economic model of crime and punishment

Economists analyze crime with the same approach they use to analyze other kinds of human behavior. Becker (1968) developed an economic model of crime and punishment, in an article that has had a great influence on subsequent research. Becker was not the first to analyze crime in economic terms; during the eighteenth century there were studies by Montesquieu (1748), Beccaria (1770), and Bentham (1789), among others, but the field had long been dormant until Becker's work, which launched the modern literature in this area.

According to the economic model of criminal behavior, a person will commit a crime if the expected benefits of the crime exceed its expected costs. Thus, to reduce crime, we must either reduce the expected benefits or increase the expected costs. To reduce the expected benefits, one might provide information to potential criminals like "Beware of the dog," or "Driver has no more than $20 in cash," or "Safe's contents are protected by time delay." The expected benefits of a crime are usually apparent, but what are the expected costs? They would include: (1) the expected costs of punishment; (2) the opportunity cost of the individual's time; and (3) the expenses of supplies used in this occupation, e.g., false identification, guns, masks, burglar tools, etc. The expected punishment cost is pf, where p is the probability the offender will be caught and convicted, and f, for "fine," is the cost to the offender of the punishment imposed upon conviction.[1]

Suppose, for example, a driver in a traffic jam on the expressway is debating whether to drive on the shoulder of the road to the nearest exit. Assume the probability that he will be caught is one in two, and the cost of his punishment is $200, the expected cost of punishment is $100. The punishment cost of $200 would, of course, include not only the amount of the ticket, but also all other adverse consequences of the conviction, including a possible increase in the driver's automobile insurance premium.

As simple as it is, this model enables us to predict the effect on the crime rate of changes in certain factors. For example, suppose the unemployment rate declines. There is therefore an increase in the opportunity cost of the time of low-income individuals, and the crime rate should fall. And the evidence shows that it does: Chiricos (1987) and Freeman (1996) found that property crime is negatively related to conditions in the labor market. Isaac Ehrlich (1975) found that improvements in the labor market had a much greater effect in reducing the murder rate than increases in the probability of execution.

The next question is how society should allocate its resources to prevent crime. In general society should seek to prevent crime so long as its social costs exceed its social benefits. If the social benefits of a crime exceed its social costs, there is no reason to prevent it; indeed in this case the crime *should* be committed. Consider the offense of double-parking outside a hospital in order to take a woman who is about to give birth into the delivery room. Here the social benefit, increasing the likelihood of a normal, healthy birth, greatly exceeds the social cost of inconvenience from temporary traffic congestion.

The preceding discussion suggests that the expected cost of punishment, *pf*, should equal the social cost of the crime, which includes not only the injury to the victim, but also all other costs of crime, e.g., the costs of maintaining a criminal justice system, and the costs of all the measures taken by people to avoid becoming victims of crime. These costs include public expenditures on police, prisons, courts, and prosecutors, as well as private expenditures on defense lawyers, locks, security guards, burglar alarms, etc.

Once we have determined the optimal *pf*, the expected cost of punishment for the crime, we must consider two further questions: (1) How should law enforcement strike a balance between *p*, the probability of catching and convicting an offender, and *f*, the cost to the offender of the fine or other punishment? (2) What is the optimal type of punishment – a fine, imprisonment, loss of driver's license, loss of voting rights, or what?

Consider once again the offense of driving on the shoulder lane of the expressway. Suppose the social cost of this crime – possible interference with police and emergency vehicles – is \$100. Then the expected cost of punishment, *pf*, should also be \$100. Table 10.1 shows different possible combinations of *p*, the probability of being caught and convicted, and *f*, the fine, that would yield this expected cost of punishment.

Note that the total enforcement costs are greater, the greater the probability of detection *p*. Increasing *p* requires a greater commitment of resources to law enforcement (police, police vehicles, radar, etc.), and more judges, lawyers, and related personnel to handle the greater number of court cases. Since the government wants to deter crime at the lowest possible cost, it should choose the combination of *p* and *f* in the bottom row: the highest fine and the lowest probability of detection. We conclude that if individuals are risk-neutral, the efficient system of law enforcement will choose the lowest feasible probability of arrest and conviction, and the highest possible fine, that together yield the desired expected cost of punishment *pf*. The expected punishment *pf* should equal the social cost of the crime. Since the probability of conviction is low, the opportunity cost of the resources used in law enforcement will be minimized.

Are there any possible defects in the preceding analysis? Indeed there are. One problem is the assumption that individuals are risk-neutral. When it comes to the possibility of losing large amounts of money – large, that is, relative to their wealth – people are likely to be risk-averse rather than risk-neutral (many people will bet small amounts on the outcome of a sports event, but will also carry insurance on their house, car, and life). If individuals are risk-averse, they will go to great lengths to avoid a large fine; that is, they will take excessive care, more care than is appropriate.

Another problem is that the analysis ignores the cost of collecting fines. In fact, the cost of collecting fines increases with the amount of the fine. Someone may readily pay a ticket

Table 10.1 Relation between a fine and the costs of enforcement

Total costs of enforcement (\$ 000)	Probability of detection and conviction, p	Fine, f (\$)	Expected fine, pf (\$)
2,000	1.0	100	100
200	0.1	1,000	100
20	0.01	10,000	100

for $100, but if the fine for the violation is $10,000, he will hire a lawyer and appear at a court hearing to contest the charge. In addition, of course, many people simply do not have the assets required to pay a very large fine, i.e., the cost of collection is infinite.

If very large fines are not feasible, and the criminal's punishment is to be imprisonment, we can still apply the preceding analysis of the optimal system of law enforcement. It is possible to have long prison terms (a large f) and low probabilities of apprehension and conviction (a low p). If criminals are risk-neutral, a p of 0.1 and a sentence of twenty years has exactly the same deterrent effect as a p of 0.2 and a sentence of ten years. However, the regime that administers two ten-year sentences has a much larger cost of enforcement, since more resources will be required to double the probability of conviction, and carry out twice the number of trials, sentencing hearings, and the like.

Up to now we have assumed that p is an unrestricted "choice variable" for the government, that is, that the government can choose whatever level of p it desires. However, we must also consider the fact that p is affected by the type of crime involved. In certain types of crimes, p is relatively low since the criminal seeks to conceal the crime. In these cases, the law generally imposes a larger f than otherwise. For example, violations of antitrust law often involve a group of firms that enter into a secret agreement to fix prices or otherwise restrict competition. Since many such "conspiracies in restraint of trade" may go undetected, the law provides that someone injured by an antitrust violation can recover treble damages, an amount equal to three times actual damages. Those who engage in insider trading of corporate securities, which can also be difficult (costly) to detect, are subject to a civil penalty of up to three times the gain derived through the trades. Another example is provided by punitive (i.e. more than compensatory) damages, which under tort law are often allowed in cases where the tortious conduct is concealed. Finally, under criminal law, premeditated murder is punished more severely than murder committed in a fit of passion. When a murder is premeditated, or carefully planned in advance, the murderer usually takes measures to avoid detection; the lower p requires a higher f.

The optimal type of punishment

The observation that it may be difficult to collect fines leads us to the second question posed above, concerning the optimal form of punishment. Fines do not seem to be a practical form of punishment for many crimes, since many criminals have little or no assets. What other kinds of punishment are there, and how should we choose among them? One way to analyze this issue is to compare the costs of different types of punishment.

One punishment that is widely used is imprisonment. The costs of this alternative include not only the cost to the prisoner of being miserable (which we can ignore since it provides the deterrent effect that any punishment must provide), but also the expense of building and operating prisons, and a loss of productivity of the offender during the period of incarceration. The individual will also be less productive after his release, because of his prolonged separation from the labor market and the stigma of conviction of a serious offense.[2] The reduction of his productivity and earning capacity will lower the opportunity cost of crime, and increase the likelihood that he will return to crime.

It is clear that, in general, the social cost of imprisonment is much greater than the social cost of a fine. A fine, after all, involves only a transfer of funds from the criminal to the government. Essentially no real resources are consumed in this transaction, and the loss to the criminal is offset by an exactly equal gain for the government. In contrast, all the costs involved in imprisonment – the reduced productivity of the offender, the expenditures on prison guards, etc., do not yield a benefit for anyone; they represent a deadweight social loss.

Recognition of the costs of imprisonment has prompted the use of many alternatives. Some initiatives are designed to increase the productivity of time spent in prison, by establishing programs for the education of inmates or increasing the scope of their work opportunities. In some areas probation or parole have been used increasingly as a substitute for incarceration, and there is more "product differentiation" of prisons into maximum and minimum security facilities, homes for youthful offenders, halfway houses, and the like. Another proposal is to increase the use of fines by allowing offenders to pay them in periodic installments from earnings. (However, a potential drawback with this arrangement is that, by reducing the offender's net earnings from legal activity, it lowers the opportunity cost of crime.) Some courts have allowed individuals to serve their jail time on weekends, so that they can hold productive jobs during the work week. Many offenders have been ordered to perform community service.

Much of the costs of imprisonment can be avoided through the use of electronic tethers, global positioning devices, and related equipment, which monitor the location and physical condition of offenders. This equipment can determine, for example, whether an individual is intoxicated, or is at home during a designated curfew period.

Some of the arrangements described above, e.g., greater use of probation and parole, involve much fewer resources, and less sacrifice of the offender's productivity, than prison, but are also less of a punishment, and thus have less deterrent effect on crime. This reduction in deterrence applies not only to future crimes, but also to crimes that may be committed during the period of the criminal's punishment. An individual on parole can commit crimes much more easily than one in a penitentiary. However technological advances are making it possible to obtain a greater deterrent effect from a given investment in law enforcement. Innovations such as the electronic tether are making it possible to impose very effective punishments at a minimal cost of resources, including the offender's productivity.

There are, of course, many other types of punishment besides fines and imprisonment. Convictions may lead to restrictions on movement and occupation, the denial of licenses, the loss of parental rights, voting rights or even citizenship. Historically, there has been a wide variety of punishments, including (apart from execution, which we consider below) branding, torture, banishment, mutilation, and public humiliation. Today, in the United States, these kinds of punishments would probably be found to be "cruel and unusual" punishments in violation of the Eighth and Fourteenth amendments to the Constitution. Whatever the deterrent effect of such punishments may be, there is an argument against them based on efficiency: administering them usually has large social costs. For example, their use may tend to breed hostility toward the government, or may lead to personal retaliation against those who impose the punishment.

An application: Megan's Laws

Let us consider one type of punishment that might be viewed as falling within the category of public humiliation, or shame. There are statutes, commonly known as Megan's Laws,[3] that require persons convicted of sexual crimes to register as sex offenders; these laws also require some type of public notification of the presence of sex offenders in the community. Most states now have web sites that provide detailed information about registered sex offenders such as their name, date of birth, physical characteristics, and sometimes a photograph. Under current federal law the minimum period of registration is ten years;

in some cases, e.g. aggravated sexual crimes or more than one conviction, registration is for life.

These laws may have some deterrent effect, since they increase the costs of sex crimes in two ways: (1) they increase the informal sanctions imposed by the public on the offender, and (2) by providing a means of notifying persons in the vicinity of the offender, they may reduce his opportunities to commit such crimes. Clearly these laws substantially increase the cost of being convicted of a sexual offense. There are two consequences of that: (1) to avoid the sanctions for sex crimes, prosecutors and offenders may agree on a plea bargain in which the offender pleads guilty to a crime that does not require registration as a sex offender;[4] or (2), in the event such a plea bargain is not made available, an offender is far more likely to insist on a trial. Another consequence of these laws has been that informal sanctions, e.g. withdrawal of social contact, ridicule, and humiliation, may be imposed on the family members of the offenders. Perhaps the major problem with these statutes is that the individuals who must register as sex offenders are less likely to be able to find or keep a job, or to maintain social relationships in the communities in which they reside. This loss of social capital and economic productivity reduces the opportunity cost of crime for these individuals, and may lead to desperate behavior; in some cases offenders have committed suicide in an apparent response to public notification.

These statutes will be supported by those who believe that the sanctions could have a substantial effect on sex crimes, both in deterring the first offense and then in deterring further crimes through the notification requirements. Others may believe that these crimes could be deterred more effectively by the rehabilitation provided by social and economic opportunities than by further punishment extending far into the future.

Let us now consider what punishment should be imposed for the most serious crimes, such as murder. Recall that in general, the expected punishment should equal the social cost of the crime. Many would argue that fines and imprisonment, even for the life of the offender, cannot equal the cost of the victim's life, so that murder should be subject to capital punishment. Nonetheless, many states restrict capital punishment to murders in which there are "aggravated circumstances," i.e., in which the social cost of the crime is especially great, such as the murder of a child or of multiple victims. Conversely, the death penalty is generally not imposed in cases where the social cost is perceived to be lower, e.g., the "mercy killing" of an individual in an advanced stage of a terminal illness.

There has been extensive research on the question whether capital punishment has a deterrent effect beyond that of life imprisonment. We review this literature in the next section. It must be recognized that there are important incentive effects of capital punishment, since it is not possible to increase the punishment of an individual who is already facing the death penalty. For example, if rape were subject to capital punishment, a rapist might be prompted to kill his victim, who will usually be the sole witness to the crime. He might believe that by doing so he could reduce the probability of detection, while facing the same penalty.[5] On the other hand, the prospect of the death penalty might deter some persons from rape. We examine these and related issues below.

The deterrent effect of capital punishment

An important watershed in the study of capital punishment was an article by Ehrlich (1975), which, although controversial, was a significant improvement on the previous literature, in that it applied economic analysis and state-of-the-art econometric methods to a large data set. His work was based entirely on the economic model of crime and punishment.

Ehrlich assumed that a potential murderer makes his decision by simply weighing the expected benefits against the expected costs. In his econometric analysis the dependent variable is the murder rate, and the independent, or explanatory variables included the fraction of the population in the labor force, the unemployment rate (both of these variables representing the opportunity cost of crime), the age composition of the population, and per capita expenditures on police. Also included were three law enforcement variables that together provided the expected cost of murder to the offender: the probability of arrest; the probability of conviction, given that the offender is arrested; and the probability of execution, given conviction. The model predicted a negative relationship between each of these probabilities and the murder rate, and also reflected Ehrlich's assumption that these variables were "endogenous," i.e., they both affected the murder rate, and were affected by it. Ehrlich used data on aggregate homicides in the United States during the period from 1933 to 1969. He found that each of the enforcement probabilities had a significant negative effect on the murder rate. In particular, he estimated that between seven and eight murders per year would be eliminated by carrying out one additional execution.

Wolpin (1978) carried out a study similar to Ehrlich's of homicides in England and Wales from 1929 to 1968. He found that four homicides per year could have been eliminated by one additional execution. His research has, however, been criticized for not considering that the immigration of different ethnic groups may have explained an increase in the English homicide rate after 1961.[6]

Ehrlich's research created something of a sensation, since no previous study had found that the death penalty had a statistically significant effect on the murder rate. Economists and statisticians who reviewed his work subsequently leveled a number of criticisms. One objection was that his results were sensitive to the period covered by his data set. At the end of that period, from 1962 through 1969, the number of executions had declined abruptly because of legal challenges, and some critics argued that these years should be excluded. Passell and Taylor (1977) did exclude those years, and found that the probability of execution was no longer statistically significant. Another criticism was that Ehrlich's results would not hold up if he had used a different econometric specification. He had used what some considered a rather arbitrary choice, a multiplicative model in which all the explanatory variables were multiplied by each other, and a different model would yield different results. Leamer (1983) and McManus (1985) estimated the deterrent effect of capital punishment in separate studies of the same data set, on murder rates across U.S. States in 1950. They each concluded that a deterrent effect could not be objectively demonstrated, and that a researcher's interpretation of the evidence would be based on his prior beliefs. It should be noted that Ehrlich (1999, 1977) has provided detailed rebuttals to the criticism by Leamer and McManus and others. All in all, it seems clear that no consensus has emerged on the issue of deterrence.

In any case, Ehrlich's research provides a stunning example of the influence an empirical study can have on the decisions of the U.S. Supreme Court. His paper, which was then unpublished, was cited in the brief of the Solicitor General (the lawyer who represents the U.S. government) in the case of Gregg v. Georgia,[7] which reviewed the constitutionality of the death penalty statutes of five states. The question whether the death penalty had a deterrent effect was a crucial issue in this case, since a finding of deterrence would provide a rational basis for a punishment being attacked as a "cruel and unusual" punishment, in violation of the Eighth and Fourteenth amendments to the Constitution. Ehrlich's article, and a number of articles criticizing it, were noted in both the opinion of the Court and a dissenting opinion, and it seems clear that the Justices writing these opinions were closely familiar with this literature. In his dissent Justice Marshall cited all the methodological criticisms of Ehrlich's work mentioned above. In the event, the Gregg decision upheld the constitutionality of three of the death penalty statutes, which provided a model of a constitutional statute that other states could follow. In doing so, the Court effectively restored capital punishment in the United States, ending a nine-year moratorium on executions.

Evaluating the system of law enforcement

Whether the criminal justice system is fair

The discussion in the preceding sections assumes that p, the probability of being caught and convicted, and f, the cost of punishment to the offender, are the same for all offenders. This assumption is of course manifestly untrue. Many observers have pointed out differences in the way the criminal justice system applies to different groups of the population. It is widely held that the system is unjust, since the quality of legal representation is higher for wealthy criminals than for low-income offenders (an observation that cannot be doubted), and thus they are less likely to be convicted. Note, however, that a lower probability of conviction could be completely offset by a larger penalty, given that the offender is convicted. Suppose that for the low-income criminal p is 1, and f is $50,000. If p is only one in two for the high-income criminal, but f is $100,000, both offenders face the same expected penalty.

This example is relevant because Lott (1992) found that high-income offenders were in fact subject to much higher penalties upon conviction, when one takes into account the reduction in earnings resulting from their conviction. High-income professionals such as lawyers can lose their license to practice their occupation, and even if they are not legally barred from their previous type of employment, they often have difficulty finding comparable positions because of the damage to their reputation resulting from a felony conviction. Lott found that the penalty imposed on earnings by conviction was highly progressive. His empirical work showed, for example, that a bank embezzler whose pre-sentence income was $16,800 would experience a decline in earnings of 39 percent, but one whose pre-sentence income was $49,400 would have a decline of 82 percent. Although Lott did not have data on differences in the probability of conviction, he found indirect evidence that, at least for the types of offenders he analyzed (those charged with embezzlement, fraud, larceny, and theft), the differences in p across income levels were not enough to compensate for the differences in f; in other words, criminals with higher incomes faced higher expected penalties pf.

Discrimination in law enforcement

The next two sections each review an empirical study of racial discrimination in the enforcement of criminal law. Both of these studies are models of how this kind of research should be done (and, unfortunately, is often not done); they each use rigorous statistical methods and a careful analytical model to investigate the issue of discrimination. The first study, involving searches of motor vehicles by police, finds no evidence of discrimination against Blacks. The second study, involving the amount of bail bonds set by judges, does find such discrimination.

Racial profiling

There are a number of interesting issues involving discrimination in the enforcement of criminal law. One is the issue of "racial profiling," i.e., the use of race as a factor in deciding who should be investigated for crimes. In Maryland, between January 1995 and January 1999, 63 percent of motorists searched by the Maryland state police were Black, but only 18 percent of all motorists on the road were Black. However, Knowles, Persico, and Todd (2001) pointed out that this disparity between the proportion of Black drivers who were searched and their proportion of all drivers did not by itself prove racial discrimination. It is likely that police make their decisions on which cars to search on the basis of many factors, and some of these factors may be associated with race. For example, one police training manual cites as possible indicators of drug activity certain characteristics such as tinted windows, cellphones, the use of leased vehicles, religious symbols (used to divert suspicion), and attorney business cards. Knowles et al. analyzed the Maryland data to determine whether police were simply trying to maximize the number of successful searches, i.e., searches that yielded evidence of crimes (generally possession of illegal drugs), or rather were motivated by an intent to harass Black motorists.

Knowles et al. develop a theoretical model that provides a way to test whether the police's decisions on whom to search are based on racial discrimination, or instead by a desire to apprehend as many criminals as possible. According to their model, if the objective of the police is to maximize the number of criminal convictions, the consequence will be that for persons of each race, the probability the individual is guilty, given that he is searched, will be the same.

To understand the basic idea of their model, suppose the population consists of just two ethnic groups, A and B. Suppose the police knew that they were more likely to uncover a particular type of crime if they investigated individuals of group A rather than individuals of group B. Then, if they wish to maximize the number of convictions for this crime, they should investigate only individuals from group A.

Now suppose they have adopted this strategy. The payoff of this strategy will soon be reduced by two factors: (1) the police will encounter the law of eventually diminishing marginal product: on the extensive margin, as they investigate more and more individuals from group A, they will be investigating people who are less and less likely to have committed the crime in question; and (2) on the intensive margin, individuals from group A will respond to the high probability of detection by committing less crimes, while individuals from group B will respond to their zero probability of detection by committing more crimes. Eventually the police will find that the probability of obtaining a conviction by checking on someone from group A is no greater (and perhaps less) than by checking on someone from group B. At this point they will stop concentrating on group A, and begin investigating individuals from group B as well. In equilibrium they will make their decisions on whom to investigate in such a way that the probability of uncovering a crime from an investigation will be the same for each group. Note, however, that this does *not* mean that the probability of being investigated will be identical for each group. Bear in mind also that we are assuming that the objective of the police is to maximize the number of criminal convictions, not to harass any ethnic group.

Thus, according to the theoretical model of Knowles et al., if police were not motivated by racial prejudice, but simply wanted to maximize the number of criminal convictions, then, for individuals of each race, the probability the individual was guilty, given that he was searched, would be the same. If, on the other hand, police *were* motivated by racial discrimination, then the probability that a Black motorist was guilty, given that he was searched, would be *less* than the same probability for a White motorist. They defined a motorist as guilty if he were found with any amount of illegal drugs. It turned out that, among motorists whose cars were searched, the proportion guilty was about the same for each race, viz., 32 percent for Whites and 34 percent for Blacks. For Hispanics, however, the guilty rate was only 11 percent, much lower than the rate for Blacks and Whites, and therefore suggestive of discrimination against this group. However the authors suggested that this result should be interpreted with caution, since there were relatively few Hispanics in the data set.

Discrimination in setting bail bonds

Another study, by Ayres and Waldfogel (1994), found that there was discrimination against Black males, in the setting of bail bonds. To understand this finding, one must first understand the procedure of setting bail and its purpose. The primary purpose of bail is to provide a reasonable assurance that the person accused of a crime will appear in court. Another possible purpose is to ensure that no one's safety would be endangered by the release of the defendant before trial, or that no crimes would be committed by the defendant before trial.[8]

After a judge decides on the amount of a bond, the defendant can either post the bond himself, or arrange to have it posted by a bail bond dealer. To arrange for bond by a dealer, a defendant must pay the dealer a fee, which is nonrefundable, and may also give the dealer some type of collateral, like jewelry or a valuable watch. If the defendant subsequently fails to appear in court, the bond dealer will become liable for the bond, and will sell any collateral provided by the defendant to help make the required payment to the court.[9]

The law of Connecticut, the state in which this study was done, requires that bond be set at the lowest amount that will reasonably assure that the defendant will appear in court. The implication is that the likelihood of the defendant's appearance increases with the amount of the bond. It is obvious that this relation would hold if the defendant furnished the amount of the bond himself, since he would lose that amount if he failed to appear; in this case it is clear that a higher bond would increase the probability the defendant will appear. However in most cases the bond will be provided by a dealer. Since the defendant's bond fee is nonrefundable, it is a sunk cost; thus it is not obvious why the amount of the bond would have any effect on the defendant's decision whether to flee.[10] Ayres and Waldfogel, however, argue that if the bond is relatively large, the dealer will make a greater effort to monitor the location of the defendant before trial, and to have him apprehended if he attempts to flee. The defendant, being aware of the bond dealer's incentives, will know that an attempt to flee is less likely to be successful, and is therefore less likely to flee, when the bond is large.

Ayres and Waldfogel found evidence that the rates charged by bond dealers are determined by economic conditions (the bond rate is the total nonrefundable fee charged by the bond dealer, divided by the bail amount set by the judge). Specifically, they found that the rates charged by bond dealers were inversely related to the number of dealers in a city. In cities where the bond dealer had little competition, the dealer generally charged the maximum rate allowed by law. In cities where there were several bond dealers, bond rates were likely to be well below the statutory maximum.

Their study includes a theoretical model which shows that, under competition, the rate charged by a bond dealer should be proportional to the probability that that defendant will flee. Suppose $B =$ the amount of bail set by the judge, $p =$ the probability the defendant will flee, $R =$ the total nonrefundable fee paid to the bond dealer, r the bond rate charged by the bond dealer, $= R/B$, $C =$ the value of the collateral given by the defendant to the bond dealer, and $\pi =$ the expected profit of the bond dealer. Then the expected profit:

$$\pi = R(1-p) + p(R - B + C) = R - pB + pC$$

The term $R(1-p)$ indicates that with probability $1-p$ the defendant will not flee, and the dealer will then gain the nonrefundable fee R; the term following it indicates that with probability p, the defendant will flee, in which case the bond dealer would still gain the nonrefundable fee R, but will also have a loss equal to the amount of the bond B, offset by C, the amount he recovers from sale of the defendant's collateral.[11]

Let us assume that competition drives the profit of the bond dealers down to zero. Then we can solve for the value of the market rate r.

$$R - pB + pC = 0 \Rightarrow R = pB - pC$$

and therefore:

$$r = \frac{R}{B} = p\left(1 - \frac{C}{B}\right)$$

Let us assume that the value of the collateral provided by the defendant is proportional to the amount of the bond, i.e., $C = kB$, where k is some constant. Then $r = p(1-k)$, so the bond rate is proportional to the risk that the defendant will flee.

Ayres and Waldfogel found that, on average, the bail amounts set by judges for Black male defendants were substantially higher than those set for white males. However, one cannot infer that this disparity indicates racial discrimination, since in setting bail, judges must consider a number of factors that affect the risk of flight, e.g., the seriousness of the alleged crime, the defendant's employment status, and whether he has relatives in the community. The severity of the crime is relevant, since defendants facing more serious charges may be more likely to flee. There may also be a greater risk of flight for someone who is unemployed, or who has few ties to the community. Although certain statistical methods, such as multiple regression analysis, can be used to control for observable factors, it is likely that the judge who sets the bail has some information about the defendant that is not available to the researcher who is analyzing the data for evidence of discrimination.

The central finding of this study is that the rates charged by bond dealers to Black male defendants were almost 19 percent lower than those charged to white males. From this disparity, the authors infer that there was discrimination against Black males by judges in setting bail. Their reasoning is as follows: if judges were impartial, they would set bail at levels such that the expected probability of flight of all defendants would be equal.[12] In contrast, a judge who discriminated against Black defendants would set the bond for them too high, so that their expected probability of flight would be lower than for other defendants. Now because of the discipline imposed by competition, the rates charged by bond dealers will be proportional to the defendant's probability of flight. Consequently, since the rates actually charged by bond dealers to Black defendants were significantly less than those charged to Whites, for Blacks the probability of flight was made too low, which means their bond was set too high.

Ayres and Waldfogel considered, and ruled out, other possible reasons why Black defendants might be charged lower rates. For example, if bond dealers had monopoly power, they might have been engaging in price discrimination, i.e. they would charge lower rates to Black defendants because they tend to be poorer than Whites. The authors found, however, that the rates charged by bond dealers were not correlated with income. This study makes ingenious use of market data to test for discrimination. Since the bond dealers are risking their own funds, it seems plausible that their assessment of the risk of flight would be as reliable as possible.

Measuring the determinants of crime and the benefits of law enforcement

The effect of police on the crime rate

To determine the optimal amount of investment in law enforcement, we would want to compare the marginal cost of the investment with its marginal benefit, e.g., the effect on the crime rate of hiring additional police officers. However, these benefits are usually very hard to measure. Hiring more police should increase p, the probability of arrest for a given level of crime, and this in turn should reduce the crime rate, through a deterrent effect and also through the effect of incapacitation.[13] That is, even if the deterrent impact is small (because, for example, criminals do not have good information about the increase in law enforcement efforts), there may be a substantial benefit from incarceration ("getting criminals off the streets"), since it is much less likely that criminals will commit crimes while in prison. Thus we would expect the crime rate to fall with an increase in the police force.[14] We might also expect that, following an increase in the police force, there would be an initial increase in the arrest rate, followed by a decline as the crime rate was reduced by the effects of deterrence and incarceration.

However, attempts to measure the benefits of a greater investment in law enforcement must deal with problems of simultaneity and possible displacement effects. The simultaneity problem arises because it often happens that more police are hired in response to a crime wave – an unusually high crime rate or recent rapid growth of crime. Thus a researcher who examines the data, but fails to take this into account, might (incorrectly) conclude that the crime rate *increases* with the size of the police force. The displacement effect arises because, for example, an increase in the police force in suburb A may well reduce crime there, but might also increase crime in adjacent communities by diverting criminals to areas where the probability of apprehension is lower.

For all the foregoing reasons the benefits of an investment in law enforcement, even if substantial, are often hard to determine from the data. However Levitt (1997) devised a method to deal with the simultaneity problem. First, he found that there were significant increases in the police force in U.S. cities in years when there was an election for mayor or governor; it appears that incumbents have an incentive to hire more police in advance of an election, to either reduce crime or at least appear to be striving to do so. Thus, if crime is indeed reduced by a larger police presence, election years should have the effect of reducing crime through an increase in the police force, but should not otherwise affect the crime rate. Using statistical methods to exploit this property of electoral cycles (instrumental variables and two-stage least squares), Levitt found that additional police had large negative effects on crime. Comparing the marginal cost of a police officer to his estimate of the marginal benefit through crime reduction, he found the former smaller than the latter, suggesting that the number of police in large cities was below the optimal level.

The effect of the prison population on the crime rate

Since imprisonment is generally the most severe punishment imposed on crimes, we would expect the crime rate to be lower when upon conviction the probability of imprisonment is relatively high, and the expected duration of a prison term is long. Of course, one consequence of an increase in these variables is that at any given time, a relatively large fraction of the population will be in prison. This raises the question whether there is evidence that the crime rate declines when the prison population increases.

Increasing a state's prison population (its prisoners per capita) might reduce the crime rate either through deterrence (potential criminals are deterred by a greater expected period of imprisonment) or through incapacitation (since persons cannot commit crimes while in prison). Studies of the effect of the prison population on the crime rate have been plagued by a simultaneity problem quite similar to the one we encountered above, when considering the effect on crime of the size of the police force: while an increase in the state's prison population may reduce the crime rate, an increase in crime caused by unrelated factors (an increase in gang activity, or in the number of single-parent families, or a decline in economic opportunities for youths) will increase the state's prison population. Thus the causation between crime and the prison population runs in both directions. This reciprocal causation makes it difficult to identify the effect of the size of the prison population on crime. Indeed, some studies have found that an increase in the prison population has been accompanied by an increase in the crime rate. Some commentators have argued that a policy of law enforcement that relies heavily on imprisonment doesn't work, since over the period 1973–1992 the crime rate in the United States did not decline much, if at all, even though the rate of incarceration more than tripled. It is therefore important to determine whether, and if so, how much, crime is reduced by an increase in the prison population.

Levitt (1996) found a way to break the simultaneity of crime and the prison population. His approach is based on the observation that many lawsuits have been brought against state prison systems based on the claim that overcrowding of prisons is cruel and unusual punishment. Not surprisingly, these lawsuits reduced the rate of growth of prison populations in the states where they were filed. Levitt noted that litigation based on prison overcrowding could, by reducing the growth of the state's prison population, increase the crime rate, but should not otherwise have any effect on crime. This insight led him to exploit a statistical technique (instrumental variables) that made it possible to isolate the effect of the size of the prison population on crime. His estimates suggested that the effect of adding one prisoner was to eliminate fifteen crimes per year.

Comparing the marginal social cost of imprisonment to the marginal benefit from reducing crime, he found the former smaller than the latter, and concluded that there should be greater use of incarceration. Levitt also stressed, however, that any increased use of imprisonment should occur at the intensive, rather than the extensive, margin, i.e., in the form of longer sentences for current prisoners, rather than by adding more inmates. His reasoning was that there is great variation among criminals, in terms of the number and seriousness of the crimes they are likely to commit if not in prison. Consequently there is a greater benefit in terms of crime reduction to be had by prolonging the sentences of the most serious offenders, e.g. those who repeatedly commit violent crimes, than by adding to the prison system those from the bottom of the crime distribution, such as nonviolent petty thieves.

The effect of abortion laws on the crime rate

The United States experienced dramatic declines in the crime rate during the period from 1991 to 2005. In the decade after 1991, homicides fell by more than 40 percent, while violent crime and property crime declined by more than 30 percent. Researchers have investigated a number of possible reasons for this development: the increased use of imprisonment, increases in the number of police officers, a decline in the use of crack cocaine, improvements in the economy, changes in gun control laws, and increased expenditures on precautions such as security guards, locks, and alarms. However Donohue and Levitt (2001) have proposed another explanation, which they find to be more important than any of the foregoing factors: the nationwide increase in abortions following the 1973 Supreme Court decision in *Roe v. Wade*. With that decision, the Court struck down state criminal laws against abortion, holding that they violated a woman's constitutional right to privacy, which included a right to terminate her pregnancy.[15]

The argument by Donohue and Levitt runs as follows. Women choose to have abortions when children are unwanted or mistimed. A large proportion of women in this situation are teenagers, unmarried, or living in poverty. Unwanted children who are born only because their mothers were unable to obtain abortions are more likely than other children to be raised in a single-parent household, to live in poverty, and to be part of a household on welfare. In addition, their mothers are more likely to have been drinking, smoking, or using drugs during pregnancy. These unwanted children are also more apt to be abused and neglected. Research shows that children born and living under these conditions have a high propensity to be involved in juvenile delinquency and later, criminal activity. Abortions prevent unwanted children from being born, and enable women to postpone births until they can provide a child with a more favorable home environment.

Donohue and Levitt examined whether differences in the crime rate could be explained by differences in the abortion rate. They used various statistical methods to analyze the effect of the abortion rate on crime, taking into account other factors that might affect crime such as prisoners and police per capita, economic conditions, state welfare payments, whether state law allowed the carrying of concealed handguns, and per capita beer consumption. Their analysis took into account that most abortions are performed six to seven months before birth would have occurred, and that the likelihood of criminal activity depends on the individual's age; thus, an increase in abortions in a given state would not be expected to have much of an impact on the state's crime rate until about fifteen years later. They found that legalized abortion was a factor of great importance in explaining the nationwide decline in crime, possibly accounting for one-half of the overall reduction in crime observed in their data.

Several studies have found other noteworthy effects of the legalization of abortion. Kalist and Molinari (2006) analyzed the effect of legalized abortion on the rate of homicides of infants (children less than one year old). They found that an increase in the abortion ratio (the number of abortions divided by live births) by 10 percent reduced the number of unwanted births by 3.5 percent, and thereby reduced the rate of infant homicides.

Another study found that the legalization of abortion reduced the rate of childbearing by unmarried teenage females. After forty-one consecutive years of increase, the rate of childbearing out of wedlock by teenage females in the United States began to decline in 1991, and by 2002 was 20 per cent below its peak. Donohue et al. (2009) estimated that the legalization of abortion in the mid-1970s caused fewer female babies to be born into situations where their parents were unable or unwilling to provide nurturing and supportive environments. The support that girls born in the 1970s received from their parents made them less likely to become out-of-wedlock mothers when they reached their teenage years in the 1990s. In other words, because abortion was available in the 1970s, the childhood background of girls who were born was substantially more favorable than it would have been for the cohort that would have been born had abortion not been legalized. Donohue et al. estimated that the legalization of abortion accounted for 25 percent of the decline in the birth rates of unmarried teenage females during the period 1991–2002.

Markets for crime

In the next three sections we consider applications of the economic model of crime and punishment to specific crimes. We first examine the market for illegal drugs, and then the economics of smuggling. Finally, we consider the effect on the theft of motor vehicles of Lojack, a recent innovation in law enforcement.

The market for illegal drugs

As part of a "war on drugs," the U.S. government has established a number of programs designed to reduce the use of illegal drugs. The objective of some of these programs is to reduce demand, through educational programs and advertising, and by increasing the penalties for drug use and possession, for example, by making those convicted of drug offenses ineligible for federal student aid. Other programs are intended to reduce supply, by providing resources for enforcement of drug laws, and increasing the penalties for the sale of drugs.

On an episode of *Nightline*, the television program, the host, Ted Koppel, claimed that the evidence showed that the war on drugs was a failure. He pointed out that the street price of cocaine and marijuana was much lower than it had been before. Koppel was assuming that the decline in price had been caused by an increase in supply, as shown in Figure 10.1. The inference was that the war on drugs was a failure. However, a fall in price could also be caused by a decline in demand, as shown in Figure 10.2. In this case the government would be winning the war on drugs, since the amount of drugs sold would be lower than before. The point is that, to determine whether the government was winning or losing the war on drugs, one would have to know whether the quantity of drugs sold had increased, as in Figure 10.1, or decreased, as in Figure 10.2.

Now suppose that the government's efforts caused a reduction in the supply of drugs, so that the supply curve shifts to the left. Recall that the industry supply curve represents the

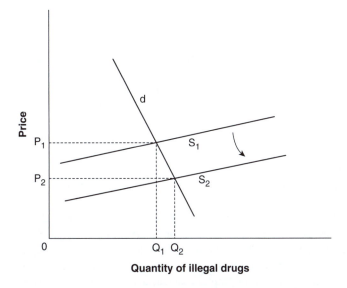

Figure 10.1 An increase in the supply of drugs.

Figure 10.2 A decline in demand for drugs.

horizontal sum of the supply curves, or long-run marginal cost curves, of all firms in the industry. The supply curve might shift upward and to the left because (1) there were fewer firms in the drug business (perhaps because the members of some drug gangs had been sent to prison), or (2) the costs of the firms still in the drug business had increased (because the expected punishment costs had increased, and the direct costs of supplying drugs may have also increased, e.g., since more shipments of drugs were intercepted by authorities). If the demand curve has not moved, the reduction in supply would cause the price of drugs to increase. It has been argued that the consequence could actually be an *increase* in the overall crime rate. Consider Figure 10.3, which shows the demand for drugs of an individual who is a drug addict. Since this individual is addicted, his demand curve is inelastic – from his standpoint, there are no good substitutes for the drug. When the price of the drug increases from P_1 to P_2, the amount purchased declines only slightly, from Q_1 to Q_2, and the amount spent by the addict increases, from area $0P_1aQ_1$ to area $0P_2bQ_2$. (We know $0P_2bQ_2$ is larger since the demand curve is inelastic.) Critics of drug laws point out that many crimes are committed by addicts who are seeking money to enable them to purchase drugs. Thus, if the price of drugs increases from P_1 to P_2, the addict must commit more crimes to raise the larger amount of money that is now required $0P_2bQ_2$. This is the economic rationale for legalization of drug use. If it were perfectly legal to sell drugs such as cocaine, the cost of providing drugs would fall, and many firms would enter the industry. Consequently the supply curve would shift down and to the right, and the price would fall, reducing the total expenditure on drugs by the addict, and the number of crimes he would have to commit to support his habit.

A potential problem with legalization arises, however, if we consider that not all the potential consumers of drugs are addicts. Some are casual or "recreational" users, whose demand is relatively elastic, and there are others who would try drugs if they were legal, but not if they were illegal and subject to criminal penalties. For such individuals a lower price of drugs would lead to much greater consumption, as shown in Figure 10.4. Their use of drugs is likely to reduce their productivity, and may eventually cause them to

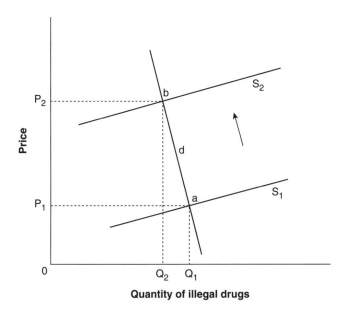

Figure 10.3 The effect of a price increase on a drug addict.

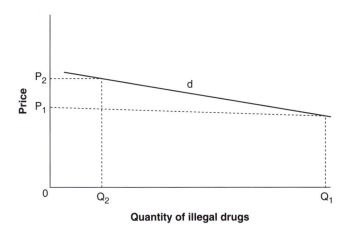

Figure 10.4 The effect of a price increase on a casual drug user.

become addicts. Increasing the price of drugs for these individuals is likely to sharply reduce their consumption, or even deter them from drug use altogether.

Thus it appears that the optimal solution may lie in a form of price discrimination: charging a low price to the addict whose demand is inelastic, and a high price to the casual user, while taking measures to ensure that the addicts cannot resell drugs to casual users. As it happens, this kind of two-part pricing scheme has been used in Great Britain. Individuals who registered with the government as heroin addicts were allowed to buy heroin from pharmacies at a low price, while the purchase of heroin was illegal for anyone not so registered. A nonaddict could only buy heroin illegally, at a much higher price on the black market.

The economics of smuggling

Governments are often prone to adopt taxes or regulations without much consideration of how these policies might affect the movement of people, firms or commodities across their borders. In certain situations, in which conditions are favorable for smuggling, the effects of these policies may be quite different from what was anticipated.

In Canada, taxes on cigarettes were increased by 167 percent between 1984 and 1992. During this period exports of cigarettes to the United States were not subject to Canadian duties; cigarettes entering the United States were subject to tax at the U.S. domestic rate, but this was about one-fifth of the Canadian tax rate. These conditions created substantial incentives for smuggling; cigarettes that were first exported from Canada to the United States, and then smuggled back into Canada, could avoid the tax on domestic cigarettes, which amounted to 75 percent of their retail price.[16] Studies have found that about 90 percent of cigarettes exported to the United States were subsequently smuggled back into Canada, often through Mohawk Indian reservations along the border.[17]

In Canada, the general availability of cigarettes on the black market reduced the demand for cigarettes sold legally, thereby reducing tax revenues for the government. After evaluating the situation, the government in 1994 decided to adopt certain measures to deter smuggling and increase its tax revenues. The government imposed duties on exports, reduced the tax on cigarettes sold domestically, and increased the penalties for smuggling as well as its efforts at law enforcement.

Figures 10.5 and 10.6 show the consequences of these measures. The expected costs of smuggling, which determine the height of the supply curve to the black market, were increased by the new duties on exports, and by the measures that increased the probability of arrest and the penalties imposed upon conviction. Thus the black-market supply curve, shown in Figure 10.5, shifts up from BMS_1 to BMS_2. At the same time the reduction of the tax in the legal market lowered the price to consumers, which caused the black-market demand curve

Figure 10.5 The effect of new government policies in the illegal ("black") market.

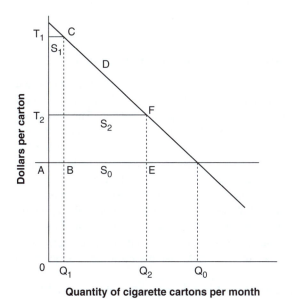

Figure 10.6 The effect of new government policies in the legal market.

to shift back to the left, from BMD$_1$ to BMD$_2$. (Legal purchases are a substitute for purchases on the black market, and a decline in the price of a substitute causes the demand curve for a good to shift back.)

Figure 10.6 shows the effects of the new government policies in the legal market. If there were no tax on cigarettes, the quantity sold would be determined by the intersection of the supply curve S$_0$ and the demand curve D, at Q$_0$. However, before 1994 there was a high tax AT$_1$, which placed a wedge between the supply curve and the demand curve; the tax can also be viewed as increasing the marginal cost of suppliers, so that the effective supply curve rose to S$_1$, and the quantity sold was only Q$_1$. When the tax was subsequently reduced to AT$_2$, the effective supply curve was S$_2$, and the quantity sold increased to Q$_2$.

The overall consequences of the new measures were a shift of sales from the black market to the legal market, and a change (possibly an increase) in tax revenues for the Canadian government. Figure 10.6 shows a change in total tax revenues from AT$_1$CB to AT$_2$FE. Of course, any increase in tax revenue was offset by an increase in the costs of law enforcement, and in any case the government was also greatly concerned with the health effects of smoking, legal or otherwise. An increase in health problems caused by more smoking would directly increase health care expenditures, but also reduce life expectancies, with indeterminate effects on the government's net revenues.

Even without the new policies adopted by Canada in 1994, if U.S. tax rates on cigarettes had been comparable to Canadian tax rates, there would have been no incentive to export cigarettes to the United States and smuggle them back into Canada. However, if the United States had raised its tax rates to the Canadian level (as Canadians often urged it to do), it would have been vulnerable to smuggling across the Mexican border. Since the Mexican tax rate on cigarettes was low, and there was no duty on exports from the United States to Mexico, a high tax rate in the United States would create incentives to export cigarettes from the United States to Mexico, and smuggle them back across the border. Thus the problem would have been transferred from Canada to the United States!

Externalities resulting from precautions taken against crime; Lojack

Ayres and Levitt (1998) point out that externalities arise from private actions taken to avoid crime. There are some forms of self-protection that are highly visible, like steering wheel locks on cars or home security systems with warning signs posted outside. These kinds of precautions have negative externalities, since they simply steer criminals to other potential victims.[18] There are, however, also invisible forms of self-protection such as silent burglar alarms. These types of precautions yield positive externalities; since criminals do not know who has taken these precautions, they have a general deterrent effect on crime.

With Lojack, a small radio transmitter is hidden inside a car. There is no indication anywhere on the vehicle that Lojack is installed. When a car is reported stolen, police remotely activate the vehicle's transmitter. By following the signal, the police can then go directly to the vehicle in specially equipped police cars or helicopters. Ayres and Levitt found that one auto theft is eliminated each year for every three Lojack systems installed in high-crime central cities.

It appeared that the most important effect of Lojack was its impact on "chop shops." These are garages to which stolen cars are taken, to be dismantled rapidly into parts. With Lojack, the police could easily find and shut down these operations.

Auto theft rings are known to have modified their practices because of Lojack. One strategy they have adopted is to leave a stolen vehicle in, for example, the parking lot of a shopping center, to see if the police come after it. If the police do not appear after a reasonable interval, they conclude the vehicle does not have Lojack and return for it.

Ayres and Levitt investigated whether the effect of Lojack in reducing auto theft was a net reduction of crime, or simply a diversion of crime into other channels. Becker's economic model of crime suggests that if there is a decline in the expected benefits of one type of crime, criminals will substitute into an alternative criminal activity that has a higher rate of return. One example of such displacement activity is the growth of chop shops. It is unprofitable to sell stolen cars, since the thief will not be able to provide the buyer a good title; only the registered owner can do that. Moreover, the thief runs the risk of being caught if the police find him in possession of a vehicle registered to someone else. Therefore the most profitable activity is to dismantle the car quickly and sell its individual parts. With regard to possible displacement effects of Lojack, Ayres and Levitt examined whether auto theft rings shifted their activities geographically, so that a decline in thefts in the central city was offset by an increase in outlying suburban or rural areas, or whether they switched from auto theft to other more promising crimes such as burglary or robbery. They found no evidence of either of these types of displacement effects, but did find a statistically significant increase in the theft rate of older vehicles that were less likely to have Lojack installed.

Ayres and Levitt found that the effect of Lojack in reducing the auto theft rate was subject to the law of eventually diminishing marginal product. The decline associated with the first percentage point of Lojack's market share (i.e., the percentage of vehicles that had Lojack installed) was two and a half times that of the second percentage point, and seven times that of the third percentage point. The apparent explanation for the diminishing returns was that soon after Lojack entered a market, auto theft rings would modify their operations (e.g., by temporarily abandoning stolen cars to see if the police were following, by moving to other

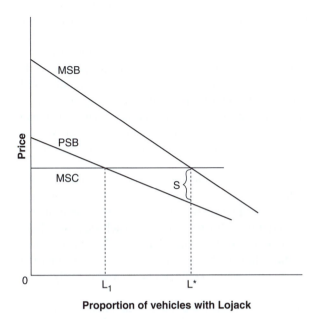

Figure 10.7 The efficient level of Lojack use with a subsidy.

locations, or by avoiding the vehicles most likely to have Lojack). Further market penetration of Lojack had a much smaller marginal impact, since the professional thieves had already changed their operations to minimize the effect of Lojack.

It could be argued that Lojack should be subsidized, since the marginal social benefit from its use exceeds the marginal benefit to the purchaser by the amount of the externality. In Figure 10.7, the efficient level of Lojack consumption is at L^*, where the curve of marginal social benefit intersects marginal social cost. This outcome will be achieved if a subsidy S increases demand from PSB to MSB.[19] Without the subsidy the equilibrium will be at L_1, where there is insufficient use of Lojack.

Factors affecting the quality of law enforcement

We have already noted that p, the probability of detection, and f, the cost of punishment to the offender, are not the same for all offenders. Thus, for the wealthy defendant, p may well be lower, but the effective f might be greater than it is for the low-income defendant. In this section we consider a number of other factors that may lead to systematic differences in p and f across different crimes and different types of defendants.

Becker and Stigler (1974) have observed that the quality of law enforcement tends to decline when there is a large disparity between the gain to law enforcement officials from obtaining a conviction, and the cost of that conviction to the offender. Consider a policeman who is prepared to arrest a major drug supplier. The gain to the policeman from this arrest may be some praise from his superiors, and some enhancement of his career; let us assume this gain has a present value of $1,000. On the other hand, the cost of conviction to the drug dealer may be $1 million. The drug dealer would be willing to pay the policeman any amount up to $1 million to allow him to go free. The difference between $1,000 and $1 million creates an opportunity for a transaction that would benefit both parties if the policeman does not place a high value on honesty and the risk of detection is low.

It should be emphasized that the decline in the quality of law enforcement results not just from corruption, i.e., a reduction of enforcement efforts resulting from exchange with the offender, but also from underinvestment of resources by law enforcement. It is usually worth far more to the major drug supplier to avoid a conviction than it is for the government to obtain it. Consequently the drug lord will hire the top criminal lawyers available to prepare his defense, while the government may assign his case to an assistant prosecutor who has just graduated from law school. With that understanding, we continue to examine corruption as an example of the general problem.

One factor affecting the quality of enforcement is whether there will be repeated encounters between the law enforcers and the offender. In activities that involve repeated violations, such as prostitution, narcotics, or gambling, the two sides will have numerous opportunities to "work things out" and maintain a long-term relationship, in which each side can rely on the other to abide by agreements. This helps to explain the development of organized crime. A criminal organization can represent many individuals who violate the law, and enter into arrangements with police, prosecutors, and judges that could not be done effectively by the individual members acting on their own.

Corruption does not completely eliminate the deterrent effect of criminal law. Suppose a law enforcer has sufficient evidence to convict an individual of a violation for which there is a $1,000 fine. The offender would be willing to pay the enforcer a bribe of up to $1,000 to be released. If the offender does pay a bribe of $1,000, he is punished just as much as he would have been if he had been convicted. Moreover, if these opportunities were fully anticipated by the enforcer, and there was no chance of detection, the enforcer would be willing to work in this job for $1,000 less than his usual wage.

There may, however, be good reasons to prevent enforcers from engaging in corruption or malfeasance. The analysis of Becker and Stigler implies that, to ensure that an enforcer does not engage in corruption, his employer must pay him a wage premium beyond the amount he could earn outside of law enforcement. The cost of engaging in corruption is that if he is caught, he will be terminated, and will subsequently have to work outside of law enforcement, so he will lose this premium. The premium must be larger the greater the potential gain from malfeasance, the lower the probability that malfeasance will be detected, and the higher the discount rate, or subjective rate of interest. (The discount rate represents the importance to the offender of immediate gain relative to future income. A higher discount rate implies less consideration of the future relative to current income.)

There is considerable empirical evidence supporting the analysis of Becker and Stigler. Police corruption is far more widespread in countries where the salaries of police are low compared to the earnings of other workers.

Public versus private enforcement of law

The preceding discussion shows that the quality of law enforcement tends to decline when there is a large disparity between the gain to the enforcer and the loss for the offender. One solution proposed by Becker and Stigler is to make the gain equal the loss, under a system of private law enforcement. Under this proposal, if a fine is prescribed for some offense, a private enforcer who discovers the violation and obtains a conviction would collect the full amount of the fine from the offender. If the offender could not pay the fine, the government would pay a bounty to the private enforcer.

There is substantial precedent for private enforcement of criminal law. In England, the national and local governments have paid bounties for the arrest and conviction of offenders for centuries. The Internal Revenue Service offers informers a reward of 10 percent of any additional taxes collected through their information. Some states offer bounties for the apprehension of offenders who have failed to appear in court or have escaped from custody.

The Becker–Stigler proposal would, of course, greatly extend the role of private enforcement in criminal law. We should therefore consider some questions that have been raised about replacing public enforcement with private enforcement. The basic problem is that since the private enforcer is paid on a piecework basis, he has an incentive to produce as much output as possible – the output in this case being crimes. He might achieve this by (1) inventing, or even committing, the crime, (2) encouraging commission of the crime through entrapment. If an offender is about to commit a crime but has not yet done so, the private enforcer has an incentive to wait until the crime is completed before making an arrest. The reason for doing so is that the fine for the completed crime is presumably greater than for a mere criminal attempt.

There may be a concern that the private enforcer will prosecute an innocent person for a crime committed by someone else, or suppress evidence favorable to the defendant. The premise is that the enforcer would be interested only in obtaining the conviction, not in whether the defendant was guilty. However, it is not obvious that a private enforcer is less sensitive to the merits of the case than a public enforcer would be. It could be argued that a private enforcer is less likely to prosecute when the case is weak, since he would have to bear the full costs of an unsuccessful prosecution. In any case, this problem would be mitigated if the enforcer were liable to the defendant for prosecutions that were both unsuccessful and unjustified (some of the abuses described above, such as entrapment and suppression of evidence, occur from time to time under public enforcement. This may be explained to some extent by the fact that there is no effective remedy available to a defendant who has been unjustifiably prosecuted by a public prosecutor).[20]

Perhaps the most serious problem, however, is that private enforcement would be much too effective. Under the current system public officials exercise considerable discretion in deciding which violations to prosecute. Police frequently disregard minor traffic violations and behavior that violates the letter, but not the spirit of the law; building inspectors ignore trivial violations of building codes. This would not happen under a system of private enforcement. Every violation for which the enforcer could be compensated would be fully pursued; a ticket would be issued to every jaywalker, and a motorist going 1 m.p.h. over the limit would receive a citation.

In some cases the enforcer might be restrained by the possibility that judges and juries would decline to convict a defendant for a trivial violation. However it is still likely that laws would have to be revised to avoid this problem of overzealous enforcement; it would probably be necessary to define illegal conduct in much greater detail. This would increase the costs of drafting legislation, and more detailed laws would have to be revised more frequently to adapt to changing conditions. Being more specific, the laws would create loopholes for conduct that should be prosecuted, and could be prosecuted under the current system, by a public enforcer applying general criminal statutes.

Bibliography

Ayres, Ian, and Steven D. Levitt, "Measuring Positive Externalities from Unobservable Victim Precaution: An Empirical Analysis of Lojack," 113 (1) *Quarterly Journal of Economics* 43–78 (February 1998).

Ayres, Ian and Joel Waldfogel, "A Market Test for Race Discrimination in Bail Setting," 46 *Stanford Law Review* 987–1047 (May 1994).

Beccaria, Cesare B., *An Essay on Crimes and Punishments* (Albany, NY: Little, 1872), originally published in 1770.

Becker, Gary S., "Crime and Punishment: An Economic Approach," 76 (2) *Journal of Political Economy* 169–217 (1968).

Becker, Gary S., and George J. Stigler, "Law Enforcement, Malfeasance and Compensation of Enforcers," 3 *Journal of Legal Studies* 1–18 (January 1974).

Bentham, Jeremy, "An Introduction to the Principles of Morals and Legislation," in *The Utilitarians* (Garden City, NY: Anchor Books, 1973), originally published in 1789.

Carter, M. Shawn, and Dennis W. Jansen, "Canada Cuts Cigarette Taxes to Fight Smuggling," 4 (1) *Economic Times* 40–41 (spring 1995).

Chiricos, Theodore, "Rates of Crime and Unemployment: An Analysis of Aggregate Research Evidence," 34 (2) *Social Problems* 187–211 (1987).

Donohue, John J., Jeffrey Grogger, and Steven D. Levitt, "The Impact of Legalized Abortion on Teen Childbearing," 11 (1) *American Law and Economics Review* 24–46 (spring 2009).

Ehrlich, Isaac, "The Deterrent Effect of Capital Punishment: A Question of Life and Death," 65 *American Economic Review* 397 (1975).

Ehrlich, Isaac, "Capital Punishment and Deterrence: Some Further Thoughts and Additional Evidence," 85 *Journal of Political Economy* 741 (1977).

Ehrlich, Isaac, "Sensitivity Analyses of the Deterrence Hypothesis: Let's Keep the Econ in Econometrics," 42 *Journal of Land and Economics* 455 (April 1999).

Freeman, Richard, "Why do So Many Young American Men Commit Crimes and What Might we Do about It?" 10 *Journal of Economic Perspectives* 25–42 (1996).

Harper, Fowler V., Fleming James, Jr., and Oscar S. Gray, *The Law of Torts* (2nd ed., Boston, MA: Little Brown, 1986).

Kalist, David E., and Noelle A. Molinari, "Is the Marginal Child More Likely to be Murdered? An Examination of State Abortion Ratios and Infant Homicide," 41 (3) *Journal of Human Resources* 611–630 (2006).

Knowles, John, Nicola Persico and Petra Todd, "Racial Bias in Motor Vehicle Searches: Theory and Evidence," 109 (1) *Journal of Political Economy* 203–229 (2001).

Leamer, Edward E., "Let's Take the Con out of Econometrics," 73 *American Economic Review* 31 (1983).

Lempert, Richard O., "Desert and Deterrence: An Assessment of the Moral Bases of the Case for Capital Punishment," 79 *Michigan Law Review* 1177–1231 (1981).

Levitt, Steven D., "The Effect of Prison Population Size on Crime Rates: Evidence from Prison Overcrowding Litigation," 111 (2) *Quarterly Journal of Economics* 319–351 (May 1996).

Levitt, Steven D., "Using Electoral Cycles in Police Hiring to Estimate the Effect of Police on Crime," 87(3) *American Economic Review* 270–290 (June 1997).

Lott, John R., Jr., "Do We Punish High Income Criminals Too Heavily?," 30 *Economic Inquiry* 583–608 (October 1992).

Mayhew, Patricia, Ronald Clarke, Andrew Sturman, and J. Mike Hough, *Crime as Opportunity*, Research Study 34 (London: Home Office, 1976).

McCormick, Robert E., and Robert D. Tollison, "Crime on the Court," 92 (2) *Journal of Political Economy* 223–235 (1984).

McManus, Walter R., "Estimates of the Deterrent Effect of Capital Punishment: The Importance of the Researcher's Prior Beliefs," 93 *Journal of Political Economy* 417–425 (1985).

Montesquieu, Charles de Secondat, *The Spirit of the Laws* (Berkeley, CA: University of California Press, 1977), originally published in 1748.

Passell, Peter, and John Taylor, "The Deterrent Effect of Capital Punishment: Another View," 57 *American Economic Review* 445 (1977).

Polinsky, A. Mitchell, "Economics and Law. Discussion," 90 *American Economic Review Papers and Proceedings* 435 (1978).

Shavell, Steven, "A Model of Optimal Incapacitation," 77 *American Economic Review* 107–110 (1987).

Teichman, Doron, "Sanctioning Sex Offenders Efficiently: An Economic Perspective on Megan's Laws," Working Paper, University of Michigan Law School (2004).

Wilson, James Q., *Thinking about Crime* (New York: Basic Books, 1983).

Wolpin, Kenneth, "Capital Punishment and Homicide: The English Experience," 68 *American Economic Review* 422 (1978).

Problems

1. The economic analysis of crime offers an explanation for why premeditated murder is punished more severely than murder committed in the heat of the moment. What is that explanation?

2. Explain why horse thieves were hanged in the American west in the nineteenth century, i.e., why the punishment was so severe.

3. "Criminal law is less of a deterrent for high-income individuals than for low-income individuals. Since high-income individuals can hire better lawyers, their expected punishment for a crime is lower." Evaluate this statement.

4. In the state of Maryland, during the years 1995–1998, 63 percent of all motorists searched by state police were African-American, but only 18 percent of all motorists on the road were African-American. Does this evidence by itself prove racial discrimination on the part of the police? If not, why not? What more information would you need to determine whether the state police were motivated by racial discrimination or instead by a desire to maximize criminal convictions (usually for the possession of illegal drugs)?

5. Explain the likely consequences of governmental action to increase the punishment of sellers of drugs, if the group purchasing the drugs (*a*) has an inelastic demand, or (*b*) has an elastic demand.

6. Suppose 20 per cent of the owners of automobiles in a city, who originally have no anti-theft devices in their vehicles buy Lojack for their vehicles. How would this be expected to affect the rate of automobile theft in the long run? How would it make a difference if a thief (a) could, or (b) could not, tell whether a particular vehicle had Lojack?

7. Consider a system of private law enforcement whereby private enforcers would receive a payment for each criminal conviction they obtained. What would be the advantages or disadvantages of such a system, compared with the current system of public enforcement?

11 Corporations and financial markets

This chapter will consider some economic issues that arise in corporate law and financial markets. Over the last four decades, research in this area has been completely transformed by the application of principles of economics and the theory of finance. Economics is now considered just as integral to the study of corporate governance and the regulation of securities markets, as it is to antitrust law or public utility regulation. We begin by examining how the characteristics of the corporation usually make it the best type of business organization to use for the purpose of raising capital.

The characteristics of the corporation

A business can be carried on through many different forms of business organization. In the United States, the most important of these forms are the corporation, a partnership (general or limited), a trust, and the sole proprietorship. Among these alternatives, the corporation is generally considered the form of business organization that is best for raising capital.

A firm can raise capital by issuing either debt securities, such as bonds or mortgages, or equity securities such as common stock. The superiority of the corporation as a means of raising capital is based on the ability to sell its stock to the public. The corporation has four features that, taken together, distinguish it from the other types of business organization. The corporation has (1) limited liability, (2) continuity of existence, (3) free transferability of ownership interests, and (4) centralized management. It is important to understand exactly how each of these features is helpful in raising capital.

1   *Limited liability*. Because of limited liability, a shareholder is not personally liable for the debts of the corporation, voluntary or involuntary; the worst that can happen is that the stock becomes worthless. In contrast, a general partner is liable for the debts of the partnership.[1] If there were no limited liability, a stockholder of the former Johns Manville Corporation would have been personally liable to thousands of individuals who had claims for personal injuries resulting from their exposure to asbestos in products sold by that firm.[2] Because of limited liability, an individual who acquires stock of a corporation does not have to be concerned about potential liability of this magnitude.

2   *Continuity of existence*. To become a corporation, a firm must file articles of incorporation in a particular state. The most popular state of incorporation is Delaware. In general, a corporation can live forever, provided that someone pays the annual franchise tax that is imposed by its state of incorporation. Thus an investor who has purchased the stock

of a corporation knows that it is quite unlikely that the corporation will be liquidated, requiring him to reinvest his funds elsewhere. In a partnership, on the other hand, the default rule is that the firm is dissolved upon the death of a partner or the transfer of his interest. However, the partnership agreement can provide that the partnership will continue notwithstanding the death or withdrawal of a partner.

3 *Free transferability of ownership interests*. This feature means that a stockholder's investment in the corporation is relatively liquid. A single share of common stock of a publicly held corporation typically has small value, and the shares are often traded frequently in large daily volume on an organized market such as the New York Stock Exchange. In contrast, a member of a partnership cannot sell his share to another without the approval of the other partners.

4 *Centralized management*. The decisions involved in the day-to-day business operations of the corporation are made by a group of professional managers who work full-time for the corporation. The shareholders are passive investors, who do not participate in the management of the firm.

Because of these four features, a business organized as a corporation can raise capital through a "public offering" in which its stock is purchased, often in small amounts, by a large number of individuals. This is generally the most effective way to raise a large amount of capital, more effective for example than a "private placement" which seeks capital from a small number of wealthy individuals. To raise a large amount of money for a business, one must usually obtain it, directly or indirectly, from a large number of investors, many of whom have only a small amount to invest.

Common and preferred stock

In general, financial interests in a corporation can be classified into two broad categories: debt and equity. Virtually any financial or security interest in a corporation is one of these, or a combination of them, or has value because of the possibility that it can become one or the other. The typical example of a debt interest, which represents a loan made to the corporation, is a bond, which has a specified rate of interest and date of maturity. For example, a bond of the Coca-Cola Company issued in 2007 has a par value[3] of $1,000, a date of maturity of November 15, 2017, and a rate of interest of 5.35 percent. Once a bond is issued, its market value fluctuates inversely with the market rate of interest, as explained in Chapter 2. As the market rate of interest increases, the market value of the bond declines, and vice versa.

The typical example of an equity, or ownership, interest, is a share of common stock of a corporation. A stockholder of a firm is often described as the residual claimant to the assets and earnings of the firm, since he is entitled to the residual profits and assets remaining after all the debts of the firm have been paid. A stockholder benefits from the earnings of a corporation either by receiving dividends, which are usually paid on a quarterly basis, or through appreciation of the value of the stock.

Preferred stock is essentially a debt of the firm, except that it usually has no prescribed date of maturity, and payment of the dividend on preferred stock, although certainly customary, is not legally required.[4] Owners of preferred stock receive dividends on the stock's par value at a specified rate, such as 5 percent per year. It is called "preferred" stock because it is preferred over common stock in two ways: (1) the holder of preferred stock has a preferred claim to the earnings of the corporation, before any dividends can be paid on the common stock; and (2) in the event the firm goes bankrupt, holders of preferred stock have a preferred claim to the assets of the company (to receive the par value of their stock), prior to that of the common stock holders (but subordinate to debt). Preferred stock also differs from pure debt in that its holders do not have the right to bring legal foreclosure proceedings against the corporation if their dividends are not paid, which will happen if the directors of the corporation decide that there are not enough earnings to pay them. Since preferred stock is subordinate to bonds, preferred stock involves more risk, so a corporation has to pay somewhat higher dividends to preferred stockholders than the interest rate it pays on its bonds.

Preferred stock may be "cumulative," which means that any arrears of unpaid dividends must be made up before holders of common stock can receive dividends. Suppose Ms. Jones has 100 shares of preferred stock with a par value of $50 per share, paying an annual dividend of 4 percent. Thus she is entitled to receive dividends from earnings of $200 per year, or $50 per quarter. Suppose the earnings of the corporation are insufficient to enable it to pay dividends in January and April of 2006, but its earnings then fully recover. If Ms. Jones's preferred stock is not cumulative, she is entitled to receive a dividend of $50 in the next quarter, July 2005, but if it is cumulative she must receive a dividend of $150 before any dividend can be paid to holders of common stock.

Shares of preferred stock may be "convertible" into common stock, i.e., the holder of preferred stock may have an option to convert it into common stock at a specified exchange rate, e.g., ten shares of common for one share of preferred. Bonds may also be convertible into common stock. Suppose Ms. Jones has a share of convertible preferred stock convertible into ten shares of common, and the current market value of her preferred stock is $100. She would probably want to exercise her option to convert it to common stock if the market value of common stock exceeded $10 per share.

Some preferred stock (and many bonds) are "callable," i.e., the company has the option to pay them off at a time before they become due (of course, as noted above, preferred stock may have no date of maturity). The company would want to call an issue of preferred stock if the market rate of interest fell below the dividend on the preferred stock, since it could then borrow the funds at a lower rate of interest. The company would be in the same position as a homeowner who wants to refinance his mortgage. Suppose a home owner has a mortgage of $200,000 with a 5 percent rate of interest, and mortgage interest rates fall to 3 percent. The home owner would then want to borrow $200,000 from a bank at 3 percent and use the money to pay off his existing mortgage; by doing so he would still have a mortgage debt of $200,000, but his interest rate would be reduced from 5 to 3 percent. If preferred stock is callable, the company is usually required to pay a premium above the stock's par value in order to call it (in the case of a bond, a premium above the bond's unpaid principal); however, the premium usually declines as the due date approaches. Of course, the right of the company to call preferred stock (or a bond) reduces the value of the security, since otherwise the holder would benefit from a gain in its market value when interest rates declined. If interest rates fall substantially so that the market value of preferred stock increases, the holder can expect the company to buy it back at the call price.

There has been a recent innovation known as "floating rate" preferred stock. In this type of security the dividend rate is not fixed. When there is an increase in interest rates, which would normally reduce the market value of preferred stock, the dividend increases to compensate for it. When interest rates fall, which would normally increase the value of preferred stock, the dividend declines. Thus with this type of security the risk of a change in interest rates is transferred from the holder of preferred stock to the issuing corporation.

Potential conflicts between managers and stockholders

The separation of ownership from control

In the modern, publicly held corporation there is a separation of ownership from control. A typical large corporation is owned by millions of shareholders, the majority of whom know very little about the firm; indeed, many shareholders (those with an interest through pension funds or mutual funds, or those who are children) may not even know they own shares of the corporation. The firm is controlled by its managers, who generally hold a small fraction of the total stock outstanding.

The responsibility of the managers is to work on behalf of the stockholders, to maximize the profits of the corporation. In the terminology of labor economics, the managers act as an agent, representing the interests of the stockholders (the principal).

However there is a principal–agent problem: it may be difficult (costly) for the principal to ensure that the agent is working in the principal's best interests; the agent may deviate from this course of action to promote his own interests. Since the managers have far more information about the firm's operations than the outside stockholders, it is difficult for the stockholders to monitor the performance of the managers; thus the managers may be inclined to shirk their responsibilities, or to use their position to enrich themselves at the expense of the stockholders. This problem was recognized by, among others, Adam Smith:

> The directors of such companies ... being the managers rather of other people's money than of their own, it cannot well be expected that they should watch over it with the same anxious vigilance with which the partners of a private [company] frequently watch over their own ... Negligence and profusion, therefore, must always prevail, more or less, in the management of the affairs of such a company.[5]

Smith thought that private companies, in which most or all the stock was owned by the managers, would remain the normal way of doing business, but in this he was mistaken; the advantages to investors of the public corporation, described above, proved to be important enough to easily outweigh concerns about self-dealing by its managers.

To minimize the temptation to deviate from profit maximization, corporations have devised arrangements for compensating executives that align their interests with those of the shareholders. For example, a manager's compensation may be determined partly by the profits of the firm. One problem with this arrangement is that it rewards a strategy of maximizing the current profits of the firm, rather than its long-term prosperity. Another frequently used method is to compensate the executive with stock, or with options to buy stock at a given price. The idea behind this approach is that the market price of a stock represents the discounted present value of the stream of future earnings of the corporation, as anticipated by the market. Suppose, for example, an executive is granted the right to purchase 10,000 shares of stock at $20 (its market value at the time of the grant) for five years. If the decisions subsequently made by the executive increase the firm's long-run earnings prospects, the price of the stock may increase to $25. The executive can then purchase the stock for $20 and immediately resell it for $25, for a profit of $50,000. On the other hand, if the executive were to take actions that artificially increased the firm's current profits at the expense of its long-term prospects, the stock price should decline.

There are also potential pitfalls with the use of stock options, however. For one thing, the stock price can be influenced by many factors beyond the control of the manager, like the general economic climate. During an economic boom a mediocre executive may be handsomely rewarded (and may therefore slack off), while an effective executive may be underpaid in a recession. Moreover, it may be necessary to compensate managers for the risk entailed in stock options. While one can imagine many other forms of contingent compensation – for example, the executive could be rewarded according to how well his company's stock does relative to other firms in the same industry – each method has its own disadvantages.[6] The more fundamental problem, however, is that the terms of contingent compensation can easily be manipulated by those in control of the corporation. For example, a recent study found that when stock options granted to top executives had proved to be unprofitable, the corporation simply replaced them with new options with a lower exercise price![7]

Given the preceding discussion of the limitations of contingent compensation arrangements, we may ask whether there are other ways to give managers the incentive to maximize profits, and prevent them from plundering all the wealth of the corporation. It is generally recognized that the divergence of interests between managers and shareholders is limited by markets: capital markets, managerial labor markets, and especially the market for corporate control. First, there is discipline from the capital market: firms that are poorly managed are likely to find it difficult to raise capital needed for investment, either by borrowing or by selling shares of the corporation. Second, there is a managerial labor market; the performance of executives is closely observed by their peers and superiors.[8] Executives who shirk, or make poor decisions, are not likely to receive raises or obtain promotions. The chief executive officer of a corporation cannot, of course, be promoted to a higher position, but if his firm prospers, he could be chosen for a high executive position in another, larger, firm. Finally, and perhaps most importantly, there is the market for corporate control, i.e., the possibility of a takeover. We analyze this form of market discipline in the next section.

The market discipline from takeovers

Many economists believe that the most effective way to induce managers to maximize profits is through the threat of a takeover. To understand why, one must first understand that all the employees of a corporation work at the pleasure of the board of directors. The board of directors has the authority to fire any or all existing managers and to hire new ones. The directors, in turn, are elected periodically by the shareholders. Indeed, the most important right of the shareholders is to vote for members of the board of directors.

Suppose the current managers of the corporation are doing a poor job; then the market will expect little earnings in the future, so the market price of the stock, which reflects the present value of the stream of future earnings, will fall. Suppose the price of the stock under poor management is $10. Some outside observers will notice that the firm is poorly managed, and will realize that under better management, the earnings prospects of the firm could improve substantially. Let us suppose that under good management the price of the stock would be $20. This situation creates a profit opportunity: an entrepreneur could buy enough shares to acquire control of the corporation (50 percent plus one share) at the current market price of $20 per share, and then vote to replace the current board of directors with his own representatives. His new directors would then fire the existing managers and hire new ones. Under the new management the firm's expected earnings would increase, and the stock price would increase to $20. The entrepreneur would thereby earn a profit of $10 multiplied by the number of shares he held.

Is there evidence to support the view that firms are managed more efficiently after a takeover? A number of empirical studies have shown that changes in corporate control yield a substantial premium for shareholders of the acquired corporation – between 21 percent and 41 percent. In many cases corporations that are taken over are actually acquired by another corporation, and there is typically only a small increase in the value of stock of the acquiring corporation. These studies provide direct evidence that the acquired corporation benefits from a change of management. There is not much appreciation of the stock of the acquiring corporation, since it is already well managed.

Regulation of takeovers

Notwithstanding this evidence of economic gains from takeovers, there is, and has been, a great deal of opposition to them. Many witnesses have testified before Congress and state legislatures of alleged hardships resulting from takeovers: termination of senior executives after many years of service, layoffs of workers and the like. Some important consequences of this legislative campaign have been the enactment of the Williams Act, a federal statute, in 1968, its amendment in 1970, and a wave of state anti-takeover statutes during the period 1975–1978.

The Williams Act required anyone who acquired 10 percent or more of the stock of a corporation to file a statement with the Securities and Exchange Commission (thereby informing the entire world)[9] that disclosed his identity, his source of funds, and his purpose in acquiring the stock. Another provision allowed the management of the target corporation to sue for an injunction (a court order) to delay a tender offer. In 1970 the Williams Act was amended to reduce the threshold of stock ownership that triggered the disclosure requirement from 10 percent to 5 percent.[10] The state anti-takeover statutes, enacted from 1975 to 1978, imposed further restrictions, and provided management of the target corporations with an arsenal of techniques to enable them to thwart or delay tender offers. Some of these statutes required that someone who planned to make a tender offer had to report his intent to do so well in advance, from ten to thirty days ahead of the tender offer. In some statutes the target corporation could delay matters by requesting a hearing before the state's securities commissioner.

The effect of this legislation was to greatly increase the costs of takeovers, by providing time, information, and opportunities for delay to stockholders, managers of the target corporation, and potential competing bidders. Returning to the previous example, a stockholder who realizes that the market value of his stock is likely to increase from $10 to $20 following a takeover will demand a higher price than $10 for his stock. Thus the entrepreneur making the tender offer will have to pay more to acquire a controlling interest, and his expected profit will be smaller. Of course, if the profit is too small the takeover will no longer be feasible.

There were two major consequences of the anti-takeover regulation described above: the number of takeovers declined drastically, and the shareholders of those corporations that were taken over received higher premiums (Jarrell and Bradley 1980). The average premiums for a cash tender offer increased from 32 percent before the Williams Act to nearly 53 percent thereafter. The state statutes increased the average premium further, from 53 percent to 73 percent. Thus this regulation did benefit stockholders of the firms that were subsequently acquired. However, by in effect imposing a tax on takeovers, it prevented many potential takeovers from occurring, resulting in losses for the shareholders of the corporations that were not acquired.[11] The only tender offers that were made after the legislation were for firms that were so poorly managed that the expected gains from their acquisition exceeded even the substantially increased costs.

The anti-takeover regulation reduced the expected gains from knowledge about the optimal use of corporate resources, and therefore surely reduced the amount of research that generates such knowledge. Also, by reducing the threat of a takeover, this legislation diluted the incentives for incumbent management to maximize profits.

Apart from changes in the law, corporations have responded to the threat of a takeover by adopting defensive measures, such as requiring that any merger be approved by a supermajority of 70 percent or even 80 percent of stockholders; creating different classes of stock to give management more voting power than other shareholders; filing lawsuits against the party attempting the takeover, alleging violations of antitrust or securities laws; and offering to buy stock back from the hostile bidder on especially favorable terms (a tactic known as "greenmail"). The most significant of such protective barriers, however, is known as the "poison pill." This term refers to a provision in the corporate charter that is automatically triggered when someone acquires a specified percentage of stock (often 15 percent of the stock outstanding), and that then gives the stockholders other than the hostile bidder the right to acquire additional stock on very favorable terms, so that the share of stock held by the bidder is greatly diminished.

These measures are often defended by incumbent managers on the ground that they protect stockholders, by preventing hostile bidders from acquiring their stock at less than its full market value, for example during a recession (note that this argument assumes the efficient markets hypothesis is invalid, and the market price of the stock does not equal its actual value). Of course, these measures can also make it extremely difficult to dislodge poorly performing managers, which works to the disadvantage of shareholders. Defensive measures such as the poison pill, in conjunction with federal and state anti-takeover statutes, have substantially reduced the frequency of takeovers in the U.S. market since the 1980s.

Compensation of investment advisors

Many controversies involving regulation of financial markets (and indeed markets for other goods and services) involve the quality of buyers' information. This is well illustrated by a case involving the compensation of investment advisors to mutual funds, Jones v. Harris Associates.[12] To understand the issues of this case, it will be useful to have some background information about mutual funds. The person who has the position of investment advisor of a mutual fund is typically responsible for determining how the money in the mutual fund is invested, and often for other management services. It is generally true that the mutual fund was created by the investment advisor. The fees paid to investment advisors are determined by the board of trustees of the mutual fund, and a federal statute requires that at least 40 percent of the trustees must be disinterested in (independent of) the advisor, and that initial decisions on the advisor's compensation be made by a majority of those disinterested trustees. The narrow legal question raised by the Jones case is whether those who own shares of the mutual fund can recover some of the compensation that was paid to the advisor if it is subsequently found by a court to be "excessive," or so large as not to be "reasonable."

The Jones court, in an opinion written by Judge Frank Easterbrook, ruled against the plaintiffs, essentially (disregarding less relevant legal nuances) on the ground that the market for mutual funds is competitive. Judge Easterbrook's rationale was that, at the end of 2002, there were over 8,000 mutual funds holding more than $6 trillion in assets, indicating that there were then, and are now, ample choices available to investors. If an investor in a mutual fund is dissatisfied with its performance, he can "redeem" the shares, i.e. have the fund buy his shares back from him at their current asset value, and then invest the proceeds in another fund. The compensation of the advisor is based on the total amount invested in the mutual fund; for example, he might be paid 1 percent of the asset value of the fund each year. Consequently if the investments chosen by the advisor do well, his compensation increases for two reasons: the market value of the fund increases, and other investors will be induced to put their money in the fund. If the investments chosen by the advisor do badly, his compensation shrinks both because the value of the mutual fund has declined, and because investors will tend to redeem their shares and invest elsewhere. Thus, in Judge Easterbrook's view, investors are ultimately protected by competition among mutual funds. Moreover, the fees paid to Harris Associates, the investment advisor in the case under consideration, were less than the fees paid to advisors by many other mutual funds. It was not a good idea to allow judges to determine whether the compensation paid to investment advisors was excessive, because judges are at a severe informational disadvantage compared to markets; the subjective opinions of judges are less reliable than the impersonal determinations of a competitive market.

A dissenting opinion by Judge Richard Posner argued, however, that the fees paid to investment advisors might well be unreasonable, because of a lack of information about fees on the part of investors, and because members of the board of directors, who often have close relationships with the advisor, have a feeble incentive to police the compensation of the advisor. In addition, studies showed that mutual funds hardly ever "fired" their investment advisors. Judge Posner pointed out that the management fees paid by the fund to the advisor were often much less than the fees paid to the advisor by independent outside firms that hired him for investment advice, e.g. pension funds. The fact that some other mutual funds paid higher fees to their advisors than Harris Associates received was not conclusive, because the same problem of close relationships and mutual back-scratching between trustees and investment advisors applied to other mutual funds. Others, citing recent research in behavioral economics, argued that it was unlikely that investors could determine whether the returns they obtained from a mutual fund were attributable to the skill of the advisor or to random chance. Thus most investors were ill equipped to evaluate the performance of the investment advisor of a mutual fund.

This controversy is typical of many involving regulation. On one side are those who contend that, without intervention by the government or the courts, markets will naturally reward those who provide goods and services of high quality and punish those who do not; regulators are likely to increase costs of production and become captives of the industry they regulate. On the other side are those who believe consumers do not have good information and are therefore unable to differentiate among firms that differ in quality. Government intervention, or the possibility of legal liability, is therefore required to protect consumers from firms that provide inferior goods at the market price, or goods of average quality at a high price.

The competition to be the state of incorporation

In the United States, individuals who wish to form a corporation can choose to incorporate their business in any one of the fifty states. The state that is chosen derives certain benefits from being the firm's state of incorporation; for example, it receives an annual franchise tax from the firm in exchange for the privilege of being a corporation.[13]

A corporation is subject to the corporation law of its state of incorporation. Many corporations obtained their charter from Delaware, and are consequently governed by that state's corporation law. Some commentators, such as Ralph Nader, argue that states compete to be the state of incorporation by enacting corporation laws that benefit the firm's incumbent management at the expense of the interests of stockholders and creditors. In this "race to the bottom," states vie to outdo each other at eliminating safeguards for stockholders, creditors, and other groups against management self-dealing. The remedy proposed by Nader is to require that all corporations be chartered by the federal government, and be subject to a federal corporation law.

Richard Posner and others have, however, argued that this is a solution for a nonexistent problem – that Nader's analysis ignores the discipline imposed by the market. They point out that a corporation that offered no protection to its creditors would be unable to borrow unless it agreed to pay very high interest rates. Similarly, a corporation that provided no protection to its stockholders would have great difficulty selling its shares. According to this view, competition for corporate charters among the states should cause corporation law to evolve toward efficient rules. There would be no presumption of efficiency for a federal corporation law, which as a monopoly would derive no benefit from the impetus for innovation provided by competition.

The prohibition of insider trading

One restriction on the activities of managers that is imposed by law is a prohibition of insider trading. Insider trading is buying or selling securities to take advantage of inside information, i.e., material information about a firm that is not available to the public. Under federal securities laws this prohibition applies to corporate insiders and their confidants or "tipees."

Some commentators[14] have argued that insider trading should be permitted. One argument is based on the efficient capital markets hypothesis – the idea that the market price of a security reflects all publicly available information, of both past events and anticipated future events. According to this view, which is widely accepted by economists, the price of a security is a public good; it is the best available measure of the value of the corporation. The more that information about the firm is made public, the better the price of its stock will be as a guide to investors and others. Allowing managers to trade on inside information gives them a powerful incentive to communicate their information rapidly to the market, through a buy or sell order.

Putting it differently, the argument is that it may be efficient for a firm to give managers, rather than stockholders, a property right in information. Through insider trading, managers can provide the public with information about the value of the firm, in situations where it is not feasible to disclose the information itself because, for example, such disclosure would be harmful to the firm. For example, the managers may have learned from a confidential report that there are valuable mineral deposits on land the firm is about to purchase.[15] Another argument is that allowing insider trading gives managers an incentive to find ways to increase the value of the firm – to create valuable information – since they would know that once the information is created, they would be able to exploit it through insider trading.

Notwithstanding the foregoing arguments, most researchers approve of the ban on insider training. Those who support the current law point out that, without a ban, managers might have an incentive to conceal information; moreover, if short selling were allowed, managers could have an incentive to reduce the value of the firm. Also, contemplation of the profits to be gained from insider trading might well distract managers from the business of managing. Finally, Posner and others have argued that insider trading does not reward good management; rather it rewards the possession of inside information. This view is supported by a cursory examination of the circumstances of many who have profited from inside information. They include a geologist who learned of major copper deposits on the firm's land; a mailroom employee, and a printer, who had advance notice of tender offers; a partner in a law firm that represented a corporation involved in a takeover (who was not working on the deal himself); and a stockbroker who obtained information from his wife, who obtained it from her mother, who had obtained it from her brother, a corporate insider.

In the chapter on contract law, we learned that for fraud cases where one party to a contract had failed to disclose information to another, Kronman proposed a distinction between information that was discovered casually, and information that was obtained by a deliberate, methodical search. In Kronman's view, disclosure should be required only in cases where the information was obtained casually or accidentally. He has also suggested that the government's ban of insider trading might be justified on the ground that most of the information acquired by managers is acquired casually.[16]

Some have argued that a ban on insider trading is futile, because it is difficult (costly) to enforce. However, there are various ways to improve enforcement; for example, the Securities and Exchange Commission pays bounties for information leading to civil penalties for insider trading. Under current (2009) law, the amount of a civil penalty can be up to three times the profit gained (or loss avoided) through insider trading. Given the widespread support for the current law, it seems unlikely that the prohibition of insider trading will be repealed anytime soon.

Conflicts among shareholders

The majority shareholders' right to "squeeze out" the minority

Under the corporation law of Delaware, a majority of the shareholders can force a minority to sell their shares to the corporation. Any minority shareholder who is dissatisfied with the amount offered for his shares is entitled to a judicial appraisal of their value. In effect, the majority shareholders have a power of eminent domain over the shares of the minority.

There may be entirely legitimate reasons for the majority to want to buy the shares of the minority. Corporations that have more than a prescribed number of shareholders[17] are considered publicly held; they are subject to extensive regulations requiring them to file periodic reports with the Securities and Exchange Commission, and disclose all material information about the corporation's future prospects in proxy materials sent to stockholders, and they are liable for fraud if these reports are deemed to be misleading. The value of a corporation may increase if it can reduce the number of its shareholders below this threshold number, so that it does not have to bear the substantial costs of complying with these regulations. The majority shareholders could, of course, acquire the shares from the minority in voluntary transactions, but there is a holdout problem: as the total number of shareholders approaches the threshold, the remaining minority shareholders could demand the entire difference between the value of the firm as a public corporation, and its value as a private "closely held" corporation. The majority's right to force a sale overcomes this monopoly problem, and the appraisal remedy ensures that the minority receives the fair market value of its shares.

Deposit insurance and moral hazard

Let us now consider a subtle example of moral hazard in financial markets. Some have argued that moral hazard is created by federal deposit insurance, which in the United States (in May 2010) guarantees the accounts of bank depositors up to $250,000. We explain below the arguments made in favor of deposit insurance, and how it leads to moral hazard.

Federal deposit insurance is a guarantee to depositors that they will not lose the money they deposited in a bank account, up to the limits of coverage, even if the bank becomes insolvent. The rationale for deposit insurance is to prevent bank runs. Banks are susceptible to runs because they make long-term loans to businesses, i.e., they lend "long," but the money they lend is from demand deposits, which can be withdrawn immediately, i.e. they borrow "short." It is efficient for banks to make long-term, illiquid loans, because many of the projects that provide the highest return to society take a long time to complete. Banks also provide other borrowers with liquidity by allowing them to put up their illiquid land or machinery as collateral in exchange for loans made to them in cash.[18] Finally, demand deposits provide liquidity to the economy because they enable buyers to make payments to sellers through bank drafts.

The mismatch between the duration of a bank's assets (loans) and its liabilities (demand deposits) works fine as long as the withdrawal activity of depositors is normal. Banks are confident that they can meet depositors' demands according to the principles of fractional reserves, namely that (1) normally only a small fraction of depositors will wish to withdraw their accounts on any given day, and (2) the range of the total amount they withdraw is, under ordinary circumstances, statistically predictable. If, however, depositors fear that the bank has insufficient funds to cover all its deposits, they will know that other depositors might demand withdrawal of all their funds, so that if they do not act quickly there may be nothing left. Thus even if the fear of bank failure is based on a false rumor, there can be a stampede of depositors rushing to withdraw all their funds – a classic bank run. If too many depositors seek to withdraw their demand deposits, the bank will not be able to meet all their demands because typically, 80 percent or more of the bank's funds are tied up in illiquid loans. Thus the bank will either have to sell off its assets at distress sale prices or become insolvent. Thus without deposit insurance, banks would not make long-term loans to projects with the highest social rate of return, and society would be worse off. If on the other hand, there is deposit insurance, depositors will not fear that their funds will be lost and there will be no bank run. Banks will then feel safe in making long-term loans.

This is the argument for deposit insurance. However, it should be recognized that deposit insurance can have costs as well as benefits. The cost is moral hazard: federal deposit insurance tends to make depositors less vigilant in monitoring the investment activity of banks, thereby encouraging banks to take greater risks, which leads to more bank failures. To see why, consider the following example: suppose the compensation of a bank manager is that he gets 10 percent of the total profits from his investment of the $10 million in funds deposited in his bank. The bank's depositors are protected by federal deposit insurance, and any premiums paid for that insurance are not affected by the level of risk of the bank's investments. There is an absolutely safe investment in federal government securities that pays 5 percent, so if the bank manager chooses this investment, he would get 10 percent of the resulting profits of $500,000, or $50,000. There is another alternative – a risky investment in an internet startup company, that with a probability of 80 percent will pay 100 percent, and with a probability of 20 percent will pay −100 percent, i.e., the company would go bankrupt and all the money of depositors would be lost. If the bank manager chooses this risky investment, his payoff with an 80 percent probability will be $10 million × 10 percent = $1 million, and his payoff with a 20 percent probability would be −$10 million × 10 percent = −$1 million. So his expected payoff is $800,000 − 200,000 = $600,000. Thus he will be sorely tempted to invest in the internet venture if the accounts of depositors are protected by federal deposit insurance. Since the depositors would not bear any loss, they do not bear the consequences of failing to monitor the bank's investments, and the bank manager would not bear the consequences of his overly risky behavior, i.e. there is moral hazard in all directions. The depositors would not care how risky the bank's investments are, because they are fully protected by deposit insurance.

If, on the other hand, there were no deposit insurance, the depositors would pay much more attention to the bank's investment behavior, and would not put their funds in a bank unless it had a reputation for prudent investment, or unless the bank paid them a premium for the increased risk to their deposits. In terms of our example, if there were no federal deposit insurance, the bank manager's payoff with a 20 percent probability might be −$10 million, because he would be sued by the depositors, his reputation would be forever tarnished and his career as a bank manger would be over. Here he bears the full consequences of his risky behavior, and there is no problem of moral hazard. In this case his expected payoff from the risky investment would be $800,000 −2 million = −$1,200,000. So he would not make the risky investment in the internet company.

Some have argued that the savings and loan crisis of the 1980s was a consequence of this type of moral hazard. Because of the problem of moral hazard, countries around the world that have deposit insurance have extensive regulation of banks, including restrictions on entry, restrictions on activities, examinations, and sanctions. To mitigate the moral hazard problem, regulation in some countries provides for either coinsurance, limits on coverage, or premiums based on the risk of bank investments.

Bibliography

Bebchuk, Lucian A., "The Case for Facilitating Competing Tender Offers," 95 *Harvard Law Review* 1028–1056 (1982).

Bebchuk, Lucian A., Jesse M. Fried, and David I. Walker, "Executive Compensation in America: Optimal Contracting or Extraction of Rents?" Working paper, University of California, Berkeley (2001).

Carlton, Dennis W., and Daniel R. Fischel, "The Regulation of Insider Trading," 35 *Stanford Law Review* 857–895 (May 1983).

Jarrell, Gregg A., and Michael Bradley, "The Economic Effects of Federal and State Regulations of Cash Tender Offers, 23 (2) *Journal of Law and Economics* 371–407 (October 1980).

Jensen, Michael C., and William H. Meckling, "Theory of the Firm: Managerial Behavior, Agency Costs and Ownership Structure," 3 *Journal of Financial Economics* 305–360 (1976).

Murphy, Kevin J., "Executive Compensation," in Orley Ashenfelter and David Card (eds.) *Handbook of Labor Economics* (Amsterdam: North Holland, 1999).

Schumann, Laurence, "State Regulation of Takeovers and Shareholder Wealth: The Case of New York's 1985 Takeover Statutes," 19 (4) *RAND Journal of Economics* 557–567 (winter 1988).

Jarrell, Gregg A., James Buckley and Jeffry Netter, "The Market for Corporate Control: The Empirical Evidence since 1980," 2 (1) *Journal of Economic Perspectives* 49–68 (winter 1988).

Kronman, Anthony, "Mistake, Disclosure, Information and the Law of Contracts," 7 *Journal of Legal Studies* 1 (1978).

Manne, Henry G., *Insider Trading and the Stock Market* (1966).

McCoy, Patricia A., "The Moral Hazard Implications of Deposit Insurance: Theory and Evidence," working paper (February 18, 2007).

Shleifer, Andrei, and Robert Vishny, "The Takeover Wave of the 1980s," 4 (3) *Journal of Applied Corporate Finance* 49–56 (fall 1991).

Smith, Adam, *An Inquiry into the Nature and Causes of the Wealth of Nations* (1776).

Problems

1. Explain why the corporation is generally considered to be the form of business organization that is best suited for raising large amounts of capital. Explain in detail the characteristics of the corporation which are useful for this purpose.

2. Ralph Nader has argued that large corporations should be required to incorporate under a uniform federal corporation law, rather than under the law of an individual state. He contends that, under the current system, there is a "competition in laxity," i.e., states compete among each other by adopting rules that benefit management at the expense of others. Evaluate this proposal critically.

3. (a) A number of studies have shown that, when there is a takeover of one corporation by another, there is a substantial increase in value of stock for shareholders of the acquired corporation, but little or no effect on the value of the stock of the acquiring corporation. Explain these effects of a takeover on stock values. (b) Two devices that are often adopted by corporations that expect to be the target of a takeover attempt are the "golden parachute" and the "poison pill." Explain what these devices are, and how they affect takeovers.

4. Under Delaware corporation law, the majority shareholders of a corporation can force minority shareholders to sell their shares to the corporation. Is there any economic justification for giving such a right to the majority shareholders?

5. What are the internal or external monitors that give managers of firms the incentive to do their utmost to ensure that the firm maximizes profits? Be specific.

12 Taxation

In this chapter we will consider the economic effects of different kinds of taxes and of various rules of taxation. First we consider how the behavior of individuals may be affected by a death tax such as the federal estate tax. We analyze the effect on private savings of changes in social security benefits, and of a proposal to replace income tax with a tax on consumption. We also examine the effect of changes in tax rules on the level of charitable giving. We analyze the economic effect of rules allowing firms to deduct from taxable income the decline in value of their machinery and equipment through depreciation. Finally, we examine the social cost of two tax preferences, the allowance of percentage depletion for minerals such as oil and gas, and the exemption from income tax of interest on municipal bonds. Before we turn to the taxonomy, as it were, of federal tax rules, it is important to understand the impact of a tax in general terms. The reader may therefore wish to review the explanations of a tax and subsidy in the chapter on the principles of microeconomics, at the beginning of this text.

We begin by examining all the possible economic consequences of a particular tax – a death tax – which is imposed on the value of the property owned by an individual at the time when he or she dies.

The effects of a death tax

Let us examine the substitution effects of the taxation of an individual's wealth upon his death. The value of all the property owned by an individual at his death is potentially subject to an estate tax imposed by the federal government and to an inheritance tax imposed by the state in which he resides. The federal estate tax is highly progressive, in that the marginal tax rate increases with the size of the estate.[1] A primary objective of the federal estate tax, aside from raising revenue, was to reduce the inequality in the distribution of income among the population by preventing large accumulations of wealth from being passed on intact to succeeding generations of family members.

There are several substitution effects that may be expected in response to the imposition of a death tax. First, one would expect that wealthy individuals would attempt to give away their property to relatives and friends shortly before their death, in order to reduce the value of their estate which is subject to the death tax. For example, an individual who intends to divide his estate equally among his children might decide to give them their shares of his property before he dies, rather than have his estate diminished by estate tax before being divided among them. This possibility occurred to the U.S. Congress, which has enacted special rules of tax law that are specifically designed to thwart this method of avoiding estate tax. There is a "gift tax" which imposes a tax on a donor who makes large gifts to individuals. The tax applies only to the amount of gifts beyond a threshold, which was $12,000 in 2009 and is progressive.

Second, since the death tax is a tax on accumulated wealth, it reduces the incentive to save. One would therefore expect that wealthy individuals would consume more of their wealth than they would in the absence of a death tax. Finally, the death tax may also induce people to do less work. On the other hand, there may be an offsetting effect on work effort, since persons who inherit substantial wealth may not work as hard as they would if they had inherited less.

The foregoing behavioral responses to a death tax do not exhaust all the possibilities. Other substitution effects are probably less important, however, since the behavior involves larger costs. For example, persons may renounce their citizenship and leave a country which imposes a large estate tax. In the United States, elderly persons may decide to move to a state such as Florida, which imposes a minimal inheritance tax.

How important are the actual effects of these taxes on behavior? One study[2] found that a high rate of estate, inheritance, and gift (EIG) taxes seemed to reduce the rate of migration into the state by the very rich elderly. These individuals have the most to gain from choosing a residence in a low-tax state, and often a low cost of doing so; for example, those with multiple homes can simply change their legal domicile with a stroke of the pen. However, this group is by definition extremely small. Another study[3] that covered a much larger portion of the elderly (65 or over) found that the rate of EIG taxes did not affect their migration decisions; those decisions were, however, positively influenced by a state's amenities (e.g., an attractive climate, shoreline, lakes, and mountains) and negatively influenced by a high crime rate or a high cost of living. Moreover, this study found evidence suggesting that there was a political effect of elderly migration on state tax policy. The states experiencing relatively large in-migration of the elderly were more likely to reduce EIG taxes than others.

An interesting feature of the federal estate tax is that property left by a decedent to his or her spouse is exempt from estate tax.[4] This provision, which is known as the "marital deduction," was designed to afford relief to widows inheriting property from their husbands. The idea underlying the marital deduction is that much of the property inherited by the widow represents the accumulation of her productive activity during the years of the marriage, even though her work may have been done primarily in the home, rather than in the market. The husband would not have been able to accumulate much of his property had it not been for the cooperative efforts of the wife in productive tasks within the household, such as the preparation of meals and raising of children.

Since this property is allocable to the wife's work effort, it should not be treated as a transfer of property from the husband to the wife. Richard Posner has noted another reason for the marital deduction; at the time of her husband's death the widow is likely to be an elderly person, and if she dies soon after her husband the entire estate would be subject to estate tax twice within a short period. This scenario would in effect result in a much higher rate of estate tax, which would induce more of the substitution effects described above.

Social security

Under the social security system, there is a payroll tax of a fixed percentage rate (currently 15.3 percent) on a worker's earnings up to a certain level, which changes each year and was $106,800 in 2010.[5] Although this tax may seem proportional, it is actually regressive, for two reasons: first, it is imposed only on wages and salaries, not on income from other sources such as interest, dividends and fringe benefits; second, earnings above the ceiling level are not subject to the tax. The marginal tax rate on earnings above this level is zero.

The original idea behind the social security program was to compel individuals to save, to provide for their retirement; after a worker reached retirement age, he would get back in monthly benefits the contributions he had made through the tax, with interest. However, because of subsequent changes in the law, the relation between the payroll taxes paid by an individual and the benefits he later receives has become more and more tenuous. There is now very little connection between the amount of the taxes paid by the individual and the value of the benefits he is expected to receive.[6]

From 1937 through 1976 there was a trend of growth in the value of social security benefits that a worker could expect to receive upon retirement. In addition, it is well known that the personal savings rate in the United States has been substantially below that of other highly developed nations. In 2006, for example, the household net savings rate in the United States was 0.8 percent of disposable household income, compared to 10.5 percent in Germany, 11.5 percent in France, 8.7 percent in Italy, and 12 percent in Switzerland.[7]

Some economists have argued that the increase in social security benefits bears a substantial share of the responsibility for the continually low rate of private saving. According to this view, an individual who is saving to achieve a given income upon retirement will reduce his savings if the government announces an increase in social security benefits, since a dollar in social security benefits is a perfect substitute for a dollar in benefits from his own retirement fund. However, this explanation for the decline in savings has been challenged by other economists, including Robert Barro. Barro argued that the level of saving undertaken by households is based on the present value of their expected wealth. Households calculate their wealth by taking into account the tax payments they will be required to make in the future. If the government should increase its spending on social security benefits without increasing taxes, the budget deficit will increase. Individuals will realize that at some point in the future the government will have to raise taxes to pay for its increase in spending. This follows from the notion that the government is subject to a budget constraint. The present value of the government's expenditures must eventually equal the present value of the tax revenues which it collects. This principle determines the effect of the increase in social security benefits. One the one hand, since these benefits have increased, an individual can reduce the rate of his own saving required to provide for his retirement. On the other hand, since the government's budget deficit has increased by the amount of the increase in benefits, individuals must increase their savings to pay for the higher level of taxes which the government will have to impose in the future. It turns out that the increase in savings required to pay the higher taxes will exactly offset the reduction in savings resulting from the increase in social security benefits. In other words, there is both good news and bad news for the taxpayer: the good news is that the government bought him a gift; the bad news is that the government paid for it with his credit card. Thus there is no real change in the wealth of the taxpayer. Since savings are based on expected wealth, and wealth has not changed, savings should not be affected.

The notion that an increase in government spending without an increase in taxes should have no effect on behavior is an example of the principle of "Ricardian equivalence," after the English economist David Ricardo (1772–1823). It should be noted that one of the assumptions underlying Ricardian equivalence is that individuals understand that their taxes will have to increase later on if there is an increase in the budget deficit. Whether, and to what extent, the growth of social security benefits may have affected the rate of private saving is unresolved, and remains a controversial issue. If a worker does not believe that he will receive the value

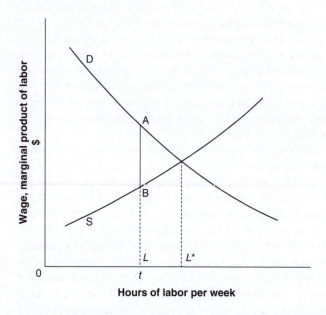

Figure 12.1 The effect of social security tax on the amount of labor supplied.

of his tax payments under the current system, the payroll tax can be regarded as a tax on labor, which will reduce the amount of work done by the individual, as shown in Figure 12.1. Because of the payroll tax the worker will work L hours per week rather than L^*, the number of hours she would work if there were no tax. As we shall now explain, because of the peculiar rules of social security, many married women are likely to consider the payroll tax on their earnings as a pure tax.

The spouse of a worker covered by social security is entitled to receive a benefit derived from the earnings of her spouse: 50 percent of the benefit earned by her spouse if her spouse is living, or, if her spouse is deceased, a survivor benefit of 100 percent.[8] Alternatively, the spouse may choose a social security benefit based only on her own earnings. Since many married women have had lower wages and fewer years in the labor force than their husbands, they are often better off choosing a benefit based on their husband's earnings. In this case, of course, they obtain no increase in benefits from all the payroll tax that was collected from their own earnings. Under these circumstances, the payroll tax is most likely to have the effect of discouraging labor force participation. One-earner couples fare the best under this system; the spouse in the labor force pays all the social security tax, and obtains a full benefit, while the other spouse collects a spouse benefit or survivor's benefit.[9]

Incentive effects of the survivor's benefit

There is another interesting incentive effect of the survivor's benefit. Suppose Mr. and Mrs. Green are long-time friends of Mr. and Mrs. Blue. Over a period of years both Mrs. Green and Mr. Blue die. Their surviving spouses, Mr. Green and Mrs. Blue, who have always enjoyed each other's company, become closer, and finally decide to live together. Will they get married? Under the law in effect before 1965, they often would not. Why not? If Mrs. Blue had already reached normal retirement age, she received a survivor's benefit equal to 100 percent of her deceased husband's benefit. If she were to marry Mr. Green, under the previous law, she would lose her survivor's benefit, and would have the right to receive only 50 percent of the benefit of her new husband, Mr. Green. This could well be a substantial sacrifice – enough in many cases to deter the couple from marrying.

The law was subsequently changed; since 2009 Mrs. Blue will not lose her survivor's benefit unless she remarries before age 60. Do economic incentives still affect the decision to remarry? Apparently so: one study[10] found a significant decline in the marriage rates of widows immediately prior to age 60 and an increase thereafter.

The effect on savings of tax rules concerning interest

The tax consequences of saving and borrowing done by individuals will have a major influence on the amount of net saving done by the population. Carroll and Summers (1987) found that around 1971 there was a divergence between the rate of private savings in Canada and the United States. In Canada the savings rate accelerated, while in the United States it went into decline. They argued that the explanation for this disparity could be found in differences between the tax laws of the two countries. In Canada the tax rules were both more favorable to saving and less favorable to borrowing. This explained the differential in the net savings rate, since net savings is total savings minus total borrowing.

It turns out that in Canada one could invest in certain savings plans, such as Registered Pension Plans maintained by employers and Registered Retirement Savings Plans maintained by individuals, under which a substantial portion of interest income was exempt from income tax. The United States eventually enacted tax laws that gave similar treatment to savings plans, such as Individual Retirement Accounts, but such plans were not widely used until 1981.

Consider a U.S. and a Canadian citizen, each of whom invests $5,000 in a bond paying interest at a 10 percent rate. Assume the U.S. citizen is in a 40 percent marginal income tax bracket. The U.S. citizen receives $500 in interest each year, but this increases his taxable income by $500, resulting in additional tax liability of $500 \times .40 = $200. His rate of interest after taxes is therefore $500 - 200/5,000 = 6$ percent. In contrast, assuming interest income is not taxed in Canada, the Canadian citizen earns an after-tax rate of interest of 10 percent.

In addition, the tax system was much more hospitable to borrowing in the United States. Until 1986 all payments of interest were deductible as itemized deductions in the United States, while interest was not deductible in Canada. Consider a U.S. and a Canadian citizen, each of whom has borrowed $5,000 at a 10 percent rate of interest. Again assume the U.S. citizen is in a 40 percent marginal income tax bracket. Each year the U.S. citizen must pay $500 in interest, but can then deduct this amount as an itemized deduction. This will reduce his taxable income by $500, which enables him to avoid paying tax of $500 \times .40 = $200. The net cost of borrowing to him is therefore $300, so the after-tax rate of interest paid is $300/5,000 = 6$ percent, compared to the 10 percent interest rate paid by the Canadian. The combination of more favorable tax treatment of savings in Canada and less favorable tax treatment of borrowing led to substantially higher net saving in Canada during this period.

The proposal for a tax on consumption

Concern about the low savings rate in the United States, documented in the preceding section, has led a number of economists to propose that the federal income tax be replaced by a federal tax on consumption. Since consumption plus savings equals income, a tax on consumption should have the effect of discouraging consumption, thereby increasing savings and promoting more rapid growth of the economy. It is sometimes argued that a tax on consumption would be regressive, since persons with low incomes consume a larger fraction of their income than persons with high incomes. However, this argument assumes that the same tax rate would apply to all levels of consumption. A Hungarian economist, Nicholas Kaldor (1908–1986), proposed a progressive consumption tax which would require no more information than that which is now required in the administration of the federal income tax.

Under Kaldor's proposal, a taxpayer would operate on a cash-flow basis. The taxpayer would keep accounts of all receipts, which would be deemed income, and of all expenditures on capital assets (including money deposited in a bank account) which would be considered "savings." Recall that a capital asset is anything which yields valuable services for a period beyond the current year. The difference between the money coming in (income) and the money used to acquire capital assets (savings) would be treated as consumption, and would determine the amount of tax which the individual would have to pay. There could be an increasing marginal tax rate on consumption, so that the tax could be as progressive as Congress wanted it to be.

Some economists have pointed out a problem which could arise in the administration of a progressive consumption tax. This problem can be illustrated by comparing the operation of an income tax with that of a consumption tax, assuming that each tax is required to raise the same amount of revenue. (This assumption guarantees that the comparison of the two taxes will be a fair one.) Suppose, as indicated in Table 12.1, that a taxpayer with income of $40,000 would pay income tax of $15,000, leaving him disposable income of $25,000. Let us assume for convenience that all taxpayers consume 80 percent of their disposable income, regardless of whether they pay an income or consumption tax. This hypothetical taxpayer would therefore spend $20,000 on consumption.

Suppose, on the other hand, that a taxpayer with an income of $50,000 would pay an income tax of $20,000, leaving him disposable income of $30,000. Since by assumption every taxpayer consumes 80 percent of disposable income, this taxpayer would have a total consumption expenditure of $24,000. The marginal income tax rate on consumption between $40,000 and $50,000 can be determined as follows:

$$\frac{\Delta \text{income tax}}{\Delta \text{income}} = \frac{20{,}000 - 15{,}000}{50{,}000 - 40{,}000} = \frac{5{,}000}{10{,}000} = 50 \text{ percent}$$

Thus there is a 50 percent marginal income tax rate on income between $40,000 and $50,000. Now suppose that the income tax is replaced by a consumption tax which raises the same amount of revenue. The taxpayer who has an income of $40,000 must now pay $15,000

Table 12.1 Comparison of income and consumption taxes ($)

	Income/consumption	Taxpayer 1	Taxpayer 2
1	Income	40,000	50,000
2	Income tax	15,000	20,000
3	Disposable income = (1 − 2)	25,000	30,000
4	Consumption = (80% of 3)	20,000	24,000

in consumption tax, leaving him $25,000 of disposable income, of which he consumes 80 percent, or $20,000. Similarly the taxpayer with an income of $50,000 pays $20,000 in consumption tax, leaving $30,000 of disposable income, of which he consumes 80 percent, or $24,000. The marginal consumption tax rate on consumption between $20,000 and $24,000 would be determined as follows:

$$\frac{\Delta \text{consumption tax}}{\Delta \text{consumption}} = \frac{20,000 - 15,000}{24,000 - 20,000} = \frac{5,000}{4,000} = 125 \text{ percent}$$

Because of the much higher marginal tax rate on consumption, there is a much stronger incentive for cheating under the consumption tax than under the income tax.[11] Under the income tax, a taxpayer who conceals $1.00 of income stands to gain $0.50 if he is not caught. Under the consumption tax, on the other hand, a taxpayer who understates his consumption by $1.00 (either by understating his income or by overstating his savings) stands to gain $1.25! Thus there is a much greater expected reward for cheating under the consumption tax. The incentive to cheat will be stronger the smaller consumption is as a fraction of income and the higher the marginal tax rate (i.e., the more progressive the tax is). If the expected benefits of cheating increase, and the expected costs remain the same, we would expect the aggregate amount of cheating to increase. Accordingly, if the income tax is replaced by a consumption tax it will be necessary to take countervailing measures to increase the cost of cheating, either by allocating more resources to enforcement of the tax laws, to increase the probability that cheating will be detected, or by increasing the penalties for those who are caught, or both.

Charitable contributions

Individuals who file a federal income tax return in the United States can reduce the amount of their income that is subject to tax by choosing one of two alternatives: (1) they may take a "standard deduction" of a specified amount, or (2) they can "itemize" their deductions, subtracting from taxable income the sum of their expenditures on certain items such as State income tax, mortgage interest, property tax, and charitable contributions. Charitable contributions are donations made to nonprofit organizations such as churches, museums, colleges, universities and other charitable organizations. It is easier for a taxpayer to take the standard deduction, since someone who itemizes his deductions must go through all his records for the year to add up all his charitable gifts and other qualifying expenditures. Nonetheless many taxpayers can obtain a larger deduction than the standard deduction by itemizing, so they find it worth while to do so.

Changes in federal income tax rates change the tax benefit of a charitable donation for taxpayers who itemize their deductions. Before 1981, the highest income tax bracket was 70 percent. If someone in that bracket donated $10,000 to the Detroit Institute of Arts, he could reduce his taxable income by $10,000, and would therefore avoid having to pay $10,000 \times 70 percent = $7,000 in income tax. Therefore the net cost of the donation to the taxpayer would be $10,000 - $7,000 = $3,000. In 1981, however, the highest tax rate was reduced to 50 percent. Now the taxpayer who made a gift of $10,000 could still reduce his taxable income by $10,000, but now would avoid having to pay only $10,000 \times 50 percent = $5,000 in income tax. Therefore in 1981 the net cost of a gift of $10,000 was $10,000 - $5,000 = $5,000. Finally, the Tax Reform Act of 1986 reduced the highest income tax rate even further, from 50 percent to 28 percent over a few years.

When the 28 percent tax rate took effect, the amount of tax savings from a $10,000 gift was only $10,000 \times 28$ percent $= \$2,800$, so the net cost of the gift to the taxpayer was then $7,200.

Charles Clotfelter (1989) investigated how these changes in tax laws affected the amount of charitable donations. On the one hand, when taxes are reduced, households have more disposable income. Recall that a consumer whose income increases will purchase more of a good if it is a "normal" good. Thus if charitable giving is a "normal" good for most people, an increase in income should lead to more charitable giving. This is what economists call the "income effect." However, we must also consider the "substitution effect" – an increase in the price of a good leads consumers to buy less of it, while a decline in price induces them to buy more. Here, for taxpayers in the highest tax brackets who itemize their deductions, the price or cost of a charitable contribution increased from 30 percent of the contribution to 50 percent to 72 percent. Thus, for taxpayers who itemized their deductions, the changes in tax rates had a positive income effect but a negative substitution effect. Note, however, that for taxpayers who took the standard deduction, the tax cuts had a positive income effect (more disposable income) but no substitution effect (no change in price).

Clotfelter found that on average there was a decline in charitable giving by the households in the highest income tax brackets (who almost invariably itemize deductions). These taxpayers had a positive income effect, but a negative substitution effect that was large enough to overcome the income effect. In contrast, those taxpayers who took the standard deduction increased their charitable giving to some extent. These results are exactly what one would expect from economic theory.

Depreciation

The profits of a business equal its total revenues minus its total costs. If a business has machinery and equipment, the costs of the business include the loss in value of those assets through the ordinary wear and tear of use or through obsolescence. This cost is known as "depreciation." There are a number of different methods of computing deductions for depreciation.[12] We will first consider the method of "straight line" depreciation.

Suppose a firm buys an asset for $2,400. This asset has a useful life of six years and no "salvage value," i.e., at the end of six years it will be worth nothing. Under straight-line depreciation, the firm would be allowed to take an annual deduction of $2,400/6 = \$400$ each year for six years after acquiring the asset. The percentage of the asset's "basis," or purchase price, which is deductible each year is $100/6 = 16\frac{2}{3}$ percent. At the end of each year the basis of the asset is reduced by the amount of depreciation which has been deducted.

The original cost basis of the asset would be $2,400, its purchase price. After the depreciation deduction of $400 in the first year, its basis would decline to $2,000. After the depreciation deduction of $400 in the second year, the basis would decline to $1,600. After the third year, the basis would be $1,200, and so forth.

Methods of "accelerated depreciation" allow the owner of an asset to take depreciation deductions which exceed those allowable under straight-line depreciation. Under current law, the maximum deductions in the early years of ownership are available under the double declining balance method. This method allows the taxpayer to take deductions at twice the rate of straight-line depreciation; however, the deduction is based on the undepreciated balance, not the initial basis of the asset. In the above example, the rate of depreciation available under the double declining balance method would be $2 \times 16\frac{2}{3} = 33\frac{1}{3}$ percent of the undepreciated balance. Under this method, the depreciation deduction in the first year would be $2,400/3 = \$800$. The basis of the asset would then decline to $2,400 - 800 = \$1,600$.

The depreciation deduction in the second year would be $1,600/3 = \$533$. The basis would then decline to $\$1,600 - 533 = \$1,066$. The depreciation deduction in the third year would be $1,066/3 = 355$. It should be noted that under this method the taxpayer has the right to shift to the straight-line method whenever he chooses to do so. Normally the taxpayer will change to the straight-line method as soon as that method allows a larger deduction than continuation of the double declining balance method.

Accelerated depreciation allows a business to postpone its tax payments. Essentially, it allows a business an interest-free loan from the government. However, this observation may not be accurate if tax rates are changing during the useful life of the asset. For example, if people expect tax rates to increase substantially in the near future, they may prefer not to use a method of accelerated depreciation. In such a case it may be better to take less depreciation now and save more for the future, when depreciation deductions would be applied against higher tax rates. During World War II and the Korean conflict, firms which acquired assets for military purposes were allowed to depreciate them over a period of five years. This provision encouraged firms in the defense industry to substitute toward assets with a long useful life. To see why, consider the effect of this provision on the depreciation of (1) an asset with a useful life of fifty years and (2) an asset with a useful life of six years. Assume that the value of each asset is $\$60,000$ and the method of depreciation is straight-line. Under this law the depreciation deduction of the longer-lived asset would increase from $\$1,200$ per year to $\$12,000$. In contrast, the depreciation deduction of the short-lived asset would increase much less, from $\$10,000$ per year to $\$12,000$.

Suppose, on the other hand, that Congress enacted a law allowing firms to deduct five years from the useful life of an asset. This would encourage firms to substitute in favor of short-lived assets. In the above example, the depreciation deduction of the short-lived asset would increase from $\$10,000$ to $\$60,000$, while the deduction for the long-lived asset would increase much less, from $\$1,200$ to $\$1,333$.

Percentage depletion

In general, a firm is only allowed to take a deduction for depreciation of assets which decline in value over time. Land is an asset which normally is considered not to lose its value over time; accordingly a firm may not take a deduction for depreciation of land. However, in certain cases a firm can take a deduction for the loss in value of land, when the firm engages in the activity of extracting minerals from the land. Since the land loses its value as the minerals are extracted over time, a firm is allowed a deduction for a cost known as "depletion."

Suppose, for example, a firm purchases a silver mine for $\$1$ million. Each year it extracts 20 percent of the silver in the mine, for five years. Under a method of accounting known as cost depletion, the firm would be allowed a deduction for depletion of $\$200,000$ per year. This amount represents 20 percent of the purchase price, or "cost basis," of $\$1$ million. It turns out that there is another method of accounting for depletion known as percentage depletion. Under this method, a firm is allowed to deduct as depletion a specified percentage of the gross value of the mineral being extracted, value being determined at the well or minehead. The percentage is different for different minerals. Under 2009 law, it is 15 percent for certain kinds of oil and gas production, and gold, silver, copper, and iron ore; other percentages apply to other minerals. It is, however, noteworthy that for many years the deduction for percentage depletion for oil and gas exploration was much higher – 27.5 percent.

Percentage depletion is an alternative to cost depletion. A firm that chooses to use the method of percentage depletion forgoes the opportunity to deduct its costs as expenses.

However, if percentage depletion allows a firm to take deductions greater than its actual costs, a firm which may use percentage depletion is subject to a lower rate of income tax than firms in other industries which do not have a similar tax advantage. In effect, then, percentage depletion may be viewed as a subsidy to firms in the business of mineral exploration. Figure 12.2 illustrates the effect of percentage depletion. Recall that a subsidy acts as a payment which is added to the amount buyers are willing to pay, to enable it to reach the amount for which sellers are willing to sell. Thus it is a wedge between the supply and demand curves, to the right of their intersection. An important consequence of a subsidy is that "too much" of the good is produced, i.e., the amount of the good produced is more than the efficient level. The same analysis applies in this case; percentage depletion has induced us to use up our mineral resources too rapidly. With the subsidy the amount of oil produced is Q_s rather than Q^*, the amount that is socially optimal.

We can compare the amount of resources that are used to obtain a given stream of income from oil exploration, when percentage depletion is used, with the amount of resources that are used to produce an equivalent stream of income in other areas of business activity. If we find that more resources are used to obtain the stream of income in oil exploration than would be required in other business activities, we will have shown that there is a misallocation of resources, in that the rate of return in oil exploration is less than the rate of return in other business activities. Clearly one could obtain the same national income with less resources, if some resources were reassigned from oil exploration to other activities; or, stating it differently, with the same total resources we could increase our national income by diverting resources from oil exploration to other areas of the economy.

Consider a stream of future net income with value equal to X. We will determine (1) the cost of resources that will be used to yield an income stream of X in oil exploration, and (2) the cost of resources that would be required to yield income of X in other economic activities. If it turns out that cost (1) is substantially greater than cost (2), we will have shown that there is a misallocation of resources, in that too much of society's resources are being invested in oil exploration. To compare cost (1) with cost (2), we will make use of

Figure 12.2 The effect of percentage depletion on the amount of oil produced.

a powerful economic principle known as an equilibrium or arbitrage condition. According to this principle, a condition of equilibrium is that the price a buyer will pay for an asset, C_1, will just equal the discounted present value of the net (i.e., after-tax) income yielded by that asset.

We will assume that, in other areas of the economy, an asset which yields income is subject to normal depreciation. The taxable income yielded by this asset in the future will then be $X - C_1$. If t is the rate of income tax on a business, the taxes which must be paid in the future are $t(X - C_1)$. Let δ be the discount factor which converts the value of a future stream of income to its present value. Then the present value of taxes to be paid in the future is $\delta t(X - C_1)$. The present value of the net (after-tax) income yielded by the asset will then be $\delta X - \delta t(X - C_1)$.

Under the arbitrage condition referred to above, the cost of the asset, C_1, will equal this amount, so that:

$$C_1 = \delta X - \delta t(X - C_1)$$
$$\Longrightarrow C_1 = \delta X - \delta t X + \delta t C_1$$
$$\Longrightarrow C_1 - \delta t C_1 = \delta X - \delta t X$$
$$\Longrightarrow C_1(1 - \delta t) = \delta X(1 - t)$$
$$\Longrightarrow C_1 = \frac{\delta X(1 - t)}{(1 - \delta t)}$$

Now let us consider an asset for which percentage depletion may be used. Let C_2 be the price a buyer is willing to pay for this asset. At this juncture it should be noted that a firm which is allowed to use percentage depletion must choose between that method and the method of cost depletion. We can think of cost depletion as being analogous to normal depreciation. Under cost depletion, all costs of an asset are deducted as expenses. As we noted above, a firm that chooses to use percentage depletion is not allowed to deduct its costs as expenses. However, we will see below that there is an important qualification to this rule.

Now under percentage depletion the tax deductions available for an asset, such as an oil well or mine, are not based on the cost of the asset; instead, they are a specified percentage of the value of the mineral which is extracted from the oil well or mine. For example, for a substantial period the deduction for oil was $27\frac{1}{2}$ percent of the value of the oil being extracted from the well (value being determined at the wellhead). Suppose under percentage depletion the depletion deduction is equal to a fraction of net income ρ. In this case, if the rate of tax on income is t, the taxes payable in the future on income of the asset will equal $t(X - \rho X)$. The discounted present value of these tax payments will then be $\delta t(X - \rho X)$. The present value of the net (after-tax) income yielded by the asset will then be $\delta X - \delta t(X - \rho X)$. We can now again apply the arbitrage condition. According to this condition, the price buyers are willing to pay for this asset, C_2, must equal the net (after-tax) income yielded by the asset:

$$C_2 = \delta X - \delta t(X - \rho X)$$
$$\Longrightarrow C_2 = \delta X - \delta t X + \delta t \rho X$$
$$\Longrightarrow C_2 = \delta X(1 - t + t\rho)$$

We can now determine the ratio of C_2 to C_1, to compare the amount of resources used in an activity with percentage depletion to the amount used in an activity with normal depreciation. This ratio will be

$$\frac{C_2}{C_1} = \delta X(1 - t + t\rho)/\frac{\delta X(1-t)}{(1-\delta t)}$$

$$= \frac{(1 - t + t\rho)(1 - \delta t)}{(1-t)}$$

Suppose $t = 0.5$, $\delta = 0.65$, and $\rho = 0.35$. These represent approximate values for these variables for much of the historical period when percentage depletion was used in oil exploration. If we substitute these values in the above expression, we obtain the result that C_2/C_1 was about 0.911 – less than 1! This result is unexpected, since it would mean that less resources are used in oil and gas exploration than in other activities to yield a given stream of income. Perhaps there is something wrong with our analysis.

It turns out that in fact our analysis is incorrect, because we have not taken into account a crucial difference of opinion between an economist and an accountant with respect to the meaning of the word "cost." Oil exploration is an inherently risky activity. Suppose, for example, that on average only two out of every ten wells that are drilled turn out to be "gushers"; the other eight are dry holes. If the cost of drilling each well was, say, $100,000, an economist would conclude that the economic cost of the two wells was $100,000 × 10 = $1 million. One could say that the economic cost of each successful well was $500,000. The tax accountant, however, would be troubled by this approach, since there is an allocation problem: it is not clear which dry holes should be allocated to which successful well. In fact, the tax accountant, unlike the economist, would conclude that the "cost" of each successful well was only $100,000 – the costs directly incurred in drilling the well itself. The tax authorities happen to agree with the accountant's interpretation of cost rather than the economist's. This is important in light of the rule mentioned above, that a firm which chooses the method of percentage depletion gives up the opportunity to deduct its actual costs. The consequence of this narrow interpretation of "cost" is that if the firm chooses to take percentage depletion on the two successful wells, it gives up the right to deduct only $200,000 in cost depletion, not $1 million. Thus the firm can not only use percentage depletion for the two successful wells, but also can deduct an additional $800,000 in expenses! This makes the method of percentage depletion much more valuable than it would be if the economist's interpretation of the word "cost" were followed.

We must therefore modify the arbitrage condition for the activity which is allowed to use percentage depletion. The net (after-tax) income yielded by the asset must be increased by the income tax which is saved because, in addition to deductions for percentage depletion, 80 per cent of economic costs are deducted as expenses. In the above example, C_2, the economic cost of each oil well, would be $500,000. Because, to the accountant, the "cost" of a successful well is only $100,000, the firm would obtain an additional deduction of 80 per cent of $500,000, or $400,000. If t, the corporate income tax rate, were 50 per cent, the firm would have to pay an additional $200,000 in taxes if it did not have this deduction. In other words, by having the deduction of $0.8C_2$ the firm saves $200,000 in tax payments. In general, the income taxes that are saved when 80 per cent of economic costs are deducted as expenses is $0.8C_2t$. Thus we must rewrite the arbitrage condition as follows:

$$C_2 = \delta X - \delta t(X - \rho X - 0.8C_2)$$
$$\implies C_2 - 0.8\delta t C_2 = \delta X - \delta t X + \delta t \rho X$$
$$\implies C_2(1 - 0.8\delta t) = \delta X - \delta t X + \delta t \rho X$$

We can now, finally, determine the ratio of C_2 to C_1:

$$\frac{C_2}{C_1} = \frac{\delta X(1 - t + t\rho)}{(1 - 0.8\delta t)} \bigg/ \frac{\delta X(1 - t)}{(1 - \delta t)} = \frac{(1 - t + t\rho)(1 - \delta t)}{(1 - 0.8\delta t)(1 - t)}$$

Again suppose $t = .5$, $\delta = .65$, and $\rho = .35$. If we substitute these values in the above expression, we obtain the result that C_2/C_1 was about 1.23. Thus oil exploration has used about 123 per cent of the resources needed to produce the same level of income. This would mean that about 23 percent of the resources invested in oil exploration have been wasted because of the subsidy provided by percentage depletion.

A number of arguments have been made on behalf of percentage depletion. One argument is based on the premise that exploration for minerals is an especially risky undertaking; the probability of drilling a dry hole is high. Accordingly, it is argued, the tax laws should allow a higher than average rate of return to firms engaged in this activity. If oil and gas exploration, for example, was really as risky as this argument suggests, one would expect that the rate of bankruptcies would be higher than average for firms in this industry. However, the data do not indicate that the rate of bankruptcy is abnormally high in this business. This argument also overlooks the possibility that firms involved in mineral exploration can and do pool risks. In fact, joint ventures are commonplace in oil and gas exploration. It is a common practice for firms to sell an interest of 90 per cent or more in wells which they plan to drill, and to use the proceeds to buy fractional interests in many other wells drilled by others. Finally, and more fundamentally, if there is freedom of entry into the business of mineral exploration, and the industry is reasonably competitive, one would expect that firms in this industry would earn no more than a competitive rate of return, regardless of the tax preferences available to the industry. Another argument made for percentage depletion is that it is necessary for national defense, since the nation needs an ample supply of oil, gas, and other minerals in the event of war. However, if these resources are needed for defense purposes, it is not clear why we should create an incentive to extract them more rapidly than they would be extracted otherwise. The consequence of percentage depletion has been that more oil and gas were available in the short run, but less were available for future use. If the objective is to preserve these resources for military purposes, it might be advisable to limit current production, and maintain known reserves of oil and gas in the ground. If, on the other hand, it is thought necessary to have these resources available for immediate use, the oil could be extracted and stored in stockpiles above ground. Whether the storage of oil and gas should be above or below ground would depend on whether the additional cost of maintaining stockpiles above the ground exceeded the benefit of having these resources immediately available for military use.

The subsidy for residential housing

The preceding section analyzed the deduction for percentage depletion, one of the subsidies provided to firms in the business of extracting minerals from land. Another sector of the economy that economists consider to be heavily subsidized is residential housing. Now, to determine whether a good is (1) subsidized (or equivalently, taxed at a lower rate than other goods), or (2) taxed (or equivalently, taxed at a higher rate than other goods), we must examine the tax treatment of both the costs and the benefits of the good. Some of the major costs of housing – the interest paid on a mortgage or home equity loan, and property taxes – are deductible from federal income tax. Also, in many cases the capital gain from the sale of a house is excluded from taxable income. In contrast, the tenant of an apartment cannot deduct her rental payments from income. This difference in tax treatment gives consumers a powerful incentive to buy a house rather than rent one.

A homeowner might object to this comparison, pointing out that he must pay property taxes. However property taxes are really payment for a bundle of services provided by the municipality: fire and police protection, schools, roads, garbage collection, sewers, and the like. Moreover these services substantially increase the value of the house.

What about the tax treatment of the benefits of a house? We can compare the tax treatment of an investment in housing with investments in other assets such as stocks and bonds. Here, as has often been noted, there is a major difference: the benefits flowing from ownership of stocks and bonds (dividends, interest, and capital gains) are taxable income, while the benefits of shelter and comfort from living in a home are not deemed to be taxable income. We know these benefits are valuable, because people are willing to pay substantial amounts for them, e.g. in the form of rental payments.

Thus, if we compare buying a house to renting a house, we find that there is a tax preference for buying a house, since the costs of buying a house are deductible, while rental payments are not. On the other hand, if we compare an investment in housing with investments in financial assets like stocks and bonds, we find a tax preference for housing, since the income from housing is not taxable, while the income from financial assets is. We may therefore conclude that home ownership is subsidized, which means that too much housing is purchased. In Figure 12.3, because of the subsidy AB, the amount of housing purchased is Q_S rather than Q^*; we have an excessive amount of housing rather than the efficient level. Too much of our land

Figure 12.3 The effect of the subsidy of home ownership.

is occupied by mansions consuming excessive amounts of energy. We could increase our national income and output by investing less in housing and more in alternative assets such as parks, office buildings, factories, schools, or human capital.

The social cost of the tax exemption of interest on municipal bonds

We saw in Chapter 2 that one of the factors affecting interest rates is the tax treatment of the interest on the debt obligation. The interest on bonds issued by state and municipal governments is exempt from federal income tax. Because of this tax advantage, the equilibrium rate of interest on these bonds is substantially lower than it is on bonds for which the interest is taxable income. For example, the market rate of interest on municipal bonds may be only 8 percent, while the rate of interest on corporate bonds is 10 percent. This differential in interest rates is in and of itself evidence of inefficiency, since it indicates that capital invested in projects of municipal governments is yielding a rate of return of only 8 percent, while capital invested in the projects of corporations is yielding a rate of return of 10 percent. Because of the law of eventually diminishing marginal product, the rate of return in a given sector will decline if additional capital flows into that sector, and will increase if capital is withdrawn from that sector.

National income could be increased if some capital was transferred from municipal projects (raising the rate of return in that sector) to corporate projects (lowering the rate of return in that sector). National income will continue to increase as more and more capital is reallocated in this way until the rate of return in both sectors is equal. At this point capital will be invested in a manner that maximizes national income.

An application to professional sports

Oddly enough, the income tax exemption of interest on municipal bonds has often affected the decision as to where the stadium of a professional sports team will be located. Around 1995 the Chicago Bears Football Club decided that the team needed a new or improved stadium. If the Bears organization built a new stadium on its own, it would have to pay interest on the funds it borrowed at the going rate on similar corporate bonds of about 7 percent. If, however, the city of Chicago could be persuaded to build the stadium and then lease it to the Bears, the city would be able to borrow the funds at a substantially lower rate of interest, about 5.75 percent. The city could lease the stadium to the Bears, for rental payments that would pay all the principal and interest on the amounts borrowed by the city.[13] The resulting savings in interest payments on, for example, a \$200 million stadium would be $(0.07 - 0.575) \times \$200$ million, or about \$2.5 million per year. This amount could be divided between the Bears and the city of Chicago.

Of course there might be considerable haggling over the terms of the contract, since this is a classic example of bilateral monopoly. The city would know that if the Bears remained in Chicago, the Bears' best alternative to dealing with the city would be to build its own stadium at a much higher borrowing cost of 7 percent. On the other hand, the Bears could threaten to move the franchise to another city if they did not get sufficiently favorable terms from Chicago.

During these negotiations the Bears threatened to move the franchise to Gary, Indiana, which would also be able to finance the stadium by issuing municipal bonds. However, Casey Mulligan (1995) argued that this threat was an empty one, since Chicago, which had a better credit rating than Gary, could therefore borrow at a lower rate of interest. Gary would probably have had to pay an interest rate of about 6.5 percent or more. Thus the Bears could obtain a greater benefit from the lower cost of borrowing of Chicago compared to Gary. In the end the Bears remained in Chicago, and came to terms with the city.

Bibliography

Andreoni, James, "Reasonable Doubt and the Optimal Magnitude of Fines: Should the Penalty Fit the Crime?," 22 (3) *RAND Journal of Economics* 385–395 (autumn 1991).

Bar-Gill, Oren, and Oren Gazal Ayal, "Plea Bargains only for the Guilty," 49 *Journal of Law and Economics* 353–364 (April 2006).

Barro, Robert J., *The Impact of Social Security on Private Savings* (Washington, DC: American Enterprise Institute, 1978).

Blau, Francine D., Marianne A. Ferber, and Anne E. Winkler, *The Economics of Women, Men and Work* (3rd ed., Upper Saddle River, NJ: Prentice Hall, 1998).

Brien, Michael J., Stacy Dickert-Conlin, and David A. Weaver, "Widows Waiting to Wed? (Re)Marriage and Economic Incentives in Social Security Widow Benefits," 39 (3) *Journal of Human Resources* 585–623 (summer 2004).

Clotfelter, Charles T., "The Impact of Tax Reform on Charitable Giving: A 1989 Perspective," Working Paper 90–7, School of Business Administration, University of Michigan (December 1, 1989).

Conway, Karen S., and Jonathan C. Rork, "State 'Death' Taxes and Elderly Migration: The Chicken or the Egg?" 59 (1) *National Tax Journal* 97–128 (March 2006).

Craig, Michael D., "Improving Jury Deliberations: A Reconsideration of Lesser Included Offense Instructions," 16 (3) *University of Michigan Journal of Law Reform*, 561–583 (spring 1983).

Donaldson, Russell G., "Lesser-related State Offense Instructions: Modern Status," 50 *A.L.R. 4th* 1081 (2006).

Feldstein, Martin, "Social Security, Induced Retirement, and Aggregate Capital Formation," 82 *Journal of Political Economy* 905 (1974).

Feldstein, Martin, "Social Security and Private Savings: Reply," 90 *Journal of Political Economy* 630 (1982).

Grossman, Gene M., and Michael L. Katz, "Plea Bargaining and Social Welfare," 73 *American Economic Review* 749–757 (1983).

Hamrick, Tracy L., "Looking at Lesser Included Offenses on an 'All or Nothing' Basis: State v. Bullard and the Sporting Approach to Criminal Justice," 69 *North Carolina Law Review* 1470–1483 (1990–1991).

Harberger, Arnold C., "The Taxation of Mineral Industries," and "The Tax Treatment of Oil Exploration," in Harberger, *Taxation and Welfare* (Chicago: University of Chicago Press, 1974).

Hoffheimer, Michael H., "The Rise and Fall of Lesser Included Offenses," 36 (2) *Rutgers Law Journal* 351–437 (winter 2005).

Kipnis, K., "Criminal Justice and the Negotiated Plea," 86 (2) *Ethics* 93–106 (1976).

Klevorick, Alvin K., and Michael Rothschild, "A Model of the Jury Decision Process," 8 *Journal of Legal Studies* 141–164 (January 1979).

Landes, William, M., "An Economic Analysis of the Courts," 14 *Journal of Law and Economics* 61–107 (1971).

Mulligan, Casey B., "Daley, Bears sack U.S. Treasury," *Chicago Tribune*, December 13, 1995, Sec. 1, p. 27.

OECD Factbook 2009: Economic, Environmental and Social Statistics (Paris: OECD, 2009).

Pattilo, Michael G., "When 'Lesser' is More: The Case for Reviving the Constitutional Right to a Lesser Included Offense," 77 *Texas Law Review* 429–463 (1998–1999).

Posner, Richard A., *Economic Analysis of Law* (3rd ed., Riverwoods, IL: Aspen Publishers, 1986), chapter 18.

Reinganum, Jennifer F., "Plea Bargaining and Prosecutorial Discretion," 78 *American Economic Review* 713–728 (1988).

Roberts, Milton, annotation, "Modern Status of Law regarding Cure of Error, in Instruction as to One Offense, by Conviction of Higher or Lesser Offense," 15 *A.L.R. 4th* 118 (2006).

Shellenberger, James A., and James A. Strazella, "The Lesser Included Offense Doctrine and the Constitution: The Development of Due Process and Double Jeopardy Remedies," 79 *Marquette Law Review* 1 (1995).

Simonson, Itamar, "Choice Based on Reasons: The Case of Attraction and Compromise Effects," 16 (2) *Journal of Consumer Research: An Interdisciplinary Quarterly* 158–174 (September 1989).

Tversky, Amos, "Elimination by Aspects: A theory of choice," 79 *Psychological Review* 281–299 (1972).

Tversky, Amos and Kahneman, Daniel, "Loss Aversion in Riskless Choice: A Reference-dependent Model," 106 (4) *Quarterly Journal of Economics* 1039–1061 (November 1991).

Volokh, Alexander, "*n* Guilty Men," 146 *University of Pennsylvania Law Review* 173 (1997).

Zitter, Jay M., "When Should Jury's Deliberation Proceed from Charged Offense to Lesser-included Offense?," note, 26 *A.L.R. 5th* 603 (2006).

Problems

1. What are all the consequences of the federal estate tax and state inheritance tax on the behavior of people?

2. There is a controversy concerning the effects on private savings of the growth of Social Security benefits since the 1930s. Explain.

3. Explain in detail why private saving behavior between the United States and Canada began to diverge sharply around 1971.

4. Suppose that when an individual's income is $80,000, his income tax is $20,000, and when his income is $90,000, his income tax is $26,000. Suppose also that the individual always consumes three-quarters of his disposable income (after-tax income). Compute (*a*) the individual's marginal income tax rate; (*b*) the marginal consumption tax rate which would apply if the income tax were replaced by a consumption tax which raised the same amount of revenue. Does this suggest a problem concerning the enforcement of the consumption tax? Explain.

5. Between 1981 and 1990 there was a general reduction in income tax rates, and the maximum marginal income tax rate declined from 70 percent to 28 percent. What was the effect on charitable giving by (*a*) high-income individuals, who generally take a deduction for charitable contributions as part of their itemized deductions, and (*b*) by those lower- and middle-income individuals who take the standard deduction?

6. Write down and explain the equilibrium or "arbitrage" condition for the purchase price of an asset that is subject to depreciation for income tax purposes. Let X equal the amount of pre-tax income yielded by the asset in the future. t equals the tax rate, δ equals the discount rate that converts future dollars to dollars in present value, and C equals the purchase price paid for the asset.

7. (*Note*. This problem requires use of the equilibrium or "arbitrage" condition for the purchase price of an asset that is subject to depreciation for income tax purposes.) There are two different business activities, projects 1 and 2. Each of these projects yields a pre-tax income of $900,000 over the same span of years. Both these business activities are subject to normal depreciation. The taxable income generated by project 1 is taxed at a 50 percent rate, while the taxable income of project 2 is taxed at a more favorable rate of 20 percent because of various tax preferences. Let the discount rate that converts

future dollars from each project to present value be 0.8. Using the arbitrage condition, figure out how much someone would be willing to pay for (*a*) project 1; (*b*) project 2. How could the allocation of resources be improved?

8.   Suppose capital gains of assets such as securities were taxed as they accrued rather than upon realization, i.e. when the assets were sold or exchanged. What problems would be solved by such a change in the law? What problems would be created?

13 Labor law

In this chapter we consider a few selected topics in labor law. We will see that these laws cannot be evaluated in a competent way without a careful economic analysis, even though it would not even occur to many people (including many federal and state government officials who must decide whether to enact such laws) that such an analysis is necessary.

Covenants not to compete are agreements made between workers and employers, in which the worker agrees that if he leaves the firm, he will not enter into competition with his employer for a specified period of time, within a specified geographical area. We examine the economic effects of these agreements, and a possible economic justification for them.

The remainder of the chapter provides economic analysis of different kinds of legislation claimed by their proponents to protect or benefit workers. We examine the economic effects of minimum wage legislation, which establishes a price floor, and also consider wage controls, a price ceiling. We consider the effects of various laws that are designed to protect workers from layoffs or termination. The United States' Occupational Safety and Health Act created an agency that issues regulations designed to protect workers from injury and illness caused by hazards in the workplace. The Americans with Disabilities Act was intended to improve the labor market opportunities of disabled persons. We consider some effects of federal regulation designed to provide protection for individuals in pension and health plans. Finally, we consider proposals based on the doctrine of "comparable worth" – the idea that, when some type of work done mostly by women is judged to be comparable to some work done mostly by men, both types of jobs should have the same pay.

Covenants not to compete

Generally speaking, the common law does not enforce contracts that would reduce competition. However an exception is made for certain agreements made between employees and employers, that are known as covenants not to compete. In these agreements the worker agrees that if he leaves the firm, he will not enter into competition with his employer for a specified period of time, within a specified geographical area. The agreement also specifies the kind of work that is considered to be competition with his former employer. For example, a person joining a veterinarian business might be asked to agree that if he left the business, he would not join or open a competing veterinarian business within a ten-mile radius for five years.

Firms often use covenants not to compete when they want to prevent an employee from leaving. This must be done indirectly, since the courts will not order specific enforcement of employment contracts, i.e., they will not order an employee to continue working at the firm. Why not? A reason often cited for this rule is that courts will not enforce contracts for involuntary servitude, which are also prohibited by the Thirteenth Amendment to the U.S. Constitution. (One could argue that this particular form of servitude is voluntary, but the courts would probably reject the argument.)

Another explanation is the administrative costs involved in the specific enforcement of employment contracts: it is very costly for the courts to monitor employees to ensure that they are arriving at work punctually, making an appropriate effort, completing their assignments on time, etc.

A firm could always sue an employee who leaves before the end of his contract for money damages. Alternatively, covenants not to compete, if enforced, can be a very effective way to retain key employees. Suppose a firm trains an employee to be a talent agent, and he signs an enforceable agreement not to work as a talent agent elsewhere within five years of leaving the firm. If he could earn a much higher income as a talent agent than in other lines of work, he may well decide to stay with the firm. The courts will generally uphold covenants not to compete[1] when they are considered "reasonable," and not too broad in terms of duration, geographic area, or scope of the activity prohibited.

Some judges and commentators oppose the enforcement of covenants not to compete, on the grounds that they restrict competition. However, others have argued that these agreements may be efficient, in that they encourage firms to provide training for, and share information with, their workers. A firm that knows an employee will not leave for several years is apt to provide him with more training, since the firm knows it will be able to share the benefit of the employee's increased productivity. To evaluate these issues, one must first consider an economic analysis of the different types of training provided by firms to their employees.

General and firm-specific human capital

There is an important economic distinction between on-the-job training that increases the worker's general human capital, and training that provides only firm-specific human capital. General human capital makes the employee more productive not only at the firm that provides the training, but also at other firms. An example is the training a medical intern receives at a hospital, or the training in litigation a lawyer receives from working in the U.S. Department of Justice or the office of a District Attorney. Firm-specific human capital, on the other hand, makes the worker more productive only at the firm where he is being trained. An example would be learning a filing system that is used only by one's employer, or learning the strengths and weaknesses of one's fellow workers.

To see why this distinction is important, let us assume a worker's career has two periods, and consider what his compensation might be in each period. Note first that in the standard static analysis of competitive labor markets, the worker's wage equals his marginal revenue product. However, in a dynamic analysis, which considers a worker's compensation over multiple periods, a worker's wage in any given period could differ from his marginal revenue product. In a dynamic setting competition requires only that the present value of the worker's compensation over all periods must equal the present value of his marginal revenue product over those periods. With that understood, let us now assume a worker's career has two periods, and his training occurs in period 1.

Suppose the productivity of a worker without training is $100 per period. The worker's employer, firm A, wants to provide training to the worker that will increase his productivity by 30 percent. There are various costs of training: the costs of diverting the firm's other labor and capital from directly productive activity to the task of training the worker, and the diminished productivity of the worker during the period he is being trained. Suppose the total

Table 13.1 Different possible sequences of wages over two periods

Salary profile	First-period wage	Second-period wage
1	100	100
2	100	130
3	75	130
4	100	75
5	88	115

cost of such training is $25. The question is who will bear these training costs – the worker or his employer.

Consider the different salary profiles in Table 13.1.[2] If the training increases the worker's general human capital, it will increase his productivity by 30 percent, to $130 at any firm in period 2. Since other firms are willing to pay the worker $130, firm A must pay the worker at least $130 in period 2, or he will leave the firm. Here the value of the worker's increased productivity, $30, is captured entirely by the worker. In salary profile 2, the firm would pay the full cost of the worker's training, since it pays him $100 even though his productivity was diminished and there were other costs of training totaling $25. However, the firm would obtain none of the benefits of the training, since all benefits are captured by the worker. We can therefore conclude that the firm would not adopt salary profile 2. The only feasible alternative is salary profile 3, under which the worker is paid $75 during the period of training and $130 in period 2. Here the full cost of training, $25, is borne by the worker, in the form of a reduction of his salary in period 1. Since the worker receives the full benefit of his training – an increase in salary equal to the increase in his productivity – he must bear its full cost.

Now suppose, instead, the training increases the worker's productivity only at firm A, i.e., the training is firm-specific. In this case after training the worker will be worth $130 at firm A, but only $100 at other firms; consequently other firms would not be willing to pay the worker more than $100. Therefore firm A knows that if it pays the worker an amount above $100 in period 2, for example $110, the worker will not leave. However, if the worker can anticipate this sequence of events, he would be aware that he would not obtain the full benefit of his increased productivity. Accordingly he would not be willing to bear the full cost of his training in period 1. In other words, the worker would demand a compensating differential in period 1 to offset the fact that he would not receive the full value of his increased productivity in period 2. Since the worker and the firm each receive a share of the benefits, they will also share the costs of the training. The worker's salary will be reduced during the period of his training, but by an amount less than its full cost. Consider salary profile 5, under which the worker is paid $88 in period 1 and $115 in period 2. Under this scenario the worker bears $12(= $100 − 88) of the cost of training in period 1, and receives $15(= $115 − 100) of the benefit in period 2. The firm, on the other hand, bears ($25 − 12) = $13 of the cost in period 1, and receives a benefit of $15 in period 2 (the worker's actual productivity of $130 minus his salary of $115). Thus this salary arrangement will benefit both parties.

Let us continue with the assumption that the worker's training is firm-specific, i.e. it improves his productivity only at firm A. What about salary profile 1, under which the worker would receive $100 in each period? The problem with this profile is that the worker would have no reason not to leave firm A in period 2; his salary at firm A is $100, and any other firm is willing to pay this amount. The worker's departure would, however, impose a substantial loss on firm A, since the worker's services in period 2 are worth $130 to firm A while his salary is only $100. There is a substantial risk that the firm would not enjoy the benefit of training that it paid for. To avoid the possibility of such a loss, the firm would instead adopt a salary arrangement like salary profile 5.

Given the preceding discussion of human capital, we would like to determine why, and under what circumstances, a firm would want to bind an employee through a covenant not to compete. We have seen that if training increases the worker's firm-specific human capital, the firm would pay the trained worker more than the wage he could obtain at other firms, so he would not want to leave. Thus there is no need for a covenant not to compete in this case. On the other hand, if training increases the worker's general human capital, his compensation in period 2 will equal his marginal revenue product, so the firm should be indifferent whether he stays or leaves. Again it is not clear why the firm would want the worker to sign a covenant not to compete.

Rubin and Shedd, however, point out that there is a case where a covenant not to compete would be desirable. Suppose the firm finds it useful to increase a worker's general human capital by sharing valuable information with him – information that, since it is general human capital, would be valued highly by other firms, and that is too valuable for the worker to pay for through a reduction of his salary. In this case the worker would not be able to pay for the general human capital while he was being trained; the only way he could do so is by receiving compensation less than his marginal product for an extended period after his training – perhaps several years. Let us assume a worker's career has many periods, and let each period be a year. Suppose, for example, the additional general human capital resulting from training increased a worker's productivity from $100 to $300. In the year of his training his productivity is reduced from 100 to 60, and the additional cost of his training, in terms of the firm's resources, is $200; thus the total cost of his training is $240. The firm might then choose to pay him $60 in the year of his training, and then $250 in each of the following four years, so that the worker would bear the full cost of his training. Note that in each of the four years after his training, he would be paid $250 even though his marginal product to the firm is $300. In this situation, a worker would be tempted to leave the firm before he had repaid the full cost of his training, since by doing so he could obtain $300 at another firm, rather than the $250 he would receive for four years from firm A. However – and this is the main point – a covenant not to compete could prevent the worker from leaving before he had reimbursed the firm for the general human capital he acquired.

There is also a possibility of opportunistic behavior by the firm. In the previous example, if the worker signed a covenant not to compete for five years, the firm might decide to pay him less than $250 per year. The courts should be alert to this possibility, and refuse to enforce covenants not to compete when the worker has already paid in full for the general human capital that he acquired.

Legal disputes involving covenants not to compete usually involve two types of information: customer lists and trade secrets. Covenants often bar a former worker from doing business with customers of the firm. In deciding whether to enforce these agreements, the courts have fashioned a distinction based on the amount of effort made by the firm to develop customers. If the names of the firm's customers are readily available to any firm in the business, or if the customers are not likely to be a source of repeat business, the courts generally will not enforce the agreement. Here the courts might be thinking that since the information is not worth very much, there is no need to compel the worker to stay at the firm to pay for his training. Enforcing the covenant might only enable the firm to take advantage of the worker, by paying him less than his marginal revenue product. If, on the other hand, a firm can show that it made a substantial investment to develop its customers, the worker who signed a covenant not to compete will be barred from using this information. The idea is that if these agreements were not enforced, firms would have no incentive to make efficient investments in developing customers.

A similar distinction is applied to trade secrets. If the information that a firm seeks to protect is specialized knowledge, the courts will enforce a covenant prohibiting a former employee from using or disclosing the information. Indeed, information that qualifies as a trade secret is protected whether or not there is a covenant not to compete. If, however, the information in question would have been acquired by an employee working at any firm in the industry, it will not be protected. The courts have refused to enforce covenants not to compete for firms such as travel agencies, or those in the car rental business, or in real estate sales, because the courts assume that a worker could have acquired the same knowledge from any firm in these businesses.

One approach the courts might consider is to apply the rules applied by firms with franchised businesses, like MacDonald's. When MacDonald's sells a franchise to a buyer at a particular location, it usually promises the franchisee that it will not sell another franchise to any other buyer within a certain distance. This standard could be applied to determine whether geographic restrictions in a covenant not to compete are reasonable from the standpoint of efficiency.

Maximum and minimum wages

Sometimes governments attempt to control inflation by instituting wage and price controls. A maximum wage is a price ceiling. In these situations a worker's productivity often exceeds his wage, and firms will take various measures to prevent them from leaving for competing firms. The firm may increase fringe benefits and payments in kind, by providing valued workers with company-owned vehicles or housing, or paid holidays. Another strategy is to reclassify workers into higher-paid positions by simply changing their job titles without changing their responsibilities.

Governments may also establish a minimum wage. The United States has had a minimum wage since 1938, but it does not apply to all workers. The federal minimum wage originally covered about 38 percent of all nonsupervisory wage and salary workers; by 1997, it covered 70 percent of such workers. States may also have their own minimum wages, and if it is different from the federal minimum wage, the worker is entitled to the one that is higher. The federal minimum wage, which in 2010 was $7.25 an hour, is specified in nominal terms, so until it is changed by Congress, it does not adjust for inflation and changes in worker productivity. Thus the minimum wage has often fallen by 10 percent or more relative to the average manufacturing wage, before being increased again by Congress.

Those who support the minimum wage contend it increases the income of low-skilled workers and reduces poverty. Those who oppose the minimum wage contend that it reduces employment and increases unemployment. Figure 13.1 shows the market for unskilled workers. If there were no minimum wage the wage would be w_1 and the number of workers hired would be L_1. Now suppose the government enacts a minimum wage w_{min}. At this wage the supply of labor, L_S, exceeds the amount of labor firms will hire, L_D. Thus there is an excess supply of labor equal to $L_S - L_D$, which we call unemployment. In addition the minimum wage causes a loss of employment $L_1 - L_D$, which we call disemployment. The reduction in employment could occur either at the extensive margin, through layoffs, or at the intensive margin, through a decline in the number of hours worked per week.

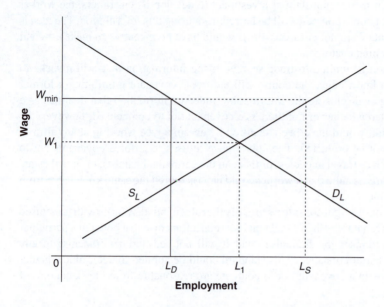

Figure 13.1 The effect of a minimum wage on the employment of unskilled workers.

Figure 13.1 assumes that all unskilled workers are covered by the minimum wage. In the United States, however, many workers are not covered, so firms in the uncovered sector may legally pay a lower wage. Consider Figure 13.2, which shows (*a*) a covered and (*b*) an uncovered sector. Suppose first there is no minimum wage, so the equilibrium wage in both sectors is W_1, L_{C1} workers are employed in the covered sector, and L_{U1} workers are employed in the uncovered sector. Now suppose the government adopts a minimum wage, W_{min}, which applies only in the covered sector. This reduces employment in the covered sector to L_{C2}. Suppose all the workers in the covered sector who lost their jobs, $L_{C1} - L_{C2}$, went into the uncovered sector. This would increase the labor supply in the uncovered sector to L_{U2} and, assuming demand for workers in that sector did not change, would reduce the wage there to W_{U2}. Thus the availability of an uncovered sector suggests that the effect of imposing a minimum wage would not be unemployment, but rather a reduction of wages in the uncovered sector. However it is quite unlikely that all workers laid off in the covered sector will look for jobs in the uncovered sector; some will remain unemployed, hoping to be rehired in the covered sector. This is especially likely for workers for whom it is costly to enter the uncovered sector – for example, because that would require a move, or because the jobs and skills required in that sector are substantially different.

The effect of the minimum wage on total wages paid to unskilled workers depends on the elasticity of demand for their services. If demand is elastic (an elasticity of demand less than −1), meaning that there are good substitutes for them, an increase in the minimum wage will reduce the total amount paid to unskilled workers. For example, if the elasticity of demand is −1.5, then a 20 percent increase in the minimum wage will cause a 30 percent decline in employment. Thus total payments of wages would be $(1.2 \times 0.7) = 0.84$, 84 percent of what they were before the increase.

Another concern about the minimum wage involves its possible effect on unskilled workers who must be trained by their employers. As explained above, workers who are acquiring

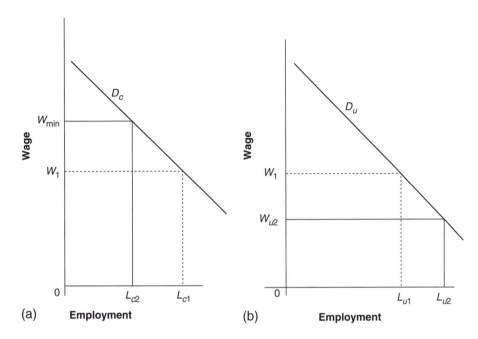

Figure 13.2 The effect of a minimum wage on wages and employment in (*a*) the sector it covers, (*b*) sectors it does not cover.

general human capital from training provided by their employer, e.g. by learning word processing skills, must "pay" for that training through a lower wage. If that lower wage is below the minimum wage, it will no longer be feasible for firms to hire and train them.

The impact of the minimum wage on individual firms will depend on the substitution and scale effects of an increase in the wage of unskilled workers. With regard to the scale effect, if wages of unskilled workers are a large proportion of a firm's costs, its costs will increase substantially, causing an increase in the price of its product, a resulting decline in its sales and a decline in its purchase of inputs. Suppose a buffet-style restaurant has relatively few unskilled workers per patron compared to a conventional restaurant, which has many servers. Since wages of unskilled workers are a larger proportion of the total costs of the conventional restaurant, its costs and prices will increase more than those of the buffet-style restaurant. This will divert business from the conventional restaurant to the buffet-style restaurant. The net effect on employment of workers by buffet-style restaurants is indeterminate. On the one hand, an increase in the cost of its unskilled workers will have negative scale and substitution effects. On the other hand, these effects may be greater for competing firms, such as conventional restaurants. The resulting competitive advantage creates an offsetting positive scale effect for buffet-style restaurants.

Employment protection laws

There are various laws that are designed to protect workers from layoffs or termination. Some countries require severance pay, in the range of eight to twelve months of pay, when an employee's termination is considered "unjust" or "unfair." Some laws give employees the right to challenge their dismissal in a formal legal setting. Some laws require employers to wait for some period of time, or give advance notice to some third party (e.g. the government, or a union) if they wish to close a plant, thereby eliminating jobs, or lay off a group of workers. Other regulations restrict employers from hiring workers on a temporary basis, or by contract of a fixed length, since these arrangements are viewed as a way to circumvent the protections against termination provided for full-time year-round workers. For example, some regulations limit the number of times a worker can be hired and rehired under consecutive contracts of fixed length. Finally, a number of countries, including the United States, have laws on unemployment compensation that require firms to pay the state premiums for unemployment insurance, where the premium is based on how many workers from the firm are unemployed.

Economists have investigated the effects of these laws on employment, unemployment, wages and average hours worked per year. In general, restrictions like mandatory severance pay are expected to reduce the flow from employment to unemployment, but since they make it harder (more costly) to dismiss employees, they may also make firms more cautious in hiring. The idea is that firms will be more willing to hire workers if they know that they can easily be dismissed if there is a decline in demand for the firm's output or if an employee simply turns out not to be a good worker.

This effect would tend to increase unemployment, by reducing the flow from unemployment to employment. Thus employment protection legislation has effects that work in opposite directions. Some studies have found that these laws have no overall effect on unemployment, but others have found an increase in the unemployment rate. An empirical analysis of Lazear (1990) suggests that an increase from zero to three months of required severance pay would increase the unemployment rate in the United States by 5.5 percent.

In a perfectly functioning labor market, the effect of any law regarding mandatory severance pay would be eliminated by offsetting market adjustments. This is so because an order from the government that A must pay $X to B can be nullified by a side agreement that B will compensate A by paying the $X back. Suppose, for example, there is no law regarding severance pay, and each worker signs a contract with a firm promising to work for two years for $20,000 per year. All workers will work the first year, but in the second year there is a 20 percent probability of being laid off. Therefore the expected income of a worker over the two-year period is $20,000 + (0.80 \times $20,000) = $36,000$. A worker who is laid off receives no severance pay. Thus a worker who is not laid off in the second year receives a total salary of $40,000 over the two years, and the probability of this occurrence is 80 percent; but a worker who is laid off in the second year receives only $20,000 over the two years, and the probability of this event is 20 percent.

Now suppose the government passes a law providing that any worker who is laid off in the second year must receive a severance payment of $2,000 from his employer. The market response would be that every worker pays for this benefit through a reduction of his first-year salary by $2,000 to $18,000 – in effect a deposit. However the worker is no worse off, because in the second year he will receive his deposit back – in the form of severance pay if he is laid off, and in the form of a salary increase otherwise. In this example, if he is not laid off in the second year, he would receive his salary of $20,000 plus a refund of his deposit of $2,000, for a total salary of $22,000 in his second year, and a total payment of $40,000 over the two years. The probability of this scenario is 80 percent. If, on the other hand, he were laid off in his second year, he would receive a refund of his deposit of $2,000, for a total salary of $20,000 over the two years. The probability of this outcome is 20 percent. Thus both workers and firms would be in exactly the same situation as they were before the law was passed. Note that the firm's cost of labor has not increased, despite the law requiring firms to pay severance pay they did not pay before. The firm has nullified its cost increase by an "agreement" with its employees. There is some evidence that this happens in the real world. One study examined the consequences of an Italian law requiring that firms with fewer than fifteen workers must make severance payments of between two and a half and six months' wages to an employee if his dismissal was "unfair." The authors found that about 44 percent of the increase in the expected firing costs was passed on to workers via a reduction in wages.

One would also expect an effect of employment protection legislation on the average hours of work of a firm's employees. Whenever a firm needs additional labor, the management must decide whether to have its employees work more hours per week, or instead to hire more employees. This decision turns on a comparison between the marginal cost of hiring an additional worker, and the marginal cost (possibly including overtime) of having its current workers work additional hours. Employment protection legislation tends to increase the costs of hiring another worker. Thus one would expect that an increase in these legal restrictions would cause firms to respond at the margin by having their workers work more overtime, and a relaxation of these restrictions might lead firms to hire more workers. One study found that in continental European countries, where the employment protection laws are relatively strict, there is much more use of overtime than in countries like the United States and Canada, where the laws are far less restrictive.

OSHA

The Occupational Safety and Health Act of 1970 established for the first time a federal program intended to protect almost all the nation's work force from job-related death, injury, and illness. The Occupational Safety and Health Administration (OSHA) was created in the Department of Labor to administer the Act, and began operations in 1971, with the mission of assuring safe and healthy working conditions for workers. The new agency had the strong support of organized labor.

Some economists have questioned whether the agency is necessary, at least if employers are liable for the costs of injuries to workers, because, they would argue, it is in an employer's interest to provide an optimal level of health and safety for their workers. Recall from the law of eventually diminishing marginal product, that as more and more units of a factor *a* are hired by a firm, holding fixed the amounts of all other factors, the additional output obtained by hiring an additional unit of factor *a* must eventually decline. This law applies to safety expenditures made to a given workplace area: the first expenditures would eliminate the obvious hazards and those that can be alleviated at low cost, such as exposed moving parts of machinery. After these are fixed, the next expenditures are likely to have a somewhat lower yield in terms of safety. At some point the marginal cost of additional safety expenditures will equal the marginal benefit, in terms of increased worker health and safety.

We must also consider compensating differentials for unsafe working conditions. A worker would be indifferent between annual earnings of $25,000 in an absolutely safe work environment, and receiving $30,000 in a workplace with a hazard that was worth $5,000 to him to avoid (i.e. the worker would be willing to pay $5,000 to avoid the danger). If the employer could eliminate the hazard with an annual expenditure of $4,000, his total costs would be $29,000 without the hazard and $30,000 with the hazard, so the hazard would disappear. If, on the other hand, it would cost the employer $6,000 annually to eliminate the hazard, he would not be inclined to do so, because his total costs would then be $31,000 without the hazard and $30,000 with it. In a perfectly competitive market, a firm that made such an expenditure would be unable to compete with a firm that did not make the expenditure: if both firms provided workers with the same level of utility, the safer firm paying $25,000 and the unsafe firm paying $30,000, the safe firm would have costs of $1,000 greater per worker and would eventually go out of business.

The foregoing argument of course assumes that both employers and workers have accurate information about the safety of their workplace. If workers were unable to distinguish between a safe and an unsafe workplace, they would choose to work at an unsafe firm paying $30,000 over a safe firm paying $29,000 even if, if they had knowledge of the danger, they would pay $5,000 to avoid it (of course, in this case, the safe firm would have a strong incentive to inform the workers about the danger at the unsafe firm).

There has been considerable speculation as to why OSHA has strong political support. Some researchers have argued that large firms support OSHA because it is less costly for them to comply with OSHA standards than it is for small firms, on account of economies of scale; thus OSHA regulations drive smaller firms out of business, eliminating competition for the large firms. Others, noting the strong support of organized labor for OSHA, have suggested that the real purpose of OSHA is to reduce the competition for unions from nonunion labor. If the unregulated level of health and safety is generally lower in nonunion firms than in union firms, unions might support an OSHA regulation that would raise the costs of the nonunion firm to those of the unionized firm. The consequence would be a negative scale effect: the prices of the nonunion firm would increase, reducing their sales and output and thus the demand for their workers, while demand would shift toward the output of the union firms, increasing the demand for their workers.

It has been argued that the decisions made by OSHA on the use of technology are influenced by organized labor. When OSHA considers proposals to protect workers from hazards to their health or safety, there are usually two alternatives: the agency can order workers to wear "personal protection devices," or can order the employer to install "engineering controls." For example, if there is danger from falling objects, the agency could order workers to wear hard hats (personal protection devices), or alternatively require employers to provide covered walkways (engineering controls). If there is a hazard from airborne carcinogens, OSHA could require workers to wear respirators, or alternatively order the employer to reduce emissions. One study argued that because of the influence of organized labor, OSHA has most often favored engineering controls, even if personal protection devices would eliminate the hazard at lower cost. (Of course, in making this comparison, it is important to consider the cost of annoyance or discomfort to workers of wearing personal protection devices.) Some have argued that unions have lobbied for engineering controls rather than personal protection devices because they increase the cost of capital relative to labor.

Figure 13.3 shows the quantity of labor hired when (1) there is no OSHA regulation (L_1), (2) when OSHA requires workers to wear a personal protection device, increasing the cost of labor (L_2), and finally (3) when OSHA instead requires the employer to use engineering controls, increasing the cost of capital (L_3). Figure 13.3 assumes that the level of output of the firm does not change, so that the firm remains on the same isoquant; this assumption is made for convenience of exposition. This diagram also assumes that requiring the use of personal protection devices would increase the cost of labor relative to capital. If, for example, workers are required to wear hard hats, the firm's cost would increase in proportion to the number of workers in the area subject to falling debris. Such a regulation would not increase the cost of capital used by the employer. The increase in the cost of labor would have a negative substitution effect (to hire more capital and less labor) and a negative scale effect (to hire less of both factors), and assuming the substitution effect was larger, the consequence

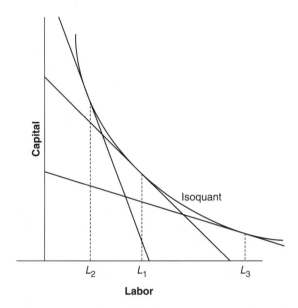

Figure 13.3 The effect of OSHA regulation on the amount of labor hired.

would be that the firm would hire more capital and less labor: L_2 is less than L_1 (the negative scale effect is not depicted in Figure 13.3: it would mean that the isoquants move away from the origin). Suppose, on the other hand, that the employer was ordered to install covered walkways instead. These costs would increase in proportion to the size of the structure, or the amount of capital employed, and would be unrelated to the number of workers employed. The increase in the cost of capital would have a substitution effect (to hire more labor and less capital) and a negative scale effect (to hire less of both factors), and so long as the substitution effect was larger, the consequence would be that the firm would hire more labor and less capital: L_3 is larger than L_1. Also, in many cases engineering controls increase the demand for skilled labor. Essentially, the argument is that choosing engineering controls will benefit unions by increasing the number of employees required to produce a given level of output.

Another argument made on behalf of OSHA is that it is necessary to offset other statutes that prevent workers and firms from bearing the full cost of injuries to workers. Federal programs like Social Security Disability Insurance pay a portion of the cost of injuries to workers, which tends to dilute the incentive of workers and firms to take efficient precautions to avoid injuries. OSHA could correct for the potential moral hazard, by imposing a specific standard protecting worker health or safety. Of course there is no guarantee that OSHA standards will provide the efficient level of protection, given that it has much less information about costs than the firms it regulates.

Laws concerning the employment of disabled persons

Disabled persons comprise approximately 13 percent of the adult civilian population aged sixteen or older. As of 1980, almost 70 percent of adults with disabilities reported that their disability prevented them from working. The propensity of the disabled not to work is likely attributable to higher fixed and marginal costs of working than able-bodied persons, and often less output per unit of work time. The fixed costs include the effort involved in preparing for work, the time to get settled at the job site, and the effort, time, and money involved in transportation to and from work. The marginal costs include the effort and exertion involved in doing tasks, many of which are routine for able-bodied persons. These costs reduce the incentives of disabled persons to acquire job market skills, and induce many to opt out of working altogether. Consequently the disabled often have less skills and invest less in training and education than able-bodied persons.

During the 1970s, the proportion of the disabled who were not working increased substantially. Over the same period there was rapid growth of payments for disability from the Social Security Disability Insurance program, which is believed to be an important factor in a decline of male labor force participation that occurred in the 1970s.

A concern over the expansion of disability benefits led the government to tighten the eligibility rules in 1980, but resulting public criticism of placing restrictions on benefits during a recession prompted Congress to change the law again in 1984 to liberalize the procedures for obtaining benefits. Between 1984 and 2001, the share of nonelderly (25 – 64) adults receiving disability benefits increased by 60 percent.

Leisure is a normal good for disabled as well as able-bodied workers. Consequently increasing disability benefits will lead some of the disabled to "buy more leisure time," by withdrawing completely from the labor force, neither working nor seeking employment. This is evidently what happened during the 1970s. By 1980 the number of disability beneficiaries was almost twice the number in 1970, and almost 70 percent of adults with disabilities reported that their disability precluded them from working. Of the 30 percent who did work, more than two-thirds worked full-time (at least thirty-five hours per week). The lack of interest in part-time work is probably attributable to the relatively large fixed costs of work faced by the disabled. It is not surprising that after making the substantial effort involved in preparing for the work day, obtaining transportation to work, etc., they do not want to limit their work time to a few hours. Between 1984 and 2001 an increase in benefits, less stringent screening, and a trend of declining demand for less skilled workers (who represent a large proportion of the disabled) induced many who could qualify for disability insurance benefits to leave the labor force.

The explosion in disability payments that occurred during the 1970s and after 1984 has been attributed to moral hazard, arising from a division of responsibilities between the federal government and the states. The Disability Insurance program is funded by the federal government, but the decisions on who qualifies for these benefits have been made by state agencies. Thus a state can be generous in determining eligibility for benefits without having to raise taxes to pay for them; the consequence has been enormous growth of disability payments, and often unequal treatment of individuals living in different states. In addition, state officials have been reluctant to classify those receiving disability insurance payments as being no longer eligible, since it was likely that these individuals would then end up on General Assistance, a state-funded program.

Paradoxically, while the Disability Insurance program has effectively deterred many from working, another statute, the Americans with Disabilities Act (ADA), which was enacted in 1990, encouraged the disabled to work by providing subsidies. A major objective of the ADA was to improve the labor market opportunities of people with disabilities. One section of the Act prohibited discrimination against disabled persons who were qualified for a job in hiring, firing, wages, promotion, and other terms and conditions of employment. This provision enabled disabled workers to sue employers for employment discrimination. Another section required employers to provide a "reasonable accommodation" for a person with a disability, such as wheelchair access. To meet the reasonable accommodation requirement, an employer might be required to modify their facilities, provide special equipment or assistance, revise work schedules, or redefine jobs.

Let us apply economic analysis to determine why, prior to the ADA, disabled workers had lower earnings than the nondisabled. In general a firm will employ workers (or any other factor of production) up to the point where their marginal cost, the addition to total costs from hiring them, equals their marginal revenue product, i.e., the additional revenue gained by hiring them. Suppose the marginal revenue product of A, a disabled worker, and B, one who is not disabled, is the same: $100 a day. Suppose the marginal cost of the able-bodied worker in earnings, fringe benefits, and providing a work space is $100 per day, but the daily marginal cost of the disabled worker is $120, because he requires a special accommodation, like a magnified computer screen for a vision-impaired person, and training in how to use it. Under these circumstances the employer would be willing to hire the disabled person, but only for $20 per day less than the compensation of the able-bodied worker. If there were no regulation, firms could "charge" for the extra accommodation expense by paying a daily wage $20 lower than that of the able-bodied worker, or the worker could purchase the equipment himself and pay for the training prior to the start of his employment. Then the marginal cost of the disabled worker would not exceed his marginal product, and the firm would be quite willing to hire him along with the able-bodied worker. However the anti-discrimination provisions of the ADA prevent any adjustment for this cost differential, through a reduction of wages or by any other means.

The reasonable accommodation requirement, combined with regulation compelling firms to hire the disabled, amounts to a subsidy for the disabled. It increases the costs of firms, and simultaneously reduces the costs of hiring disabled workers, with both substitution and scale effects. Since the costs of the firm increase, the prices of the firm's products or services will increase, reducing output and thus the demand for various inputs, including labor, disabled or otherwise. One consequence will be a decline in demand for nondisabled workers who are good substitutes for the disabled (the substitution effect). If the supply of these nondisabled workers is inelastic, their wages will fall (and the wage reduction will be larger, the larger the supply of disabled workers entering the market). If the supply of substitute workers is elastic, some of them may leave the labor force or work for fewer hours. Also, since there has been an overall increase in the cost of labor, firms may substitute away from labor toward more capital-intensive methods of production.

The effect of the ADA on different types of nondisabled workers depends on whether they are substitutes or complements for the disabled. Part of the subsidy will benefit those who are complementary with disabled workers, such as medical personnel and therapists, supervisory and training staff, and workers in firms that produce the accommodation goods.

If a law like the ADA requires the employer to pay the same compensation to both disabled and nondisabled workers, the employer is likely to respond by not hiring disabled workers; since the marginal cost of the disabled worker exceeds his marginal revenue product, the employer would lose profits of $20 by hiring him. If the law requires the employer not only to provide disabled workers the same compensation, but also to hire them, the employer will respond by hiring as few disabled workers as possible – just enough to avoid sanctions for violating the law.

Consistent with this analysis, some studies have found that the ADA actually reduced the employment of the disabled. These researchers argued (contrary to the subsidy interpretation) that the cost of providing accommodations increased the cost of hiring disabled workers, and that, plus the expected cost of being sued by disabled employees, deterred firms from hiring the disabled. For example, the antidiscrimination provision that allows disabled workers to sue their employers for wrongful termination may have been intended to protect their employment, but it is an increase in the cost of firing that induced employers not to hire the disabled in the first place (employers can also be sued for a failure to hire the disabled, but these lawsuits are less costly to firms than lawsuits for termination or layoffs). However, some researchers have arrived at a different conclusion. For example, Jolls (2004) found that the decline in employment following the passage of the ADA was only temporary, and attributable to disabled persons leaving work in order to return to school. She argued that the ADA, with its promise of increasing wages and employment of disabled persons, increased the returns to education for them, and thus encouraged them to invest in further education.

Public accommodations

Sometimes provision of public accommodations for the handicapped are justified on the grounds of network externalities or economies of scale. For example, it is not cost-effective to put wheelchair lifts on buses unless a large fraction of city buses can be equipped with them and there are a substantial number of riders in wheelchairs. We must also consider that there are usually several ways a public accommodation can be provided, and it is important to calculate the costs and benefits of each alternative before choosing one. Requiring lifts on buses is expensive not only in direct cost, but also in the time lost for nondisabled passengers. This type of accommodation would not be efficient in small cities, where there are few potential users. In such areas it would be better to use alternative methods of transportation, like special vans or taxi service. These considerations indicate that it is inappropriate to have uniform national standards, and that one must consider local conditions to determine the optimal type of accommodations.

Regulation of pensions

There are two types of pension plans, defined benefit plans and defined contribution plans. A defined benefit plan determines the amount the worker is entitled to upon retirement through a formula, which is usually based on his earnings, how many years he has worked for the employer, and his age at retirement. For example, teachers in public secondary schools in Michigan get an annual pension equal to (1.5 percent × number of years of service × the average of their three highest consecutive years of compensation), which are usually their last three years of work.

A defined contribution plan, on the other hand, establishes a separate account for each worker covered by the plan. Often contributions to the plan are made by both the worker and the employer, in accordance with a specified formula. For example, Wayne State University in Detroit will contribute to an employee's plan twice the amount the employee decides to contribute, up to a maximum of 10 percent of the employee's salary. Thus if the employee contributes 5 percent of his salary, Wayne State will contribute an additional 10 percent to his account. If the employee contributes only 3 percent, Wayne State will contribute 6 percent. Defined contribution plans typically give the worker a number of choices as to how his money shall be invested – whether in stock, bonds, real estate, and so forth – and he may also be able to choose investments of different levels of risk. When an employee retires, he is entitled to all the money that has accumulated in his account, which is the sum of the contributions made by him and the employer and any interest, dividends, and capital gains earned on those contributions. He may receive this amount in a lump sum, or as an annuity with monthly payments based on his life expectancy. The employee might also choose an annuity that will provide income to him and his spouse for the rest of their lives. Note that in a defined contribution plan the risk of gain or loss from investments is borne by the worker, while in a defined benefit plan the risk is borne by the employer or the plan.

Pension plans provide substantial benefits to both workers and employers. First, there are important tax advantages. When an employer in the United States makes contributions to the plan, they are exempt from both payroll and income tax. In addition, earnings made through the investment of contributions made to the plan are not subject to income tax. Thus a pension plan has tax benefits for the worker compared to other financial investments. The worker is not subject to income tax until he receives distributions from the plan on retirement, and never pays payroll tax. Since income tax rates increase with income, the tax advantages of a pension plan are greater for high-paid than for low-income workers. Ippolito (1986) found that pensions can reduce lifetime income taxes by 15 percent or more for middle-income workers, and by more for high-income workers.

Different types of plans offer additional benefits to workers. As previously noted, the market risk of investments is shifted from the worker to the employer by a defined benefit pension plan. Some plans have cost-of-living adjustments to protect retirees against the risk that their benefits will be eroded by inflation. Workers might also be concerned that their Social Security benefits will be cut in the future. Accordingly some plans integrate pension benefits with Social Security benefits; if Social Security benefits should decline, pension benefits will automatically increase to compensate for the reduction. The administrative costs of pension plans are usually low, at least in a large company, because of economies of scale. Although some economies of scale may be realized by other pooled investment vehicles such as mutual funds, the costs of record-keeping and marketing are usually lower in a pension plan, since the employer already has extensive information on its workers.

There are other important benefits of pension plans having to do with incentives, turnover of workers, and the timing of retirement decisions. To understand these effects, one must know that contributions made by the employer to a pension plan are not nonforfeitable, i.e., owned by the worker, until they are "vested" (contributions made by the worker himself are always owned by him). In the United States, under previous law, a plan could provide that a worker would have no vested pension benefits until he had worked for the employer for ten years, whereupon he would be fully (100 percent) vested. This was known as cliff vesting. Alternatively, a plan could provide that a worker was 25 percent vested after five years, and his percentage of vesting would increase every subsequent year until full vesting at fifteen years. However, the rules on vesting have changed, and under 2009 U.S. law, all pensions must be fully vested after six years.

Consider the previous example of a defined benefit pension plan, with cliff vesting after ten years. An employee who quit or was terminated before ten years would have no pension. This kind of deferred compensation arrangement tends to screen out workers who don't intend to stay with the employer long (at the extensive margin), and also gives workers an incentive not to shirk, lest they are dismissed before their pension vests (the intensive margin). Both effects reduce the turnover of workers, giving the employer an incentive to invest more in firm-specific training.

Pension plans are just one example of what seems to be a common practice, whereby firms pay young workers something less than their marginal revenue product and older workers more. This scheme of compensation gives workers an incentive to stay with the firm and to refrain from shirking, so that they will be around to enjoy the higher compensation that comes in their later years of service. When this is the compensation arrangement, a worker might be concerned that even if he performs well, the employer will take advantage of the situation by firing him just before he would receive the higher compensation, or just before his pension vests. The risk of this type of "cheating" should be less when the employer is concerned about its reputation; if the word gets out that workers for a company have been systematically deprived of their pensions, new workers will discount any promises of pension benefits made to them, and demand higher current compensation. Although abuses of this type seem to be rare, a few companies apparently have discharged workers just before they became eligible to receive their pensions. These were typically firms that were on the verge of bankruptcy, and therefore more concerned about short-term survival than long-run effects on their reputation in the labor market.

There may also be abuses of pension plans by employees. Suppose, for example, the worker's pension benefit is determined by a percentage of the average of his three highest consecutive years of compensation. Some workers will arrange to work an enormous amount of overtime in their last three years, to jack up their pension. This type of abuse is more common in government jobs than in the private sector, since excessive costs have a larger impact on shareholders than on individual taxpayers.

Historically, firms have used pension plans as a device to induce employees to retire at a certain age. Firms naturally will want employees to retire after their compensation exceeds their marginal revenue product, once they have met their implied contractual obligations to the employee. They were able to induce employees to retire at normal retirement age by constructing defined benefit plans so that the employee's future pension benefits would lose value if the employee stayed on after the prescribed age of retirement. Before 1989 more than one-half of the participants in defined benefit pension plans in the United States received no credit for service after age sixty-five (Gustman et al. 1994). Similarly, with a defined contribution plan, the employer would discontinue its contributions after the employee reached normal retirement age. However, recent regulations have made it much more difficult for firms to use pension plans to provide incentives for employees to retire at a given age.

The mix of pension plan types has been changing over the last twenty-five years. The defined benefit plan used to be the dominant mode, but most pension plans now are defined contribution plans. One reason why the defined contribution plan is gaining in popularity is that it shifts investment risk from firms to employees; another is that it is more suited for accommodating employees with diverse preferences. Some employees will want to save less for retirement than others because of their family or career situations. With a defined contribution plan an employee can usually choose the amount and type of investment, and the level of risk that he chooses.

Comparable worth

Some have argued that there is substantial discrimination against women in wages, hiring, and promotion. Others contend that even if women in the same type of job were treated equally in terms of wages, discrimination would persist, since women in predominantly female professions are paid less than men in predominantly male professions, even if the work in each profession requires the same level of skill and effort. This is the basis of the doctrine of comparable worth – the idea that when some type of work done mostly by women is judged to be "comparable" to some type of work done mostly by men, both types of jobs should have the same pay. Advocates of comparable worth contend that predominantly female jobs, such as those in child care and elementary education, can be matched with male jobs in, say, truck driving and vocational education that have essentially the same required level of education, stress, interaction with customers, and level of responsibility. They also cite studies showing that, other things equal, the wage of a job is lower the higher the proportion of women in that job. This fact, they argue, is attributable to discrimination. Jobs that are comparable, they argue, should have the same wage.

Labor economists would generally respond that differences in wages are often attributable to factors other than discrimination, such as the worker's level of education, region, age, years of work experience, union status, restrictions on entry into the profession, compensating differentials for working conditions, and the like. They would also point to problems that can arise when wages of different occupations are set by law rather than market forces. Consider the salaries of professors in two different departments of a university – art history and electrical engineering. An applicant for a position in either department must have the same level of education – a Ph.D. degree – and professors in each department are expected to do research, teaching, and departmental service activities (serving on committees and the like). One could therefore argue that these two jobs are comparable.

Suppose that at first professors in these departments are paid the same salary W_1, and supply equals demand in each market. N_{1E} professors of electrical engineering and N_{1A} professors of art history will be hired. Subsequently there is an increase in demand by students for classes in electrical engineering, and a decrease in demand for classes in art history. This increases the demand for professors in electrical engineering from D_{1E} to D_{2E}, and reduces the demand for professors of art history from D_{1A} to D_{2A}. Figures 13.4–5 show that at the original wage W_1 there is now excess demand for professors of electrical engineering in the amount $N_{2E} - N_{1E}$ and an excess supply of professors of art history in the amount $N_{1A} - N_{2A}$. The normal market response would be that the wage of electrical engineering professors

Figure 13.4 The market for professors of electrical engineering.

Figure 13.5 The market for professors of art history.

would increase to W_{3E} and the number of them hired would increase to N_{3E}; meanwhile, the wage of art history professors would decline to W_{3A} and the number of them hired would decline to N_{3A}. Suppose, however, that the president of the university is a firm believer in the doctrine of comparable worth, and orders that the wage for each type of professor remain at W_1. In this case the university would be offering an above-market wage for art history Ph.D.s and a below-market wage for electrical engineering Ph.D.s. One would expect that, as a consequence, the university would be able to hire professors of above-average quality in art history and professors of below-average quality in electrical engineering. Thus even though wages would remain unchanged, the price per unit of quality would have increased in the electrical engineering labor market and declined in the art history market. Note also that the point at which W_1 intersects each supply curve has not changed. Therefore one consequence of applying the comparable worth approach is that the numbers of the professors hired, and thus the number of courses offered, would not have changed to adjust to the change in demand of the students.

Bibliography

Autor, David H., and Mark G. Duggan, "The Rise in the Disability Rolls and the Decline in Unemployment," *Quarterly Journal of Economics* 157–205 (February 2003).

Deleire, Thomas, "The Unintended Consequences of the Americans with Disabilities Act," 23 (1) *Regulation* 21 (2000).

Ehrenberg, Ronald G., and George H. Jakubsen, "Advance Notification of Plant Closing: Does it Matter?," 28 (1) *Industrial Relations* 60–71 (winter 1989).

Gustman, Alan L., Olivia S. Mitchell, and Thomas L. Steinmeier, "The Role of Pensions in the Labor Market: A Survey of the Literature," 47 *Industrial and Labor Relations* 417–438 (1994).

Ippolito, Richard, *Pensions, Economics and Public Policy* (Homewood, IL: Dow Jones-Irwin, 1986).

Jolls, Christine, "Identifying the Effects of the Americans with Disabilities Using State-law Variation: Preliminary Evidence on Educational Participation Effects," 94 (2) *American Economic Review* 447–453 (May 2004).

Kearney, John R., "Social Security and the 'D' in OASDI: The History of a Federal Program Insuring Earners against Disability," 66 (3) *Social Security Bulletin* 2005–2006.

Lazear, Edward P., "Job Security Provisions and Employment," 105 (3) *Quarterly Journal of Economics* 699–726 (1990).

Leonardi, Marco and Giovanni Pica, "Employment Protection Legislation and Wages," IZA Discussion Paper 2680 (March 2007).

Lester, Gillian, "Restrictive Covenants, Employee Training, and the Limits of Transaction-cost Analysis," 76 *Indiana Law Journal* 49–76 (2001).

Miller, James C., III, "Is Organized Labor Rational in Supporting OSHA?," 50 *Southern Economic Journal* 881 (1984).

Oi, Walter Y., "Work for Americans with Disabilities," 523 (1) *Annals of the American Academy of Political and Social Science* 159–174 (1992).

Robinson, Derek, *Wage Drift, Fringe Benefits and Manpower Distribution* (Paris: OECD, 1968).

Rosen, Sherwin, "Disability Accommodation and the Labor Market," in Carolyn Weaver (ed.), *Disability and Work: Incentives, Rights and Opportunities* (Washington, DC: American Enterprise Institute, 1991).

Rubin, Paul H., and Peter Shedd "Human Capital and Covenants not to Compete," 10 *Journal of Legal Studies* 93–110 (1981).

Problem

1. Suppose two workers employed by Z Co., A and B, will each receive some on-the-job training. The cost of training each worker, which includes the cost of instruction and the worker's reduced productivity during the training period, is $20. Assume the training will be done in period 1, and each worker is employed for two periods. Without training the marginal revenue product of each worker would be $100 in each period. The training received by worker A increases his marginal revenue product by $25, but only at Z Co., not at other firms. The training received by worker B increases his marginal revenue product by $25 at Z Co. and at all other firms. Table 13.2 shows the salary profiles at Z Co. Which profile is most likely for each of these workers? Explain exactly why.

Table 13.2 Different possible salary profiles for workers A and B

Salary profile	First-period wage	Second-period wage
1	100	100
2	80	125
3	90	115
4	125	80

Glossary

Action   Lawsuit.

Arbitrage   Exploiting a difference in price by buying an asset at a low price and selling it at a higher price. Suppose bank A will trade euros for dollars at a rate of €0.75 per dollar, and bank B has a rate of €0.80 per dollar. For an individual with dollars, euros are cheaper at bank B. If one spends $1,000 to buy €800 at bank B, and then immediately sells them to bank A, one obtains $(1.00/0.75) \times 800 = \$1,066.67$, making a profit of $66.67.

Additur   A procedure by which a court orders that the plaintiff will be granted a new trial on the issue of damages unless the defendant agrees to an increase of the trial court's award by a specified amount.

Adverse selection   The tendency for less desirable or low-quality types to enter a market and for more desirable or high-quality types to leave it because of the inability of an uninformed participant on the other side of the market, whether buyer or seller, to distinguish one type from the other. Americans who wish to adopt babies from an underdeveloped country, and do not insist that the baby's health be evaluated by an independent medical expert, are more likely to be offered babies with serious but unobservable health problems.

Affirmative defense   A defense that raises new facts and arguments that, if proved, will preclude civil or criminal liability even if the allegations of the plaintiff or prosecutor are true. Examples of affirmative defenses are duress, assumption of risk and contributory negligence (in a civil case) and insanity and self-defense (in a criminal case). In a civil case the defendant has the burden of proving an affirmative defense.

Assumption of risk   Conduct on the part of the plaintiff that indicates he assumed the risk of injury, either by express agreement, i.e., a waiver of liability, or by implied acceptance of the risk. It is an affirmative defense to a claim of negligence.

Attorney work product   The doctrine that a lawyer's notes, memoranda and anything else that reflects the lawyer's "mental impressions, conclusions, opinions, or legal theories" about a case cannot be obtained by the opposing party through pre-trial discovery.

Average cost   The total cost of production, divided by the amount produced; cost per unit of output.

Average tax rate   The average income tax rate is the total income tax liability, divided by total taxable income.

Bona fide purchaser   An individual who bought property in good faith, i.e. without reason to believe it had been stolen.

Capital   Anything, other than a free human being, that yields productive services in future years as well as the present. It includes such things as machinery, equipment, and human capital, an individual's endowment of skills, productivity, and earning capacity, which can be increased through education or on-the-job training.

Cartel A group of independent firms that attempt, by collusive agreement, to behave as a collective monopoly. A cartel may agree to fix prices, to limit output, or divide territories among firms.

Cause of action A valid legal claim that is the basis for a lawsuit, or action.

Challenge for cause A challenge by which the defense or prosecution can eliminate a potential juror if the circumstances raise a question about his ability to hear the case impartially. For example, a person would be excused for cause if he were a close relative of the defendant, the victim, or one of the lawyers, or if he already had a firm opinion concerning the guilt of the defendant.

Choice variable A variable in a mathematical model, the value of which is chosen to optimize an objective function. For example, the objective of a firm is to maximize profits. The firm wishes to choose a level of output that will maximize profits. Here the level of output is the choice variable. Compare with **parameter**.

Class action A single action filed on behalf of numerous individual plaintiffs (sometimes millions of them) who have similar claims against the same defendant or defendants. The plaintiffs who are named are deemed to represent the interests of others who are similarly situated. The great majority of plaintiffs are not named individually but rather are described in terms of their eligibility to participate, e.g., all retail purchasers of a specified brand of steel-belted radial tire purchased new at retail and installed on a vehicle in the United States between January 1, 1985, and January 6, 2002.

Collateral benefits rule, or collateral source rule A rule of the common law (sometimes modified by statute), under which the damages for which the defendant is liable are not reduced by any payments the plaintiff may receive from sources other than the defendant, such as the plaintiff's own accident insurance.

Collateral estoppel The doctrine that determines whether a decision made on issues arising in one case will be binding when the same issues arise in another case, when at least one party, or someone closely related to the party, is involved in both litigations.

Common law The body of law provided by all published judicial decisions, i.e. the body of all legal precedents. It is a stock of knowledge about legal rules and obligations.

Community property In eight States of the U.S., the law is derived from the Spanish legal system, rather than from the common law. In these community property States each spouse acquires an immediate one-half interest in amounts that the other spouse earns during the marriage.

Comparative negligence A law of negligence that is an alternative to traditional common-law negligence. Under a regime of comparative negligence, responsibility for an accident is apportioned between plaintiff and defendant, and the plaintiff's damages are then reduced by his share of responsibility. For example, if the plaintiff's damages are $1 million, the court may determine that he bears 25 percent of responsibility for the accident, so that the defendant is 75 percent responsible. In this case the plaintiff is entitled to recover only $750,000 from the defendant.

Compensating differential An upward or downward adjustment of the wage, reflecting any amenities or disamenities of the job. Nurses on the night shift receive a wage premium (a compensating differential), since working at night is disruptive to sleep and to interaction with others.

Condemnation The government's exercise of its power of eminent domain, i.e., its right to take private property for public use, upon payment of its market value.

Consumer surplus The difference between the value of a good or service to the consumer and the amount she must pay for it. If the price paid for a new coat by Ms. X was $200, and she would have been willing to pay as much as $300 for it, her consumer surplus from this transaction is $100.

Contributory negligence   Conduct on the part of the plaintiff that contributes as a cause to the harm he suffered, and that falls below the standard he is required to conform to for his own protection. It is an affirmative defense to a claim of negligence. If the defendant can prove that the plaintiff was contributorily negligent, the defendant will not be liable for negligence unless there are certain narrowly defined extenuating circumstances. (See **Last clear chance**.)

Contingent fee   A compensation arrangement, whereby a lawyer receives a specified fraction of the recovery she obtains for her client, whether obtained through out-of-court settlement or court award.

Coase Theorem   According to this theorem, if there are no costs of bargaining and property rights are well defined, two or more parties who have a conflict will be able to reach an efficient solution by themselves, through their own negotiations. They will arrive at such an outcome regardless of how property rights are assigned among them.

Copyright   A property right in creative work granted by law to one who creates written work, choreography, motion pictures, photography, sound recordings, or other art forms. In the United States, the term of copyright protection is now the life of the author plus seventy years. The prerequisite for a copyright is that the creative work meet a "modest threshold of creative activity," and under the statutes of many countries the work must also be fixed in a tangible form.

Cost   In general, the cost of an action is the value of the best opportunity that is sacrificed by taking that action. For a producer, the cost of output is the value of everything that is used to produce that output. The *total cost* of producing some specified quantity of a good is the area under the supply curve (a curve of marginal cost) from the origin to that amount.[1] If the supply curve is for a firm, this area represents the total cost to the firm of producing that quantity of the good. If the supply curve is for a market, this area represents the total cost to the market of producing that quantity of the good.

Cross-price elasticity of demand   The elasticity of demand for one good, X, with respect to the price of another good, Y. This elasticity equals the percentage change in the amount of X demanded, divided by the percentage change in the price of Y. It is positive for goods that are substitutes, and negative for goods that are complements.

Curtesy   At common law, a widower had the right to a life estate in all of his wife's inheritable land if a child was born of the marriage.

Demand curve   There are demand curves for individual persons, or firms, and there are market demand curves, aggregating the demand curves of all individual persons in a market, or of all firms in an industry. In general, the demand curve for a good shows the amount of the good that is demanded at different prices, holding constant other factors (income, the prices of substitutes and complements, expectations about future prices, etc.) that affect the amount demanded. Equivalently, it shows the maximum amount that someone is willing to pay for the unit of the good in question. **Individual demand curve** A curve which shows the marginal value of the good, i.e., the value of each additional good to the individual, over the period of time covered by the demand curve. "Value" means the maximum amount the individual is willing to pay for the unit of the good in question. **Market demand curve** A curve which shows the value of each additional good to the market, i.e. the value of that additional good to the individual in the market who values it the most, over the period of time covered by the demand curve.

Dicta Short for "obiter dicta," "things said by the way") – an incidental observation or remark made in passing, which is not binding as a precedent upon future courts.

Diminishing returns, diminishing marginal product According to the law of (eventually) diminishing marginal product, as a firm increases the use of an input, holding fixed the amounts of other inputs, the marginal product (the increase in output resulting from an additional unit of input) will eventually decline.

Discovery This is short for "pre-trial discovery." In the process of discovery, each party prepares for trial by obtaining information from the other side by various means, such as interrogatories (written questions); oral depositions, in which witnesses are required to testify under oath; and the discovery of documents and things (physical evidence). These methods of discovery enable both sides to become fully informed about the merits of a case.

Dower A common-law doctrine that a widow had the right to a life estate in one-third of the husband's inheritable lands.

Easement The right of a person to go on to land in the possession of another and make some limited, specified use of it. Often the local electric utility has an easement enabling its workers to enter the private property of others to check and repair power lines, read electric meters, and the like.

Economies of scale There are economies of scale when the long-run average cost of production declines with the amount produced. There are economies of scale if it is possible for a firm to double output without doubling the total costs of production.

Economies of scope There are economies of scope when two products can be produced at lower cost within the same firm than if they were produced by two firms, each producing one product. For example, a firm that produces both beef and leather may be able to do so at lower cost than two firms, one producing only leather and the other producing only beef. The reason would be that the hide is a byproduct of the slaughter of cattle.

Efficient An allocation of resources is efficient if any change in that allocation that makes someone better off has to make someone else worse off. An efficient allocation of resources gets the most out of those resources; it maximizes the sum of consumer and producer surplus. An allocation of risk is efficient if it assigns risk to the person who is best suited to bear the risk, e.g. from someone who is risk-averse to another who is risk-neutral or less risk-averse.

Efficient capital markets, Hypothesis of The theory that prices of securities in financial markets fully reflect all available information.

Elastic Having a price-elasticity of demand between -1 and $-\infty$. If the demand for a good or service is elastic, the amount purchased changes substantially if its price changes. The demand for a good is elastic if there are very good substitutes available for it. In an area where there are many gasoline stations, the demand for, say, Marathon gasoline is elastic, since there are many good substitutes available for it (e.g., gasoline from ExxonMobil, Shell, BP, etc.).

Elasticity When this word is used by itself, it usually means the elasticity of demand with respect to price, which is, for some good X, a fraction, equal to (1) the percentage change in the amount of X demanded, divided by (2) the percentage change in the price of X. The idea is to measure how much the amount demanded is affected by a change in price. There are many different elasticities, for example the elasticity of demand with respect to income, the elasticity of supply with respect to price, the cross-elasticity of demand for good A with respect to the price of good B. Every elasticity is a percentage change in something, divided by a percentage change in something else.

Elasticity of supply   A measure of how responsive the amount supplied of a good is to its market price. The elasticity of supply of a good equals the percentage change in the amount supplied to the market, divided by the percentage change in its price.

Eminent domain   The government's right to take private property for public use, upon payment of its market value.

Equilibrium   A situation where all the agents in the economic model, whether persons or firms, are doing the best they can, and there is no tendency toward change. A pendulum is in equilibrium when its bob weight is in a downward vertical position – a 90° angle relative to the earth's surface. It is out of equilibrium if its weight is at, say, a 60° angle relative to the earth's surface.

Endogenous   An endogenous variable is one that is determined within the model in which it appears. It is not a constant, not taken as a given. In a model of the supply and demand for wheat, the price and amount of wheat produced would be endogenous variables. A choice variable is an endogenous variable. For example, the amount of orange juice bought by a consumer is chosen to maximize her utility.

Exogenous   An exogenous variable is one that is taken as a given, i.e., a constant, a parameter of the model. For a firm in a perfectly competitive market, the price of the good it produces is exogenous, because decisions made by the firm on how much to produce will have no effect on the price.

Expected value   The mean or average value; the weighted average of all possible values, where the weights are the probabilities.[2] If the possible outcomes of a jury trial are an award of $10,000 with probability 1/4, of $100,000 with probability 1/2, and $300,000 with probability 1/4, then the expected value of the verdict is:

$$(10,000 \times 0.25) + (100,000 \times 0.50) + (300,000 \times 0.25) = \$127,500.$$

Extensive margin   A change on the extensive margin is a change in participation: either entry into the market, or exit from it. If the wages of nurses increase, an individual who had left the nursing profession might choose to re-renter it; this is a change on the extensive margin.

Externality   A transaction generates a positive or negative externality if it has a positive or negative impact, respectively, on others not directly involved in the transaction. A manufacturer that dumps toxic chemicals into a river, thereby reducing the fish population, imposes a negative externality on fishermen who fish downstream from the manufacturing plant.

Fair use   A doctrine of copyright law, under which persons may use portions of a copyrighted work without obtaining the author's permission. In most cases of fair use, only a small part of the work is used and the author is acknowledged. An example is a quotation from a copyrighted book in a book review.

Fellow-servant rule   A common-law doctrine that a worker's employer was not vicariously liable for injuries caused by the negligence of a coworker. The doctrine has been generally abrogated by workers' compensation statutes.

Fixed costs   Costs that must be paid by a firm regardless of the amount it produces. Fixed costs must be paid even if nothing is produced.

Free rider problem   When a number of people share something of value, e.g. property or an experience, some of them may avoid paying their share of the costs; this is the free rider problem.

Hearsay Testimony of a witness concerning an event that he did not personally observe, but was informed about by another. Under the "hearsay rule," such testimony is inadmissible under the rules of evidence unless it falls within one of the exceptions to the rule. For example, A can testify that he saw a gun in the car of B, the defendant, but cannot testify that C told him there was a gun in the defendant's car. The principal arguments for the hearsay rule are that the statements made by C to A were not made under oath (and thus subject to penalties for perjury if false) and were not subject to cross-examination, which might reveal that C was joking, or only saw a metallic object that he assumed was a gun, or undermine C's statement in some other way.

Heirs Those entitled to inherit the property of a person who dies. If the deceased individual has a will, her heirs are those designated in her will. If the individual dies intestate (without a will), her heirs are those designated in the statute of intestacy.

Holding The rule of law announced in a reported judicial decision that becomes the precedent established by the case.

Holdout problem The problem that arises when the owner of an asset, negotiating with one who wishes to acquire the asset for a more valuable use, demands compensation that would extract some of the profit to be obtained from the more valuable use. The holdout problem is that such demands may prevent assets from being acquired for more valuable uses, an inefficient outcome.

Human capital The endowment of ability and knowledge that determines an individual's real income, productivity or earning capacity. It is increased by education and on-the-job training.

Income effect The effect on consumption of a change in an individual's real income, or purchasing power, resulting from the change in a price. If the price of gasoline increases sharply, those who buy gasoline have less real income, and this negative income effect is greater the more gasoline one normally buys.

Income elasticity of demand The income elasticity of demand for a good is the percentage change in the amount of the good demanded divided by the percentage change in income. Those goods for which this elasticity is positive are called normal, and those for which it is negative are called inferior goods.

Inelastic Having a price-elasticity of demand between 0 and -1. If the demand for a good or service is inelastic, the amount purchased is not much affected by a change in its price. The demand for a good is inelastic if there are not good substitutes available for it. For example, the demand for insulin is inelastic, since a diabetic will not reduce his consumption of insulin much when its price increases.

Inferior good If a good or service is inferior, an individual buys less of it when his income increases, and more of it when his income declines.

Injunction A court order directing a party to perform a specified act, or refrain from performing some act. A party who disobeys an injunction may be held in contempt of court, and sent to jail until she agrees to obey the court's order.

Inputs or factors of production All the things used to produce output, such a labor, capital (including machinery and equipment), and natural resources.

Intensive margin A change on the intensive margin is a change in the level of activity by those currently participating in the market. If a nurse's hourly wage increases, she may choose to work more hours per week; this is a change on the intensive margin.

Joint and several liability Under the common law, if two or more persons were liable for the harm done to a third person, their liability was "joint and several," so that each defendant was potentially liable for the entire damages. If, for example, a plaintiff obtained a recovery against five co-defendants for $1 million, he could collect the entire amount from any one of the defendants, or could collect a different amount from each defendant in any combination of amounts, so long as the total amount collected equaled $1 million.

Joint tenancy　A form of joint ownership of property, whereby all the tenants (owners) have the right to use and possession of the entire property. Under a joint tenancy there is a "right of survivorship," i.e. if one joint tenant dies, her interest expires and the property is owned entirely by the surviving joint tenants.

Last clear chance　Under this doctrine of common-law negligence, the defendant is liable if, even though the plaintiff was negligent, the defendant had a "last clear chance" to avoid the accident, i.e., the defendant could still have prevented an injury to the plaintiff by the exercise of reasonable care.

Lessor　The owner of property, who enters into a lease agreement with the lessee.

Life estate　An estate in property under which one (called the "life tenant") has the right to use and possess the entire property only during his lifetime. The interest disappears on the death of the life tenant; thus the life tenant has no interest to leave to his heirs.

Marginal cost　The cost of producing one more unit of a good, at the current level of output. Marginal cost is the increase in total cost resulting from the production of one more unit of the good.

Marginal product　The increase in total output obtained by adding one more unit of an input, holding fixed that amount of all other inputs. The marginal product of labor is the additional output a firm would obtain by hiring one more worker.

Marginal revenue　The additional revenue a firm could gain by selling one more unit of the good.

Marginal revenue product　The additional revenue a firm could gain by adding one more unit of an input, holding other inputs constant. The marginal revenue product of labor is the additional revenue, or sales, a firm would gain by hiring one more worker.

Marginal tax rate　The marginal income tax rate between two levels of income is the change in the income tax, divided by the change in income. Alternatively, it is the fraction of an additional dollar of income that must be paid as tax.

Monopoly　A pure monopoly is when a firm makes a product or provides a service for which there are no good substitutes; also there are substantial barriers to entry that prevent competition by other firms.

Moral hazard　The inefficiency that arises when someone does not bear the full cost of (or responsibility for) his actions. In the context of insurance, moral hazard arises because a person's behavior will change once he is insured in such a way as to increase the probability or amount of a loss.

Nash equilibrium　A set of strategies such that each player adopts the best strategy available to her, given the strategies that she believes will be chosen by the other players, and the beliefs of each player as to what the other players will do are borne out. (Note that this observation is true for every player in the game.)

Normal good　If a good or service is normal, an individual buys more of it when his income increases, and less of it when his income declines.

Nuisance claim　A claim that has no legal merit.

Parameter　A quantity or relation in a mathematical model that is given, or exogenously determined. For example, a firm may have a production function $Q = 5K^{0.5}L^{0.5}$, where Q is the number of sweatshirts produced per day, K is the number of machines used to produce sweatshirts, and L is the number of workers employed. The numbers 5, 0.5 and 0.5 in the production function are parameters because they are given; they are a fact of life for the firm. They are not a matter of choice for the firm, at least under the assumptions of the model. Compare with **Choice variable**.

Parol evidence rule   A rule of contract law that prohibits the use of oral or written evidence to vary or contradict the terms of an "integrated," i.e., apparently complete, written contract.

Patent   An exclusive right granted by the government to an inventor, to use and sell her invention for a prescribed period of time (currently in the United States twenty years from the date of application for the patent).

Peremptory challenge   A challenge by which the defense or the prosecution can eliminate potential jurors without being required to explain why they find the juror objectionable.

Precedent   Under the doctrine of precedent, or *stare decisis* (to stand by things decided), a court is obliged to follow an earlier published decision made by another court if that decision basically involved the same legal issue as that arising in the case at bar.

Price-elasticity of demand   The elasticity of demand with respect to price. (See **Elasticity**.)

Prisoner's dilemma   A game in which two prisoners are interrogated separately about a crime they committed, and the police need more evidence to convict either prisoner. The strategy that is privately optimal for each prisoner is to confess, in order to obtain a lighter sentence than the other prisoner; however, both prisoners would be better off if they could cooperate, so that neither confessed. The prisoners' dilemma is a parable for the problem of chiseling that arises in a cartel. In a cartel in which the firms agree to restrict output, the firms collectively would maximize profits if each firm restricted its output in accordance with the cartel agreement. However, any firm could make a greater profit by producing more than it is supposed to.

Producer surplus   Profits.

Property right   A right to the exclusive use of a thing, i.e., a right to exclude all others from its use.

Public good   A good with the property that, when it is used or consumed by a person, the use or consumption does not reduce the amount of the good that will be available for others. A theorem of mathematics is a public good, since A's use of it does not in any way prevent it from being used by B.

Punitive damages   Damages beyond compensatory damages, i.e., beyond the amount required to compensate victims for their loss. The courts have stated that the goals of punitive damages are deterrence and punishment.

Real property   Land, including any "improvements" such as buildings, on it.

Remainder interest   An estate in property following a life estate. If A has a life estate, and B a remainder interest, the property is owned outright by B upon the death of A. If the property in question is land, on the death of A, B owns the property in fee simple absolute.

Remittitur   A procedure by which a court orders that the defendant will be granted a new trial on the issue of damages unless the plaintiff agrees to a reduction of the trial court's award by a specified amount.

Res ipsa loquitur   Latin for "The thing speaks for itself." Under this doctrine, certain circumstances are deemed sufficient to support a finding of negligence, e.g., amputation of the wrong leg by a surgeon. Some courts have given the rule an additional procedural effect, by having the burden of proof on negligence shift to the defendant.

Residuary clause   A clause in a will that gives all the remainder of the estate, after the specific bequests of personal property and devises of real property are satisfied, to one or more of the beneficiaries; a provision in a will that disposes of all property not specifically disposed of by other provisions of the will. A typical clause would be: "I give all the rest, residue, and remainder of my estate to my husband, Steve. If he does not survive me, I give my residuary estate to those of my children who survive me, in equal shares, to be divided among them and the descendants of a deceased child of mine, to take their ancestor's share per stirpes."

Respondeat superior   Latin for "Let the superior answer for it." Another term for the doctrine of vicarious liability.

Risk-averse   A person who is risk-averse is willing to pay some amount to avoid risk. That is, he prefers a certain amount to a risky alternative that has the same expected value. Rather than take a gamble with a fair coin, with a payoff of $20 for heads and $0 for tails, he will accept some amount less than $10.

Risk-neutral   A person who is risk-neutral is indifferent between a fixed payment and a risky alternative that has the same expected value. He is equally willing to accept a payment of $10, or take a gamble with a fair coin, with a payoff of $20 for heads and $0 for tails.

Risk-preferrer   A person who is a risk-preferrer would rather take a gamble than a fixed payment that has the same expected value as the gamble. He would prefer to take a gamble with a fair coin, with a payoff of $20 for heads and $0 for tails, rather than take a certain payment of $10. He would not take the fixed payment unless it were some amount greater than $10.

Settlor   A person who creates a trust by giving real or personal property to a trustee for the benefit of beneficiaries. If the settlor is alive at the time he makes the transfer, the trust is called an inter vivos trust (*inter vivos* is Latin for "among or between the living"). If the settlor has died, and thus makes the transfer into trust via a will, the trust is called a testamentary trust, and the settlor may be referred to as the "testator."

Shadow price   The opportunity cost of a good or service, often provided when the market price is unavailable or incomplete. For example, the shadow price of oil and gas takes into account environmental costs such its contribution to pollution and global warming as well as the direct costs of production.

Statute of Frauds   A statute which requires that certain kinds of agreements, such as an agreement to sell land, must be in writing to be enforceable contracts.

Substitution effect   The effect on consumption of a change in price remaining after one removes the income effect. The substitution effect is the effect of a pure change in price.

Sunk cost   a "cost" that has already been incurred, that cannot be recovered, and is consequently irrelevant to a decision currently being considered. It is in fact not a cost of the action under consideration. Mr. X, who has completed medical school, is considering whether to become a screenwriter in Hollywood. In deciding which career to pursue, he should consider the potential risks and rewards of being a screenwriter, compared to those of being a physician, an occupation for which he has completed his training. He should not consider the tuition and expenses he paid for medical school.

Supply curve   There are supply curves for individual firms (or persons), and there are market supply curves, aggregating the supply curves of all firms (or persons) in an industry or market. In general, the supply curve of a good shows the amount of the good that will be supplied to the market at different prices, holding constant other factors (the cost of inputs, expectations about future prices, etc.) that affect the amount supplied. Equivalently, the supply curve shows the minimum amount the supplier will accept to produce the unit of the good in question. **Firm supply curve** A curve that shows the marginal cost of the good to the firm, i.e., the cost of producing each additional good, over the period of time covered by the supply curve. Equivalently, the supply curve shows the minimum amount the firm will accept to produce the unit of the good in question. **Market supply curve** A curve that shows the cost to the industry of producing each additional good, i.e. the cost of producing that additional good for the firm or firms that can produce it at least cost, over the period of time covered by the supply curve.

Takeover The acquisition by an outside group of a controlling interest in a corporation's stock. When the incumbent management opposes the attempt at a takeover, it is called a hostile takeover bid.

Tenancy in common A form of common ownership of property, whereby all the tenants in common (owners) have the right to use and possession of the entire property. Under this form of ownership, there is no right of survivorship, so the heirs of a deceased tenant succeed to her interest. See **Joint tenancy**.

Testator A person who dies leaving a will.

Tort A wrong, other than a breach of contract, that subjects the wrongdoer to civil liability under the common law or a statute. Two important examples of torts are negligence and strict liability in tort.

Trademark or trade name A property right in a name, word, symbol or design that is used to identify the product of a particular firm and distinguish it from competing products. The owner of a trademark or tradename has an exclusive right to use the symbol or name to refer to the product, and is protected from an infringing use.

Transaction costs All the costs of carrying out an exchange or making an agreement. These costs including the costs of identifying the parties with whom one must negotiate, the costs of getting together with them, the costs of the bargaining process itself (e.g. the stress involved in negotiations), and the costs of enforcing the resulting agreement.

Trust A form of ownership of property in which assets are delivered by an individual to another party, called the trustee, who holds legal title to the assets and manages them for the benefit of others, who are known as the beneficiaries. The person who delivers the assets into trust is called the settlor (since he is making a "settlement" of property), if he is alive at the time, and the testator, if the trust is established upon his death.

Value The value of a good or service to a person is the maximum amount she would be willing to pay for it. The **total value** of some specified amount of a good equals the area under the demand curve (a curve of marginal value), from the origin to that amount. If the demand curve is for an individual, this area represents the total value of that quantity of the good to that individual. If the demand curve is for a market, the area represents the total value of that quantity of the good to the market.

Variable costs All costs of production that are not fixed.

Vicarious liability Under this doctrine, an employer is strictly liable for any torts committed by its employees when acting within the scope of their employment (however historically there was an exception, known as the fellow-servant rule, that applied when one employee committed a tort against another). Thus if a physician is employed by a hospital, the hospital is strictly liable for medical malpractice (negligence) on the part of the physician.

Voir dire The process of questioning potential jurors, to decide which of them will actually serve on the jury. *Voir dire* is a French phrase meaning "to speak the truth."

Widow's forced share In many States there are statutes, known as "forced share" statutes, providing that a widow cannot be completely disinherited by her husband. Under a typical forced-share statute, the surviving spouse (whether male or female) is entitled to claim a one-third share of the decedent's entire estate.

Notes

Introduction

1 Ellickson (2000).
2 Grant Gilmore, quoted in Kelso (1982), at 642.
3 William of Occam (or Ockham) was an English philosopher and theologian. He maintained that theories should be parsimonious, and that one should not make any more assumptions, or introduce more definitions, than the minimum needed for the analysis. "Occam's razor" is used to "shave off" unnecessary and redundant concepts and constructs that are not required by one's theoretical model.
4 Richard Musgrave, quoted by Orley M. Ashenfelter in Parkin (1990) at 378.
5 Pre-eminent journals that specialize in law and economics include the *American Law and Economics Review*, the *European Journal of Law and Economics*, the *International Review of Law and Economics*, the *Journal of Law, Economics and Organization*, the *Journal of Legal Studies, Research in Law and Economics*, and the *Supreme Court Economic Review*. Two other journals, although not limited to this field, have published much important work in law and economics: the *Rand Journal of Economics* (formerly the *Bell Journal of Economics*), and the *Journal of Law and Economics*. Other papers in this area have been published in general journals in economics such as the *Journal of Political Economy*, the *Quarterly Journal of Economics, Economic Inquiry* and the *Southern Economic Journal*. Finally, many contributions to economic analysis of law have appeared in specialized field journals such as the *Journal of Economic History*, the *Journal of Forensic Economics*, and the *Journal of Empirical Legal Studies*.
6 66 N.Y. 2nd 576, 498 N.Y. Supp. 2nd 743, 489 N.E. 2nd 712 (1985).
7 For simplicity, we ignore tax issues. However, we may note in passing that (1) income, and possibly payroll, taxes would have to be paid on these additional earnings; (2) Mrs. O'Brien would not be taxed on the property distributed to her in the marital property settlement; and (3) any income she subsequently derived from investment of her share of property might be subject to income tax.
8 Polinsky (1989).
9 By the time the excellent text by Cooter and Ulen (1988) came out I had crossed the Rubicon.
10 Some reviewers were skeptical as to whether this chapter belonged in the text, but I believe it is an essential supplement to the other chapters. For example, it helps to explain how the determination of damages for personal injuries based on lost earnings should take into account that those earnings would have been taxed.

1 Principles of microeconomics (I)

1 Evans and Zhang (2007).
2 Here we are assuming that it does not matter to workers how they dry their hands. If this assumption is incorrect, and, for example, they prefer paper towels to electric hand driers, an employer who uses hand driers must provide its workers some additional compensation to compete with businesses that provide paper towels for their workers. This would represent another component of the cost of hand driers.
3 For simplicity we assume the rate of interest Mr. X could receive by investing the $300,000 in a bond is the same as the rate he would pay if he borrowed it.

4 To prove this, we would have to determine the optimal inventory for each store. We will not undertake this task, but it is straightforward if one knows the costs and benefits of holding inventory. With regard to benefits, the larger a store's inventory, the less likely it is that the store will have to turn a customer away, which would cost not only that sale but a loss of goodwill. On the other hand, the store's costs are larger the larger its inventory, since a larger inventory requires more storage space, more capital invested in inventory, etc. The point is that the optimal inventory of the small store is larger relative to its sales than the optimal inventory of the large store, because it faces greater variation in the demand of its customers. Intuitively, it is clear that the risk of turning the customer away is greater, the more the variation in demand.

5 Strictly speaking, this definition of a demand curve assumes that a buyer is in a competitive market, i.e. he is not such a dominant figure among buyers that he has leverage with sellers to influence the price. Below we provide an alternative definition of a demand curve, namely that its height represents the value of an additional unit of the good. This definition is correct under any circumstances.

6 Actually, the word "customary" is a bit of an understatement here. Any economist who violated this convention, by putting quantity on the vertical axis, would be considered by his colleagues to have taken leave of his senses!

7 According to tradition, all economists follow this convention because the great British economist Alfred Marshall drew his diagrams this way Marshall (1890).

8 Alternatively, marginal cost is the increase in total cost resulting from the production of an additional unit of the good.

9 Smith (1776), Book I, Chapter 10.

10 Rosen (1992), at 219; see also Pashigian (1977).

11 Rosen (1992), at 231.

12 More precisely, the slope of $q = f(a)$ is the limiting value of $\Delta q / \Delta a$ as $\Delta a \to 0$.

13 Note also that we have analyzed an excise tax, i.e., a tax of a fixed dollar amount per unit, and there are other types of taxes, such as an ad valorem tax (from Latin for a tax "on value"), which equals a specified percentage of the price for which the good is sold. The analysis of an ad valorem tax is essentially the same, but in this case, the amount of the tax (the size of the wedge between supply and demand curves) increases with the height of the demand curve.

14 Here again "demand" can refer to the demand of an individual consumer, or to the total demand of all the consumers in a given market.

15 Some even contend this elasticity may be negative, on the ground that the perceived brutality of capital punishment incites people to violence.

16 More precisely, the cost of taking an additional hour of leisure time is the reduction in after-tax earnings and fringe benefits resulting from reducing work time by one hour.

2 Principles of microeconomics (II)

1 Recall that the price-elasticity of demand equals the percentage change in the quantity demanded, divided by the percentage change in the price. For the perfectly competitive firm, a very small positive percentage change in price (in the denominator) leads to a percentage change in the amount demanded of -100 percent (in the numerator). Thus the price-elasticity of demand (the overall fraction) approaches $-\infty$.

2 *United States v. Consolidated Laundries Corp.*, 291 F. 2d 563 (2d Cir. 1961). It is, however, important to note that in some cases the division of markets can actually increase competition rather than reduce it. See Posner (2001).

3 By George Stigler. His precise language is "anything (other than a free human being) which yields valuable services over an appreciable period of time" Stigler (1966), at 275.

4 Sometimes the word "capital" is used in an entirely different sense, to mean "money" or "the resources that can be purchased with money," as in "The firm could raise capital through a new public offering of stock." This usage is confusing, but is probably too deeply embedded in the language to be stamped out.

5 World Bank (1997), Table 3.3, cited in Ehrenberg and Smith (2003). The wealth estimates for 1994 are expressed in dollars for the year 2000.

6 Ehrenberg and Smith (2003), at 318.

7 In Appendix 2.1 to this chapter, we consider what the accumulated value would be if interest were compounded more frequently than once a year.

8 See, for example, the discussions of the doctrine of unconscionability in the chapter on contracts, of municipal bonds in the chapter on taxation, and of the Beard hypothesis in the chapter providing an introduction to the legal system.

9 More fundamentally, the real interest rate on an asset is the rate at which its real value increases over time.

10 After Irving Fisher (1867–1947), a monetary economist of great distinction who first pointed out the relation between expected inflation and interest rates.

11 There is a good discussion of efficient markets in Mishkin (1998), at 692–701.

12 Some textbooks flatly state that a good must be nonexclusive, in order for it to qualify as a public good. The author, and many other economists, believe that this definition is too restrictive, and that the true defining characteristic of a public good is that its use by one person does not reduce the amount available to others.

13 Here we ignore the cost of fuel, and the (negligible) physical impact of the vehicle on the bridge. Note that the bridge is not a nonexclusive good, since it is easy to prevent persons from crossing the bridge if, for example, they do not pay a toll.

3 Introduction to the legal system

1 For simplicity, we ignore the variation in the rules of mediation across different courts. In state courts in Michigan, for example, a party who rejects the mediation award is liable for the other party's expenses unless the trial verdict is more favorable to him by a margin of more than 10 percent.

2 One study found that in cases where the mediation award was not accepted by both parties, but the case was later settled, the settlement payment was exactly equal to the mediation award over 13 percent of the time. See Spurr (2000).

3 The Federal Circuit Court of Appeals, which was established in 1982, has jurisdiction over certain types of specialized cases such as patents and international trade. Unlike the other U.S. Circuit Courts of Appeals, its jurisdiction is not defined by geographical boundaries.

4 In some rather narrowly defined situations a case can be reviewed by the Supreme Court through an alternative channel of "appeal" or "certification," but these methods are much less important than the writ of certiorari.

5 The Court's practice is to grant a writ of certiorari if at least four Justices vote in favor of it.

6 In the state court system only the decisions of appellate courts are published. In the federal system the decisions of the trial court (the federal district courts), as well as those of appellate courts, may be published, but many are not. For example, only 20 percent of the decisions by the federal Circuit Courts of Appeal in the year 2000 were published; Hannon (2001).

7 A final possibility is that a court could determine that the rule of a prior case was applicable, but simply refuse to follow it rather than overrule it. This could happen, for example, if the force of the prior case as precedent was weakened by the fact that it was decided in a different jurisdiction, e.g., another state or country.

8 Similarly (according to informed opinion), predictions of a major snowstorm are more likely to be wrong than predictions that the winter storm system will pass by the local area.

9 Beard (1913). A concise summary of Beard's legacy is provided by Tushnet (1987–1988).

10 In Shays' Rebellion, indebted farmers petitioned the state senate of Massachusetts to issue paper money, halt foreclosures of mortgages and prevent their own imprisonment for debt. When the Senate failed to act, Daniel Shays led an armed insurrection, using force to prevent courts from sitting to enter judgments for debt. The rebellion was quickly put down. The leaders were convicted of treason but were subsequently pardoned.

11 *Everson v. Board of Education*, 330 U.S. 1 (1947).

4 Property law

1 This example is from Posner (1986).

2 Howlett (1999).

3 Although we have not yet defined efficiency (we will consider several alternative formulations of it below), it can be achieved by using all available resources, including human resources, to maximize value.

4 Named after the Italian mathematical economist Vilfredo Pareto (1848–1923), who derived the conditions for efficiency.

5 Kaldor (1939).

6 Hicks (1940).

7 It should, however, be noted that recent research has raised serious questions about the historical accuracy of this story; Casadesus-Masanell and Spulber (2000). For a defense of the conventional interpretation, see Klein (2000).

8 If the individual were risk-averse, so that his marginal utility declined with income, the $100 tax would provide a greater incentive than the $100 subsidy, but this is a detail.

9 The fact that the demand curve facing the rancher is horizontal indicates that his ranch operates in a competitive market, i.e. he is a "price-taker."

10 The clause was so named because it permanently reserved a player's services to the first team that signed him, until he was either traded or released.

11 The Fifth Amendment to the U.S. Constitution provides for "just compensation" in the event private property is "taken for public use." The just compensation requirement applies to the states through the due process clause of the Fourteenth Amendment. The property in question may be real or personal property. The rifle that was used to assassinate President Kennedy was the subject of an eminent domain proceeding.

12 See, e.g., Kelo v. City of New London, 545 U.S. 469 (2005).

13 Griggs v. Allegheny County, 369 U.S. 84 (1962).

14 Berman v. Parker, 348 U.S. 26 (1954).

15 Poletown Neighborhood Council v. City of Detroit, 410 Mich. 616, 304 N.W. 2d 455 (1981).

16 However, this decision was subsequently overruled by the Michigan Supreme Court. Wayne County v. Edward Hathcock et al., 471 Mich., 445 (2004).

17 Munch (1976).

18 It might also be considered a transaction cost, owing to the parties' inability to negotiate with parties who cannot yet be identified – namely, other factories who may enter the area in the future.

19 Spur Industries Inc. v. Del E. Webb Development Co., 108 Ariz. 178, 494 P. 2nd 700 (1972).

20 Boomer v. Atlantic Cement Co., 26 N.Y. 2nd 219, 257 N.E. 2nd 870 (1970).

21 Note that if the Court had awarded title to the Guggenheim, the buyers could still recover the value of the painting from the gallery through a claim for breach of contract (breach of warranty of title); Bibas (1993).

22 Shavell (2003, chapter 9) notes that there are informational benefits of a registry. The government might use it as a source of information for the purposes of taxation, or (if one considers, for example, the registration of motor vehicles or guns), in the enforcement of criminal law or safety regulations.

23 Article I, Section 8, U.S. Constitution.

24 The Statute of Anne (1710).

25 The leading case in this area is State Street Bank & Trust v. Signature Financial Group, 149 F. 3d 1368 (Federal Circuit 1998).

26 Compare the discussion of the effect of the Williams Act on hostile takeovers, in the chapter on corporations.

27 Raskind (2001).

28 Note, however, that once a work has entered the public domain it can no longer be copyrighted.

29 Shavell (2003), chapter on property law.

30 Varian (2000).

31 If the owner of, for example, a patent has a property right, he can go to court and obtain an injunction (a court order) preventing anyone else from using his invention without his consent. If the patent were protected only by a rule of liability, someone else would be able to use the invention without the owner's consent, but would then be liable to the owner for money damages. See the discussion of these alternative remedies in the preceding section, "How disputes are decided by law."

32 It should, however, be noted that one can obtain a property right in a distinctive mark without registering it.

33 Senate Report No. 1333, 79th Congress, 2nd Session (1946).

34 Under the Lanham Act, a mark that is similar to an existing trademark cannot be registered if its use is "likely, when used on or in connection with the goods of the applicant, to cause confusion, or to cause a mistake, or to deceive" 15 U.S.C. 1052(d).

35 This example is from Kaplow and Shavell (2002).

5 Problems of incomplete property rights

1 The operation was performed by Dr. Joseph E. Murray at Peter Bent Brigham Hospital in Boston. In 1990 he received the Nobel Prize in Medicine for this achievement.
2 In 2001 the number of organ donations from living persons surpassed those from the dead; Strom (2003).
3 This estimate was made by the United Network for Organ Sharing. *New York Times*, December 3, 2001, p. A14.
4 Sunstein and Thaler (2008).
5 Thaler (2009).
6 *New York Times*, December 3, 2001, p. A14.
7 Some couples choose to adopt rather than bear children because of concern over a genetic defect that the child might inherit. In addition, some married couples with natural children choose to adopt others. There are also adoptions by single persons.
8 In 1971, about 21 percent of nonrelative adoptions were done as independent adoptions; Landes and Posner (1978).
9 We are assuming that the owner of the oyster bed operates in a competitive market, so his price equals marginal cost.
10 In Virginia, the annual catch fell from 1.9 million bushels in 1964 to 64,500 bushels in 1993.
11 McPherson and Nieswiadomy (2000).
12 The discussion in this section is based on Simmons and Kreuter (1989) and McPherson and Nieswiadomy (2000). After controlling for a number of variables that affected the elephant population in 35 African countries over several time periods, McPherson and Nieswiadomy found a 19 percent higher growth rate for the elephant population in countries that vested some form of ownership in their citizens through a national program. There were also some indications that political instability and undemocratic forms of government, which tend to make property rights less secure, had a negative effect on the stock of elephants.
13 Wines (2007).
14 Cones (1977).
15 Ibid.
16 Iraq claimed that its invasion of Kuwait, which led to the Persian Gulf War in 1991, was justified since Kuwait was extracting more than its share of a common pool of oil underneath the two countries; Perloff (2001).
17 Under the doctrine of fixtures, any improvements made by the tenant that are attached or "affixed" to the premises, e.g. cupboards, fences, carpeting (but not rugs), become the property of the landlord unless the lease provides otherwise. This common-law rule is efficient, since the removal of such improvements would be likely to damage the property.
18 See, e.g., Griffin (1985).
19 La Fond v. Detroit, 357 Mich. 362 (1959).
20 See Annotation, 25 ALR 3d 736.
21 Coffee v. William Marsh Rice University (1966, Texas Civil App.), 408 S.W. 2nd 269.
22 In re Rood Estate, 41 Mich. App. 405 (June 1972).
23 Langbein and Waggoner (1987).
24 Curnutte (1989).
25 Langbein and Waggoner (1987).
26 They are Arizona, California, Idaho, Louisiana, Nevada, New Mexico, Texas, and Washington.

6 Informal creation of property rights

1 See Eckert (1979) and Biblowit (1991).
2 Gilson and Mnookin (1985), pp. 350–352.
3 The full name of this group is the United Society of Believers in Christ's Second Appearing. They were called the "Shaking Quakers" or "Shakers" because, in their worship rituals, they shook and trembled to rid themselves of evil influences.

7 The law of contracts

1 15 U.S. (2 Wheat.) 178 (1817).
2 66 Mich. 568, 33 N.W. 919 (1887).

3 L. N. Jackson & Co. v. Royal Norwegian Government, 177 F. 2nd 694 (2nd Cir. 1949), cert. denied 339 U.S. 914 (1950).
4 Krell v. Henry, 2 K.B. 740 (1903).
5 In fact these "waivers of liability" are often not enforceable under state law, but a customer who is shown this language may believe that he has no claim against the parking garage.
6 Schwarz and Wilde (1983).
7 Macaulay v. Schroeder Publishing Co. (1974) 1 W.L.R. 1308 (H.L.).
8 In Williams v. Walker-Thomas Furniture Co., 350 F. 2nd 445 (D.C. Cir. 1965), a consumer had made payments of $1,400 for a number of items bought separately with a total purchase price of $1,800. When the consumer defaulted in her payments for a stereo set, the store sought to reclaim all the items. The Court of Appeals held that the consumer's defense of unconscionability had to be considered by the trial court.
9 The next two sections bear an obvious debt to Polinsky's (1983) chapter 5, on damages for breach of contract, which in turn is based on a model developed in Shavell (1980, 1984).
10 9 Ex. 341, 156 Eng. Rep. 145 (1854).
11 Note, however, that a defendant employer that wishes to reduce its damages has the burden of proof on the issue whether its former employee could have found work.
12 The court may also order a party to do something similar, but not identical, to what the party promised to do. The court can also order a party not to perform services for anyone other than the party who was entitled to performance under the contract; Cooter and Ulen (2000).

8 Torts

1 "Tort" is a Norman word meaning "wrong."
2 There may also be civil liability created by statute, e.g., under the Civil Rights Act or the Clean Air Act.
3 This idea was originally developed by Guido Calabresi (1970).
4 Learned Hand (1872–1961) was a federal judge in New York, and is regarded as one of the foremost judicial contributors to economic analysis of law in the history of the United States.
5 Another characteristic of an affirmative defense is that it raises new facts and arguments that, if proved, will preclude liability, even if the plaintiff's allegations are true. In contrast, a defense that takes issue with the plaintiff's allegations, like a denial that the defendant's conduct was negligent, is not an affirmative defense.
6 Restatement (Second) of Torts, Sec. 402 A.
7 Polinsky and Shavell (2009).
8 However, the employer is not strictly liable when one employee commits a tort against another. This exception to vicarious liability is known as the "fellow servant" rule.
9 Blyth v. Birmingham Water Works, 11 Exch. 781, 156 Eng. Rep. 1047 (1856).
10 248 N.Y. 339, 162 N.E. 99 (1928).
11 In the chapter on contracts, we saw that there is also a requirement of foreseeability under contract law. Note, however, that under tort law this requirement goes to the issue of liability, while under contract law it concerns only the measure of damages.
12 81 Vt. 471, 71 A. 188 (1908).
13 At common law there was generally no duty to protect a trespasser.
14 This and the previous example are taken from Posner (1986).
15 However, as of 2002, the common-law rule had been abrogated by statute in four states. These statutes generally impose a duty to render "reasonable" assistance when it can be done without danger to the rescuer; failure to intervene is a misdemeanor; White (2002), at 512–513. In most European nations there is a duty to rescue; Silver (1985).
16 The restatement imposes a duty where the potential rescuer has a special relationship with the victim. Restatement (Second) of Torts Sec. 314A–B (1965).
17 However, compensation may be available to a rescuer who is injured. The "rescue doctrine" recognized in many U.S. jurisdictions permits an injured rescuer to recover from a defendant whose negligence caused someone to be placed in peril. The defendant could be the imperiled victim, or a third party who was responsible for the danger; White (2002), pp. 508–509.
18 This form of comparative negligence is used in important federal statutes like the Federal Employers' Liability Act (involving railroad injuries) and the Jones Act (involving maritime injuries).

19 We are assuming here that a jurisdiction with modified comparative negligence retains the doctrine of last clear chance in situations where the plaintiff would otherwise be barred from recovery. There is variation among states in this regard. See generally Harper et al. (1986).

20 Sloan et al. (1997); Bovbjerg et al. (1997). These programs cover lifelong expenses of medical and custodial care; payments are made as expenses are incurred. All collateral sources (public and private) are offset. There is no explicit compensation for pain and suffering. Physicians who participate in the program are charged a flat annual fee.

21 Frequency is the total number of paid claims, including court awards and out-of-court settlement payments, and severity is the average amount per paid claim.

22 At common law, claims based on the premise that the patient was inadequately informed of the risks of a procedure were brought under the theory of battery. (The tort of battery applies to the harmful touching of a person without justification, consent or excuse.) Today informed consent cases are usually based on negligence.

23 By 1986 such funds had been created in at least eleven states; Posner (1986).

24 Recall that the intensive margin refers to changes in the level of an activity by current participants, while the extensive margin refers to individuals or firms who enter or leave an activity.

25 This section is based on the analysis in Easterbrook et al. (1980).

26 Ibid.

27 Earnings are also subject to payroll taxes, but with respect to amounts withheld for social security one could argue that there is an offsetting benefit – the increase in social security benefits received on retirement. Thus amounts withheld for social security might be considered more like a contribution to a pension plan than a tax. However, as we will see in the chapter on taxation, the link between social security contributions and benefits is imprecise at best, and for some, e.g., married individuals whose spouses have greater earnings, there is no gain derived from their contributions.

28 It should, however, be noted that if the damages for the victim's lost earnings are reduced by the taxes that would have been paid on them, it is appropriate to discount these amounts to present value by the market rate of interest on a security the interest on which is tax-exempt. The objective is to award the victim an amount that would enable him to purchase a security that yields a stream of income that will fully replace the after-tax earnings. If the income from the security is itself subject to tax, the victim will be undercompensated.

29 This statement of course disregards the argument made above, that it is appropriate to use the interest rate on tax-exempt securities when damages are based on after-tax earnings. One could use the interest rate on U.S. government obligations to discount damages based on pre-tax earnings, and make adjustments for the difference in tax treatment between earnings and interest on U.S. obligations.

30 Similarly, forecasts of future medical expenses should take into account both inflation and expected changes in the real cost of medical treatment.

31 The *Journal of Forensic Economics* is entirely devoted to research on issues like this, involving the determination of damages.

32 Viscusi (1993).

33 The law generally provides that a requirement for punitive damages is that the defendant has acted in a reprehensible manner – egregiously, maliciously, or with reckless disregard for others – and many courts suggest that the amount of punitive damages should be greater the more reprehensible the defendant's conduct has been; Polinsky and Shavell (1998), at 905.

34 BMW of North America v. Gore, 517 U.S. 559 (1996), *on remand* 701 So. 2nd 507, 31 Ala. B. Rep. 2135 (Ala. 1997).

35 In re the *Exxon Valdez*, 270 F. 3d 1215 (9th Cir. 2001).

36 Exxon Shipping Co. et al. v. Baker (554 U.S. 2008).

37 See, e.g., Polinsky and Shavell (1998), and Hylton (1998).

38 Compare the discussion of the plaintiffs' lawyer "selling out the class" in class actions, in Chapter 9, on the economics of litigation.

39 See the discussion of "Factors affecting the quality of law enforcement" in the chapter on criminal law.

40 To be precise, a loss in earnings for more than a year that is not compensated by other insurance.

41 O'Connell and Joost (1986) divide no-fault states into two groups: "add-on" states, in which no-fault benefits supplement the right to claim under tort law, and "no lawsuit" states, in which accident victims who receive no-fault benefits are barred from bringing a tort claim.

42 Gaudry (1988); Devlin (1988).

9 The economics of litigation

1 329 U.S. 495 (1947).

2 To gauge the magnitude of the distortion resulting from this problem of asymmetric information, Levitt and Syverson (2002) compared home sales made by real estate agents to sales by agents of their own homes. They found that the homes owned by agents sold for about 2 per cent more than other houses, and remain on the market about ten days longer.

3 There is some evidence that referrals among lawyers are more common when the legal claim requires specialized knowledge, e.g., claims based on medical malpractice or products liability, or those arising under admiralty law.

4 In re General Motors Corporation Pick-up Truck Fuel Tank Products Liability Litigation, 55 F. 3d 768 (3rd Cir. 1995). In one class action approximately one million class members had the opportunity to obtain coupons worth several hundred dollars toward the purchase of a Ford vehicle, but only seventy-five individuals redeemed the coupons.

5 Helland and Klick (2007).

6 In re Auction Houses Antitrust Litigation, 197 F.R.D. 71 (S.D.N.Y. 2000).

7 Eisenberg and Miller (2004).

8 Many statutes adopt the rule of indemnity half-way, in that the prevailing plaintiff, but not the prevailing defendant, may recover his legal fees from the losing party. In this section we will assume the fee-shifting can go in either direction, not just for the benefit of the plaintiff.

9 Although the case of Jarndyce v. Jarndyce is fictitious, Dickens, who was familiar with the Court of Chancery, noted that it was an accurate depiction of many lawsuits: "… everything set forth in these pages concerning the Court of Chancery is substantially true, and within the truth. … At the present moment [in August 1853] there is a suit before the Court which was commenced nearly twenty years ago; in which from thirty to forty counsel have been known to appear at one time; in which costs have been incurred to the amount of seventy thousand pounds; which is a *friendly suit*; and which is (I am assured) no closer to its termination now then when it was begun" Dickens (1951).

10 Studdert et al. (2006).

11 Frye v. United States, 293 F. 1013 (D.C. Cir. 1923).

12 509 U.S. 579 (1993).

13 This argument was made by Ellickson (1989) to explain the general adherence by whalers to whaling customs.

14 Implicit in Posner's analysis is the assumption that the determination of the law by the Supreme Court is more accurate than that of a Circuit Court. This assumption is probably reasonable, given that (1) the Supreme Court has at its disposal all the materials that were available to the Circuit Court, plus the benefit of its own research; (2) the law clerks for the Supreme Court Justices are of very high quality; and (3) it is likely that the best analysis of the nine Supreme Court Justices who hear a case is better than the best analysis of the three Circuit Court judges who would normally decide a case. We might also consider the dictum of Justice Robert H. Jackson, who noted that "… we are not final because we are infallible. We know that we are infallible only because we are final."

15 Rubin himself has essentially abandoned his previous argument, contending that common law and statutory law were both efficient in the nineteenth century, but that by the early twentieth century each had become inefficient. The reason for the change was the emergence of professional interest groups, who sought to make the law maximize their own private benefits; Rubin (1982).

16 Levine (1999) and Levine, Loayza, and Beck (1999).

17 Or someone in "privity" with the party, i.e. someone who is deemed to be closely related to the party.

18 James, Sec. 7.4, at 241.

19 James, Sec. 7.2, 238–239.

20 The Sixth Amendment provides the right in criminal prosecutions, and the Seventh Amendment provides the right in civil cases where the amount in controversy exceeds $20.
21 Williams v. Florida, 399 U.S. 78 (1970) (six-member juries in state criminal cases), and Colgrove v. Battin, 413 U.S. 149 (1973) (federal civil cases).
22 399 U.S. 78, 101 (1970).
23 A federal grand jury, by statute, may not have fewer than sixteen nor more than twenty-three persons.
24 However, the Supreme Court has placed some restrictions on the right to use peremptory challenges. In Batson v. Kentucky (1986), the Court held that prosecutors could not use peremptory challenges to exclude persons on the basis of their race, and in James E. Bowman v. T. Bowman (1994), the Court held that peremptory challenges could not be used to exclude potential jurors on the basis of their sex.
25 This rule applies if the crime is punishable by imprisonment for more than one year. However, if the crime is punishable by death, each side is entitled to twenty peremptory challenges. Rule 24, Federal Rules of Criminal Procedure (1997).
26 These decisions were Apodaca v. Oregon, 406 U.S. 404 (1972) (ten-to-two guilty verdict allowed); Johnson v. Louisiana, 406 U.S. 356 (1972) (nine-to-three verdict allowed); and Burch v. Louisiana, 441 U.S. 130 (1979) (five-to-one verdict not constitutional).
27 In some states the jury makes a recommendation concerning the death penalty to the judge, who subsequently decides the sentence.
28 Witherspoon v. Illinois, 391 U.S. 510 (1968).
29 From survey data, Kadane concluded that group a3 was approximately 11.3 per cent of the entire population, but that group a2 (those who would always vote for the death penalty) amounted to only one per cent.

10 Criminal law

1 For simplicity we are assuming there is a cost to the offender only if he is convicted. In reality, once he is charged with a crime, he must bear the cost of the criminal proceeding, including the expense of a lawyer, whether or not he is ultimately convicted.
2 The stigma is based on the inference that the individual has committed a serious crime, not the fact that he has been in prison. It should be noted that the offender's loss of income resulting from the stigma may not be inefficient, assuming the conviction was justified. It is not necessarily inefficient for an embezzler to find diminished opportunities in the banking industry, nor for the sex offender to find few openings in child care.
3 It is clear that the major impetus for these laws was the murder on July 29, 1994, of Megan Kanka, a seven-year-old girl who lived in New Jersey. Megan was brutally raped and murdered by a neighbor of the Kanka family, a convicted sex offender who lived across the street. See Teichman (2004).
4 One state legislature has acted to thwart strategy (1) by enacting a statute that requires registration if the defendant was initially charged with an offense for which registration was required, if he was subsequently convicted of a different offense "arising out of the same set of circumstances." One possible consequence is that in some cases, judges or juries who believe that the sanctions are excessive will simply refuse to convict defendants. See Teichman (2004).
5 There are, however, two countervailing considerations that may affect the criminal's behavior: he may believe that the probability of being apprehended is greater if he also commits murder, holding other things constant, and he may have some regard for the welfare of his victim.
6 Another criticism is that Wolpin, who acknowledged the limitations of his data, did not consider the possibility that the average prison sentence for homicide might have declined over the same period that execution rates declined; Polinsky (1978).
7 428 U.S. 153 (1976).
8 Ayres and Waldfogel argue that this potential objective of bail is not relevant to their study, since (1) under the law in effect at the time, judges were not supposed to consider the possibility of pretrial crime as a factor in setting bail, and (2) if, notwithstanding the law, a judge was concerned about this possibility, he would presumably set a bail bond high enough to prevent the defendant from making bail. However their sample included only defendants who were released on bail.

9 More precisely, the bond dealer will be liable if the defendant cannot be found for six months, and in that case will be liable for the amount of the bond × the forfeiture rate, which in Connecticut was 55 percent of the bond.

10 Note, however, that the defendant's decision whether to flee would be affected if the collateral obtained from the defendant increases with the amount of the bond. In this case the defendant would have less incentive to flee as the bond increases, since he would lose more collateral.

11 Here we assume for the sake of exposition that the forfeiture rate is 100 percent. The results do not depend on this assumption.

12 A technical note: the authors do allow for the fact that judges might want to make the expected probability of flight different for different crimes. They estimate a regression in which the dependent variable is the log of the bond rate, and the independent variables are the severity of the crime, the type of the crime, and the characteristics (race and sex) of the defendant.

13 On the economic theory of incapacitation, i.e. imposing sanctions such as imprisonment that prevent offenders from being able to harm others, see Shavell (1987).

14 McCormick and Tollison (1984) found that the addition of a third official in college basketball – a 50 percent increase in the number of enforcers – reduced the number of fouls committed by players by 34 percent.

15 *Roe v. Wade*, 410 U.S. 113 (1973). The Court held that the due process clause of the Fourteenth Amendment protected against state action on the right to privacy, including a woman's right to terminate her pregnancy.

16 Carter and Jansen (1995).

17 Ibid.

18 In a study of public law enforcement, Wilson (1983) found that one consequence of increasing evening police patrols in New York City subways was an increase in subway robberies during the day.

19 There may already be a subsidy, if police departments purchase the equipment needed to trace the vehicles that have Lojack installed.

20 There is a tort of malicious prosecution, but for almost all cases its requirements are too onerous to be satisfied by a potential plaintiff. The elements of the tort include malice, a lack of probable cause for the prosecution, and successful termination in favor of the accused. Moreover, officers of the state such as prosecuting attorneys may have an absolute immunity. Harper, James and Gray (1986), Sec. 4.1, 4.3.

11 Corporations and financial markets

1 A general partnership has only general partners. A limited partnership has limited partners, whose liability is limited, and must have at least one general partner, whose liability is unlimited. Often, however, the general partner is a corporation. Whether the partnership is general or limited, the management decisions are made only by its general partners.

2 Consider also the potential liability of the shareholders of the Union Carbide Corporation if there were no rule of limited liability. On December 3, 1984, more than 3,000 people in Bhopal, in central India, were killed when a deadly gas was released from a storage tank at a Union Carbide plant. The tank released 40 tons of methyl isocyanate gas, killing those who inhaled it while they slept. Thousands more subsequently died from the aftereffects. *New York Times*, July 7, 2008, p. 1.

3 The "par value" of a security is the dollar value shown on its certificate.

4 Because payment of the dividend is not a strict legal obligation, the law considers preferred stock to be an equity security.

5 Smith (1776).

6 It may be difficult to determine the scope of the relevant industry. Also, if an industry is declining, the best managerial decision might be to leave it and enter another industry.

7 Bebchuk et al. (2001), pp. 73–76.

8 Jensen and Meckling (1976).

9 These statements are now available on the SEC web site.

10 The amendments also extended the coverage of the Act, by applying it to "exchange offers," which are tenders offers in which some or all of the consideration is stock or bonds of the acquiring corporation. (The original statute had applied only to cash tender offers.)

11 Indeed, Bebchuk (1982) argues that there is a net benefit to stockholders from this regulation, since they receive higher premiums, and the increased costs to bidders do not significantly reduce the number of takeovers. However, most researchers support the position of Jarrell and Bradley summarized above, that there is a net loss to shareholders resulting from the decline in takeovers and the protection of inefficient entrenched management. See, e.g., Schumann (1988); Jarrell et al. (1988); Shleifer and Vishny (1991).

12 537 F. 3d 728 (7th Cir. 2008).

13 Another possible benefit of incorporations is an increase in demand for the services of the state's lawyers.

14 See, e.g., Manne (1966); Carlton and Fischel (1983).

15 Carlton and Fischel (1983).

16 Kronman (1978).

17 Corporations with more than $5 million of assets and at least one outstanding class of securities that is held by more than 500 shareholders of record are subject to special regulation under the Federal Securities Exchange Act of 1934. The regulations under this statute require the corporation to register that class of shares with the SEC and periodically make public disclosure of financial information.

18 This section closely follows McCoy (2008).

12 Taxation

1 The highest marginal rate of estate tax was 45 percent in the year 2009.

2 Bakija and Slemrod (2004).

3 Conway and Rork (2006).

4 The marital deduction was formerly subject to a ceiling of one half of the decedent's "adjusted gross estate." This ceiling was eliminated for estates of persons dying after 1981.

5 To be precise, this tax has a component, known as the medicare or hospital insurance portion, which currently (in 2010) applies to all wages, without any limitation on the amount. However, only this portion of the tax applies to wages beyond $106,800.

6 It should be noted that the link between retirement contributions and benefits has been preserved in some countries. For example, in Chile a worker may choose to have between 10 percent and 20 percent of his pretax income deposited in a fund, the earnings on which are not subject to income tax. The fund is earmarked for the worker who contributed to it, and is distributed to him upon his retirement.

7 OECD Factbook 2009.

8 Blau et al. (1998). Former spouses who were divorced after at least ten years of marriage are entitled to the same benefits.

9 A spouse may obtain a survivor's benefit based on her spouse's death, regardless of whether she has previously elected to receive a spouse benefit, or a benefit based on her own earnings.

10 Brien et al. (2000).

11 The astute reader may question why, in this example, an individual's consumption is the same under a consumption tax as it is under an income tax, given that the whole point of a consumption tax is to increase saving, by reducing consumption. This is a valid criticism, but does not detract from the point of the example. We have made the assumption for convenience in exposition.

12 Tax law changes constantly, and this section should not be viewed as a guide for determining one's deduction for depreciation under current U.S. tax law. Rather, our purpose is to show the economic effects of some depreciation rules that have often been used.

13 One could argue that the Bears would be better off building their own stadium, since they would then own the stadium outright rather than have only the right to use it under a lease agreement. However the lease could be written in a way that would confer all the important advantages of ownership on the Bears. For example the Bears could be granted a long-term lease, perhaps with an option to buy the stadium at the expiration of the lease.

13 Labor law

1 However, in some states, such as California, covenants not to compete are not enforced.

2 Strictly speaking, all the salary profiles being compared should have the same discounted present value – the value determined by competition in the labor market. Any firm that offered a salary

profile with a lower present value would be unable to attract any workers, and any firm that offered a profile with a higher present value would be overpaying, and thus would make less profit than other firms. We ignore this point for convenience of exposition.

Glossary

1 A technical detail: if the supply curve is for the short run, we must also add to this area any fixed cost to obtain total cost.
2 Here we assume for simplicity that the random variable is discrete.

Index

Note: Page references in italics relate to the glossary; references followed by "n" relate to notes